ACADEMICS IN RETREAT

ACADEMICS IN RETREAT
The Politics of Educational Innovation

by Joseph Fashing and Steven E. Deutsch

ALBUQUERQUE
UNIVERSITY OF NEW MEXICO PRESS

LA
227.3
.F3

© University of New Mexico Press, 1971.
All rights reserved.
Manufactured in the United States of America.
Library of Congress Catalog Card No. 78-153940.
First Edition.

This book is for Katie in the
year of our liberation with
great affection and many thanks
for all of the important lessons
for which she is alone responsible
—J.F.

Contents

Prefatory Remarks
    I By Steven E. Deutsch   xi
    II By Joseph Fashing   xix

Acknowledgments   xxi

I The Challenge for Educational Change   1
    American Society and Higher Education   1
    Educational Problems in Retrospect   6
    Assault on the Campus: Protest and the
        Recent Educational Climate   9
    University Response to Demands for Change: The Record   11
    Organizational Structure and Resistance to Innovation   14
    Change in Higher Education   19
    Patterns of Innovation   22

	The Political Context of Change	25
	Introduction to Case Studies	28
II	**The Hazards of Being Number One**	**31**
	Educational Development at Berkeley	33
	After the Free Speech Movement	34
	Education at Berkeley: The Muscatine Report	37
	Approaches to Innovation	42
	Experimental College	43
	The Board of Educational Development and Center for Participant Education	46
	The Third World College	54
	Governing the Multiversity	58
	May 1970: Crisis and Regression	63
	The Challenge of Educational Change: Conclusions from the Berkeley Case	66
	Neo-McCarthyism and Anarchist Hysteria: California Politics Since FSM	69
III	**War and Peace on Campus: San Francisco State College**	**76**
	Community Action in the Search for Relevance	80
	Altering the Educational Experience: The Experimental College	82
	Pressing for Recognition: The Issue of Legitimacy	85
	Ethnic Studies and the Third World College	93
	A Further Word on the Historic Strike	98
	Shifting Internal Leadership and the Response to Cross-Pressures	101
	After the Strike: The End of Innovation and the Death of a College	110
IV	**Successful Innovation and the Challenge of Change: University of Oregon**	**114**
	Counterculture, Radicalism, and Bombings: A Changing Milieu	114
	A University at the Crossroads	116
	Conduct Codes: Student and Faculty	119
	The Student and the University Government	121
	The Student and the Curriculum: SEARCH	128
	Addressing the Problem of Racism	139

Contents

	The Presidential Search: Pushing the Issue of Student Participation	146
	The Wider Context of Educational Innovation	150
V	Alternative Models for Excellence: Western Washington State College	156
	Institutional Growth and Alternatives to the Multiversity	157
	Fairhaven College	161
	Expanding the Satellite Concept: Huxley College and the College of Ethnic Studies	168
	Reforming the Remainder: Northwest Free University	171
	Students and Institutional Policy	174
	Protecting Institutional Freedom	176
VI	Exploring the Possibilities of Freedom: University of California at Los Angeles	179
	The Multiversity in the South	179
	Combatting Alienation and Apathy: Development of Educational Innovations	183
	Beginnings of Special Education	183
	University Response to the Cry for Relevance	185
	Experimental College	186
	Committee for the Study of Education and Society	188
	Summer Task Forces and the Further Development of New Programs	193
	Institute for the Study of American Cultures	199
	Faculty Participation in the Innovative Process	201
	Students as Agents of Innovation and Change	203
	Innovation Without Confrontation	206
	In Search of Excellence	208
	Relations with the Outside Community	209
VII	Tranquility to Trashing: The Transition at Stanford	212
	The Experiment and Its Failures	216
	Study of Education at Stanford (SES)	220
	Black Studies at Stanford	229
	Self-Satisfaction and the Absence of Urgency	232
VIII	Political Processes and Institutional Change	237
	Organization and the Innovational Process	238
	Observations on Experimental Colleges	245

The Innovation in Ethnic Studies: An Assessment	248
Catalysts for Change: Who Are the Innovators?	258
Curricular Innovation and the Problem of Institutional Governance: Substantive vs. Procedural Issues	265
Student Power and Its Potential	271
The Politics of Higher Education	277
The University in the Larger Political Arena	280
Postscript: An Admonition	284
Appendix A Note on Methodology	286
Gathering Data	289
Notes	292
Index	316

Prefatory Remarks

I

It has often been said that writers identify the beginning of the New Left in America as the time in which they joined "the movement." There is some truth in the notion that we all tend to place events in relationship to our own experiences rather than the other way around. I concur with Alvin Gouldner and others that the social analyst needs to appreciate the inputs which have affected his thinking. (See my essay in the *American Sociological Review,* April 1971.) It is in this light that I offer a brief autobiographical note.

Along with a whole generation of Americans, I was the product of the Depression with its legacy of economic insecurity, quest for material success, and continued emphasis on the Puritan values that formed the basis of this country's consciousness. As a college student during the so-called quiet 50s, I sensed the middle-class acceptance of education as the vehicle for insuring success and the striving for upward mobility characteristic of the working class youth who made it to college. Amidst the acquiescence and the timidity that was manifest in the McCarthy period, however, there was the embryo of concern which was to be articulated in the expression of the movements for racial justice and in opposition to the rabid militarism and anti-communist ideology which increasingly characterized domestic and international policies. Students in relatively small numbers were politically expressive and the stirrings of discontent within the educational systems were evident. At that time I began to wonder about the compatibility of traditional approaches to teaching and learning and the various conceptions of self-direction and growth. I pondered the role of education as a vehicle for mobility in industrial society, while noting the essential homogeneity of race and class at my college. When I then spent some time at a commuter college in a major downtown metropolitan area, I came to appreciate the locking-out function that American higher education was increasingly to assume.

The stirrings out of apathy which began in the mid-fifties were expressed largely in concern over Russian intervention in Hungary, U.S. troop deployments to Lebanon, nuclear testing in the atmosphere, and the host of other issues associated with the Cold War—as well as the struggle for social justice. The sputnik phenomenon was felt educationally in terms of an increased emphasis upon science and applied technics, along with the further subordination of humanistic studies. The appreciation of knowledge in the service of the state became pronounced.

My own political involvements at the time were tied to the pacifistic peace movement, the formation of the Student Peace Union, and the efforts to integrate schools and to compel public accommodations to serve within the letter of the law (the major objectives of the then active groups, NAACP and CORE). Yet, like most graduate students in the 1950s, my attention within the university was focused on things such as ROTC, not on student participation in governance or on what kind of learning went on in the university or even how it was taught. The first lunch-counter sit-in in North Carolina, the expansion of civil rights effort in the South, and the formation of the Northern Student Movement, however, ushered in the 1960s and directed energies into ways of relating the university to the struggles in the society.

Prefatory Remarks xiii

Perhaps it is the experience of being on the other side of the podium that leads many to understand the power dynamics of the educational institution. The experience of starting my university teaching career ten years ago was especially important in leading me to think seriously about the nature of the student-teacher relationship, the way in which learning was structured in the university, and how the function of the university in the society was reflected in how the institution was run.

It was at the beginning of the 1960s as a young faculty member that I began to challenge the role of the university, to see more clearly the military-industrial-educational complex, and to examine critically the way in which the university was run. Perhaps the issues became clearer than they might have otherwise, since I taught first at Michigan State University just at the time when some of its faculty were beginning to write and talk about that particular university's role in Vietnam. Michigan State President John Hannah accepted the invitation of Vice-President Richard Nixon in the 1950s to develop a CIA-linked university project to support a puppet government in Vietnam. In the late 1960s President Richard Nixon appointed Hannah to head the U.S. Agency for International Development which handles most university contracts for overseas projects.

It is possible that Michigan State University was the clearest prototype of what American universities were becoming. But what was to be the consequence? In the words of conservative writer and former Michigan State faculty member Russell Kirk:

> . . . is it the Hannahs [M.S.U. President] of our time who have discredited the university, and so raised up a turbulent generation of students, at once ignorant and passionate, who nevertheless sense somehow that Hannah's idea of a university is not quite John Henry Newman's idea of a university? Having established academic collectivism, having overwhelmed academic community, having severed the intellectual and moral roots of the higher learning, people like John Hannah are chagrined to discover the proles are restless [in Weaver and Weaver, *The University and Revolution,* p. 70].

In the beginnings of the most significant movement of students on the Left, Students for a Democratic Society talked a good deal about participatory democracy, the idea of persons organizing to control their fate in ways that have been articulated in Yugoslav systems of self-management or what some writers have discussed as community government (discussed in Deutsch and Howard, *Where It's At: Radical*

Perspectives in Sociology). This thinking arose out of a concern for alternative systems of power and decision making and a belief that in American society all institutions were structured to facilitate the interests of the military-industrial complex. Throughout the decade of the 1960s the broader philosophical ideas were carried by students into these realms of education. Many asked, if we expect to change America and to make it better, more humane and more consistent with these values, then where better to begin but in the institution through which all pass in one way or another?

My own thinking was shaped in part by the educational philosophies of writers such as Paul Goodman, by S.D.S. positions, and by my conditioning in the classroom and as a faculty member. I found that the idea behind Friends World College, captured in the phrase "community of scholars, some younger, some older," best fit my own ideal. I recall my enthusiasm two years ago when I read Harold Taylor's book *Students Without Teachers* which characterized many of my thoughts as well. But in the effort to sort out my own educational philosophies and in attempting to fit what I was doing as an educator to my broader philosophies and ideologies, I noted several curious inconsistencies. For example, I had taught for a few years in the mid-1960s at an expensive, private, urban university on the edge of one of the most restive Black ghettos in the country. While active and in support of the United Freedom Movement and the effort to desegregrate and upgrade Cleveland schools, I was teaching privileged white youth. While demonstrating to prevent the construction of inferior all-black public schools, I was a part of the locking-out system of higher education. While researching and writing about the problems of ghetto youth and the needs for change in education (my chapter in Beggs and Alexander, *Integration and Education*), I was not personally a part of the few experiments developing in higher education which admitted students not on the basis of achievement, but potential, and which measured the quality of colleges and universities by their products not their students' achievements before entering. At this point I began to take an interest in institutions of higher learning which were experimenting with admissions and programs designed for minority youth. I began to ponder what the possibilities were and what impact such efforts would have in the larger picture.

By 1965 I began to note the growing shift in faculty-student relationships and the experimental efforts which took various forms including the student-initiated curricular efforts at San Francisco State College. In the winter of 1966 I learned firsthand of the San Francisco State developments, and I pursued my inquiry after moving to the West Coast that fall. I continued to be intrigued by the experimental effort there and visited the campus several times, including the convocation held in the fall of 1967. By 1968 I was aware that student-initiated curricular efforts were being developed throughout the country and I pondered whether the dramatic departure from traditional faculty prerogatives of fixing the curriculum would spill over into other areas of the university, not only programmatically but politically in terms of decision-making power and governance.

During the mid-1960s one of my major research interests addressed the international developments in higher education. I was struck by the commitments made by American colleges and universities to international programs ranging from admissions of substantial numbers of foreign students to the international training of U.S. students to institution-building programs abroad. I initiated my research at a time when most educators supported internationalizing the curriculum in an effort to make American students more sensitive to the rest of the world. It was a time when the idealism of the Peace Corps was matched by the optimism many felt as a result of President Kennedy's American University speech suggesting a major thaw in the Cold War. Yet, as my research continued, I became more aware of the strategic considerations which lay behind virtually all governmental support for international educational and cultural affairs, and I sensed increasingly the problems of reconciling the total function of the university in our society with the pleas for expansion of the international dimension. In my book *International Education and Exchange: A Sociological Analysis*, I tapped some of the dimensions of the problem but only superficially touched upon some of the critical concerns which later became more apparent.

I continued to be intrigued by how policies were made and by what shaped the programs of colleges and universities in the international dimension. This furthered my interest in relating what Harold Taylor called "The World As Teacher" to "the university as American reality." That is, I saw the support for international programs coming less from idealistic world federalists and peace makers, and more from the State Department planners concerned with preserving America's position in the world. Another question which occurred was whether universities were operating out of a moralistic altruism or out of sheer expediency in opening admissions and developing minority student programs. Furthermore, as the universities more and more became the servants of power in the society, their critical roles were diminished and only dramatic restorative efforts—such as the Teach-Ins Against the War in Vietnam—moved the universities back to positions of autonomous criticism.

By 1968 I was aware that the major developments in American higher education were potentially a force for fundamental change in the academy. In particular, the student-initiated experimental colleges and the ethnic studies programs went to the heart of what the student movement for change was calling for. First, students challenged faculty prerogatives and pushed for shared power in determining what should be taught at the academy and who should do the teaching. Second, this not only led to a substantive change with the introduction of action-oriented courses, courses concerned with war, imperialism, militarism, racism and the range of issues discerned by students, but it opened up important matters of policy commitments by the colleges and universities. These radical curricular developments seemed particularly significant. While I had San Francisco State especially in mind, many widely publicized developments seemed illustrative, for example, the Berkeley course which had students in Washington, D.C. with the Poor People's Campaign. As part of a study I was doing for the University of Oregon's School of Community Service and Public Affairs, I had occasion to visit a number of university campuses in 1968 and explore their experimental efforts, including various cluster colleges. The more I observed what was happening and pondered the relationships between on-campus educational reforms and off-campus politics, I appreciated the degree to which educational experimentation was the link. In short, experimental colleges and ethnic studies programs tied together the demands for community relevance, the calls for a redirection of university resources, the arguments for restructuring power within the university, and appeals for altering the curriculum itself. These developments *had* to be the most important thing going on in American higher education in 1968, and there seemed to be virtually no research into these problems.

While I had some theoretical ideas about what the focus of a study should be, the character clearly had to be experimental in nature, calling for a research design and methodology appropriate to the effort (discussed in the Appendix). It seemed clear that it would be useful to

Prefatory Remarks xvii

gather systematic evidence as to what was happening on typical campuses in which educational innovations seemed to be developing into significant parts of the institution. More importantly, the major question seemed to be: What impact, if any, do radical curricular developments have upon the political structures of colleges and universities? Tied to this was the matter of educational reform as an approach to achieving structural change. I was convinced that such efforts were ill-conceived in the educational system of the country, and I argued (*Sociological Inquiry,* winter 1970) that the prime use of social science, in fact, had been to develop strategies for reform which obscured the wider picture and prevented basic structural changes from developing. Would this same phenomenon occur in experimental colleges and ethnic studies? Would they diffuse student discontent and divert energies into impotent reformist enterprises while leaving the fundamental features and functions of the academy untouched and unaltered? This seemed to be a critical set of questions in 1968, as the first cadres of "McCarthy kids" were being recruited by SDSers who educated them as to the diversionary tactics of the American establishment or as they dropped out and took up hip cultures and retreated into drug or other ecstatic states of withdrawal.

Joseph Fashing and I got together to develop the strategy for this study in the summer of 1968. He had been working on a study of citizen support for minority programs in the public schools and had a background of research and programs in educational sociology. Through an increasingly involved and challenging intellectual relationship, we came together to articulate the problem for this study as we pondered the thrust of American higher education and the challenges of innovations, governance, and the dynamic of change on the campus and in the society. We launched our investigation and initiated campus visits in the fall of 1968 and have just completed the most recent visits in the early months of 1971.

Many of the questions which struck us in 1968 have been answered to a considerable extent by now. We see what has happened in terms of the crisis in legitimacy with the young's overwhelming rejection of such societal laws as those on drugs, sex, draft, and abortion. While there have been signs of relative political quiescence, events of May 1970 clearly affect the total academic community, which now includes eight million students. As these words are written in April 1971, the campus and the nation are responding to the American-supported invasion of Laos, three years after a man won election to the Presidency of the country on a pledge to extricate the United States from Indochina.

This study of the politics of educational innovation does not address all facets of higher education, nor are the points today in direct response to the questions asked at the initiation of the study. Furthermore, our confidence in making predictive commentary about students or the academy is sharply reduced. This is not due to our sense that we will make the same ideological assumptions that led sociologists to celebrate the fulfillment of the American Dream and the "end of ideology" in the 1950s and thus fail to anticipate either the student or Black liberation movements of the 1960s. I am convinced that the commentary and analysis in this book *is* close to the pulse of what is going on in American higher education. However, situational factors such as the Cambodian invasion of May 1970 shape American college and university life in a way that none of us can predict. This study explains some of the developments in the past six years and suggests some implications for now and for tomorrow, but the reader surely must put all this into a context that more and more obviously affects the nature of college and university life in America. A humane, democratic, and idealistic university requires a compatible society.

Steven E. Deutsch

II

In the past few years, the gulf between the various constituencies of the university has grown dramatically. The ideal of the community of scholars, held by many in the academic world, now seems more distant than ever. The frustration induced by the gap between what the university is and what I personally feel that it could be is what engendered my interest in the project that led to this book.

At the time we undertook the study I was straddling the fence between the world of the faculty member and that of the student. In the last stages of my graduate study, I had been given the opportunity to teach, and I was forced to face the issues about which I had had much to say as a student. To translate my own educational dreams into some semblance of reality is a more formidable challenge than I had once imagined it would be, but I remain convinced that it is not impossible.

My initial concerns did not arise out of any systematic examination of the structure of educational institutions or of their role in the society but simply as a consequence of a mixed variety of educational experiences. Some of these experiences were happy indeed, but others were disastrous. At the time, and in frequent reflections since, I have asked myself if these disparate experiences were necessary. Would it not be possible to construct learning situations in which there really was some sense of communality? Are such things as schools without failure a real possibility—at every educational level? Is it necessary for the university to act as a clearinghouse, sorting the worthy from the unworthy, the "bright" from the "dull," the talented from the untalented? Must the accent remain on competition rather than on learning? The answers to these and a host of other questions have remained more or less problematic, but I am convinced that the possibilities have only begun to be explored.

This study represents, to me, the beginning of a search for answers about the possibilities. My concern is heightened, as everyone's is, I suspect, by the current rapid disintegration of the academy. In the face of a growing cynicism about the possibilities for reform of the university, I am not convinced that the battle has been lost—although I will concede that it is a formidable task that lies ahead. Part of the reason that I have not given up is my conviction that radical and liberal critics have not yet taken the kinds of initiatives that are necessary if meaningful change is to be achieved. We have not met impressively the challenge of giving substance to our rhetoric. We have created our own credibility gaps at every level in the university, and it should not be surprising that we find widespread disaffection as a response. To lead the way in the construction and implementation of alternative models of education is not a task which many of us have taken seriously. To the extent that we have not, we have contributed to the polarization on campus.

There are those who argue that the university is simply a reflection of the larger society and that reform of our institutions can only follow a transformation of the larger society. The heart of that issue is whether the university should remain in its position of follower rather than leader. A position of leadership requires a willingness to assume the role of exemplar—to practice what we preach. If we lack the capacity and the will to transform our own small sector of society, then our claims to a larger leadership role will necessarily ring hollow. Initiatives for change must begin somewhere and why not the university? In the last analysis, it is a simple question of attending to our own admonitions. If we can do at least that, perhaps we can restore some hope for the future. At this point I remain hopeful, but the time is short. In any case, the construction of viable alternatives to our current educational institutions is the most urgent task of the concerned academic.

Joseph Fashing

Acknowledgments

This book is the product of numerous conversations held with many of our colleagues around the country, far too numerous to mention. Several have been particularly helpful as informants and consultants of various sorts and, while acknowledging the many, we especially thank: George Rothbart, Richard Brown, Troy Duster, Robert Kinsman, Maurice Foisy, and Lee Zeigler. Gail Kunselman, Carolyn Norman, and Carol Mitchell are among the many others who helped us in a variety of ways and to whom we express our appreciation.

The Institute of Scholarly and Scientific Research of the University of Oregon Graduate School gave us the initial support for the study, and we are most grateful. Additionally, the Department of Sociology at the University of Oregon was most supportive in terms of facilitating the research and providing needed assistance.

To the many persons who were willing to talk with us, to those who allowed personal and telephone interviews, we express our appreciation. We might indicate that as in all such field research, the fact is that the study would not have been done without the cooperation of the informants and respondents. We hope that their trust and cooperation will have been warranted in this book.

We dedicate this book to the proposition that institutions of higher education must change and that they need to fulfill their potential in bringing about a more humane, decent society.

Joseph Fashing
Steven E. Deutsch

I
The Challenge for Educational Change

American Society and Higher Education

At no time in our history has there been a crisis comparable to the one in which we currently find ourselves. It became increasingly clear during the 1960s that the institutions of the United States had experienced a fundamental breakdown bringing on a crisis in legitimacy which ushered in the 1970s. By the middle of the decade there were regular urban disorders (race riots and rebellions), the massive rejection of an illegal and genocidal war, and widespread disillusionment with electoral politics and nonviolence as methods of social change. There was substantial disaffection for major institutions—the "death of God" controversy in the church, a great deal of marital dissolution, and manifestations of work alienation. Perhaps most notable in this period of crisis has been the chaos in education.

As Americans began to read James Conant and other writers on slums and schools, their concern grew for the quality of education. Blacks took to the streets and concern became more widespread. The struggle for racial justice shook the moral foundations of the society, but the commitment of the young provided inspiration and hope for the country. Out of this mood, a new moral thrust was emerging which led to efforts towards a thaw in the Cold War. It provided impetus for the rediscovery of poverty and the effort to reexamine pervasive social needs. In a more general sense, it inspired young people not only to search for a more perfect world, but to work for one.

The era of political timidity, a legacy of the McCarthy years with its witchhunts and intimidation, was changing even before the decade had ended. With the civil rights struggle beginning in the 1960s, there was a profound shift in ideological mood. The emphasis on conservatism declined and a growing challenge to liberalism replaced it.[1]

The sixties began with the election of John Kennedy, the personification of youth, liberalism and optimism, and a commitment to "get the country moving again." The Peace Corps and the end of atmospheric nuclear testing heralded a new hope. As the president appointed his brother U.S. Attorney General, the nation witnessed the first sit-in in North Carolina opening massive efforts to open public accommodations in the South. Millions of Americans saw Bull Connor's dogs in Birmingham working to preserve the control of power by the white ruling class. Meanwhile, festering tensions in the cities of the North and West grew and our national failures became more apparent. Early Kennedy supporters joined Students for a Democratic Society in an effort to meet the challenge to remake the society.

Jack Newfield, a chronicler of the New Left, observed that what was happening was "not that the country [was] becoming more conservative, but that liberalism [was] becoming more conservative."[2] Students recruited into the movement began to recognize that the Kennedy-Johnson variety of Democratic liberalism was making only hollow gestures at liberating repressed minorities and depressed poor. The call for world peace rang false in the face of threats to destroy mankind in a nuclear showdown in Cuba and the extension of American military involvement in Southeast Asia.

As these events transpired, the proportion of the population under the age of twenty-five was expanding and approaching one-half of all Americans. The number of young people in school was increasing steadily and enrollments in colleges and universities skyrocketed. With the expansion of the college community students came to play a more critical role in supporting the politics and programs of state welfarism and liberalism.

The Free Speech Movement at Berkeley had given witness to the growing alienation of university students. At the same time SDS projects (ERAP—Educational Research and Action Projects) in Cleveland and Newark and projects in the South during Mississippi Freedom Summer were showing the long-range commitment of students. Student activists who returned to the campus came with a new sensitivity and social concern. Foremost among these concerns were such issues as the role of military training and war research in the universities and the failure of the universities to mobilize resources to meet the needs of minority and poor communities. By mid-decade, the escalation of the war in Vietnam and rising draft calls fanned the discontent and disillusion of growing numbers of American youth.

In 1965 the Teach-In Movement was born, an event which heralded the concept of restructuring the university. One important by-product of this movement was a considerable alteration in faculty-student relationships on many campuses. Many persons have since come to realize that 1965 was truly a turning point for the American university. This year ushered in the wide range of demands for change which have characterized the period since.

If there was a coming-of-age on university campuses, it was marked by the recognition of a fundamental truth: institutions of higher leaning are a reflection of the wider society. Though faculty and students may act as if they reside in an ivory tower, they occupy a central place in the total societal machine. In this respect, we cannot examine colleges and universities outside the context of the larger society. As we move into the seventies, the United States is in a period of monumental crisis. Its survival, and that of the entire planet, are no longer taken for granted. This crisis exists on the campus as much as anywhere. Although our concern is primarily with the politics of the college and university undergoing change, a sensitivity to the wider context in which these changes are occurring is a must.

Immanuel Wallerstein has pointed out, quite correctly, that the university is political in any posture it assumes, whether it is in support of the government, indifferent to the government, or in opposition to the government.[3] What is critical is the political policy the university has at any particular moment. He notes that, "it is not surprising . . . that the university, perpetual ground of conflict, should be beset by disorders as the importance of the institution has suddenly become so visible and widely recognized. What seemed just and sensible action twenty-five years ago, even five years ago, is now being challenged by many within the university." [4] By the end of the 1960s, "a politically aroused student population, led by anti-capitalist, anti-imperialist groups, has made it clear that its fundamental target is the role the university plays in the social order." [5]

Characteristic of the assault on the role of the university were the events of the 1968 academic year. That year saw massive demonstrations across the country, including the uprising at Columbia. There were comparable attacks at Chicago and other universities which were involved in the Institute for Defense Analysis and whose administrations were increasingly moving against the poor and minority populations in the resident communities surrounding the campuses. This was only the beginning of what was to be an extremely turbulent year on the nation's campuses. "During the Columbia anniversary spring of 1969, one researcher counted student disruptions on 83 separate campuses from San Francisco State to City College of New York. On a single day in April 1969, student demonstrators were occupying buildings on 17 American campuses." [6]

Perhaps another reason that 1968 illuminated the significance of the push for changes on the campuses is that it was a traumatic year for the nation. There were the assassinations of Martin Luther King and Robert Kennedy, the brutality of the Democratic Convention, and the collapse of faith in electoral politics for masses of people, especially the young. The growth of the New Left was substantial and 1968 was a harbinger of things to come. By 1969 the *New York Times* reported "635,000 radical students and fellow travellers studying on the campuses. That the anti-left *Times* would report the tabluation is significant, and the numbers, even if understated, speak for themselves." [7] In 1970 the surveys show that freshman students are increasingly leftist in their orientation.[8] There is evidence that a shift has occurred so that the constituency of activist left students has expanded.[9] The mood for change in 1968 was indicative of things to come.

During the 1960s problems, collectively referred to as "the campus crisis," reached the stage where they are now counted among the most pressing issues in a nation besieged with troubles. At no time in our history has the climate on the campus reflected such a general disaffection and alienation among America's students. This is not to say that the nation has never experienced comparable difficulties on the campus, only that the magnitude has never been so great. Although campuses were generally quiet as the 1970-71 year began, the mood of students was still sullen. Professors commonly observed that the quiet reflected a sense of futility and despair. The atmosphere was morose—as if hope had been abandoned. Nevertheless, the issues that generated the crisis wear on. As the proportion of the students attending colleges and universities grows, the campus crisis is magnified in the national mind.

The importance of higher education in this country has grown immensely in the last few decades. Today there are nearly eight million students in this country's colleges and universities and the prognosis is for continued, though perhaps slower, growth. Since 1960 this growth has been extraordinary. Many major state institutions doubled their enrollment in less than a decade. While universities managed to keep pace physically by accommodating burgeoning numbers of students, the rapidity of this change outdistanced the immediate capacity of most institutions to respond to the problems attendant to such growth. There is a growing feeling that the educational process is suffering as a consequence of current developments affecting the campus. According to one college administrator, "studies of American higher education, both in the teaching and learning process, and in the administration of the large and complex university, reveal a record with many failures." [10]

Considering the magnitude of the problems facing higher education, there has been relatively little systematic study of the change process and its response to these problems. In the past decade, for instance, there has been very little study of the process of educational innovation in colleges and universities, and almost none with reference to some of the most important developments. Among these are student initiated experimental colleges, other experimental units, and ethnic studies programs. While it appears that these are among the most rapidly developing innovative programs in American higher education, comparative study of their development and of their impact on the institutions in which they have emerged has been negligible. It was our intent in undertaking this study, to begin such a comparative analysis. Our central focus is on the sources of educational innovations, the politics of development of such innovations, and, particularly, their impact on the governance of the institutions in which they are undertaken.

Educational Problems in Retrospect

Many of the problems often considered peculiar to mass education in the mass society are not particularly new ones. Throughout the history of American education, the themes of the critics and of the student protestors show a remarkable consistency. If one examines some of these past critiques of higher education, or looks at the types of issues that have moved students to protest, one is immediately struck by the parallels between analyses of the problems of a half-century ago and those examining the current situation. As far back as 1918 Thorstein Veblen, in *The Higher Learning in America*,[11] a book that has become a classic in American educational criticism, railed against the neglect of the undergraduate student in the new universities. He criticized the university for its bureaucratic organization and for what he called a system of "scholastic accountancy" which bears a startling resemblance to the contemporary problem usually referred to as "publish or perish." Veblen's thesis was that the university was no place for the undergraduate and that mimicry of a university education as a substitute for a sound undergraduate education in a liberal arts college was absurd.[12] There is a lingering suspicion that many university faculty share this idea and reflect it in the attention which they give to their undergraduate students.

Only a few years later Upton Sinclair, reflecting on his own educational experience, spoke of the "irrelevance" of higher education. He laments:

> I look back now, and see myself as I was, and I shudder—not merely for myself, but for all other products of the educational machine. I think of the things I didn't know, and of the pains and perils to which my ignorance exposed me! I knew nothing about hygiene and health; everything of that sort I had to learn by painful error. I knew nothing about women; I had met only three or four besides my mother, and had no idea how to deal with them. I knew as much about sex as was known to the ancient religious ascetics, but nothing of modern discoveries or theories on the subject.
>
> More significant yet, I knew nothing about modern literature in any language; I had acquired a supreme and top-lofty contempt for it, and was embarrassed when I happened to read "Sentimental Tommy," and discovered that someone had written a work of genius in my own

time! I knew nothing about modern history; so far as my mind was concerned, the world had come to an end with the Franco-Prussian war, and nothing had happened since. . . .

Most significant of all to me personally, I was unaware that the modern revolutionary movement existed . . . I knew, of course, that there had been Socialism in ancient times, for I had read Plato, and been amused by his quaint suggestions for the reconstruction of the world. Also I knew that there had been dreamers and cranks in America who went off and tried to found Utopian commonwealths. It was safe for me to be told about these experiments, because they had failed. I had heard the names of Marx and Lassalle, and had a vague idea of them as dreadful men, who met in the back rooms of beer-gardens, and conspired, and made dynamite bombs, and practised free love. That they had any relationship to my life, that they had anything to teach me, that they had founded a movement which embraced all the future—of this I was as ignorant as I was of the civilization of Dahomey, or the far side of the moon.[13]

Nor are these the only parallels. Robert Hutchins, in assessing the problems at the University of Chicago and other great universities more than thirty-five years ago, discussed in one or another context each of the following: the alleged overemphasis on research to the exclusion of teaching; deficiencies in the preparation of college instructors; and consignment of classes to teaching assistants who are either ill-prepared, ill-motivated, or both.[14]

At the same time James Wechsler related the tale of the "student revolt." The revolt included, among other things, a radicalization of the student population as the result of experiences with the labor movement, especially in the border states. Students began to attack major national interests, struck at Columbia University over the expulsion of the editor of the student newspaper, began active efforts to resist compulsory ROTC training, and staged national student strikes for peace in 1934 and 1935 reputed to have rallied 25,000 and 175,000 participants respectively. The issues were very much the same as those which compel today's student activists. Predominant themes were anti-war, anti-military, and prolabor. Neither was the response from the university and the public unlike today's. There was panic, attempted repression, red-baiting, and charges of professional agitation while patriotic groups like the Daughters of the American Revolution and the American Legion fomented the red (Communist) scare.[15]

The issues and the parameters of the current problem have been articulated clearly by Clark Kerr in *The Uses of the University*. The nature of the modern "multiversity" is somewhat different than that of the traditional university. This difference, Kerr argues, is a consequence of the demands imposed upon institutions of higher learning by an advanced industrial and highly technological society such as our own. He points out that federal research programs spawned during World War II with the establishment of wartime laboratories, which subsequently developed into such "continuing government financed research centers as the Lincoln Laboratory at the Massachusetts Institute of Technology, the Argonne at Chicago, and the Lawrence Radiation Laboratory at California," [16] have contributed to the increasing emphasis on research in the multiversity. Kerr is not among the critics of these developments, however, and he goes on to point out that we can expect such an emphasis to continue given the demands and needs of our society for continued technological and scientific development.

The shifting emphasis upon research has brought about a concomitant shift in the nature of priorities within many institutions' instructional programs. Harold Orlans, in a study of the impact of federal aid on the colleges and universities, concluded that federal research aid "has accelerated the long-standing depreciation of undergraduate education at large universities." [17] It is this issue, the claimed deterioration in the quality of undergraduate education, which constitutes one of the more pressing problems of the modern university.

The issue of shifting emphasis and educational deterioration has been accompanied, in the past ten years, by the demands of ethnic and radical minority communities that the university use its resources to seek solutions to minority problems in this country. As a first step they appealed to the university to discard its oppressive role in a number of urban areas.[18] In this respect, minority spokesmen demanded, not only research of minority problems, but that the university provide an education for those community members traditionally excluded by standard university selection procedures and by economic barriers.

These kinds of demands impose obligations which the university has rarely addressed with relish. Perhaps the most important of these obligations is dealing with the particular needs of the minority student which may have implications for the entire university in terms of curriculum revisions, the necessity of directing scholarship into new areas, and the conduct of remedial or preparatory programs which were traditionally seen as the function of the junior college, if they were addressed at all.

There appears to be general agreement that, because of the nature of the reward system in American higher education, undergraduate instruction, whatever its aims, receives a relatively low priority. Whatever objective measures we might choose would probably support this contention. The average professor spends less time in the undergraduate classroom than ever before; the ratio of students to regular faculty continues to grow; and graduates assume responsibility for instruction in an increasing proportion of the undergraduate curriculum.[19]

Assault on the Campus:
Protest and the Recent Educational Climate

Events of the past few years have made it abundantly clear, however, that the climate among college students is not one which will allow the progressive deterioration of the university's instructional mission. Increasingly larger classes and an increasingly impersonal and mechanical environment are no longer the objects of passive complaint. These and other problems have become the targets of direct action on an unprecedented scale.[20]

Perhaps the most significant events in the recent history of American higher education transpired at the University of California's Berkeley campus early in the fall of 1964. The outbreak of the Free Speech Movement at Berkeley is synonymous for many with the beginning of the "student movement" in this country. Since the events at Berkeley, similar, and sometimes more dramatic, confrontations between students and other segments of the academic community have occurred on a number of campuses. Indeed, there are few major institutions which have escaped without at least token confrontations between dissident students and other campus factions. These confrontations have, in effect, signalled the end of the student's willingness to sit by passively while the rest of the university community adopts policies and programs which he defines as antithetical to his own interests. Students have been formulating demands on a number of fronts which have a common theme—that the university devote considerably more attention to their education, both in terms of its general "quality" and in terms of its "relevance" in the framework of current local, national, and international conditions.

The general aim of much recent student activism has been vaguely defined general reforms oriented toward solving the problems already outlined. On other fronts, of course, the issues have extended well beyond the bounds of the campus even though they were often of singular importance in the university community. Among these issues have been the war, the universities' involvement in defense (or offense) research, and the universities' relationships with the larger community, especially the ethnic minorities. Here again though, it is often difficult to separate campus issues from broader ones since faculty commitments to these broader issues and to the moral questions they raise has quite direct implications for the classroom experience of the student. Many contemporary student demands are concerned with establishing innovative approaches to the variety of problems facing him. They include such ideas as: experimental curricula; student participation in university decision making; special attention to the curriculum and related needs of black and other minority students; a general reduction in the size of classes; insured consideration of quality of instruction in the promotion and tenure of faculty; a general humanization of the university's bureaucratic directive machinery; and a withdrawal of the university from cooperation with governmental military and paramilitary operations.

The demands of student dissidents have generated a variety of responses from the larger institutions. Many of these responses are still in the stage of recommendations by faculty committees and have yet to be acted upon.[21] Others, however, represent initial attempts to deal with problems at the heart of many student complaints. The most frequent innovative program appears to be that which falls under the label of the "experimental college." Such programs often consist primarily of credit and non-credit student-organized seminars and courses calculated to revitalize the curriculum by increasing its interest and making it "relevant" to the lives and experience of the student. In other cases, the experimental college has involved a more formal institutional commitment with a separate faculty, separate facilities, and a totally independent curriculum.[22]

In another problem area there are growing numbers of programs for campus minority communities such as institutes for black and ethnic studies. Also residential colleges now operate within the larger university which are specifically designed to combat problems of depersonalization and alienation, students have been introduced to committees making decisions on various facets of university operation, and assorted other remedial enterprises have been initiated. There are few institutions without some form of program addressed to university problems. A few, like Antioch, have, in fact, experimented with the operation of the total institution; but most have been considerably more modest in the scope of their approach to problems.

Despite the modesty of their resources, however, experimental colleges and other innovational programs have had a considerable impact on many institutions. In some cases they have enrolled large numbers of students and, perhaps, have acted as a catalyst for additional programs. Often other institutions, looking for alternative modes of response to pressing problems, have looked to such experimental colleges as possible models for educational reform. On the other hand, despite the enthusiasm among a number of constituencies and despite the immense pressures for change, innovation and reform programs continue to be modest in both resources and scope. In cases where various campus constituents have clashed over the underlying issues, such programs have faltered and often collapsed. Where hostilities have progressively escalated and lines hardened as in the more celebrated cases like San Francisco State and Berkeley, reprisals from governing boards and legislatures alike have virtually destroyed the programs and along with them the impetus toward reform.

University Response to Demands for Change: The Record

To the casual observer Berkeley would appear to be among the vanguard of forces for change. There is little, however, despite the much publicized Muscatine Report [23] or the *Report of the Faculty Committee on University Governance*,[24] which would suggest that there have been significant changes since the fall of 1964. Such a judgment is corroborated by Nathan Glazer who comments:

> Four years after the Free Speech Movement exploded in Autumn 1964, the world does look very different, and the FSM looks like a prophetic turning point; but the University of California looks very much the same. . . . [25]

This condition continues despite what almost everyone would concede is one of the most active student bodies in the nation in pushing for reform, and despite apparent commitments on the part of faculty and administration to generalized change and improvement. But the problem is not one that is peculiar to Berkeley; it has national and even international dimensions.[26]

The immediate question emerging from all of this is why, given these sorts of commitments, has there been so little significant change? Or, to put the question into a positive framework, how is it that changes are wrought in the modern college and university structure, and beyond that, what are their implications?

While there has been an apparent organizational rigidity within the university in this country, it has not been totally unresponsive to demands for change. The nature of such change has rarely, however, been oriented toward the actual or perceived needs of students, but to the more general demands of the outside community, especially government and industry. With regard to the basic educational process, there has been little alteration except in the faculty-student ratio, since the very beginning of American higher education. Frederick Rudolph, a historian of American higher education, suggests that:

> Resistance to fundamental reform was ingrained in the American collegiate and university tradition, as over three hundred years of history demonstrated. A historian of the University of Rochester described the traditional policy of his institution as one of wise conservatism modified by the spirit of liberal progressivism when warranted by circumstances. This was also, except on rare occasions, the historic policy of the American college and university: drift, reluctant accommodation, belated recognition that while no one was looking, change had in fact taken place.[27]

On the opposite side of the coin, however, one can argue that the university has been overwhelmed by forces from the outside and that such forces have drastically altered the nature of its internal priorities. Kerr argues, for instance, that "two great impacts, beyond all other forces, have molded the modern American university system and made it distinctive." [28] The first of these forces was the Morrill Act of 1862 and the other was the federal support of scientific research begun during the Second World War. Each of these, he points out, were in response to perceived national needs, the first to increased needs for agricultural development and the second to problems of weapons research and national defense. The Morrill Act led to change in curricular structure and to "democratizing" higher education, while federal support of defense research shifted rather firmly the nature of priorities within the institution. The university's relationships with outside private and governmental agencies developed into a form of mutual interdependence with a large part of the university's operating budget being exchanged for scientific and technical expertise.[29]

Thus while the university cannot be characterized as having been totally unresponsive to the demands for change, it is exactly in those areas where it has been responsive that the problem lies. The acceptance of research funds, often necessary to maintain the general level of affluence in the university community, is a continuing source of controversy because of the consequent impact on institutional priorities and its implications for undergraduate education. In addition, despite rather widespread contentions regarding the political neutrality of institutions, the willingness of the university to participate in many projects has clear-cut implications. The most offensive of such projects such as nuclear or biochemical warfare research, counterinsurgency studies, and explorations of exotic tactics for social control are unacceptable to significant segments of the university community.[30]

Along with its declaration of political neutrality, some critics argue that the limitation of the search for truth to only "those truths which are rationally discernible" has rendered the contemporary university incapable of dealing with the most compelling issues of the time.[31] This has led, in fact, to a declaration of moral non-responsibility of a large portion of the academic community. The declaration is usually rendered in the form of claim to value-neutrality.[32] What this has usually meant is a refusal of the academic community to come to grips, or at least make an attempt to come to grips, with moral issues such as war, racism, and poverty, which are perhaps more than ever impinging on the average student's consciousness.[33]

The unchecked growth of institutions along what have often been haphazard or ill-planned lines has also been a matter of concern for both students and faculty. Further, the fact that the huge multiversity with its peculiar problems and priorities has become the model to which other institutions aspire, compounds the problem.[34] Despite these issues, however, and despite the growing numbers of student disorders which stem directly or indirectly from them, the pattern of resistance to change in the university community continues.[35]

The pattern of resistance to change is not only an empirical reality, but an important ingredient in the picture. For example, although many universities have established self-study committees, there is evidence to suggest that these often become devices for draining away pressures for real change.[36] At Berkeley it was argued that students' realization that the FSM did not effect change led to increased alienation a few years afterward.[37] The recognition has emerged that the university's response to demands for change has typically been one of co-optation and, in the words of one writer, "one should fight for the specific things one wants the university to do, and not for 'structural reforms' which always turn out to be meaningless."[38] Thus, from the initial arguments for structural change have come some more recent calls for substantive shifts, focusing on what is decided rather than who makes the decision. Yet the structure of the university does affect the response to demands for change.

Organizational Structure and Resistance to Innovation

Clark Kerr identified the fundamental paradox of the nature of the university when he quipped, "Few institutions are so conservative as the universities about their own affairs while their members are so liberal about the affairs of others; and sometimes the most liberal faculty member in one context is the most conservative in another."[39]

While the conservatism of the university regarding its own structure and function is often scored, there is little that would lead us to expect large-scale change in the immediate or foreseeable future. In fact, we believe that there is strong evidence that trends of the past several years suggest a strengthening of internal conservatism, rather than a weakening. In the first place, there is little, if any, consensus about what changes are desirable or required in the university. The very nature of university organization, splitting units along narrow disciplinary lines, makes the formulation of a generally accepted program of reform very nearly impossible. Self-interest, plus a rather myopic view of the needs of others, often leads departments to define what is good for the university in terms of what is good for themselves.

In the not too far distant past, the organization of the university was very much along hierarchical lines with the decisions reserved largely for top administration and the governing boards of institutions. In theory, at least, the recent trend has been toward a more democratic form of university government.[40] In certain areas, for example curriculum and personnel matters, the members of the faculty or their representatives play an important part in decisions. A fundamental remaining problem, however, is that the university has probably established more official interest groups than any other organization in existence.

What we now have in the university, perhaps more than any other organization, is a vertical dimension of the inherent conflicts of interest which Dahrendorf describes as a fundamental feature of hierarchical organization.[41] In Dahrendorf's model this conflict is limited to various competing organizational strata inasmuch as there are no built in organizational features which introduce other dimensions of divisiveness. In the university, however, the inherent divisiveness of the departmental arrangement often overrides the forces toward unity at the level of the general faculty. This is especially true in institutions which have reached a point where the departmental system is elaborate and administrative power has been limited or offset by the growing power of increasingly distinguished lower-level units.[42]

The additional problem of completing institutional and professional demands has been confronted in a variety of contexts.[43] In the framework of the modern university, this conflict centers around the commitments to professional advancement, on the one hand, and the welfare of the institution on the other. While these are not necessarily incompatible ends, there are a variety of circumstances under which they may very well be, and these are what concern us here.

The organization of the university has been such that departments are often put in the position of competing directly with one another for available resources. In this respect, the needs of a particular department for additional staff and equipment often supersedes questions of the needs of the larger university. This may be attributed, in part at least, to the combination of departmental parochialism and the fact that most institutions have no clear-cut vision of what the particular mission of the college or university is, or ought to be—except, of course, for some very vague generalities found in the first page of the bulletin or permanently engraved over the entrance to the administration building or library. While this point may be open to debate in the sense that certain expressed institutional goals might rally greater or lesser support from the collective faculty, it remains a fact that few institutions have clearly expressed and articulated goals against which they might somehow measure their achievement.

The failure to articulate clear institutional goals may be functional in the sense that it allows faculty to decide on their own particular order of priorities and therefore to operate with a maximum amount of latitude, but it provides a relatively ambiguous organizational milieu and makes institutional planning and direction more difficult. Edward Gross points out that there appears to be some intrainstitutional consensus on priorities across a broad range of possible goals, but that these may often conflict with "official policy."[44] A case in point is what Gross refers to as the "prestige university" where goals having to do with undergraduate education rank at the very bottom of a long list of possible organizational priorities.[45] It would be safe to assume though, that few, if any, institutions with significant undergraduate enrollments are likely to issue an official statement notifying students and the public that undergraduate instruction ranks last, or very nearly last, in the institutional priorities. It is more likely the case that the "official" position of the university will be embodied in some vague general principles like those alluded to earlier. What this means is that there is rarely a larger institutional commitment which can overcome the competitive and divisive interests peculiar to individual departments. Attempts to translate the cliches that pass for an institutional policy into some sort of coherent guideline or general educational plan that does more than allocate a "group requirement" to various departments would be likely to generate massive internal squabbling and perhaps bloodletting. Departmental interests are usually so entrenched that efforts to transcend them frequently meet with stiff resistance.

While there are decided disadvantages, there is the counterargument that the lack of clear-cut goals or educational plans has the positive function (from the point of view of a large majority of the academic community) of giving individual faculty members a degree of freedom seldom found outside of the academy. What this freedom has meant in a number of major universities is "an undergraduate program—that [does] not interfere too much with the real business of academic men."[46] This "real business" can be translated as research, publication, and consultation. It further entails, in larger and more distinguished institutions, the business of building the reputation of one's department by bringing to it men of great scholarly reputation. The orientations of most of the university departments can thus be said to be focused outside of the university and toward a national or international professional community of particular disciplines.

To the extent that the focus of the faculty of the various disciplines is so constricted by narrow disciplinary interests and to the extent that they are unwilling or unable to address the problems of the larger university community, there is likely to be a situation in which nothing is altered even under intense pressure. This is often so because: 1) nobody is interested in the larger problems; 2) the faculty member's energies are so taxed with the problems revolving around discipline and department that there is nothing left for more general problems; or 3) factional disputes severely limit, or make altogether impossible, a resolution of general community problems. One is tempted to argue, in fact, that the only time the university faculty approaches consensus is in the face of a crisis which is interpreted by many as impending doom for the institution, such as the Free Speech Movement, the Columbia crisis, or the events precipitated by the United States invasion of Cambodia.

An interesting illustration of the kind of pervasive inertia that seems to ensnare the university community is pointed out by Martin Trow in an assessment of the celebrated University of California Muscatine Report. Trow notes that one of the reasons that it is so widely acclaimed within the academic community is that it has "the virtue of not affecting anybody who does not want to be affected by it." He goes on, "If the Report is notable for the lack of dispute it has occasioned, it is largely because virtually all of its many recommendations can be ignored by those who are simply not interested." [47]

The kind of neutralization of the possibility of directed change which appears to be one of the features of the organization of many contemporary universities is accompanied by a rather pervasive notion identified by Trow as "laissez faire with romantic overtones." [48] There seems to be a widespread general faith in the ability of institutions to successfully meet the challenges posed by many of our current educational dilemmas. Given the widespread and increasingly hostile confrontations between various sectors of the academic community, it would seem that such optimism is perhaps unwarranted—or perhaps premature since there has been so little in the way of study of educational innovation and its implications that we have little basis for judgment. While there have been a few descriptive articles in the journals of higher education, most of these are simply outlines of programs proposed or begun. There are immense gaps in the literature with regard to such issues as the problems involved in implementing innovations and the political impact of innovation—both internal to the institution in which it occurs and in the larger political arena.

There have been a few recent efforts to study the organizational characteristics which affect the nature of change in colleges and universities.

These have tapped several dimensions. One conclusion which emerges is that historical, contextual, and idiosyncratic features play critical roles in the particular conditions on a campus. Qualitative comparisons of student-centered experimental and ideological colleges oriented toward undergraduate teaching suggests that the total ethos matters considerably in shaping the educational experience on the campus.[49] In one discussion Clark examines the distinctive colleges of Reed, Antioch and Swarthmore and notes that personnel, leadership-charisma, social base, student subculture and ideology all are important as they affect change in the institution, whether it emerges in a new revolutionary or evolutionary context.[50]

Perhaps one of the starkest statements is Franklin's observation that the elite control of institutions of higher learning—be they private like Stanford or public like Berkeley—prevents them from adapting to the challenges for change. His suggestion is to end the cries for faculty power and give power to the people; he argues that the ruling class control of universities can only mean that irrelevant shifts will occur and that internal reform is not the issue. The issue is rather a basic restructuring of the universities.[51]

Beyond many calls for general overhauls of universities, which are unlikely due to elite control of the organizations, what evidence is there that various universities react differently to the demand for change and the push for reform? There is a variety in the response pattern which colleges and universities have given to the student protest movement, although some trends may be discerned, especially in terms of the substance of concessions granted and types of changes allowed.[52] There is a critical question generated by the studies of response to protest: Is change possible without disruption, violence, and confrontations?

Hefferlin's study—perhaps the most relevant one recently added to the literature—does not discuss the mode of change, but points out that "while the responsiveness of an institution to change can be significantly affected by internal factors, the institution will seldom alter its function without external influence. Outsiders initiate; institutions react." [53] In his examination of 110 colleges and universities Hefferlin noted that university purposes and support are basically conservative; that within higher education, institutional reputation is not based on innovation; and that academic institutions are deliberately structured to resist precipitant change.[54] Although all constituencies in the university claim to be change initiators, Hefferlin found that students were most influential in adding courses, faculty carried most weight in introducing programs of study, administrators had most control over adding units changing requirements, and trustees and outsiders most affected changes in the status of institutions.[55] While not finding that poor schools are stagnant or change out of desperation or that prestige schools rest on tradition and reject change, he did observe some contrasts between most and least dynamic institutions. For example, he observed that from a structural view reform is inhibited by inflexible, old, untenured faculty structure, conservative presidents and external supports, along with attitudinal conservatism by faculty and students.[56] Yet, there is no one factor which distinguishes the dynamic from the static schools; rather, a series of interrelated factors seems to operate to permit and force change. Dynamic institutions tend to be small, urban colleges, to have limited tenure for chairmen of departments, and to have more young and untenured faculty than static ones.[57] Static institutions tend to be large, private, prestige universities, to manifest an ethos of self-satisfaction, and to have more conservative presidents than dynamic institutions. In sum, we have in Hefferlin's analysis the suggestion of some possible patterns; but mostly it rejects the idea of key causative factors in favor of a number of related, facilitating institutional features as sources of academic reform.

Change in Higher Education

While there is a well-developed literature in the area of innovation and its diffusion in the realms of secondary and elementary education, there is no counterpart to this in higher education. Even though studies of the change process in lower level school systems might provide useful theoretical insights, there is little empirical evidence that suggests that the university can be viewed as an analogue of other levels of education and that findings applicable at one level might be extrapolated to another.[58] In fact, quite the opposite would appear to be the case; the unique features of higher education vis-a-vis other levels require an analysis in their own right.

In the first place, the organizational structures of higher education and elementary and secondary schools are not even remotely comparable. Arrangements within most public school systems, if not rigidly hierarchical, at least tend to lean in the direction of centralized administration, uniform policy, predetermined curricula, and so forth. "Normal" university operation would, however, be guided by administrative principles considerably at variance with these. In the better American institutions, university administrators are viewed at best as a necessary, but often frustrating, evil. At worst the administration is cast in the role of a servile lackey of modest intellectual capacity whose sole raison d'être is to facilitate the faculty's pursuit of their peculiar individual interests—whether or not these happen to coincide with institutional interests. In any case, faculty and student views of the administration tend to vary widely, and one could certainly expect disparate appraisals from any sample of the university community.

The evaluation of the actual and the ideal role of the administration in any institution will probably differ considerably because of the peculiarities of contemporary university organization. Legally, it is almost universally the case that all power is vested in the institution's trustees. In turn, however, such powers are delegated to and exercised by the institution's chief executive officer.[59] In the reality of university politics though, it is clear that such power must be exercised gingerly. Not only is the possibility of an internal faculty revolt a restraint, the possibility of attracting top caliber faculty may be jeopardized where administrative officials gain a reputation for being heavy-handed.

In addition to the problems of recruiting and staff development occasioned by an authoritarian administration, the whole ethos of professional autonomy and academic freedom limits effective control of administration over departmental units.[60] This raises a serious problem, not only of administrative effectiveness, but of basic governing philosophy. There is clearly a point at which democratic organization is an extremely conservative force in that it reduces the capacity to take action because of the difficulties of generating consensus. In addition, such administrative styles may also serve to protect entrenched vested interests which are incompatible with the best interests of the university community. In balancing institutional and individual interests, it may be important for the administration to have a measure of power in order to assume direct control in those instances where departments are unable or unwilling to resolve such conflicts. Just what constitutes the optimum in administrative as opposed to departmental power, however, is an issue which few, if any, institutions have resolved. Major universities, and most others with aspirations for excellence in terms of the new multiversity model, operate on a kind of laissez-faire principle with regard to the operation of individual departments except in those cases where there are generally recognized problems or weaknesses. Such a principle of operation partially includes some departmental control of hiring and promotion, of tenure decisions, of curriculum, of departmental degree programs, and of most of the pedestrian decisions regarding the day-to-day operation. While the president is, in theory, expected to exercise some kind of authority, to take charge where there is demonstrable incompetence, and to veto poor decisions, the actual possibility for such administrative action is curtailed by traditions of autonomy and freedom. Such administrative capacities are further reduced in those communities where these traditions have been established and recognized for a long time.

Finally, the principles governing change in higher education will vary from those at lower levels because of the different nature of the relationship with the community at large. In this respect the relationship of the college to the general community in this country has always been one of moderate hostility. Although there has been a great deal of talk recently about the democratization of higher education, American colleges still retain an elitist flavor, though less than other Western societies. Only recently has the number of high school graduates going on to college passed fifty per cent. Those who finish college remain a minority, and their ultimate success or failure is linked closely with a number of extra-educational factors (race, income, socioeconomic status, and so on). Because it has not been an institution "of the people," higher education from its very beginning has been viewed with some antagonism by the general public.[61]

Higher education has also been traditionally more resistant to control by the outside community than public schools have been. This tradition of resistance is reinforced by the differences in nature of these two kinds of institutions. The whole history of public education at the elementary and secondary level in this country is bound up with philosophical principles of local control by the community, usually through the mechanism of an elected board. There appears to be a prevailing sentiment that such local school systems should reflect the educational philosophy and, to some extent, the prevailing political ideology, as well as the moral ethos of the community. The extent to which this is the case can be readily verified by an analysis of the platforms of candidates for local board positions. These invariably contain a range of positions which reflect commitments regarding what is and is not appropriate in school curriculum, dress, and general behavior which would be considered unwarranted infringements on academic and personal freedoms at higher levels of public education. These include, for instance, positions for and against such things as sex education, teaching or "espousing" theories of biological evolution, minimal acceptable length for skirts, and the appropriate length of a male student's hair.

While it is true that higher education is not altogether free from attempts to impose these types of sectarian standards, the extent to which it is considered legitimate is reflected in the nature of choosing governing boards for public institutions. For colleges and universities, these boards are generally appointed rather than elected, for the express purpose of removing them from the vagaries of direct political pressure. That such a system is imperfect, at best, is amply reflected in those states, such as California, where higher education has become the arena in which political fortunes are won and lost. In any case, attempts to suppress particular curricular offerings or to dictate the content or substance of any course are likely to be not only less frequent, but to meet with considerably greater resistance as one moves up the educational ladder. While attempts to assert such direct controls on the university may be on the increase, especially in those states where disruption and confrontation have been more frequent, they remain less formidable than at lower educational levels. Such interventions are mitigated to some extent, too, by virtue of the differences in clientele and because of the fact that governing boards of colleges and universities are often less uniformly parochial in their perspectives than the average local school board though this may change as political leaders move to consolidate their control over higher education.

These differences, then, suggest that the similarities between local public educational institutions and colleges and universities are not likely to be significantly greater than those between the university and a whole range of complex non-educational organizations. Given that this is the case, the long-time failure to confront the problem of change in higher education has been a singularly significant oversight.

Patterns of Innovation

Reviews of the published material on the innovation process or on innovative programs at most colleges and universities suggest that such programs are not only limited in their scope, but that they are usually set apart as a distinct unit from the "normal" university enterprise.

While such units have proliferated rapidly, they are often given little in the way of financial backing and usually placed last in terms of priority for classroom or facilities space.[62] In a period of continuing budget crises, the fate of many such programs appears to be imminent death or at least severely arrested development. Their problems are compounded by the fact that few appear to have direct connections with the university's administrative apparatus, suggesting that their potential for generating more general reform on the campus or even for influencing the course of university development in more modest ways might be quite limited. What we will examine in the following chapters are forces which generate innovative programs of one or another variety, and the ways in which such experimental enterprises do, in fact, affect the larger university system. Specifically, the focus is on the impact of radical pedagogical innovations on the larger institution. The question of particular interest is the effect that such innovations have on the procedures and apparatus of governance and decision making.

The reason for considering the apparatus of governance is that the implication of the nature of many innovations currently being attempted is clearly political. In experimental colleges, ethnic study programs, and other curricular innovations the emphasis has been on two particular themes: curricular relevance and student participation. While it may be difficult to pin down an exact meaning for curricular relevance since it may have become a shibboleth for attacking all of the perceived evils of the university community, it is not so difficult to pin down a meaningful definition of student participation. Within the framework of curricular innovation, participation usually entails a voice in formulation of policy regarding subjects to be pursued; the nature of examination procedures, *if any;* content of the course, especially in those cases where such decisions are made on the basis of the instructor's interests rather than what he as a professional considers essential; and the conduct of the classes themselves in terms of format, supplemental materials, lecture or seminar approach, and whatever else may be considered of moment. This procedure presupposes a radical alteration from the traditional roles of the academic community. Faculty no longer hold a position of unquestioned authority nor are they necessarily considered the court of last resort in disputes in any fundamental sense, although they may *in fact* occupy such a position in the eyes of the vast majority of students.

The kind of participatory democracy we have described could conceivably be used as a model for the entire university community.[63] Most students who become deeply involved in innovative programs appear, in fact, to have this end result in mind—that is to transform the entire university community. In this respect then, critics who see such developments as a threat to traditional faculty controls over such decisions are quite correct. Dispute evolves out of fundamental disagreements about how such decisions ought to be made, not about the intent of reformers. Inherent in the logic of almost any curricular experimentation is a commitment to institutional reform if the experiment proves worthwhile. The central issue here is to what extent such changes actually follow; that is, to what extent is the institution altered or affected by experimental programs, especially those which have implications for the governmental apparatus? Is there in fact a link between experiment and change, or do the two occur independent of one another? Do innovation and experiment embody any commitment to possible alternative educational modes, or are they simply mechanisms for "cooling the student out?" [64]

It may be after all that such experiments are, intentionally or unintentionally, no more than stopgap measures designed primarily to ameliorate the hostility of dissident students or to give them something which—from the faculty-administrative standpoint—is a "constructive" outlet for their energies. This kind of perspective would, of course, require no commitment to fundamental or broad scale changes, but simply a recognition that something had to be done to resolve the immediate problem of internal institutional conflict.

There is certainly more than ample reason to suspect that innovations are often attempts to restore a modicum of equilibrium without making changes having widespread impact. Such attempts move to restore equilibrium without altering established procedures or units in any significant way. The establishment of "new" departments or programs are a case in point. Such moves can be interpreted as means to temporarily avoid the central issue—reform of already existing ones. In addition, experimental programs or departments often have limited life-spans and are in no sense considered permanent additions to the institution. Basic alterations should be differentiated from a relatively simple expansion of the educational system. There is a substantial qualitative difference between fundamental alteration of existing programs and adding new programs which may or may not turn out to be permanent institutional appendages.

The Challenge for Educational Change

Along this same line there is a well established strategy of appointing study commissions or committees in any organization when its members attempt to avoid confronting basic issues.[65] In such cases there is a type of resistance in which "the very preparations for action are transmuted into devices for postponing action." [66] Such "Hamletic" strategies may well include the appointment of committees on educational innovation or curricular reform which appear periodically on almost every campus. The recommendations of such committees may fill volumes while the changes they generate are miniscule. One way of assessing the commitment of an institution to change is to determine to what extent they have taken action to implement the proposals of such committees or to what extent they have failed to move on them.

In the wake of recent student dissidence, all of these questions take on an added interest. The whole issue of the mechanics of educational change is of critical importance for those who seek alternative and more effective educational models. Given the magnitude of higher education and the increasing discontent with current organization and performance, colleges and universities must address themselves to the problem of intelligent educational change. The alternatives of growing unrest and increasingly precipitous confrontation between faculty and administration and students are unacceptable.[67]

The Political Context of Change

College enrollments will probably increase another fifty per cent in the next decade, thereby compounding the problems of the mass education process. As pointed out in the beginning of this chapter, one cannot discuss higher education out of the context of the society. Considering the fact that the university has become the center of intellectual focus in this country [68] and considering the impact of the college in terms of the intellectual and personality development of the student,[69] it is in the public interest to insure that the system of higher education does not deteriorate into an entirely soul-deadening enterprise which might successfully expunge the last trace of intellectual curiosity and appetite from its students. It may be argued that expunging intellectual curiosity and appetite from students directly meets the needs of a social structure characterized by contemporary America's corporate liberalism; however, increasing numbers of critics are attacking the university's complicity in this regard. With the growing recognition that internal repression of minorities and dissidents and international adventures and counterrevolutionary efforts like Vietnam are not accidents, pressures on higher education to snap out of its lethargy are growing,[70] and it is imperative that higher education reorient itself to meet the needs of twentieth-century students compelled to face these types of realities.

Perhaps most fundamental among all of the issues confronting us in this enterprise is the question of the potential for change within the university. We pointed out earlier the inherent conservatism of higher education which has been recorded on a number of fronts.[71] Despite the generally pessimistic outlook regarding the potential for changes from the current model of the multiversity or miniature variations on this same theme, it seems that there are a number of assumptions which are buttressed by relatively little empirical evidence. The comparatively static nature of university education may find its source in the organizational arrangements of the university; but, although the possibility must certainly be entertained, it is not entirely clear that alternative arrangements or the introduction of basic changes, despite current organizational impediments, is impossible.

If the university is to continue to function in a milieu which is itself constantly changing and imposing new demands, it must be capable of some sort of alteration if it is to survive. In the language of the systems theorist, the university must be an "ultrastable" system—one capable of self-correction or of generating alternatives on the basis of feedback through a variety of communication channels. Such feedback includes information regarding external pressures and considerations which might retard its operations or prevent it from attaining its goals.[72] We must take into account the conflicting pressures brought to bear on the university to change in inconsistent directions. It may be impossible, given limited resources, for an institution to increase its research while at the same time improving the quality of undergraduate teaching. It is obviously not possible to provide additional faculty time for work and consultation with governmental agencies at all levels while returning the professor to the classroom for a greater portion of his time.

These competing pressures suggest that the direction of change in the university is, in part, a function of the type of pressure brought to bear for change and the power of those exerting the pressure. One might argue that the pressures which the student can exert on the

The Challenge for Educational Change

university or college for reform can only be successful to the extent that they are not countered by pressures for change in other directions. If there are such counterpressures, we might argue that the direction of change is then dependent on which pressure group is the strongest or at least the most crucial to the continued operation of the organization.

These gross questions of power are mitigated to some extent by the nature of the institution. In some sense, the university is bound to pursue its stated goals or charter obligations in spite of pressures to exercise other alternatives. There must be some minimal attention paid to the students. As in any large organizational enterprise, however, especially public bureaucracies, those who administer the affairs of the university run the risk of losing sight of its original goals and becoming caught up in activities having little or nothing to do with the purpose for which the institution ostensibly exists.[73]

It may also be easier for different institutions to channel their innovative efforts in one direction than in another. If one looks at the state college system in California, for example, one finds an organization officially committed primarily to the undergraduate education with research and public service occupying a lesser role.[74] This is not to say that research and public service are not concerns of state college campuses. They are. The difference between the state college and the university, however, is in priorities given to various tasks. Since the university is the center of research activities and graduate education within the state's comprehensive system of higher education, undergraduate education there definitely assumes a second place in institutional priorities.[75] The success of pressures to improve undergraduate education, research, or public service depends, then, to some extent on the officially defined role of the institution.

If we take the question of improvement of undergraduate instruction as only one example, we might suspect that the state college system can adapt itself more readily to the demands of dissident students because its goals are more generally in line with those of the students; namely, there is a stress on teaching and on the disseminative aspects of education. The public university, on the other hand, has more disparate goals, many of which have nothing to do with the student, and some of which may be directly contrary to his interests as he perceives them. Private institutions may have constructed very similar priorities in terms of their goals, stressing one or the other functions of higher education. They may also be under pressure to excel in more than one area, especially since they may be dependent for income on sources that want the prestige of a faculty distinguished by its research but are unwilling to sacrifice educational excellence for such an objective.

The problems are not as simple as one might assume at first glance. It might be argued for instance that those institutions like the California state colleges which are "committed" to the teaching of undergraduates are in their own way more rigidly traditional and less receptive to the possibilities of change than some of their more illustrious counterparts. One reason for this may be that they are the "institution of the people" to the extent that this can be said of any college or university. They may be therefore, more directly subject to outside pressures by the masses than are the more prestigious universities. This situation is reflected in a curriculum which includes disciplines such as police science or industrial arts which many universities would consider inappropriate but which are an important part of the overall program of the state college. These kinds of institutional differences then, give rise to an important question: What is the potential for different kinds of changes in institutions with varying commitments?

Introduction to Case Studies

In the chapters which follow, we will explore in detail the issues discussed in this introduction. The focus, as we have pointed out, will be on the kinds of impact which radical curricular innovations have on the larger institutional community, especially in the area of governance and decision making. Innovation, in the context of this study, is restricted to those kinds of educational programs which alter the conventional roles of faculty and student: that is, redistribute the prerogatives, rights, and obligations of the program participants. In some cases, there may be claims of such alterations, or the extent to which such alterations actually occur may vary to a considerable extent. In each of the case studies, such variation will be an important point because it may have political implications for the internal operation of the institution. It may also be well to reiterate here that the kind of organizational changes that are of interest are those which have implications for the distribution of decision-making power. These may include, but are not limited to, the introduction of students to faculty or administrative committees, a rearrangement of the institutional gov-

The Challenge for Educational Change

ernment to include students in the final decision-making process (e.g., membership in the academic senate), or other variations designed to redistribute the decision-making power within the institution.

Specifically, the kinds of issues addressed in the context of the study include the following:

1. A description and analysis of the processes by which change is brought about in the university or college community. The analysis includes the identification of the forces which generate change as well as the sources of opposition on the campus and in the community at large. It includes also an examination of the tactics of implementation and delay of proposed innovations.

2. A description and analysis of the processes via which changes are institutionalized; the ways in which innovation or experimental programs become a continuing feature of the university or college structure; the extent to which innovative programs judged successful are incorporated into the regular institutional structure and under what conditions; and, if not incorporated, the factors that result in the death of innovative programs that we assume merit retention.

3. An analysis of the implications of radical curricular or program change for the university's governing bodies and procedures, how radically altered roles in one sphere alter roles in other spheres; how they alter perceptions of the form of appropriate relationships in other spheres; and the extent to which the principles of decision making in such experiments serve as a model for decision making at a more general level.

4. An analysis of the politics of innovation pursuing such questions as the commitment of institutions to internal reform and change, or the extent to which curricular innovation can be seen as a "safety-valve" tactic or a "cooling-out" mechanism to divert energies away from attempts to radically alter the entire university structure. As a variation on this same theme we focus on the question of whether innovation and experimentation are tolerated only as long as they don't infringe on the interests of other members of the university community.

5. And finally, an analysis of the political implications of change in the context of the larger community. This will include, of course, an exploration of the relationship of higher education to the political machinery of the state as well as to the public which it ostensibly serves.

These questions were developed in the setting of field studies in selected institutions during the years 1968–71. In particular, we initiated an inquiry into the impact of radical curricular innovations at the

Universities of California at Berkeley and Los Angeles, Stanford, Oregon, San Francisco State College, and Western Washington State College. We call the reader's attention to the Appendix in which there is a fuller discussion of the procedures and methodology and rationale for the field study.

In the subsequent chapters we examine these questions in each institutional setting. The concluding discussion attempts an interpretation based on the summary of findings and explores their theoretical and pragmatic implications.

II
The Hazards of Being Number One

In the late 1950s, even as some writers were celebrating the American success and the "end of ideology," the collective manifestations of social concern leading to the Black liberation and student movements were beginning to appear. Nineteen-sixty saw the first major sit-ins by Black students in the South. At the same time, there were demonstrations against HUAC (House Un-American Activities Committee) in San Francisco centering, in part, around the academic communities. No matter where one pinpoints the beginning of the New Left (many see 1956 as the critical year), the University of California's Berkeley campus is a focal point in its brief but dramatic history.

In the early 1960s a New Left philosophy evolved, emphasizing decentralization, individual control of life destiny, communal expression of concern for others, and commitment to social justice and equity. Participatory democracy was advanced as the mode for achieving a more perfect set of social relations, improved and more humane organizations, and an altogether better society. The Port Huron Statement, advanced by Tom Hayden and others at the formation of Students for a Democratic Society (spring 1962), was a call for new systems of decision making in which each person participated in decisions affecting his (or her) life.

A depersonalized and excessively bureaucratized society had created mass universities which trained cadres of passive recruits for the military-industrial complex. Such institutions, epitomized by Berkeley, gave students no effective voice in the decision-making process and increasingly emphasized efficiency to the virtual exclusion of concern for self-actualization or personal fulfillment.

The growing criticism of American social institutions, including universities which housed millions of alienated young men and women, was to become even more sharply articulated in the next few years. In this period of the early sixties, college and university students left campuses and joined the struggle for racial justice.[1] As a consequence of such experiences, students who had been noted only for their quiescence in the 1950s began to challenge universities to become more relevant in developing solutions to the social ills of the society. It was in this context, in the wake of an administrative decision prohibiting fund raising and recruitment for off-campus political activities, that the Free Speech Movement (FSM) was born.

One of the chief tactics used by leaders of the original Free Speech Movement was to attempt to educate large numbers of students concerning the sources of their alienation and the objectives of the new movement. Before the idea of teach-ins or suspension of normal university activities to address critical issues, the FSM was arguing that a major educational effort on the campus had to be made by students for students.[2] The issues that emerged related to control of the university and its decision-making processes, the nature of the curriculum and its relevance, and the functions of the university—including the use of campus resources for such questionable "educational" enterprises as military training and defense research.

It is clear that 1964 was a pivotal year in which a major new effort was launched on American university campuses. It came as the expression of a new generation of American youth that had begun to break with many of the ideological legacies of the past. Unlike their counterparts of a decade before, they began to display a well-developed sense

The Hazards of Being Number One

of social responsibility and a concern about the society in which they lived. The Free Speech Movement (FSM) was born out of a mood of anger, of disaffection, and of alienation; yet, it was the expression of committed and concerned youth who wished to develop an affirmative response to developments affecting the quality of their lives. The university, the institution with which they were most intimately involved, became the focal point of their efforts. Their immediate goal was the reconstruction of institutions of higher education according to their developing image of a new ideal.

What can we now say about the impact of the Berkeley Free Speech Movement? A good deal has been written of the events at Berkeley, collecting the facts and analyzing the dynamics of the FSM, but in educational terms we might note that the efforts were directed toward specific changes and that the results have been, at best, disheartening. In part this may be true because of idiosyncratic developments at Berkeley, the politicization of higher education in California, and the peculiarities of the institution. On the other hand, the current despair and disillusionment among the educational reformists of the mid-1960s appears to be widespread and deserves more intensive analysis. Berkeley is perhaps the prototype, among American universities, of frenetic activity, grandiose planning, dramatic pronouncements, and virtually no change. There is little in the areas of control of the university, the role of ROTC, defense research, and curricular reform that has changed since 1964, despite massive organizational efforts and highly publicized confrontations between students and police and military authorities.[3] To better understand the experience at Berkeley, we should look now at the first of our case studies.

Educational Development at Berkeley

The brightest star in the University of California's multicampus system is Berkeley. Located across the bay from what is generally acknowledged to be one of the nation's most exciting cities, the University of California's oldest branch is situated in an appropriate environment for an institution of such immense intellectual prestige. Boasting a brilliant, urbane, productive faculty and a student body that ranks with any in the nation, the University of California has long been considered one of the country's most stimulating intellectual centers.

In addition to its other appealing features, the Berkeley campus recently claimed the distinction of being rated as the best balanced distinguished institution in the country with regard to its overall graduate program.[4] Since graduate programs are the base on which distinguished reputations are built in university circles, this, in effect, gave Berkeley the distinction of being proclaimed our finest university.

It is not a particularly profound observation that all is not well on the Berkeley campus. Perhaps more than any other, this campus has been besieged by a series of disorders involving confrontations between all of the various campus factions—student, faculty, and administration—and between students and the police and national guard. The People's Park episode, most serious in a continuing series of incidents dating back to the late summer and autumn of 1964, resulted in hundreds of arrests and scores of injuries and claimed the first Berkeley student life when a young man watching events in the confrontation was shot by one of the local police.[5]

After the Free Speech Movement

There is no question that the Free Speech Movement (FSM) marked the beginning of a continuing escalation of hostilities among students, faculty and administration at Berkeley. Although difficulties had been increasing at the institution for many years, analysts both inside and outside of the institution act now as if almost all of Berkeley's history, at least its significant history, has occurred since the Free Speech Movement. In fact, the FSM takes on such significance in the eyes of the campus community that literally every person interviewed as part of this study, from the most conservative faculty and administration to the most radical student, traced the genesis of current problems to the events of 1964.[6]

The beginnings of the Free Speech Movement in 1964 and the issues that initiated the controversy can be readily identified. Certain critics notwithstanding, the issue was indeed one of free speech.[7] The issue erupted with students protesting the administration's action in enforcing a campus regulation prohibiting political advocacy in an area by the south entrance to the campus after many years of ignoring the rule. As the controversy grew, many other fundamental issues that had existed in a latent form exploded as the battle between students and the administration escalated. While free speech or political advocacy remained salient, issues of the impersonal university ethos, of inadequate undergraduate instruction, of exploitation of graduate students, of university research priorities, of links with military and other governmental agencies, and innumerable others were introduced.

The free speech issue itself was one that had been boiling off and on for several years on the campus and had been a source of student-administration contention throughout Clark Kerr's administrative tenure. In one recap of the political issues on the Berkeley campus prior to the Free Speech Movement, it was pointed out that the issue of campus speakers and political advocacy on campus dated back to 1958 when Clark Kerr assumed the presidency of the university and before his tenure as chancellor at Berkeley.[8] During most of this period the contest was between the administration and students. The faculty were largely disengaged from the controversy. Apparently faculty interest was aroused during the 1961-62 academic year when Kerr sought to extend rules regulating student political activity to members of the faculty in the form of a suggestion to the Academic Senate that they adopt a regulation that faculty be forbidden to "identify themselves as professors at U.C. whenever they took part in non-educational activities."[9] The result, according to some observers was a year of "incessant debate among students, faculty, and administration as each sought to preserve his rights and protest his position."[10] Debate was supplemented by more direct strategies, especially the use of illegal rallies and vigils on campus, thus apparently setting the stage for the culmination of the controversy in the historic events of the fall of 1964. These were the first manifestations in this period of the tactics and strategy which have become identified with the new generation of student activists. Students in this case were undoubtedly supplemented by Berkeley's famous non-student fringe culture which is characterized by a much higher degree of political involvement and activism than the regular student body.[11]

When looking at the history of events leading up to the FSM it is clear that Clark Kerr was a central figure from the beginning in establishing the whole series of rules and regulations governing student conduct that were the focus of the controversy. Insofar as one is able to evaluate Kerr's motives, it is unlikely that his moves during the course of events were prompted by malevolence or even inherent conservatism. What appears to have happened is that Kerr and his administration were seized by a kind of post-McCarthy trauma. The result was a general timidity and an unwillingness to directly challenge legislative and other government forces which had singled out the university for attacks reminiscent of the McCarthy era from which the nation had only then emerged. Heirich and Kaplan point out that a survey of universities of comparable size conducted by the Associated Students of the University of California (ASUC) at the time, indicated that only one other in the nation had policies as restrictive as Berkeley regarding the issues of speech and advocacy on the campus. They also add that increasing pressure was being brought to bear on the university by members of the state legislature.[12] Even then, the swing to the right that has been characteristic of state politics, and in which California has assumed a position of leadership, was showing strength. The California state counterpart of the House Un-American Activities Committee issued the Burns Report, named after the president pro tem of the state senate, Hugh Burns, a rabid "red-baiter" who spearheaded the anti-left forces in the legislature. The report announced that " 'apostles of class struggle' use the academic freedom of the university to camouflage themselves and take part in Communist-front organizations . . . [and] that pro-Castro committees and former leaders of SLATE [a left-wing campus party] are now running gigantic fronts for Communist movements.' "[13] Under such outside pressure, Kerr was not the first or the last to attempt to get the critics off his and the university's back with repressive regulation of student political activity.

Unfortunately for Kerr, his efforts in this direction backfired inasmuch as students escalated their political activity and increased their attacks on his administration. Faculty later joined in the controversy on the side of the students. Kerr ultimately found himself caught in the middle of an irreconcilable conflict. Students first, and then faculty, challenged the legitimacy of Kerr's authority to regulate their political activities. Although he had the power of the police to enforce his dictates, that power was not adequate for the task which Kerr faced. Later, with the Free Speech Movement behind him, Kerr began a progressive retreat from his hardline stand against student activism during the early days of the FSM. Although he managed to recoup some faculty support lost during the FSM with this later maneuver, it further raised the level of antagonism among the regents. The regents' hostilities were finally consolidated under the leadership of Ronald Reagan who had been elected to the California governorship in 1966 on a platform that promised to "clean up Berkeley." Reagan needed only three weeks in office to secure Kerr's dismissal.

The Hazards of Being Number One 37

Before his demise, Kerr had replaced key administrative officials at Berkeley in an attempt to restore a peaceful environment, but changes in the administration at Berkeley did not soften the conflict and the hostilities had continued to escalate. Politicians were more adamant than ever and students expanded the issues to increasingly sensitive areas. It was in such an environment that the faculty and administration began casting about for solutions to the "multiversity's" multi-problems. On March 8, 1965 in one of their most heralded moves, they appointed the Select Committee on Education under the chairmanship of English Professor Charles Muscatine.

Education at Berkeley: The Muscatine Report

In the aftermath of a trauma such as the Free Speech Movement one is tempted to suggest that if there is anything that the university did not need, it was a study committee. The problems of Berkeley were so patently obvious that the appointment of the Muscatine committee was interpreted by many as a stall. Nevertheless, despite these widespread feelings, perhaps no faculty committee has ever been greeted with such universal acclaim nor, probably, has any generated as much anticipation.

The charge of the committee was broad indeed. The Emergency Executive Committee of the Academic Senate listed these purposes in the resolution calling for the appointment of the Select Committee:

(a) to find the ways in which the traditions of humane learning and scientific inquiry can be best advanced under the challenging conditions of size and scale that confront our university community;

(b) to examine the various changes in educational programs currently under consideration in the several schools and colleges; to seek by appropriate means to communicate information concerning these programs to the wider campus community; and to consider the implications of these programs in the light of (a) above.[14]

The enthusiasm for the founding of the committee was exceeded only by the anticipation of its recommendations. Consistent with the gravity of the problem and the necessity for quick action, the committee, according to its chairman, was delighted to be able to extend its recommendations to the university community less than one year after its first meeting.

At one level the report was received as enthusiastically as perhaps any university committee report in history. According to faculty and administration on the campus, the report was hailed by all sectors of the campus community. In the press it was described as a "milestone" and compared to similar famous reports on other campuses which had preceded it. At a much less widespread, and certainly a less well publicized level, there has been a continuing criticism of the report. It is interesting to note some of the major criticism in this discussion of the impact of the report in the years following its issuance.

In any assessment of the impact of the Muscatine Report, it is necessary to bear in mind that it was in no sense radical. Its recommendations were meant to foster "the permanent health of [the] academic community . . . to see it change gradually and continuously rather than having to suffer the shocks of drastic adjustment following periods of quiescence." [15] While there was a recognition of some of the basic problems of the Berkeley campus, there was also ample recognition of Berkeley's elevated stature. The committee noted:

> . . . nowhere do we suggest a diminution of the research activity of the faculty. Research (or creativity) is of the very character of this campus; without it Berkeley would be indistinguishable from other kinds of schools. In a state system itself devoted to a pluralism of educational institutions, the Berkeley campus has an obligation, indeed, to maintain its eminence in research.[16]

The committee went on to point out that ninety per cent of the undergraduate student body expressed agreement with the statement: "Taking everything into account, Cal is a good place to go to school," and that four-fifths of the students surveyed indicated satisfaction with courses, examinations, and professors.[17] They did recognize, however, that these findings contained a certain ambiguity, especially in light of the fact that a majority of the students expressed dissatisfaction on a variety of more specific indices of satisfaction with their educational experience. Only a minority of the students felt that the grading system was an adequate indicator of actual "knowledge and understanding" of the course content; forty-six per cent felt that professors spent too little time with the students; half expressed a desire for more time for non-academic activities; and nearly eighty per cent agreed with the "popular cliche that the University operates as a factory." [18]

Continuing their discussion of the Berkeley student, the Committee addressed itself to the problem of the dropout. The problem is a particularly disturbing one at Berkeley inasmuch as less than one-half of the entering freshmen matriculate at the end of four years. Many leave because of dissatisfactions of one sort or another, but many are academic casualties succumbing to the pressures, the rigor, or the difficulty of intense academic competition. The ambivalence of the committee regarding its task can be seen in their analysis of the dropout. They stated:

> The drop-out is the extreme case of the student whose education here has been unsuccessful. Some leave because of failing grades, but others do so without such a clear academic reason. That students are admitted who prove incapable of meeting our standard is a disturbing phenomenon and calls attention to the need for reviewing our admission procedures and our liaison with high school and junior college advisors. Not all the fault lies here, of course, for students may do poorly not because of inability but because they are emotionally upset.[19]

Although the authors of the report must be given credit for agreeing that there were problems at Berkeley, the failure rate is one which they apparently felt could be resolved by better selection procedures and more adequate counseling. Nowhere did they come to grips with the possibility that student failures might be due, in part at least, to some failure on the part of the university or its components other than the admissions officers or the counseling center.

Despite this approach, Professor Pimentel, in his appended minority report, stressed what he felt was a fundamental failure of the committee—their failure to stress sufficiently that innovation, and not reform, was the goal since Berkeley occupied a position of unquestioned excellence. In fact, he belabored the point that Berkeley is one of the jewels in the University of California's crown and that the overall excellence of the university is epitomized by Berkeley.[20] It is unlikely that any of the committee would have disagreed with his characterization of the Berkeley campus, and highly probable that many in the campus community would have joined in his criticism of this feature of the report.

In spite of their ambivalence, the Select Committee did make forty-two recommendations. These ranged from a recommendation to take steps to insure that the quality of teaching performance would be an important consideration in promotion and tenure deliberations to a greater allotment of faculty teaching time to lower division instruction and from greater solicitation of student viewpoints on policy considerations to new types of professorships. They covered an assortment of topics including admissions, teaching, independent studies, professional requirements, mechanisms for the introduction of curricular innovation, and the nature of graduate programs. There is almost no imaginable pertinent area which the committee did not examine and make recommendations for.

Two years after the report was released the faculty had adopted seventeen of the original forty-two proposals. Another two were withdrawn because they were redundant in view of others passed. In addition to those passed, a number were referred to various committees for consideration, a few were passed as "sense motions," and the remainder were "received and placed on file." The exact implications of the latter two categories could not be ascertained. It is certain, however, that they do not obligate the university community to comply with or move on any program. But in many respects, the same can be said for those recommendations which were adopted.

In assessing the impact of the report the reaction of those interviewed is uniform. Almost without exception, when queried on the impact of the Muscatine Report, informants responded that it had established the Board of Educational Development. The board, which will be discussed further on, functions as an independent unit and therefore has no direct impact on the affairs of departments or colleges. The problems with the report and with the charge and authority of the committee were many, but in a particularly critical commentary on *Education at Berkeley,* Martin Trow argues that it was exactly what the majority wanted. He says:

> *Education at Berkeley* has the one (for Berkeley surely the highest) virtue of not affecting anybody who does not want to be affected by it. If the Report is notable for the lack of dispute it has occasioned, it is largely because virtually all of its many recommendations can be ignored by those who are simply not interested. They do not really even affect the life of the departments; the best evidence for that would be how few departments have debated any of its recommendations in their own meetings. The Report leaves people alone to get on with their work. That is what the Berkeley faculty wants of an undergraduate program—that it not interfere too much with the real business of academic men. What the Report adds to this phi-

losophy of education is that if a faculty member should really want to do something new or unusual with an undergraduate course he should be able to do so, and, it is hoped, not be penalized for it in a promotion committee.[21]

The assessment of the faculty position on the issue of undergraduate educational reform as one of general antipathy was corroborated repeatedly by those whom we interviewed whether they were faculty, student, or administrator. One faculty member pretty well summed up the prevailing sentiment with the comment: "It's no secret that the faculty doesn't give a damn about what the student does."

That the Select Committee did, indeed, allow those who did not want to be affected by the report to ignore it, is readily apparent in the language used in the recommendations adopted by the Academic Senate. They remained recommendations. Almost none, except those having to do with establishing the Academic Senate committee or changing the procedures of existing committees, carried the weight of a binding directive, nor could they be so interpreted. Consider the following example: "Departments with markedly low levels of faculty participation in their lower division courses should restructure their patterns of teaching in order to give greater faculty attention to the lower division." [22] Nowhere is there a procedure for insuring that departments did, in fact, reallocate their time. Perhaps it is unrealistic that they should be so "directed." The point is that such recommendations, adopted by faculty vote, in this case as a "sense motion" without any real substance, simply exacerbate the existing strains between students and faculty. Although no one expected a panacea, the results of the recommendations of the Select Committee were a bitter disappointment to those who had great expectations. In the intervening period since the issuance of *Education at Berkeley,* its central issues have frequently been the focus of new deliberations of faculty or joint faculty-student committees.

The two chief committees were a Study Commission on University Governance to address the issue of appropriate student participation in university policy affairs and a Special Committee on Academic Program which was appointed in 1965 almost simultaneously with the Select Committee on Education and interacted extensively with it. The Study Commission on University Governance did not appear until January 1967.

The best that can be said for the product of the efforts of the Special

Committee of Academic Program is that its recommendations were a reshuffling of the status quo. The recommendations involved altering the format but not the substance of existing general education or "breadth" requirements. In this respect its recommendations ran counter to those of the Select Committee which would have dispatched existing breadth requirements in favor of a more permissive arrangement allowing students greater individual freedom in determining their curriculum.[23] A student group, which included individuals later active in the Center for Participant Education, scored the committee's report (the Herr Report), as a rehash of a report issued ten years previously by a similarly constituted faculty committee. Using their own interpretation of the recommendations of the Muscatine Report, the student group presented a proposal.[24] To date, as far as anyone seems able to determine, most of the suggestions are being taken under advisement by the administration and the Academic Senate.

In the spring of 1970, a Division of Interdisciplinary and General Studies was established, apparently as a response to the Herr Report. Its chief innovation, however, has been the establishment of a six-quarter humanities sequence which is to be team taught by professors from the English and the comparative literature departments. Course content runs very much parallel to that of the Tussman program (discussed below) albeit on a reduced scale. Aside from this, the new division's only concession to innovation was to allow students a voice "in the selection of at least *one* important text relevant to their aims and interests."[25] Needless to say, the program did not elicit a particularly warm response from student activists.

Issued in January of 1968, the latest in the series of epic reports, *The Culture of the University: Governance and Education*[26] was greeted more favorably by the student activists. But if their reception was favorable, their expectations were also tempered. According to one professor who has been a central figure in many of the controversies, "It was a good report but none of it has been implemented." He didn't think that it was likely that it would be in the near future.

Approaches to Innovation

If one looks closely at any institution of higher learning, one can surely find numerous cases of attempts to innovate on a small scale: individual professors or groups of professors, isolated students, occasionally whole departments. This is probably as true of Berkeley as of any institution of similar size and character. The major attempts at innovation since the Free Speech Movement have, however, been focused in two programs—the Experimental College and the Board of Educational Development (BED). Whenever one mentions innovation at Berkeley on another campus, the likely response will be to ask if you are talking about the Experimental College. Although very few are familiar with the detailed workings of the Experimental College, a great many have heard it mentioned in some context. Many confuse it with the Board of Educational Development. The Board of Educational Development itself is probably the lesser known of the two enterprises; however, one of its courses, Social Analysis 139X (the fall 1968 Eldridge Cleaver course), gave the BED national notoriety.

Experimental College

Although both of the above programs fall into the general category of innovation when compared with most other campus programs, they are probably as disparate in nature as possible within the same institutional framework. The Experimental College is particularly interesting now because its philosophy and operation run directly counter to most of what is currently generating enthusiasm on major campuses, especially Berkeley.

Based on an interest he developed as a student of Alexander Meiklejohn, Joseph Tussman, a philosophy professor, developed the Experimental College. Occupying the student's first two years, the Experimental College is what Professor Tussman describes very precisely as an educational "program" as distinguished from a "series of courses." [27] The program consists of a highly structured and carefully planned period of study focusing on the ancient Greeks and seventeenth-century England in the first year and on America in the second. The program is certainly more rigorous than most, attempting to build discipline in the student, and it allows little latitude. Curricular decisions are the exclusive prerogative of the faculty, and there is no place for independent study outside of the framework of the common curriculum except as an extra-curricular enterprise. As Tussman puts it, "There are some games we refuse to play. 'Solitaire' is one; 'participatory democracy' is another. Each, in its own way, destroys the learning community which is the essence of the Experimental Program." [28]

One of the most interesting features of the Experimental College is that practically all of its major operating principles run counter to the movements currently in vogue in the rhetoric of educational reform. This is a feature of which Tussman is well aware, and one which he argues is one of the major assets of the Experimental Program. Furthermore, he believes that most of the faculty at Berkeley, and at most institutions for that matter, are so locked into the conventional educational arrangements that the guiding philosophy of the Experimental College is beyond their comprehension. For this reason, his procedures in initiating the college often skirted the university conventions and generated some antagonism on the part of his colleagues. His rationale for skirting the conventions is instructive.

Tussman relates that he first went directly to Clark Kerr with the idea in order to obtain some sort of minimal commitment. He was convinced at the time (just before the FSM) that you "don't try to start it with a committee." If a committee were appointed to implement the idea, he felt that it was certain death. His procedure from the beginning, then, was to handle it himself. When he began to pursue the idea seriously, he talked to the Dean of Letters and Science who was receptive and then to the Chairman of the Philosophy Department. His progress was hampered at this point by the fact that the FSM was "interfering with administrative access." To further complicate matters, he suggests, there was no climate for reform on the campus at the time of the FSM. His feeling was that Kerr saw the Experimental College as the "beginning of a revolution from below." He characterized the administration as receptive to innovation in a very broad general sense "but not concerned with quality."

When Tussman finally got to the point of approaching the appropriate faculty committees, a move which usually precedes appeals to the higher administration, he had decided that he would not submit a detailed syllabus outlining the program to the committee because he "didn't have that much faith in the educational judgment of the committee." He then appealed over the committee on courses, directly to the faculty and he contends the faculty voted without knowing what it was. Tussman consistently maintains that almost no one understands what the Experimental College is all about. The faculty are all, in his opinion, captivated by the mentality of the specialist, which doesn't allow for any model of education outside of narrow professional development.

In any case, the college "establishment" voted in favor of the Experimental College. The vote, however, was characterized as insignificant inasmuch as the faculty was indifferent. There was no substantive interest in the idea. In fact, he argues, the university was almost unanimously disinterested, and they continue to adopt the same attitude toward the program. He doesn't believe that many, or any, will read his book, nor that they will understand it if they do read it. "The only intelligent audience," he says, "are colleagues and students who've been through it."

At this point Tussman has no intention of expanding the Experimental College. He simply wants to get it authorized as a permanent unit in the university and then to maintain it in its present form. He feels that the program "needs to be fanatically defended against faculty and student attempts to change it into something else." He wants no part of alternative types of educational programs and does not believe that the Experimental College will set the tone for other innovative programs. Rather he sees the university as drifting toward increased professionalism with student specialization coming increasingly early in their careers. This will include the abolition of breadth requirements and the beefing up of the majors. In addition, he foresees a whole "glut" of student-initiated courses. All of this will happen, he argues, in the context of an environment where "the faculty doesn't give a damn about what the student does."

All of this adds up to the fact that the Experimental College has had no impact, in Tussman's opinion, in terms of opening the way for a variety of possible innovations. There was no real impact because nobody really wanted to do anything fundamentally different. When the Board of Educational Development (BED) was founded, he notes, the faculty didn't go to the BED with new courses; it was entirely the students. Furthermore, the ideological support for BED was not, in his opinion, parallel to that for the Experimental College. BED was a "substitute for real educational development." It has not been competitive in any sense. "Things like the BED become centers for small business decisions. The small business, anti-trust mentality has taken over."

This then has been the framework in which the Experimental College has been developed. It is no exaggeration to say that it has been the work of one man. One dean commented that "It works better if Tussman has a group of 'lesser lights' around him, not colleagues who will argue." The point is that Tussman is intent on preserving what he sees as the fundamental integrity of his program. It has, in this framework, become an isolated experiment, perhaps better known than most, but having little impact on the campus, except for those directly involved. The program's national impact is difficult to assess, but it would appear modest. There have been some comparable efforts to develop interdisciplinary programs, and Tussman has influenced the pattern at San Jose State College and the newly developed Evergreen State College (Olympia, Wash.) by working with an enthusiastic colleague in sociology. Although many have "heard about it," Tussman's observation that "few know what it's all about" appears to be correct.

The Board of Educational Development and Center for Participant Education

The Board of Educational Development was by far the biggest single development from the Muscatine Report. The board was created with the enactment by By-law 15 of the Berkeley Academic Senate on March 13, 1966. The new bylaw specified that the board would consist of six members serving three year staggered terms and that its duties were:

1. To stimulate and promote experimentation in all sectors of the Berkeley campus, and to support innovation wherever it is needed. . . .

2. To receive, encourage, and authorize experimental instructional proposals for which neither departmental nor college support is appropriate or feasible. . . .

3. To initiate and sponsor the securing of extramural funds for the support of experimental courses and curricula, and to administer such funds. . . .[29]

The essence of the charge to the board was to act as a service unit which would facilitate experimentation in all areas on the campus.

Just exactly how the BED was to move in facilitating innovation was not entirely clear. According to the Dean of Letters and Science, the board had no budget nor administrative machinery of its own allowing support. There is general agreement that the lack of budget funds made it most difficult for the board to carry out its charge. In its reports to the Academic Senate, the board continually calls attention to difficulties resulting from lack of funds.[30] According to the former Assistant Chancellor for Educational Development, the first critical decision was that the board would have no separate budget; as he sees it, the administration wanted to control it. The result of the

The Hazards of Being Number One

arrangement finally developed was that the board was forced to act in a relatively narrow range of activities given its original charge, and that its potential as an innovative force was severely limited. It became an agency which did nothing but review proposed experimental courses and then help to find the resources to conduct them if this had not already been arranged. Consequently, the interesting aspects of the board were not so much its role as an innovating force on the campus, but the extent to which it became the central agency in the developing political maneuvers of students, faculty, administration, and outsiders.

It is no accident that the BED became the center of political activities inasmuch as the whole question of educational reform was one that became highly politicized during the Free Speech Movement. The former Assistant Chancellor observed, and many others seem to agree, that "even at the time of Muscatine, those seriously interested in improving the quality of their education was very small, especially compared to those interested in the questions of politics and governance." To the extent that this observation is accurate, questions of educational innovation are of interest only insofar as they are politically relevant. The political relevance of the issue is tied, however, to a number of situational factors, not the least being such items as course content, format, and faculty. Furthermore, the question of the political relevance of educational innovation is intimately associated with the development of the Center for Participant Education (CPE).

The Center for Participant Education, a program sponsored by the Associated Students, appeared in 1967, following the Board of Educational Development. Its initial objectives were relatively simple: to provide a mechanism whereby students could initiate courses on any topic of their interest. Its consequences were not so simple, and its activities led directly to another in the series of confrontations between students and administration.

When the BED began, it required rather substantial proposals for courses before approving them for credit. The immediate result was that of the first ten course proposals submitted only two were accepted. This led to a meeting between the BED and students who constituted much of the original nucleus of CPE with the result that an additional two courses were approved. From this point on, CPE became more cynical and manipulated the BED to loosen up, with the result that an increasing number of proposals were approved with each passing term.

Given the student interest in the program, the CPE would appear to have been a natural development since there was no provision for student membership on the Board of Educational Development. In fact, there was no provision for student participation in any way, even in an advisory capacity. The procedure of excluding students from faculty committees had continued to be the norm at Berkeley although this has not been the case at other University of California campuses. To date students sit on only one Academic Senate Committee, the Committee on Student Affairs.[31]

The informal arrangement between the BED and CPE was amicable and worked fairly well at the beginning. Then, according to Rick Brown, acknowledged "founder and guru" of CPE, there was a shift in the nature of the courses. As Brown sees it, students were not interested in educational reform in the beginning. They were simply interested in pursuing their fancies and getting credit for it. The result was a variety of course content ranging from the "touchy-feely" to the political. Later, however, CPE began to develop its own courses with what Brown refers to as a political content. The political content had to do with issues revolving around the nature of the university, reform issues, and the like. As these courses were developed and CPE itself became more politicized, political groups saw CPE as a useful vehicle and began to exploit the opportunities to introduce courses with a higher politicized content.

As the nature of the courses began to change, one involved professor argues, antagonism developed in state political circles and among the regents toward courses which had overtones of political action. In the spring of 1968, just prior to the beginning of the controversy over the Cleaver course, the BED was getting negative feedback on a course in which students spent an entire quarter studying the Poor People's Campaign. Students involved spent much of their time in Washington, D.C. observing the development of the campaign first hand and living in Resurrection City with the campaigners. Perhaps this course, more than any previous one, sensitized the politicians and regents and alerted them to the "political implications" of the BED.

The culmination of all this was, of course, the development of the now famous Social Analysis 139X featuring a series of weekly lectures by Black Panther leader, Eldridge Cleaver. Some of the more spectacular results of the Social Analysis 139X controversy are common lore in the academic world by now, but a look at some of the less publicized details is instructive.

The course itself was proposed by a student active in the Center for Participant Education. He had enlisted four faculty members as sponsors and submitted a detailed proposal replete with all of the required syllabi, testing procedures, and so on. The course was approved by the BED. With the announcement that the course would be offered, the regents called the chairman, another member of the BED, and the student organizer to discuss the course with their Educational Policy Committee. Following the discussions, the regents considered the issue at length and passed the following two resolutions, both of which are quoted in their entirety because of their salience and intrinsic interest:

A. Four-part Hitch resolution as amended.
   1. Effective immediately for courses offered in the fall quarter, 1968–69, no one may lecture or lead a discussion for more than one occasion during a given academic quarter on a campus in courses for University credit, unless he holds an appointment with the appropriate instructional title. This applies whether or not the speaker is paid by the University.
   2. If Social Analysis 139X cannot be restructured to satisfy the policy stated in Recommendation #1 prior to the commencement of instruction in the fall quarter, 1968–69, Course 139X shall not be offered for credit in the fall quarter, 1968–69. The Chairman of the Berkeley Division of the Academic Senate shall make the determination as to whether the restructuring of this course meets the conditions of the policy stated in Recommendation on #1 and shall report his findings to The Regents, the President and the Chancellor of the Berkeley campus.
   3. Recognizing both the desirability and the problems of experimentation in courses and curriculum, The Regents direct the Academic Senate and each of its Divisions to formulate a set of explicit academic standards for the planning, staffing, conduct and evaluation of experimental courses. The Academic Senate is required to transmit to The Regents a single report or separate report of each Division describing and justifying such standards. The reports are to be available for consideration at the January, 1969 meeting of The Regents.
   4. While recognizing the primacy of the Academic Senate in approving courses and curricula, The Regents direct the President

to initiate an exploration with the Academic Senate of the appropriate role of the administration in this area of joint concern.

B. Censure Resolution

Inasmuch as The Regents of the University of California in 1920 delegated to the Academic Senate authority over approval and and supervision of courses and curricula; and

Whereas, this delegation is in the finest academic tradition and has served the University well; and

Whereas, recently the Board of Educational Development of the Berkeley Division of the Academic Senate, under its delegation from the Division, has approved a course, Social Analysis 139X, for the fall quarter 1968, which in the opinion of The Regents has been improperly structured; and

Whereas, The Regents consider that in this instance the trust that must follow such a delegation to the Senate has been abused;

Therefore, The Regents censure those within the Berkeley Division of the Academic Senate and the Board of Educational Development who were responsible for this action.[32]

The four-part Hitch resolution was, of course, a direct response to the controversy developing out of the approval of Social Analysis 139X. The rules were specifically designed so that Cleaver could not be used as a regular lecturer. But more than this, such rules had the immediate effect of crippling efforts to innovate, especially in terms of demands for relevance in the classroom since they severely hampered the instructor in making use of available outside resources and limited his freedom to structure classes according to the dictates of his own judgment. The new regulation thus impinged on one of the most cherished prerogatives of the individual faculty member, the right to plan his classes without any interference. The tradition of freedom in planning one's courses had traditionally dictated noninterference by members of the university community as well as outsiders. The regents, although the governing body, were clearly cast in the role of outsiders in this case and their action was seen as a direct affront to these principles. The fact that Charles Hitch, President of the University, introduced the first motion did nothing to repair the deteriorating relations between the faculty and administration. The censure motion simply exacerbated the situation by adding a further dimension of insult to the injury already rendered.

The Chairman of the Board of Educational Development noted in his report to the Academic Senate, that the actions of the regents made the already difficult job of the board even more formidable. Since the BED had no financial base or faculty, it was necessary to operate to a large extent on voluntary efforts by faculty. In the light of the regents' action, such voluntary efforts would be harder to obtain. Even more important, according to the BED chairman, was the fact that "student participation in educational innovation was threatened." [33] What actually happened in this regard is that the arrangements that had developed between BED and the CPE were ultimately destroyed. Now, instead of a complementary structure, the two groups had become antagonists in an increasingly bitter student-administration battle.

The reaction of the faculty to the events surrounding the controversy over Social Analysis 139X was one of mixed consternation and ambivalence about the appropriate course of action. There was agreement on the part of all administrators, faculty, and students interviewed that the faculty was upset over what they regarded as an unwarranted infringement on their academic freedom. But while they were upset over the violation of the principle, most faculty members were not enthusiastic about fighting the battle over the particular course. Students and strong faculty supporters of the CPE felt that the faculty was basically in agreement with the regents on the inappropriateness of Cleaver's role in the proposed course but were upset by the implication of the regents' action for the future of academic freedom on the campus. Apparently the faculty felt strongly enough about the principle to fight the decision to the extent of waging a court battle if necessary. Reports indicated, however, that the battle was not spirited. Many of the faculty apparently felt that they had been forced into a position of defending the course and pursued the issue in a fashion that indicated their lack of enthusiasm.

As a consequence of the relatively spiritless action on the part of the faculty and what was interpreted as a capitulation on the part of the BED, positions of the various factions hardened. During the following months, students attempted to initiate a strike against the university, the chairman of the BED resigned, and the administrative director of the board was changed. In an attempt to test the BED, CPE submitted twenty-two course proposals the following term of which only eight were accepted. The result was an open split between the two units with the CPE declaring its intention to sever whatever relationships it had had with BED in the past.

In severing its relationships with the BED, CPE did not cease to operate. Rather it adopted a new strategy by manipulating existing procedures for independent or group studies. Since any faculty member can sponsor an independent studies project for a student or a group studies program, the CPE enlisted the participation of sympathetic faculty in order to continue their efforts without having to work through the BED. Part of the strategy was of course to strip the BED of its legitimacy in student eyes and to provide an alternative for students still interested in educational innovation. Among courses initiated using this technique was one called the New American Revolution, featuring Tom Hayden, founder of Students for a Democratic Society, in a role similar to that occupied by Eldridge Cleaver in Social Analysis 139X. The immediate consequence of this new course was the introduction of a motion in the California Senate by fourteen senators urging the regents:

> . . . to terminate all delegation of authority to the Center for Participant Education to propose credit courses, and to its faculty members to accept courses proposed by this group, which has now demonstrated for a second time its academic irresponsibility and unhealthy interest in rioting and anarchy. . . .[34]

While the resolution itself apparently died in committee, its influence, or that of its perpetrators, was not without consequences. The regents subsequently ordered the Academic Senate to begin an investigation into what it felt were abuses of the independent and group studies programs. It should be noted that the regents' action in this regard was also motivated by the fact that the independent studies option was used by a sympathetic professor to give credit to students taking Social Analysis 139X even though the course did not comply with the new regents' rulings.

As a direct result of the controversies surrounding the experimental courses and the faculty and regent response, there were several significant changes. Control of experimental courses was shifted from the BED to the newly created Division of Experimental Courses controlled by the chancellor rather than by the faculty. At this point, the BED's mandate was shifted from a concern with experimental courses to the seeking of funds; control of the administration of a large foundation grant for educational innovation remained in the hands of the chancellor. The BED spent the 1969–70 academic year concerned with the general issue of experimentation, but not with the specific development of courses. Student response during this year was expressed in continued cynicism, while the new Division of Experimental Courses never was activated or appointed a chairman. For the most part, student activists in CPE abandoned their efforts at curricular reform and expanded their strategy of "working with the system," for example using the special alternatives outlined earlier. Even though they continued to function, the number of CPE-sponsored courses has dropped drastically in the past year or so. Others who were committed to the ideal of experimentation took their efforts off-campus, or at least outside of the university's credit offerings.

The Faculty Committee on Courses, apparently somewhat committed to the concept of experimentation, continued to gain support from liberal faculty, but student cynicism increased here too. Proposals for students to teach experimental courses are to be acted on by departments and, in some cases, favorable action apparently has been taken. More often, however, departments have simply procrastinated. In addition to these efforts, the possibility of some sort of informal arrangements for students to obtain field studies credits with a research institute located in Berkeley but not affiliated with the campus were explored. The university, however, resisted establishing such links even though it was likely that a substantial grant would be available from the Ford Foundation to implement such an arrangement. Meanwhile, one of the early faculty sponsors of experimental efforts (including the Cleaver Course) who had continued to look for ways of addressing student demands for experiment and curricular relevance became weary and resigned. Some saw his resignation as a symbolic expression of defeat underscoring the cost to faculty who continued to support educational reform.

The new Division of Experimental Courses has not, to date, secured a chairman, nor have any courses actually been generated. The BED which, at this time, had not met since the spring of 1970, has been declared dead by one of its members. Its role in the use of the large foundation grant mentioned earlier had been relegated to a purely advisory one. Since, according to one of the members, their recommendations apparently did not carry any weight with the administration, the chairman resigned. Another faculty member who had been solicited by the administration to take the place of the chairman noted that he would accept the post only if the BED were given control of the half-million-dollar grant. Six months later he had not yet received an answer from the administration.

Although early in 1971 students may still do independent work with faculty, even this avenue of experiment is under attack by the regents. For all practical purposes experiment with the Berkeley curriculum has come to a halt which is particularly distressing from an educational standpoint. Although our concern is primarily with the organizational consequences of educational innovation, the issue of educational philosophy is crucial. If we stress the desirability of students being active rather than passive in their educational experience, then experiments such as those early ones at Berkeley provide an important test of our educational theories. In this light, it is fortunate that at least one careful study was done of students taking the student-initiated CPE courses at Berkeley in 1968. The conclusions of the study which compared students in CPE courses and students in the traditional curriculum suggest that those who participate in the design of their educational experiences score higher on psychological tests of autonomy and independence, are better students, are more politically active, and are generally less instrumental or career-oriented in their approach to learning.[35] All these, of course, are qualities which we profess to value in our students.

While this study does not tell us much about the organizational dynamics of the University of California curricular experimentation, it is an important commentary on this type of educational innovation supporting the claims of students and faculty interested in developing such experiments that they will, indeed, improve the overall quality of the student's educational experience. Such conclusions also tend to dramatize the shortsightedness of those who have led the assaults on programs which emphasize student participation.

The Third World College

Although it was the center of a major controversy in the spring of 1969, we have not yet discussed the Third World College. Because ethnic studies programs are among the most widespread innovative programs and because they are so often the center of controversy, it is appropriate to examine Berkeley's separately. The record of Berkeley relative to some of the other colleges in the state of California which we have studied is poor. Development of an ethnic studies program began seriously there, as it did on many campuses, in the spring of 1968 following the assassination of Martin Luther King. The first impetus for such a program came from the Afro-American Student Union which presented a proposal for a Black studies program to the university administration.[36] The immediate response of the administration was to appoint a Black faculty member from the School of Social Welfare to the position of Assistant Chancellor for Academic Affairs with a responsibility for guiding the development of a Black studies program. By the fall of the 1968–69 school year, five courses which were to be a part of the Black studies curriculum were offered.[37] The approval of a comprehensive program or the authorization of a degree, however, had not been obtained.

While members of the Afro-American Student Union kept up pressure for a formal approval of the Black studies program during the fall and winter terms of the 1968–69 school year, the office of the assistant chancellor began a more comprehensive plan for a Third World College to include programs in Mexican-American, Oriental-American, and Native-American studies.[38] The issue of the Third World College became a source of conflict in the early spring of 1969, when student supporters of the San Francisco State College strike attempted to mount a similar strike at Berkeley. The net result was to generate another in the series of confrontations between students, university administration, and political forces in the state and, according to one faculty observer, to further the general deterioration of morale in the university community.

While the strike may not have accomplished anything positive, it did help to clarify the position of some of the antagonists. One professor who was interviewed relates that he had previously interpreted the position of the chancellor and the Dean of the College of Letters and Science as in between that of the conservative faculty and the more "progressive" members of the campus community. His judgment was based on events transpiring at the time of the issue of the Cleaver course in the fall of 1968. In the spring of 1969, however, when the issue of the establishment of the Third World College crystallized, he saw the chancellor and dean as having moved to the right.

In March of 1969, after the new series of disturbances, it was moved that the faculty refuse to give an ethnic studies college any more autonomy than any other unit of the university—the issue of autonomy had of course been a point of contention at Berkeley as it has almost everywhere in the development of ethnic studies programs. The faculty, however, rejected the motion whereupon the chancellor, arguing that the faculty was motivated not by principle but out of a desire for peace, essentially ignored the faculty decision and denied autonomy to the ethnic studies program. Apparently this happened after he had used the faculty as an excuse for not giving autonomy to the program. Initially what this move suggests, of course, is a kind of administrative opportunism in which key persons in authority have tried to escape assuming responsibility for actions which were clearly in line with their own judgments about the way things should be. To the extent that this is true, exposing the strategy further reduces the credibility of the administration and intensifies the existing hostilities all around.

In the time since the initial controversies, some progress has been made, but it has been miniscule. In other respects, the program has been set back. One important change was the change from a Third World College to a Department of Ethnic Studies. This shift is significant inasmuch as departmental rather than college status means that the program enjoys considerably less freedom of movement than might have otherwise been the case.

While some might consider the very fact that a Department of Ethnic Studies with four functioning program heads a distinct victory in itself, such feeling must be tempered by the course of development the department has taken. To begin with, only one of the program directors (Black studies) has a regular professional appointment. All others in the Department of Ethnic Studies have appointments as lecturers, and to anyone familiar with the university system, such a title has distinct implications of nonpermanence. One faculty member who has been at the center of activities surrounding the development of the department interprets these appointments as a move by the administration to avoid having any stable faculty members in the department even though there is a budget with twenty-three faculty slots assigned. The degree of the administration's commitment becomes even more obvious when examining the strength of their recruitment efforts. One well-known Black professor, for instance, was offered a salary of $5,000 less than his current position to come to Berkeley. This was interpreted as a clear attempt to cool out the appointment in the face of fears that the proposed new faculty member would be too radical.

The administration's fear of potential radicalism in the ethnic studies programs was underscored by one Black faculty member whose aid had been recruited by the administration. Although they were forced to seek his help, he noted, the administration viewed him as "chief Panther in residence." This was the more interesting in light of his observation that to the radical Black students, he was "chief counterrevolutionary in residence." In addition to the administrative fears, his comments demonstrate in a dramatic way the difficulties faced by minority faculty in the development of such programs. The pressures from both sides, students and administration, are incredibly intense. Because of these difficulties many minority faculty have chosen to avoid any association with such programs at Berkeley and other schools around the country.

Currently the status of the Department of Ethnic Studies is about as ambiguous as ever. Although a commitment from the administration has been extracted, implementation of the program lags. Intensive recruitment of minority faculty, a must if the program is to succeed, has not begun. The top Black administrator who initially gave direction to the Third World College plans has left for another university. Minority students remain very much underrepresented in the student body. Further compounding the problem of representation is a charge by one Black graduate student that those minority students who are recruited are sought primarily for their potential exploitation. He charges, for instance, that the sociology department actively recruits Black graduate students primarily to facilitate research by white faculty in the Black community. Even with such usefulness, he notes that Blacks currently comprise less than four per cent of the graduate student body.[39]

Even if charges such as those above were not true, and one is forced to concede that the arguments are compelling, the progress at Berkeley has been singularly unimpressive. Given its resources and its ability to develop on short notice other types of programs to which it is committed, the university's performance gives the ring of truth to critics' charges that it ultimately intends to strangle the ethnic studies program. The frustrations which led to the resignation of the first assistant vice chancellor charged with responsibility for the program, are obviously infecting other minority faculty who have chosen not to become involved or who have also withdrawn after similar experiences.

Failure of the university to move in this crucial area may heighten the tensions in other areas and further enhance the probability of future difficulties despite the current quiescence. Once again, the initiative has been taken, not by the administration, but by other campus factions. To the extent that the administrators find themselves continually in the position of reacting rather than leading, it would appear that they significantly limit their potential for resolving major dilemmas.

Governing the Multiversity

Although there has been a considerable amount of turmoil on the Berkeley campus, shifts in decision-making procedures have been negligible. Not only have students continued to be excluded from major aspects of university governance—curricular and personnel decisions, for example—but even from future planning. The Academic Plan, a long-range blueprint for the operation of the Berkeley campus, is the expression of the Academic Plan Steering Committee. "The Academic Plan Steering Committee had no student members. It did not consult representatives of the student community, nor any individual within it. The Plan is, by fiat, a negation of the principles and recommendations of the Foote Report on University Governance (*Report of the Select Committee on University Governance,* 1968) and the Muscatine Report (*Education at Berkeley,* 1966)." [40]

The nature of university governance at Berkeley has remained essentially unaltered during the tumultuous years since the 1964 Free Speech Movement—there is still no place for students. Two political scientists, Sheldon Wolin and John Schaar, long-time Berkeley faculty members and analysts of campus events, have observed that fundamental changes have not been forthcoming at Berkeley. There has been no revolution. Rather, there is a continuing ". . . rebellion against the established forms and holders of authority and search for new modes of authority." [41] As a result, no institution in America is more famous than Berkeley for the difficulties involved in its administration. The list of controversy and conflicts in the past seven years has been continually growing and the level of hostilities escalating. In many respects, the problems of governing the multiversity are not unlike those involved in governing many large political units. In this regard, the number of conflicting interest groups and the cross-pressures on administration are so extreme as to make effective action very nearly impossible. An active attack on a problem in one area almost invariably sets in motion counterattacks designed to emasculate moves in the direction of reform.

The posture of significant numbers of students has alternated between pushing the limits of student power and abandoning the campus entirely in favor of "counterinstitutions." The feeling is growing that legitimate student interests will not be served through the traditional mechanisms. At one time the push for student power may simply have meant agitation for educational reform, but this is no longer a defining limit. Students are now interested, as one professor points out, in control of all aspects of the university. They do not want to be left out of the decision-making process any longer on any issue at any level. They assume that all of the areas in which the university operates have implications for the student both as a student and as a participant in the large society.

A particularly good example of the kinds of areas in which students want to have an effective voice is in research commitments by individuals and by the university. Many students would withdraw the substantial university commitment to war and war-related research as an immoral endeavor and therefore outside of the purview of the legitimate university enterprise. Furthermore, many students would act to realign the priorities of the institution with regard to the whole general question of research. It is the contention of these students that it may often be impossible to balance one's research commitments with the obligations of competent classroom teaching performance, and they would argue that the first obligation is to the teaching enterprise since the university exists, ostensibly, to educate the student.

It is irrelevant that the student position on pushing the limits of student power is a minority position. The minority is significant and student activists have been able to rally support far exceeding their numbers on almost any issue on which they have confronted administration or faculty.[42]

In the wake of the increasingly hard line being adopted by students, the relationships between the faculty and students which one student activist suggested had previously cast the faculty in the role of heroes has broken down. Observers now take the position that, while the hostility between the students and faculty has not reached nearly the level of that between student and administration or between faculty and administration, students no longer expect the faculty to adopt a strong supportive position on any issue or to take effective action.

Part of the reason for the breakdown in the relation between students and faculty is the open recognition, after a long history of denial, of inherent conflicts of interest between the two groups. In reporting on the kinds of obstacles that they had encountered in attempting to foster innovation and experimentation on the campus, the Board of Educational Development was prompted to make the following observation:

> All of the evidence indicates that our faculty values research over teaching, and possibly values professional activity, consulting, etc. over teaching as well. Consequently, when it comes to critical deci-

sions, faculty members may cut corners in their teaching, rather than in other areas. From the standpoint of the work of the Board of Educational Development, this means that we have less manpower than necessary for an effective program of campuswide educational experimentation. We realize that a great deal of experimentation occurs within the departments; but for our experimental programs, we rely on the very small margin of surplus faculty energy.

The criteria employed in recruiting and promoting faculty members reflects faculty attitudes. Most departments and review committees are aware of the official importance of teaching as a criterion for advancement, but they are more casual in gathering information on teaching than in documenting research, and give teaching less weight than published research in their own evaluations. Imaginative teaching experiments are usually not rewarded, and indeed, faculty members are likely to be punished for devoting time to teaching and working with students at the expense of producing publications. This conflict is especially destructive for assistant professors, many of whom are effective and enthusiastic teachers, but all of whom are under the greatest pressure to conduct and publish research. This rigid system of academic rewards and punishments erodes the motivation for educational experimentation.[43]

It has become increasingly apparent that faculty and student objectives are often in direct conflict at Berkeley. Although many of those to whom we spoke suggested that this has led to an increasing polarization on the part of faculty and student groups, one professor characterizes the relationship as being somewhat ambivalent. He says, "They're polarized, but they're not. They're enemies, but they're not. There are conflicts of interest, but they need one another."

Perhaps the last comment is the most revealing. The students talk of self-education and independence, but they are also aware of a need for guidance and teaching. They want to develop close relationships with knowledgeable, interesting faculty, and they probably want a certificate of completion or license when it's all over. On the other hand, they don't want to grovel or beg for instructor time, and they want humane treatment. They don't want to be a part of an amorphous computerized mass; they want to be treated as individuals and to be taken seriously. This doesn't mean that they demand individualized tutoring programs in all areas. It does mean that they would like to know some faculty and be known in turn before they leave. All of these objectives are often impossible in the current campus environment, and they do not even include the more exotic issues that are being raised on campuses like Berkeley. Questions of official mendacity and intellectual honesty, of institutional commitments and institutional neutrality, and of outside interference and resistance to governmental tampering add complicating dimensions that further strain the faculty-student relationship.

Faculty, on the other hand, while virtually universally proclaiming a strong commitment to teaching including undergraduate instruction are faced with intense pressures for research and publication. These pressures are not, however, manufactured outside of faculty agencies. Such pressures are the product of their own subculture; the heavy demands on faculty for research are a consequence of norms built by faculty groups at a national and local level. Certainly no one who comes to Berkeley comes with any illusion about priorities or the types of demands to be put on him. Therefore one must assume the faculty initially has a very high level of commitment to research. In addition, the inducement to devote time to non-classroom activities is compounded by the opportunities for such activities as outside consulting which can be extremely lucrative and status-enhancing and which can be undertaken without jeopardizing one's income from the university. Not infrequently such arrangements are taken as indicators of one's prowess in his particular area and may enhance the possibilities of promotion up the institutional ladder. It is easy to see that the amount of time the professor is able to devote to the student is directly affected by these other activities, and, when we add a significant commitment to graduate teaching, we can see that time allotted to undergraduates is even further curtailed.

The resulting ethos at Berkeley has been one of mixed hostility and resentment tempered by the recognition of mutual interests or needs. As issues become more clearly articulated and as the intensity of feelings increases, the pressures on faculty to commit themselves heighten. Since the FSM, however, the willingness of faculty to commit themselves to student causes appears to have steadily decreased. Students, faculty, and administrators alike have concurred with one faculty member's observation about faculty that "when the going gets rough, they'll be where faculty are supposed to be, and that's not with the student." Even on those issues where there has been a rather clear community of interest, faculty and student groups have usually acted independently and almost never as a coalition.

Student-administration and student-faculty enmity is only two-thirds of the problem. There has also been a history of faculty-administration antagonism in the institution which, according to one administrator, reached its zenith at the time of the FSM and has been maintained at this peak ever since. He in fact interprets faculty action during the Free Speech Movement as a retaliation against the administration as much as a show of support for the students and the issues involved.

In the more recent episodes, the ill-will between the two groups has been fanned by administrative actions surrounding the BED and its work. In the first place, the administration appointed the Assistant Chancellor for Educational Development an ex officio member of the BED, an apparently unprecedented action representing the first case in recent history where a member of the administration has been appointed to a faculty committee. The faculty has apparently cherished its autonomy vis-a-vis the administration and regarded such an appointment as a challenge to this autonomy. Furthermore, the administrative role in events resulting from the Social Analysis 139X controversy was to back the dictates of the regents and to remove the prerogative of appointment to academic positions from the faculty where it had nominally rested. Along with these moves, the administration retained the right to review any proposed courses approved by BED with the apparent power to overrule such approval. These decisions greatly eroded whatever rights or areas of jurisdiction the faculty believed were their sole responsibility. The decisive blow came of course when the administration transferred responsibility for educational experimentation from the BED to the assistant vice chancellor, usurping at that point any faculty power in the realm of educational experimentation.

Factionalism, dispute, hostility, bitterness, and suspicion have been the heritage of the events of the past several years at Berkeley. There has been no indication of a lessening of estrangement or a closing of ranks among the various groups except perhaps briefly as a result of the People's Park battle. Even in this case, however, where reports from every sector picture administrative and political rigidity of the most absurd order, there was only a limited consolidation of the university community. Perhaps it would be more accurate to suggest that the lines of battle forced the formation of coalition between previously independent factions, but the coalition remained weak. While two hundred faculty issued a declaration of refusal to teach,[44] hundreds of others remained voiceless. Furthermore, the nature of faculty action during the meeting of the Faculty Senate on May 23, 1969 betrayed the continuing ambivalence of the majority of faculty. When a motion was introduced calling for the removal of the chancellor, it was defeated decisively by a vote of 737 to 94 with 99 abstentions [45] in spite of his central role in precipitating the disaster by ignoring the advice of the Committee on Housing and Environment and reclaiming the park without negotiation.[46] Furthermore, while passing a series of resolutions calling for a cessation of the hostilities, the faculty appears to have exerted no more direct collective pressures. Meanwhile, as hundreds of students, nonstudents, participants, and bystanders were arrested, one onlooker killed, a shopkeeper permanently blinded, and scores of others seriously injured, the chancellor is quoted as declaring in a television interview that "we have not stopped the rational process." [47] That same day the executive vice-chancellor declared in a published interview, "Our strategy was to act with humor and sensitivity." [48]

The "rational process" and the "humor and sensitivity" of the administration were evidenced by the fact that they had brought police to the campus several hours in advance of the outbreak of hostilities.[49] Furthermore, by assuming a rigid stand which at that point was certain to lead to a demonstration, the administration must surely have been able to anticipate the events which followed. The governor had several times issued declarations of emergency and called the National Guard for demonstrations over the past several months.[50] If rationality and humor had ever been a part of the administrative style at Berkeley, both had dissipated rapidly in the wake of the Free Speech Movement. Never were such adjectives used to describe the events surrounding the park controversy, except by university administrators.

But if the events of the People's Park generated profound despondence and thorough pessimism, the next spring was to bring at least a temporary resurrection of hopes for reform.

May 1970: Crisis and Regression

In 1970 the majority of American college students had lived most of their lives with a barbaric war in Indochina, a permanent system of military conscription, and an increasing awareness of the racism, sexism, and social injustices in our society. Radical politics as a response to the conditions which have created the current dilemma are increasingly appealing to such students. As Harold Taylor points out, they are a generation of students without teachers. They seldom have any meaningful interaction with their professors. For many, if not most of them, the educational experience is so highly specialized, so carefully segmented, and so narrowly circumscribed that it is almost entirely removed from contemporary reality. If the position of faculty as teachers is coincidental to the external factors impinging on students' lives, then perhaps in times of crisis something very peculiar happens. Such seems to have been the case in the spring of 1970.

Without consulting the American people, the full Congress, the House or Senate Foreign Relations Committees, or apparently even his Cabinet, President Nixon ordered U.S. troops into Cambodia. This act, characterized as a move to "win the peace," triggered a national response more volatile than any other in the course of the Vietnam war. Within days, hundreds of colleges and universities altered their schedules, suspended normal operations, and acted as well as reflected on the incursion into Cambodia and the killing of students at Kent State University and Jackson State College.

At the University of California there was a huge response. The first convocation on May 6, drew 17,000 persons. It is estimated that 10,000 students, faculty, and staff participated in a variety of political activities and that two-thirds of the eighty departments at Berkeley had some antiwar activities in operation.[51] A rash of departmental resolutions were passed concerning the war, political repression at home, student killings at Kent and Jackson State, government harassment of the Black Panther Party, and regents' action against UCLA faculty member Angela Davis. In addition to off-campus political activities, there were a number of faculty actions regarding the Berkeley campus. In one cathartic upheaval, academic credit for ROTC was suspended, course requirements in liberal arts reduced, and increased student participation was approved by faculty in many departments.

The consequences of the May 1970 events have received widespread publicity and commentary. Anyone on a college or university campus at the time experienced some of them. Perhaps the most typical response was some form of suspension of normal activities. Such suspensions commonly led to the abandonment of normal class schedules to allow times for political action or discussion of events. At Berkeley, however, despite the positive reaction in the spring, the aftermath has been disciplinary hearings for ten faculty charged with "not meeting academic responsibilities."

The hearings are only a part of a major reversal of the mood affecting the campus in early May. Regental pressure, plus a sharpened awareness of what they as faculty had done, prompted the Berkeley faculty to react in a form of backlash. One commentator noted a growing anticipation by faculty of the potential impact of their decisions on students. He argues,

> This fall (1970) the genie may be out of the bottle on academic reform. Kids on several campuses are asking, "Hey, if we could do away with grades and lectures and the traditional curriculum because Nixon invaded Cambodia, why can't we do away with them because they get in the way of learning?" [52]

In early spring of 1970 faculty at Berkeley had judged students to be cynical, despairing, and apathetic. True, they were concerned about the Chicago Conspiracy Trial and a host of community political issues, but concern with educational reform, curriculum, and governmental change at the university had dissipated perceptibly. The May events generated dramatic and spontaneous reactions by the university community—faculty and students—to national and international events. But here, even as in normal circumstances, the students were relatively impotent to effect changes—and, where faculty had acted, they soon demonstrated that they could also react. The temporary mood of crisis, the sense of a need for reform, and a heightened concern for students quickly subsided. Faculty conservatism and regental action returned the campus to a mood comparable to that before Cambodia, Kent State, and Jackson State. Sheldon Wolin and John Schaar, temper the optimism of some with the comment:

> It remains to be seen whether the crisis of the spring of 1970 amounted to a critical experience which could launch a whole new generation of political activists and a whole new style of political action. A few voices did rise above the anxious but self-congratulatory din of the new converts to the antiwar cause and tried to call attention to the profound crisis in the state. A few others tried to call teachers and students to the larger task of redefining the aims and structures of higher education so that we might produce educated men for whom knowledge, personal identity, and public commitment are part of the same quest.

> It may be that the campus effects of Cambodia will be comparable in the long run to those produced by the civil rights movement. It may also be that the aftermath of Cambodia will confirm that we are truly in an iron cage.[53]

As far as Berkeley is concerned, the evidence suggests that students at least are still very much in an iron cage. The political context and subsequent events in California make this clear despite the temporary breakthroughs of spring 1970.

*The Challenge of Educational Change:
Conclusions from the Berkeley Case*

Although the University of California has received worldwide attention because of its student activism, the fact is that the student movement is now a national and international phenomenon. While Berkeley was an early focal point, student protests against the universities on issues ranging from governance to military-industrial ties to academic reform, have been widespread. One recent survey showed 292 major student protests on 232 campuses during the first six months of 1969.[54] The issues included racial justice and race-related campus demands, Vietnam, the draft, the universities' role in war activities, and a range of issues peculiar to the local setting. There is a widespread student concern about the major issues of the day and they are demanding that the university respond to these concerns.[55]

The developments on other campuses have generally decreased attention to Berkeley, yet some critical questions were initially raised on its campus. In examining the impact of events of the past decade, we should note some of the potential consequences for other campuses, as well as those things which are more peculiar to the Berkeley experience.

While no one challenges the excellence of the University of California, the issue of the possible demise of its stature has often been raised, partly as a result of the general crisis in financing higher education but relating more directly to the politicization of higher education in California. The years since the FSM have seen fewer and fewer untenured faculty speaking out for student interests. Supporters of educational innovation who may have become weary and disillusioned have resigned to less conflict-ridden environments. Ironically, one such refuge for them was Harvard which experienced severe student disorders at the end of the sixties. Such experiences underscore the fact that student unrest is a generalized phenomenon and cannot be escaped by moving from one campus to another.

As we assess the impact of the past decade, several major points become clear. First, there has been a significant shift on major campuses away from the emphasis on student participation in running the university. While the notion of participatory democracy challenged students early in the history of the student movement, the stress on institutional government has abated somewhat. As one student analyst notes,

> Student participation in the governance of the university (read: student control of our own alienation) is not the goal of the educational revolution. In order to achieve a utopian vision of what a university must be, the society must also be transformed. As the university is an integral institution in the society, a permanent challenge to the university-as-it-is becomes a permanent challenge to society-as-it-is. Once students gain veto power (i.e., if the students and faculty don't agree on something, it doesn't get done) the revolution will have begun in earnest.[56]

Although the Berkeley community generated several responses to the FSM, the fact is that in the early part of the 1970s there is no model of governance which student activists find uniformly appealing. Emphasis is falling more upon *what* decisions are made rather than *who* makes them. As well as a simple despair among student activists of ever achieving parity with other campus constituencies, such events may reflect a growing recognition of the potential conservatizing effect of student participation over the long haul. Student participation per se will not guarantee progress toward the more idealistic projections of what a university might be like. Indeed, such participation may pose a serious threat, at least to the extent that student participation in a bad decision might nevertheless lend such a decision even greater legitimacy in the eyes of the larger campus community.

Perhaps the failures at Berkeley are due, in large measure, to a problem which became more obvious as the conflicts on the campus increased. A major theoretician for Students for a Democratic Society wrote, "We know we cannot win the kind of university we want without a complete transformation of society. . . . "[57]

The issue shifts then, between internal reform of the university and more general concerns about societal change. Thus the emphasis moves from the broad issue of governance as such and focuses more on the nature of specific decisions. To have faculty abolish ROTC and defense research becomes an important student objective even though the decision makers remain faculty. The vision of what might be is not entirely clear, however, for the limited objective of ending military training is not equivalent to an alternative curriculum meeting demands for relevance.

Earlier we noted that the mood of Berkeley students at the beginning of the seventies is one of intense cynicism and apathy. Even a sketchy inventory of specific actions over the past years make the reasons obvious. The push for radical curricular alteration has been a failure. Student-initiated experimentation in the curriculum was short-lived and quickly relegated to the status of an historical curiosity. Furthermore, the system of governance, as we have so often pointed out, is fundamentally unchanged. Student participation in decision making, be it the curriculum or long-range planning, is virtually nonexistent. The multiversity is still doing what the critics in the early sixties decried, namely, training technicians for the nation's military-industrial apparatus and performing wholesale applied research for industry and government.[58]

Perhaps the most important outcome of all this has been a loss of faith by students, even in students themselves, fostered by lack of progress in university reform and by recognition of the capacity of the system, be it the university or the larger society, to absorb and defuse the best efforts of those who see themselves as agents of change. Assaults on the university have led to study commissions whose recommendations can be conveniently ignored. Students, meanwhile, have been conveniently "cooled out" in the intervening period. Adding to their frustration is the fact that off-campus activities such as working for peace candidates in elections have been an exercise in futility. The Hubert Humphreys have been nominated while the peaceniks were getting their heads smashed in the streets. But there is a major additional factor which has contributed to the resignation and despair on the Berkeley campus—the reality of power relationships in the university. As Wolin and Schaar conclude,

> When the Berkeley faculty voted to modify ROTC programs, the Regents' response was to approve a resolution to explore the possibility of introducing ROTC units at the four campuses which do not now have them.
>
> After the Berkeley faculty had voted to request the termination of the relationship between the campus and two laboratories which, according to an official report, "encompass every aspect in the process of developing nuclear weapons," and over which the campus had virtually no control, the Regents pass a resolution (July 17,

1970) reaffirming the importance of research for national defense and vowing to continue to sponsor such programs.

What this all adds up to is not a series of attacks, but a rollback which threatens the modest measure of academic freedom previously enjoyed and promises a greater increase of bureaucratic controls. It represents, too, a denial of all that has happened, not only at Berkeley, but throughout the country, between 1964 and 1970.[59]

Neo-McCarthyism and Anarchist Hysteria: California Politics Since FSM

It is perhaps the case that California particularly illustrates the degree to which higher education became a political issue in the late 1960s partly due to peculiar characteristics of the state: a rapidly expanding population with substantial proportions of retired persons who typically fail to support educational development; large numbers of minority and low income workers in pursuit of the American Dream of upward mobility through education; and the radical political traditions of California, especially in the Bay Area. In addition though, it is clear that the dramatic events of the 1960s and Berkeley's reputation as a center of student activism created a climate which polarized the California electorate.

Ronald Reagan was not the first California politician to meddle in the affairs of the university but he was the first to be elected on a platform which consisted largely of promises to "clean up Berkeley." The result of his election in 1966 and the events that have followed under his leadership have been an unmitigated disaster for the university. During his tenure the university must surely hold the record for time spent under occupation by police or National Guard troops. His involvement in university affairs has not, however, been limited to martialling the troops. Reagan's has been a much wider and more varied involvement.

Officially the University of California is supposed to be freed from the problem of political interference by virtue of the creation of an independent corporate body, the regents, charged with total responsibility for the affairs of the institution. Of the twenty-four regents, sixteen are appointed by the governor for sixteen-year terms. The other eight positions are ex officio and include the Governor, Lieutenant Governor, Speaker of the Assembly, State Superintendent of Public Instruction, President of the State Board of Agriculture, President of the Mechanics'

Institute, President of the Alumni Association, and the President of the University.

Four of the ex officio members are high level state politicians and two others represent clear-cut political interests. In addition, appointment to the regents has never been considered an apolitical act. Many, if not most, of the regents are appointed because of political involvement or commitments to the governor in office at the time a vacancy occurs. In this respect the attempt to free the university from political influence or control has been only partially successful; while it has eliminated the possibility of direct control by the legislature, it has not circumvented the fact that appointment to the regents is a form of political patronage, and it has most certainly not assured that the regents' actions are devoid of political content or meaning.

The election of Reagan and the popularity of the president of San Francisco State College S. I. Hayakawa as a potential political candidate in 1970 demonstrate that in California at least political fortunes can be made and lost in the educational arena. In speaking of the problem of political interference, the first chairman of the BED summed it up with a comment that "the problems were compounded by the fact that the most powerful political act is not chasing Communists, but chasing students." In the 1960s students have superseded Communists in California political rhetoric as the number one enemy of the people. But while the principles have changed, the political tactics are reminiscent of the McCarthy era.

Incipient anarchy is a charge frequently leveled at the University, and the charge that Communist subversion is behind the student movements is also frequently heard. What is more, however, this kind of charge has not been the sole prerogative of the political community. Clark Kerr, during the height of the FSM appeared on national television charging that leadership had fallen into the hands of "followers of the Maoist and Castro lines." Although Kerr later retreated from this stand, the fact that he would adopt such a position publicly in the first place is indicative of the kind of pressures to which the university president is subjected in almost every instance where there is a confrontation on the campus.

The interference of the legislature and governor's office has not been limited solely to crises. The State Committee on Un-American Activities has, as we pointed out earlier, leveled periodic charges at the university as a center of Communist enterprise. Pressures have been brought to bear on the regents through legislative resolution on the one hand and through threats to cut the university's budget substantially on the other. The threat has not been an idle one. The regents, who are keenly interested in maintaining the reputation of the university as the finest in the land, are not immune to such pressures. The governor, too, has not hesitated to use the media to publicize his intentions of taking a hard stand on law and order in the university which apparently had its impact on the regents, as one member pointed out when they passed a regulation allowing the governor to declare a state of emergency in order to activate National Guard troops and bring in outside police help to stem campus disorders. He noted that while opposed to the new regulation in principle, he could not vote against it because he would risk looking like he was voting against law and order. Thus the governor is able to bring multiple pressures, both through publicity and through legislative control of funds, and is in a strategic position to manipulate the regents' action across the whole range of issues. His power can particularly be seen in an act like the firing of Clark Kerr. Although it is clear that Kerr's position with the regents was tenuous, until Reagan's accession to office he had always weathered attempts to dismiss him with a relatively substantial margin of safety. The shift after the change in administration required four more votes than those by the new officers in order to reverse this margin.

Politicial pressure on the university has increased since the demise of Kerr not just because of subsequent events at Berkeley, but probably because of the spread of disturbances to other campuses. Berkeley suffers here in two ways: first, it is assumed by large numbers of the public that if it were not for Berkeley setting the style for campus politics, such disturbances might not have occurred; and second, governmental hostility has been focused on Berkeley for so long that anything which exacerbates the chagrin of politicians with regard to higher education in general, is likely to have repercussions for Berkeley.

As a consequence of the liberal or radical political activities of so many of the students and non-students on the Berkeley campus, the posture of the legislature and the governor with regard to campus issues has been to lift events on the campus out of context of simple campus politics and place them in the larger political arena. When students become embroiled in a confrontation with the Berkeley administration now, it is assumed that the enemy includes the regents and the state political machinery. In many respects they are correct in their assessment. To the extent that this pattern of outside interference and political intervention in university affairs continues, it is almost certain that internal problems of the university community will not be resolved. As a result of this likelihood, everyone with whom one speaks on the campus characterizes the current ethos as one of complete demoralization. While for some this may mean withdrawal from the political arena, for others it means the introduction of new, and less conventional strategies.

An important consequence of these events, in addition to the polarization of constituencies, has been a situation in which student leadership is being forced to become increasingly militant and radical. One professor notes that "Rhetoric is now so far removed from political reality, ability to deliver, that it's taken on a life of its own. . . . The spokesmen get further and further out on a limb, then when they can't deliver, they're discredited." Along these lines, the issues of the People's Park was elevated to the stature of a holy war. Talk of "bringing down the fence" and of making the park "Reagan's political burial spot" was not infrequent. What is even more significant, is the increasing consolidation of the student body behind radical and activist leadership.[60] As the students continue to assume an offensive position in bringing issues to the administration, the repressiveness of the governmental machinery appears certain to increase. Caught in the middle of the squeeze is a university administration which can expect little in the way of active support from the faculty no matter what their response to these pressures. One of the signs of such pressures in recent years has been the mobility of top university administrators. The American Council on Education recently pointed out that the annual turnover of college presidents jumped nearly eighty per cent in the last three years.[61] The University of California at Berkeley has experienced considerable turnover in the top administration, ranging from the pressure on Clark Kerr which removed him as president to the recent resignation of Roger Heyns as chancellor. Heyns gave personal and health factors as the reason, but what is significant is that in his parting address he choose not to stress the quality of the university, its experimentation with governance, or other significant accomplishments, but rather he stated that the "most significant achievement of my ten years was to keep the university open."

Such is the current state of affairs. The university has been rendered almost totally incapable to taking action in any sphere. The smallest change internally takes on a highly political character as officials labor under the close scrutiny of their multiple adversaries. The only time when there has been a modicum of peace and order on the campus during the past few years has been when literally nothing was happening, and even this situation eventually generates new pressures from one or another of the campus constituencies. Without the consolidation of campus forces it would appear that the almost continuous state of hostility and bitterness will continue to escalate. Even in the face of such a highly improbable eventuality as a general consolidation of university forces, it is not likely that the state political forces or the electorate will retreat now.

Despite Governor Reagan's success, however, a considerable number of ambiguities remain in the California political situation. While Reagan could argue in his initial bid for the governorship that the state administration had been lax and that the universities had to be shaped up, he failed to make headway on some important fronts. There is evidence, for instance, that by 1970, when he won an overwhelming victory for re-election, the universities were less accessible than ever to the working class from which he drew substantial support. Other politicians with equally conservative political images, most notably Max Rafferty (State Superintendent of Schools) and Senator George Murphy, were defeated by substantial margins, raising the important question of Reagan's ability to maintain his credibility with the voters while his partners in conservatism were so thoroughly discredited.

Perhaps a part of the explanation lies in the central role that the governor's office has played in the continuing controversy in the University of California. Other politicians, while they might jump on the bandwagon, were perhaps identified with broader issues and political failures in California. In the case of Rafferty, there was his abortive attempt for the senate in 1968 coupled with a hint of scandal concerning his selective service record and a series of controversies in the public schools deriving from the issue of desegregation. Murphy, of course, was faced with serious questions concerning his health and the collapse of the defense industry in the state—a collapse for which he was held partially responsible by the electorate.

But Reagan's popularity cannot be tied wholly to the issue of the university. Perhaps more important than his performance is the fact that he has become increasingly identified in California with many of the values and traditions whose demise a substantial proportion of the electorate find threatening. It should be pointed out that one characteristic of the Bay Area during the early portion of Reagan's first term in office, while later to be shared by other parts of the nation, was relatively unique—it had become the hip capital of the country. During the "love summer" of 1967 tens of thousands of youths had come to the Bay Area, many to remain and swell the ranks of the street people and non-students in the university's fringe areas.[62] This too was translated into a political issue as the governor blamed the laxity of the university administration and faculty for attracting the parasitic community of street people whose values and behavior were intensely offensive to California's hardworking, mobility-oriented populace.

The youth culture with its challenge to puritanical traditions of personal conduct has been seen as a new mode of political subversion. Those who have interpreted it as such are no doubt correct at least to the extent that the counterculture erodes the acquisitive values of a consumer-oriented society which glorifies its economic-occupational structure and measures progress in terms of a technocratic increment in output.[63] In California, and particularly at Berkeley, the counterculture of non-students has generated political support for forces seeking to curb the autonomy of the university and to strengthen the traditional values of higher education.

What we have suggested then is that the political context of the current cultural strains in California have been fundamental in shaping the recent history of the university. While the 1960s saw demands by students for a voice in running the university, they also saw events such as the Declaration of the Berkeley Liberation Front at the time of the People's Park crisis which may have been more threatening than any of the internal crises of the university, but it was clearly linked in the public mind with the university community. In their cry for a free liberated zone adjacent to the university in which self-government would be the order of the new era, the hip community gave substance to the larger community's fears of incipient anarchism. So it was that efforts for university reform became inextricably tied to the larger revolution of the youth culture.

The people of California quite probably voted for a credible challenge to the new counterculture. In this sense, Reagan has literally become California's counterrevolutionary leader. At the same time, he has consolidated his control over a university which his constituents are convinced has made inappropriate concessions to student demands for a role in running the institution and to minority students whom they see eroding universal standards of educational excellence. On this last point, we should emphasize that working- and middle-class whites are opposed to special education and ethnic studies programs not because they oppose equal opportunity but because they are convinced that inequities and racial favoritism are endemic in the new minority programs. This segment of the citizenry rejects racial guilt and opposes concessions to minority students because of the links which they perceive between education and occupational and economic mobility. In this context, the aspirations of minority students represent a definite threat to the interests of the white community.

Such is the condition in which a battle-weary university now finds itself. Increasingly demoralized, cynical, and embittered as a consequence of their experiences with one another and the outside community, students, faculty, and administration at Berkeley may have finally abandoned the last vestiges of constructive effort at educational reform. It is not inconceivable that the university has passed beyond the point of salvation—at least if it is to retain any semblance of honor. Whether this matters any more appears doubtful.

III
War and Peace on Campus: San Francisco State College

A short drive across the Bay from Berkeley lies the San Francisco area's other major institution of higher learning, San Francisco State College. Although relatively quiescent for most of its history, San Francisco State challenged Berkeley in the recent past for recognition as the most troubled campus in America. In most other important respects, however, the two institutions are as different as night and day. It should be recognized, too, that their differences are not accidental. They are products of the allocation of the state's educational resources and of San Francisco State's role within the framework of California's *Master Plan for Higher Education*.[1]

Anyone who has visited the two campuses recognizes the differences immediately. The contrasts are not limited to the classroom and what goes on there; they affect every aspect of the life of the two institutions. While Berkeley's campus occupies a spacious park-like setting encompassing a variety of impressive structures, State's space is limited and the buildings are uniformly dull and painfully practical in appearance. The immediate impression is that the Berkeley setting is appropriate for fostering soaring feats of intellect while State's is designed for the no-nonsense, practical educational orientation that is its mission.[2]

There are few hideaways for idle reflection, and the continuing building program is rapidly depleting whatever open spaces remain on the campus. The only spots for student gatherings are a student union which is depressingly like an industrial cafeteria, an adjacent forum building, and a series of dilapidated old army-type huts which serve as the offices for student activities.

Although it began as a teachers college and still has a very large teacher-training program, State has long since abandoned the image of a teacher-training institution. The overall demand for college-trained personnel in California has helped to transform the campus into a multipurpose, general institution catering to the needs of a wide variety of students.

While the State students are not among the academic elite in terms of the conventional standards, neither are they academic incompetents. The state of California, because of its multilevel approach to higher education is quite selective in admittance to the state colleges, especially in comparison to the admission requirements of a number of other states. Because the elaborate junior college system allows the student who has performed at a less than admirable level in high school to demonstrate his ability to perform at the college level, enrollment in the state colleges is limited to the top one-third of the state's high school graduates.[3] Because of the difference in the types of programs offered at State, its reputation as a center of educational innovation, its relative convenience of the college campus for commuters, and its location in San Francisco, the quality of the student body is reputed to be higher than at many of the other state colleges or higher than one would expect given what is a more or less official designation as an inferior institution in the *Master Plan.*

Like the student body, the faculty is reputed to be a cut above that of the other state colleges and superior to many institutions of relatively higher status. Again, the mystique of San Francisco, the reputation for innovation, and the promise, perhaps, of less pressure for research and publication have been drawing cards.[4]

In contrast to many of the other state colleges and perhaps to all of the branches of the University of California, the average age of the undergraduate at San Francisco State is twenty-four. This fact in itself says much about the character of the campus. A far larger than normal percentage of the students have jobs which engage them either full or part time. The college is only infrequently the center of the student's world. As Riesman and Jencks pointed out nearly ten years ago, the State student who has not been exposed to the world of work is a rarity,[5] and this does not appear to have changed significantly in the intervening years. According to many of the college administrators, more State students are dependent upon their own resources than is the case at Berkeley or other state institutions. This fact alone may account in great measure for the lack of a collegiate environment and the relative lack of identification of the student with the institution. But, as Riesman and Jencks also note, the fact that so many of the students are devoting a major portion of their time to an occupation means that many do not identify with the role of student; that is, few think of their primary role as that of a student [6] which may explain in part what appears to be a greater affinity of the State student for off-campus activities rather than for conventional extra-curricular activities. It may account in part, too, for the reputation of the institution as a center for innovation since the links with the community seem unusually elaborate because of student activities. Another force for some creativity or innovation may be the fact that many of the conventional student activities (e.g., interest groups, fraternities, and so on) have been replaced by activities centered in the departments of the student's majors.[7] An example of the type of departmental activity to which Riesman and Jencks refer is currently found in the college's School of Education. Here, according to faculty and students, a special program dealing with the strategies for teaching disadvantaged youth was implemented largely because of the efforts of departmental majors working through their department organization and the Experimental College.

As pointed out earlier, the differences between Berkeley and San Francisco State are not accidental. The university is charged with responsibility for the education of the academic elite in the state and for graduate education and research. San Francisco State, on the other hand, is charged with the education of the second level of academic excellence and has only limited responsibility for graduate education. The difference in the charge of the two institutions is reflected in the state's commitment of resources to them.

Studies conducted before the *Master Plan* was developed indicated that the state was allocating almost exactly twice as much to the university as to the state college system, independent of capital outlays. At the time (1958–59) the enrollment was very nearly equal with the state colleges holding a slight edge. The result was a state expenditure of almost exactly two-to-one in favor of the university. When outside resources were added, the balance in favor of the university increased to nearly three-to-one.[8] The projected allocations from state funds to the two systems indicate the intention of retaining the formula of two-to-one. Allocations for 1965–70 indicate that the university had been earmarked for one and a half times as much money as the state colleges while having an anticipated enrollment of only three-fourths as many students.[9] Since such differences are clearly spelled out in the *Master Plan,* faculty and administration might be expected to be committed to the educational objectives of the institution in terms of its role in the state's overall program of higher education. There is universal recognition, however, that this is not the case.

There has been a long-standing feud between the state colleges and the university over the issue of graduate education. To date, and for the foreseeable future, the university has jealously guarded its prerogatives with regard to providing advanced graduate training. The state colleges cannot award doctorates, nor are there plans for them to do so in the future. There is a provision in the *Master Plan* for joint doctoral programs with the university, but these are with the clear understanding that control lies in the hands of the university. Even under this provision, there has been very little in the way of doctoral training in the state colleges and the lag in this area has been a source of hostility.[10] The result has been a situation in which the ambitions of state college faculty have been continually frustrated, particularly true of San Francisco State with its superior faculty, many of whom have matriculated at the nation's distinguished graduate institutions, including the neighbor across the Bay.

In effect, the faculty's ambition for the institution is a built-in barrier to effective operation within the parameters laid out in the *Master Plan.* Riesman and Jencks describe this ambition, apparent even ten years ago, as pressure to become a lower-order Berkeley or UCLA.[11] The result has been a continuing tension within the institution revolving around this and associated issues such as the nine-hour teaching load, faculty salaries, more adequate provisions for research, and expansion of the graduate program at the masters level.[12] What exists is, in reality, an unwillingness on the part of the faculty to consign itself to what one student describes as the institution's "official second-rate status."[13] It has been argued, however, that without the *Master Plan's* unambiguous limitation on graduate programs, there would probably have been little incentive for the development of the innovative programs which have made the college famous.

While faculty do not like their official designation as second-rate, or the kind of differential allocation of resources that this entails, there is some evidence that growing numbers of students are also unhappy about it. Although Riesman and Jencks play down the invidious comparisons between institutions and their consequences in terms of the student's aspirations, these have probably become a source of increasing irritation in the intervening ten years. With the growing emphasis on higher education and the increasing number of students attending San Francisco State who have ambitions for advanced graduate and professional education, the same conditions that anger faculty often anger students. Many of the brighter students especially resent the differences in the resources and prestige of the two institutions.

It is within this environment of a growing student population that is increasing in quality, of growing faculty ambitions, of greater pressures for higher education, and of increasing concern of students for the quality and content of their education that San Francisco State College developed some of the innovative programs for which it is now famous.

Community Action in the Search for Relevance

Although State's reputation for innovation apparently goes back many years as a consequence of special programs revolving around different kinds of occupational specialities, the beginnings of the kinds of innovation which have been recently the center of attention are found in a series of community action programs begun in the early 1960s.

As early as 1963 students interested in the problems of the minority and disadvantaged communities began the first tutorial program.[14] It was from this program that a much larger and much wider range of programs was later to emerge. Interest in this type of program apparently increased between 1963 and 1966 as students with experiences particularly relevant to such areas began to enroll at State. According to a former president of the college, a large percentage of students in this early group had done civil rights work in the South or been Peace Corps volunteers. This new type of student was united with other students with whom he had a common experience with the disadvantaged and was among the first to express the new concern for relevance in his educational experience.

As interest in community action programs began to increase and the areas of concern expanded, there developed a push for credit for the activities in which the students were engaged. This kind of pressure was probably the result of two factors, the relationship of the kind of work that students were doing in the community to their career aspirations and the need for some kind of formal recognition of their activity if they were going to be able to maintain an intense commitment to the program while progressing at a satisfactory rate in school.

The first efforts to obtain credit for community activities were channeled through the independent studies program available to undergraduates which simply required finding a professor who was willing to take the student under his guidance for some sort of a specially designed project. The procedure had a long history in California higher education and obtaining three credits for a community action project was, according to students, relatively easy.

As interest in community programs continued to grow, the students formalized the coordination of the various projects by developing the Community Services Institute (1966–67) which was intended to facilitate the organization of student projects, to serve as an information clearing house, and to help secure credit arrangements for those interested in working in the community.[15] In addition to these kinds of activities, the institute staff was engaged in the preparation of new and increasingly ambitious programs and in the development of a coherent philosophy of education revolving around the notion that:

> . . . educational institutions have failed to develop constructive alternatives which would provide a relevant educational experience for students who are faced with the problems of living in a rapidly changing urban society.[16]

The objective of the institute was to provide these constructive alternatives.

The student interest in a new kind of educational experience which led to the development of the Community Services Institute was also an impetus for the now famous Experimental College. The expansion of community action programs dovetailed neatly with the beginning of the Experimental College in the spring of 1966. From that point, the programs developed simultaneously in a mutually complementary relationship.

Altering the Educational Experience: The Experimental College

By far the most publicized of State's many programs has been the Experimental College. The new program attracted national attention with its founding in the spring of 1966 as a model for responsible educational change. The idea for the Experimental College developed out of the deliberations of a continuing student-faculty-administration seminar which had engaged approximately forty participants in the fall semester of 1965.[17] The "group," as it was called, had begun its meetings at the same time as three other small noncredit experimental seminars for freshmen and sophomores sponsored by the Associated Students. The group's discussions, according to former student body officers and founders of the Experimental College, centered around issues of student government and the shortcomings of the contemporary college educational experience, especially at San Francisco State.[18] Students participating in the discussions decided near the end of the fall semester, 1965 to organize the Experimental College around the format of the free university. The idea of the free university is simply that any individual who has an interest and can find someone to pursue the interest with him organizes a course. The free university courses differ from others in that anyone who can contribute teaches, but it is not part of a credit and degree-granting university program. The total experience is one of learning together, sharing interests, and teaching one another. The formal teacher-student relationship where the teacher is an authority figure is taboo. Everyone is an equal. There is also a notable absence of the traditional constraints which confine the curriculum of the traditional university within relatively narrow boundaries. Issues of academic legitimacy or controversial content are irrelevant. The accent, as the name implies, is on freedom.

The Experimental College departed from the free university concept only in that it was to be an integral part of the institution rather than a separate entity. It was hoped that the Experimental College would provide, in the student organizers' words, "a full-scale practical testing ground for their educational theories." [19] The students hoped to better approximate the ideal of the free university than had other groups by de-emphasizing the political and ideological issues in a standard educational format. They adopted the slogan "Anyone can organize a course," and set out to experiment not only with content, but with creative formats and procedures.[20] They were given the use of the college facilities and began to advertise the idea through the student newspaper. Most of the students involved in the planning also organized courses that first term.

Although the idea for the Experimental College was unique, it had little trouble winning the support of the student government. A leader in organizing the college was elected student body president on a pro-Experimental College platform. Students active in the early community action programs and very much interested in the objectives and potential of the Experimental College won student government elections. Consequently a major thrust was given to these efforts, as national news media began to notice the experimental developments.[21]

Perceptions of faculty response at the time the Experimental College began its operation are mixed, ranging from enthusiasm to indifference. Nowhere, however, were the faculty characterized as hostile, except perhaps for isolated individuals. The majority of those interviewed suggested that the faculty were favorably disposed toward the idea.[22] It should be remembered, however, that there were no immediate provisions by the Experimental College for credits. Students were asked to participate out of commitment to the idea and their own interests.

While there was no poll of faculty opinion at the time the Experimental College began, the student organizers felt that they had tacit approval from the faculty for such an enterprise in the form of a faculty policy toward student activities which had been adopted in 1961. The policy was quite progressive for that time, especially when compared with other state institutions like Berkeley. It stated in part that:

> At San Francisco State College, students are respected as adults and citizens of the community and, as such, have all the rights and responsibilities of adults and citizens to participate in college and com-

munity affairs. These rights and responsibilities are to be jealously guarded.[23]

The extent of faculty libertarianism with regard to the activities of students when the Experimental College was founded can be seen in the fact that students had already been admitted as members of the Academic Senate, and held voting membership on six faculty committees. Although some universities have since followed suit in this regard, at the time such a recognition of students was very nearly unprecedented, especially in state institutions.

The climate for educational initiatives on the part of the students was further strengthened by the appointment of John Summerskill to the San Francisco State Presidency. The new president came to San Francisco from Cornell, where as a vice president he had built a reputation as an innovator. He endorsed the idea of the Experimental College and was an active supporter of the program from the beginning. The extent of his commitment to educational innovation can be seen by the fact that he authorized the cancellation of all college classes for a two-day period during the spring of 1967 in order to allow the Experimental College to conduct an educational conference to discuss such topics as the curriculum, student participation in the college's decision-making machinery, and the college's relationship to community and national issues.[24] In the fall of that same year, classes were suspended by Summerskill for an unprecedented week-long convocation to discuss the issues involved in the Vietnam war.

In the spring of 1966 during the first semester of operation, the Experimental College enrolled over 300 students in twenty-two courses. The courses ranged from Zen Basketball, personal development and sensitivity sessions, and Introduction to Frisbee to seminars on politics and ideology, the arts and humanities, and the pure and applied sciences. Although the initial enrollment was modest by later standards, some reflection of the impact of Experimental College on the campus is seen in the outcome of the student body election that first spring of the college's operation. In the largest turnout ever recorded, a slate of pro-Experimental College candidates swept every office in the student election by a three-to-one margin.

After a summer of planning and workshops by approximately twenty students, the Experimental College began its second semester of operation. These student organizers had put in so many hours working on the Experimental College that one faculty member observed that, while some colleges worry about football players who do not attend classes, "at S.F.S. one needs to be concerned that the students most heatedly and seriously concerned with education, haven't the time for their own education, at least not the book and library and classroom end of it." [25] Many of those who were most prominent in initiating the college were literally spending full time in the enterprise. This time more than 1200 students enrolled in approximately seventy courses, a four-fold increase over the first semester's operation. Part of the increase can probably be attributed to the success of the first semester and the added publicity, but perhaps a major portion of the increase was due to the fact that several identifiable groups involved themselves in the operation of the college and developed special courses appealing to a broad range of student concerns and special interests. These groups had organized the activities of the Experimental College around seven areas, urban communities, Black arts and cultures, personal development, arts and letters, styles of thought, communications and the arts, and the Institute for Social Change.[26] At least three of the groups—urban communities, Black arts and culture, and the Institute for Social Change—merged with or became integral parts of already existing independent programs of community action and politics.

As the program of the Experimental College grew, however, the problems attendant to its development also grew. Complaints about course content, coming largely from outside the institution, the issue of course credit, and the allocation of student fees were among the more important problems the college encountered. As one writer put it, "in a sense San Francisco State's Experimental College was too successful." [27]

Pressing for Recognition: The Issue of Legitimacy

During the first full year in operation the problems which subsequently plagued the Experimental College began to appear. Perhaps the most fundamental continuing problem centered on the question of credit for the courses offered under its auspices. At approximately the same time that the Experimental College was beginning its operations, the faculty enacted a policy setting aside a series of special numbers for course experimentation. Using the "77 sequence" (course numbers

77, 177, 277), as the special courses came to be known, any faculty member could introduce a course into the curriculum that had never been offered before. It could be taught without obtaining the usual permission or going through the process of securing the approval of the various college committees which governed the curriculum. All that was required was departmental approval. Each course introduced under this procedure could be offered for only one semester before it was necessary to obtain approval through the regular procedural channels. Everyone assumed that these courses would be innovative or experimental in some respect. What became an issue, however, was the subsequent use of the courses and the initial intent of the faculty in establishing the policy.

The students who founded the Experimental College contend that adoption of the experimental 77 sequence constituted equivalent approval of the Experimental College, and was meant to encourage it by offering a mechanism through which students could readily obtain credit for many of their courses. Faculty, however, were apparently divided over what the experimental sequence was supposed to accomplish. A former president observed that tensions began to develop early in the 1966–67 academic year over the issue of the 77 courses. It was his interpretation that these courses were established, not to facilitate the Experimental College, but to help change the general education requirements by allowing experimentation with alternative types of courses to those required at the time. The academic vice president viewed the situation similarly. He felt that the students were confusing the experimental sequence within the regular curriculum with the Experimental College, a confusion which subsequently aroused some faculty antagonism.

Although there was this initial lack of clarity, the students, according to the former president, went from one faculty member to another until they found sponsors for their courses who would get them credit through the experimental sequence provision. Some students, he believes, interpreted the 77 sequence as a carte blanche, and some departments approved experimental courses without discrimination. In many cases there were students listed as course instructors for credit courses, interpreted by the former president as a violation of the intent of the sequence leading to the observation that "a few of the faculty were literally subverting the purposes of the college [State]."

Lest one conclude that this man was not sympathetic to the aims of the Experimental College, it should be pointed out that he was one of the first supporters of the program when he was a professor of education, prior to assuming the college presidency. In addition, the education department, hardly true to the tradition of its counterparts on most other campuses, was one of the most cooperative in establishing special programs which were complementary to many community action programs and enjoyed one of the best departmental relationships with the Experimental College. In fact, the directors of the college asked this individual to accept a position as a half-time consultant. He declined because the Experimental College insisted on autonomy. He was not opposed to the principle; however, he did not wish to be held accountable for the organization's activities when he had no real authority. Accordingly, a fundamental operating principle of the Experimental College remained that faculty were to act as peers, not as superiors, and faculty did not assume positions of authority.

The former president's observations on the problems of the legitimacy of the course content were even shared by some of the founders of the Experimental College. One of the central figures in the original group of founders is said to have described the Experimental College as a failure after its first year of activities.[28] She is quoted as saying that the courses "lacked intellectual discipline" and that "the hippies took it [Experimental College] over." [29] It had apparently been her conviction that if the Experimental College were a true success, it would disappear because it was no longer necessary, having led to a total institutional reform. The general deterioration of the program's content from her perspective rendered such an eventuality unlikely. However, by the fall of 1967 one commentator was led to conclude:

> State students who have been involved in the Experimental College for any length of time feel generally discouraged. But one wonders how they could possibly see the venture as in any way a failure. San Francisco State itself, in large part because of prodding from the Experimental College, now offers experimental courses which a faculty member can create for a trial semester, with only departmental approval. It has a much loosened general education program, with a student-faculty committee working to revise it still more. It is considering a Work-Study degree program, growing in part out of the Urban Communities and Change area of the Experimental College. And when one considers the thousands of State students who were stimulated by direct or indirect contact with the

E.C. to question the roots of their education, failure seems hardly the term.[30]

Throughout the 1966-67 academic year, tensions continued to increase. The primary issue continued to revolve around the question of academic standards, and provisions for securing credit for the Experimental College courses became an increasingly sensitive item. But along with the question of academic standards, another point of contention developed around the provision of salaries for the Experimental College directors and directors of associated programs in the Community Service Institute.

As the Experimental College developed, staff members devoted increasingly greater amounts of time to work related to the program which is of course no problem if the student is being supported by a parental allotment or some other kind of subsidy. For most of the active participants, however, such support was apparently not available. Thus the question became one of a salary for their Experimental College activities or abandoning these activities for a more conventional job to support themselves while going to school. Since students active in founding the Experimental College were in control of the student government, the problem was resolved with relatively little difficulty. The Experimental College was allocated a budget of $23,000 and student directors were paid modest salaries which allowed them to exist at a subsistence level.

Although the salaries were obtained without difficulty, the idea of paying students for activities which were defined as extra-curricular violated existing protocol. The idea of salaries still might not have aroused too much interest except for a combination of factors which brought the matter to public attention. The first of these was that the student newspaper's editorial staff during 1966-67 was apparently hostile to the Experimental College and is reputed to have attacked the student government regularly for diverting the funds away from "legitimate student activities" and "into their own pockets."

The problems emanating from the appropriation of student funds were compounded, according to the former president, by the fact that the issues were raised during the period of Ronald Reagan's gubernatorial campaign and immediately after his accession to office in January 1967. As with the Regents of the University of California, the new governor also became an ex officio voting member of the State College

Board of Trustees. The trustees, always more conservative than the regents, moved even further to the right than the regents with Reagan's victory. Under his leadership they began to question the ideological content of Experimental College courses. They also began to look at related issues, among them, the question of student salaries. Although the issue receded for most of the 1967–68 school year with the election of a student government which cut back more than three-fourths of the Experimental College budget, it arose again in 1968–69 and became a key factor in the confiscation of student government fiscal powers by the trustees, who charged the Associated Students with misappropriation.

The apprehensions of the trustees over the questions of course content and the responsibility of the college for the "integrity" of its courses and the maintenance of its standards, subsequently led to the issuance of a report by the chancellor's office in June 1968 on experimental colleges at all of the state college campuses.[31] The substance of the report was clearly intended to be conciliatory and to establish the legitimacy of the activities being carried on both within the framework of the conventional innovative mechanisms of the regular college and the extra-curricular activities of the student government.

While the report covers the activities of experimental colleges on all of the nine campuses where they had been established, it appears that San Francisco State was clearly the campus which had generated the apprehension. The course that finally provoked the investigation was offered in the spring of 1968 and was entitled Seminar in Guerrilla Warfare.

The trustees were apparently not alone in their anxiety over the course. The academic vice president observed that some faculty were becoming increasingly sensitive to many features of the Experimental College and reacted negatively to the course. The result was what he described as a parallel in many ways to the Cleaver course controversy at Berkeley but without the immediate disastrous consequences. As at Berkeley, the immense popularity of the Experimental College appears to have been interpreted by the faculty as a threat to the regular curriculum and therefore to their own interests and stature in the institution.

The sensitivity of the whole issue is apparent in the report from the chancellor's office. The report stresses the fact that State resources were not used, except in the case of Fresno State College where there was some faculty allocation and credit for all courses. It is noted further that experience had been largely positive but also that the experience suggested a need "to develop policy guidelines for experimental learning activities in the California State Colleges, both system-wide and by faculty and students on the individual campuses." [32] After briefly describing the official mechanisms for innovation and the Experimental College at San Francisco State, they present a "Fact Sheet on the Seminar in Guerrilla Warfare. . . . " [33] The fact sheet emphasizes the non-credit status of the course, its "academic" rather than "practical" character, the "qualifications" of the instructor, the reading material, and the fact that no state funds were involved. While the report defended the course within the framework of a legitimate experimental effort, the defense was unquestionably meant to allay the trustees' fears that the college was being used as a training ground for guerrilla activities and to placate those who were outraged by the ideological direction in which the course seemed to lean.

As the external problems regarding the direction that the Experimental College was moving were increasing, so were the internal difficulties. What had initially been an indifferent attitude on the part of the faculty was changing, in some sectors, to an overt hostility toward the Experimental College. President Hayakawa attributes this growing hostility to what he interprets as a "shock spirit which vitiated the possibilities of sound intellectual substance coming out of it." His assessment is no doubt true in part. Attempts at innovation incur certain costs as well as benefits. But it would also appear that part of the negative reaction was as a consequence of the kinds of adverse sentiment that Experimental College courses, especially those which were clearly political, generated in the outside community.

Given the facts that the Experimental College might have been seen as a threat to faculty stature and that many defined the institution as disadvantaged vis-a-vis the state's more favored university system, it is not surprising that activities which might reflect adversely on its standards, or in some other way reduce the academic legitimacy of its image in the public eye, would arouse the ire of a significant portion of the faculty. The activities of the Experimental College in encouraging the kinds of community activities which often exacerbate already hostile relations with certain sectors of the public, compound many of the college's "image problems," which are hardly irrelevant, especially in California, when one recognizes that they may ultimately affect faculty ambitions for greater resource allocations, advanced graduate or other special programs, teaching loads, and improved salary schedules. In many ways the college can be said to be in direct competition with the other educational institutions in the state for its share of the resources. In effect, the kinds of problems generated by the Experimental College, are interpreted by some factions at State as having put them at a competitive disadvantage. If the faculty is committed to the educational principle involved and willing to risk the potential consequences, the problems generated by an innovative program are not irritating. It is clear, however, that this kind of commitment was lacking among the faculty. Perhaps the rationale of many of the faculty is expressed in the comment of a president of a small university campus in another state: "The only thing that we have to offer the legislature in competing with the other campuses is the fact that we don't have any radicals or hippies. We want to keep it that way." Undoubtedly, there are very few at State who would adopt a position quite as defensive as this, but the operant principle may be much the same. The pressures in this direction must be increasing rapidly in California's increasingly reactionary political climate.

In addition to the potentially adverse consequences of the Experimental College's mobilizing a negative public sentiment, there were other issues arising internally which began to escalate in the fall of 1968. These had to do primarily with student pressures at the departmental level to give greater support to the activities of the college and its allied action programs. Students were beginning to organize in departments for the purpose of obtaining recognition and participation in the development of departmental policies so that their leverage for promoting innovative programs would be improved. Although the legitimacy of student participation had long since been established at the institutional level, it had apparently not carried over to the departmental level in most cases. The objective of the students was to establish a base within the departments from which to legitimize the activities of the Experimental College and to expand programs carrying regular academic credit. According to the students, reactions at the departmental level were mixed, ranging from highly positive and supportive to absolute refusal to consider student overtures.

At one departmental meeting where the issues were being discussed by students and faculty, the reaction of the faculty was generally supportive but cautious. It was interesting, however, to observe the dynamics of the meeting and note the reactions on both sides. The meeting in question was called to discuss the issue of the relevance of the curriculum of the Sociology Department. Students and faculty were exploring ways of altering the curriculum so that relevancy could be obtained without jeopardizing academic legitimacy. Apparently the students were surprised initially by the fact that one faculty member, who had been an active supporter of the Experimental College program, made it known that he was disturbed by the frequent lack of academic integrity in its courses, including some which he had sponsored in the past. Additionally, many of the faculty present were oriented toward containing the proposed community action program within conventional bounds. A recurring theme of this faction was the "potential for abuse" that the suggested format offered, and all wanted some assurance in advance that there would be ways of protecting the academic integrity of the program.

Students, on the other hand, appeared to resent the questions which faculty raised regarding the academic legitimacy issue. In trying to assess the students' actions, it appeared that they were having some difficulty in addressing the issues raised by the faculty. It looked as if they had not anticipated the types of objections which were raised, or perhaps more correctly, had dismissed them beforehand as illegitimate. The latter interpretation is corroborated to some extent by the student comments afterward that faculty questions or objections were a sign of bad faith. They were stalling.

Although the results of the meeting were generally unsatisfactory as far as the student participants were concerned, the Sociology Department was one which had provided a relatively high degree of support in the past, and which, by any conventional standards, could be said to have had an amicable relationship with the Experimental College. But as difficulties at every level became more obvious, the relationships between the groups became increasingly strained. This was probably no less true in other departments which were beginning to feel the pressures from inside as well as outside the institution. Most had also had sufficient experience with the Experimental College to see some of the more important problems as well as the obvious positive features of the program.

There was also an interesting interpersonal development that points out a source of strain in the relationships between students and faculty in a venture like the Experimental College. The attitude of the students toward the faculty was, in certain respects, automatically hostile. The slogans of the student movement have often collectively defined the faculty as morally inferior, and student activists frequently react to resistance on the part of faculty with a disdain that the individual professor finds offensive. One faculty member summed it up neatly after the departmental meeting with the students when he said that he was sick and tired of being "flagellated by self-righteous middle class students who are feeling conscience stricken about the evils that they see around them." His feelings are undoubtedly shared by many faculty who feel that they are being asked by students to risk more than the students are willing to risk or that they are being unfairly labelled as unsympathetic to important student concerns.

While all of these considerations were heightening tensions on the campus, they were not inherently irreconcilable. The issues became more sharply defined, however, and less amenable to conventional reconciliation when a series of events, including the dismissal of a black instructor and the alleged procrastination on the ethnic studies program, erupted in massive strike of the winter and spring of 1969.[34] Among the casualties of this historic event was the Experimental College.

Ethnic Studies and the Third World College

The most publicized events in the recent history of San Francisco State have been those evolving out of the issue of the ethnic studies program or the Third World College. The ethnic studies program itself was not the issue which sparked the conflict, but once the lines of battle had been drawn it became one of the central points around which demands and negotiations revolved.

The incident that set in motion the events of the winter and spring of 1968–69 was a series of speeches by George Murray, a Black graduate student and an instructor in the English Department. Murray had been the center of an earlier controversy in the spring of 1968 when he and other members of the college's Black Student Union had assaulted members of the staff of the student newspaper, the *Daily Gator*, charging that their editorial policies had been racist. It was alleged by those who argued for Murray's dismissal that, in talks on the campus free speech area early in the fall 1968 semester, Murray had urged the Black students on the State campus to bring guns to the campus, ostensibly for purposes of "revolution and anarchy." The interpretation of those who supported Murray was that he had warned

Black students that they would have to arm themselves in order to protect against the dangers of racist society. San Francisco State was singled out as an example of institutions supporting and buttressing the white supremacist policy of the larger society and was therefore dangerous. Whatever was in fact said has never been very clearly established although the tone was undoubtedly revolutionary.[35] But in this case the facts of the matter were in effect irrelevant. The press and the political forces in the state widely publicized the first version.

Given the political climate in California, the demands from the political sector for Murray's dismissal were not surprising. The fact that the events transpired in the weeks immediately preceding the November 1968 general election may have somewhat increased the stridency of the expressions of outrage. Max Rafferty, state superintendent of schools, for instance, incorporated allusions to both this and the earlier Cleaver course incidents at Berkeley in the advertisements for his U.S. Senate campaign. In any case, this episode is a classic example of the kinds of difficulties which colleges and universities face in trying to deal with internal issues in the context of intense pressures from the political arena for decisive action within narrowly circumscribed limits. In this case the only action acceptable to the political forces was to summarily dismiss Murray.

The problem was of course not as simple as the governor and other members of the state's directorate would like to have believed. Aside from the issue of the prudence of Murray's comments, there were important questions of free speech, academic freedom, and, certainly most important in this particular case, racial implications. The result was that the acting president refused to dismiss Murray without following the procedures which had been established for handling such cases. He was willing to entertain charges that Murray had acted irresponsibly in his classes and to investigate these charges through the channels that had been established to deal with such situations. Many faculty felt that Smith wanted to fire Murphy, but that he was committed to maintenance of existing procedures. But his actions were not satisfactory to the governor or the chancellor. The chancellor issued a directive that Murray should be dismissed. The order of course violated all of the canons of academic freedom and due process which had been established not only at San Francisco State, but at any number of institutions around the country. The order provoked a reaction on a number of fronts.

Smith notified Murray that he had been dismissed at the direction of the chancellor.[36] The faculty immediately protested the move as a violation of due process and of State's autonomy and passed a resolution calling for the chancellor's resignation. Black students, white radicals, other ethnic minorities, and a complement of other students and faculty representing a wide range of opinion began a series of independent activities which finally culminated in the strike in an atmosphere of enmity, violence, and controversy that remained most of the year. We should make clear that early support for the strike, initially called by the Black Students Union (BSU), was not particularly widespread. In fact, one reporter points out that many, if not most, on the campus were hostile because of some of the tactics employed by the BSU.[37] Hostility, however, rapidly turned to support when police were introduced to the campus in mid-November 1968. A subsequent attempt by Smith to close the campus and convene a convocation to discuss the demands of the BSU and the Third World Liberation Front was overruled by Governor Reagan and the trustees who met in emergency session in Los Angeles. Their order called for Smith to " 'open the campus immediately,' and further ordered him not to negotiate student grievances until 'order is restored and the educational processes resumed.' " [38] Smith flew immediately to Los Angeles and resigned. From that point the strike activities and general hostility escalated, and five months of periodic violent confrontation between strikers and police ensued. In the words of one faculty member, "The students [were] responding with physical violence to the ideological violence of a capricious authority that [had] no concern for fundamental liberties or basic human rights." [39]

The precipitating issue was of course the dismissal of Murray, but the strike quickly developed other issues which had been continuing points of debate prior to the Murray incident. The latent issues that now surfaced were encompassed in the famous "fifteen demands" presented by the strikers to the administration. Foremost among these was the establishment of a Third World College of which the Black Studies Program was to be a part. The Black Studies Program in particular had been a source of controversy.

Prior to the events of the 1968–69 school year, students in the BSU had been pressing for a Department of Black Studies for some time. The legitimacy of the request was not an issue at that point. What had led to an impasse of sorts, aside from financial issues, had been the question of the autonomy of the program and the nature of controls.

The BSU had argued in favor of autonomy, but it is not entirely clear what this would have entailed; it appears, however, that the chief interest of the students was to retain the power of appointment in the department. Although the procedure was not irregular, it was a source of some tension since it seemed clear that the kinds of appointments that the students had in mind were not limited to those with the conventional academic credentials. This posed a threat on two fronts: one, the administration where the appointment of certain militant types would be sure to generate governmental and trustee reaction; and, two, the faculty where an admission of the legitimacy of the principle of appointment without "appropriate" credentials might be interpreted as another threat to the status and security of regular faculty.

The problems of the program's development were undoubtedly irritated by the appointment of Nathan Hare, a Black sociologist who had been terminated at Howard University because of his outspoken advocacy of the cause of Black militance. An administrative officer at San Francisco State contends that former president John Summerskill appointed Hare although "everyone was opposed to the appointment." The extent to which this was true may be questionable, but there can be no doubt that there was some adverse opinion regarding the appointment, and some contend it was created by the administrator in question. If for no other reason, adverse opinion existed because the appointment represented a commitment to a direction in the proposed Black Studies program that many would not support. Hare had previously argued and has continued to argue for a "militant" Black Studies Program.[40] What the consequences of such a program might be is open to a variety of interpretations, but the fact is that such a stand is threatening to a great many members of the college community for reasons ranging from autonomy and academic standards to attitudes projected from a racist cultural perspective.

As the level of conflict between the strikers and the administration increased, the establishment of the Department of Black Studies undoubtedly became increasingly problematic. Opposition to the program among the San Francisco State faculty probably consolidated and hardened during the conflict. Certainly public sentiment, if the popularity of President Hayakawa in the spring 1969 opinion polls is an accurate indicator, became increasingly negative. While the administration could grant the legitimacy of the request on the one hand, the symbolic consequences of moving ahead rapidly on the program in light of what had happened would be interpreted by a hostile public as capitulation. As the strike dragged on, the potential for a satisfactory settlement became increasingly dim. Even if the administration were to grant the demands on paper, the time for recruiting faculty for the program had passed long before the "settlement" was arranged.

The settlement therefore, may have been specious in many respects. Assuming that the administration acted in good faith, they nevertheless will not be able to meet many commitments adequately or to resolve many of the problems contributing to the initial outbreak of hostilities. Aside from the recruitment problem in the area of Black studies, four of the college's six Black administrators resigned in June 1969 because of what they regarded as a lack of commitment at the administrative and governmental level. In the wake of a budget dispute in the legislature, the governor cut funds allocated for special programs for the disadvantaged, indicating that such skepticism was probably warranted.

But even these may not be the most severe immediate difficulties. One of the Black administrators who resigned argued that the proposed Black Studies program would fold because of a lack of resources and of substance. His interpretation of the program was that it is "thirty-five courses with Black in front of them" which, he pointed out, does not constitute a viable Black Studies program. Whether or not his is an entirely fair description of the proposed program, he does highlight a difficulty that must be faced eventually: the program must attract students and faculty if it is to sustain itself. This dean's fear was that the program might fail for lack of student support, putting the administration in a position to say that they gave the Black students their program and then they did not want it. Given this possible eventuality, he stressed the necessity for astute planning in order to assure a continued demand. But even if this contention with regard to the program was not true, he argued, the program would not have adequate resources to be successful in any case. He suggested that ultimate collapse was almost assured.

Besides testing the thesis of a collapse from a lack of resources or substance, there are a number of difficulties and unresolved issues. Among the most sensitive of these is the status of Nathan Hare and perhaps that of George Murray. Murray's contract was terminated early in the 1968–69 year and Hare's was not renewed after it expired in June 1969. President Hayakawa reiterated his intentions in this regard after the strike settlement.[41] According to Hare, on the other hand, he and the students were not prepared to accept this judgment. In the end, the BSU and other Black students were to have a critical role in the selection of faculty for the Black Studies program, and it would be up to them whether or not they wanted to hire either him or George Murray. The implication was clear that he expected students to move in this direction. Events since 1969 suggest that he miscalculated the students' designs, since they appeared to be unwilling to engage in another prolonged conflict in order to establish the principle of the program's autonomy—at least using this as an issue.

Black administrators seem agreed that the students lost their best chance to obtain important concessions when they became tied-in to their own rhetoric during the strike. The Assistant Dean of Students and Dean of Undergraduate Instruction both pointed out that the students had an important strategic advantage early in the winter when they literally had the college on its knees. Students refused to negotiate at that point, they suggest, because they were afraid of being co-opted by the administration. One of them explained that most had never negotiated with anyone and that in fact the students were worried that they would be outfoxed by "whitey" at the conference table. The result was that they became tied to the unconditional demands ploy and later lost their advantage. In the face of declining support for the strike, they ultimately settled, but the settlement, according to most of the observers, was not as good as it might have been earlier.

A Further Word on the Historic Strike

A great deal has since been said about the San Francisco State Strike, the longest and most dramatic of its kind in the history of U.S. higher education. Although we have not developed the full etiology of the events of 1969, we have traced some of the major ones. Particularly important were the Murray case and the range of Third World concerns which linked community service efforts with the Black Studies and Third World College proposals. In the context of the growing politicization of higher education in California, the events at San Francisco State College did not assume a character peculiar to itself. Some important features of the total events merit some elaboration.

Although the precipitating factors surrounded the firing of George Murray and the BSU strike began on November 6, 1968, the college chapter of the American Federation of Teachers did not go out until

January 6, 1969.[42] The continuing drama of December and January was unique. Six hundred police were deployed on the campus. Picket lines were set up and physical confrontations were frequent. During the first thirty days of President Hayakawa's administration more than 600 persons were arrested. It became blatantly obvious during that time where the power resided at San Francisco State College, and the despair, demoralization, and polarization which followed continues as a heavy pall over the campus.

The AFT strike was settled on March 3, 1969, but it did not include a settlement of the BSU strike which officially ended almost three weeks later on March 21 although all active picketing was halted even before the AFT settlement. A major agreement in the resolution of BSU grievances was the provision for the development of a Black Studies Department and School of Ethnic Studies. In fact, however, the six full-time faculty members already in the Black Studies Department were not re-hired.[43] In spite of the administration's commitments, the thrust of early BSU efforts had been lost.

While some of the immediate factors contributing to the outbreak of hostilities have been discussed, a number of more basic theoretical and ideological considerations remain. Among the most important of these was the race and class character of San Francisco State. Half of San Francisco's population is reportedly Third World, and this was an important factor in determining the strikers' position. It was not just the cultural nationalism of some which generated the cry for a Black Studies program; rather the thrust of the Community Services Institute and Experimental College was toward opening the doors of the college to more Third World people. Even more important was the attempt to transform the educational experience in order to make it more relevant to the lives of Third World students. Some modest advances were made in terms of special admissions of minority and low-income students; however, the ceilings for such programs were set very low by the administration.[44]

A second factor was the increasingly obvious class and caste character of the various types of institutions of higher education resulting from the *Master Plan*. Two-thirds of junior college students came from families with incomes under $10,000. Furthermore, at San Francisco State College there was a decline in Black student enrollment during the 1960s from twelve to three per cent,[45] while well over one-half of the city's high school students were non-white.[46] One of the most important substantive questions that emerged in the strike concerned the consequences of the educational program of the state and of San Francisco State College for minority and low-income students. Third World students were joined by white students, faculty strikers, organized labor, and the minority communities in support of the BSU and AFT strikes. The issue became one of whom the college served as well as what went on educationally inside its doors.

While we have not elaborated the entire range of arguments advanced during the strike, one important overall theme which emerged is grounded in a fundamental educational issue. Specifically, the question is whether or not faculty and administration in higher education can accept the idea that, "[they] be judged not by the quality of students [they] take in, but the quality of those [they] turn out." [47] Lest we imply that this was the only issue, let us make it clear that this was only one of many, but it was one which was perhaps more clearly articulated at San Francisco State than at any other of the episodic college and university crises in the past few years.[48] While there have been hundreds of protests over the functions of the university and its educational program, the strike at San Francisco may have been the most important in raising the race and class bias of higher education and the educational barriers that buttress this bias at every level.

In fact, even before the strike, one writer admonished the college in the following fashion:

> Why is San Francisco State, with its tradition of student freedom, its liberal president [Summerskill] who is generally sympathetic to student causes, and its innovative educational atmosphere, destroying itself?
>
> One reason is that SF State has made almost as little progress in finding solutions to the dilemma facing the black man in white America as has the country as a whole. And, since nearly all of the students at SF State live and work off campus and cannot, therefore, tuck themselves away in the never-never land of academe, the crisis of America is a very real crisis on that campus.[49]

As a final factual note, the consequence of the strike during the 1968–69 year was horrendous as far as the academic progress of students was concerned. In addition to the substantial depletion in enrollment in the fall of 1969, vast numbers of students found it difficult to obtain transcripts for admission to graduate schools and so forth. The wider implications of the strike will be discussed further on, but perhaps the spring 1969 conclusion of the United States National Commission on the Causes and Prevention of Violence which examined the strike at San Francisco State College is indicative:

> Today at San Francisco State the groups involved in the conflict for the most part are polarized. The students are committed to their struggle as no generation of students has ever been. The faculty is fragmented, often unhappy, and increasingly militant over its rights and responsibilities. The administration is charged with the duty to manage, but is essentially powerless to act, caught between the conflicting pressures of other groups. Trustees of the State colleges are determined to take a stand at San Francisco State; it has become for them a watershed of decision, the crucial point as they see it in a struggle for the preservation of the institutions of higher education.[50]

Shifting Internal Leadership and the Response to Cross-Pressures

We have pointed out that San Francisco State College had long enjoyed a reputation for being at the vanguard of educational innovation. This early recognition was primarily the result of pioneering special programs and of innovation within relatively narrowly defined limits. The early innovative efforts were in no sense comparable to the kinds of programs developed in the Experimental College.

Those who were around long enough to know indicated that in earlier times educational leadership had been exercised primarily by the faculty. As time went on, leadership passed from the faculty to the administration and then finally to the students. In part, the transfer of educational leadership is probably a consequence of a shift in the general position of faculty, not only at State, but across the nation. As the importance of higher education has increased, there has been a parallel move toward increasing specialization and professionalization in the academic community. The shift has been accompanied by a decreasing emphasis on the disseminative aspects of the educational enterprise and increasing pressures for research and publication as the measure of excellence. Although change in this direction has occurred at the most rapid rate in the nation's major universities, the impact of the change is felt to some degree in almost all institutions.

Probably in the early days, when State was primarily a teachers college or even later while the stress was still on terminal education, the ambitions of the faculty were quite different than they are at present. As the professional movement has accelerated and spread, however, faculty orientations have shifted, focusing more than ever on research, writing, and associated professional activities. It is not surprising that leadership in the area of educational innovation shifted out of their hands. To the extent that there was to be any leadership, the immediate heirs apparent were the administration.

In the recent past, however—perhaps the last five years—educational leadership at State shifted again, this time to the students. Part of the reason was probably the fact that there was a lack of continuity in administrative leadership during the past seven years in which the college has had five presidents. Although he might have assumed a position of leadership under different circumstances, John Summerskill, a key figure in the developments, was appointed president after the major innovational decisions (for example, the Experimental College and Community Services Institute) had already been made. Because of this, he was cast in the role of a facilitator rather than a leader. Although he could provide the climate in which innovations could flourish, he had arrived too late to play a major role in determining the character or the course of innovation on the campus. More important perhaps than the lack of continuity were the political climate, which has been continually deteriorating with respect to the governmental attitude toward higher education, and a student body bringing an even wider range of experience and sophistication to the campus.

It is no secret that the government and the public in the state of California have been particularly hostile to higher education since the time of the Free Speech Movement. Although Berkeley was the early target of these hostilities, much of the ill will has been generalized to other campuses. In the particular case of San Francisco State, matters have been complicated by the fact than an ex-president is now the chancellor of the State College System. Some contend that he was personally hostile toward State because of a continuing enmity between himself and the faculty. Whether or not this was the case, there has been a problem similar to that at Berkeley where former chief administrators from the campus have not adopted a hands-off policy in the course of transferring responsibilities. The difficulties of administration on the campus have been compounded by the continued interference of outside executive leadership.

The problem of interference has not been limited to the chancellor in this case. Just as at Berkeley, the trustees have interjected themselves directly into the affairs of the campus, frequently issuing directives with regard to particular individuals or events. Although the Murray case is the most sensational example of trustee intervention, it was apparently not limited to this episode. One of the deans interviewed contends that the interference, made easier by the failure of the administration to assert its autonomy, has rendered solution of the college's growing internal problems impossible. He suggested that unless the administration could make it clear to the trustees that theirs was a supportive and not a directive role, the college could not move forward. Whether the administration could make such an assertion is questionable inasmuch as the trustees have demonstrated their willingness to replace the top campus administrators at frequent intervals in response to attempts to assert this autonomy. The result has been an untenable situation for any administrator at State whose position does not happen to coincide with trustees.

As has been suggested in the discussion of Berkeley, there has been a general trend towards legislative, gubernatorial, and regental interference. Over 200 bills were introduced in the state legislature concerning matters ranging from student-initiated courses to faculty tenure.[51] But the situation is demonstrably worse for the state colleges within the California system of higher education than for the university system.

> [The state colleges] have not only been legislated into second-rate education but also seem most vulnerable to economic reprisal and ideological attack by pressure groups and state officials. Though rightists also assault the university, it retains some considerable autonomy because of its traditional status and its service to, and partial funding by, the national technostructure and the military. The junior colleges are under local control and retain some petty autonomy, though hardly anyone takes them seriously as more than custodial institutions. The state colleges carry on the main work of technical training and indoctrination for submissive service in the middle ranges of corporate and state hierarchies. Thus the righteous control.[52]

While these changes with regard to the faculty and administration have been taking place, the student body has not been a static entity. As the college has become a more general purpose institution and the student body has changed in its composition, more graduates, undergraduates with greater educational aspirations, and activists are appearing. If it were true, as one observer suggested, that State has been a repository for frustrated faculty who had aspirations for working at Berkeley, the same might be said for the student body. The attraction of the Bay Area and the reputation of State have undoubtedly appealed to many of those who could not make it to Berkeley for one reason or another or who simply chose State as a better alternative. The combination of a rapidly growing and changing student body and a faculty with growing aspirations in the face of shrinking resources is hardly a recipe for tranquility. The potential for conflict at State has steadily increased.

Until the time of the latest administration, tensions appeared to be developing at the greater rate between faculty and the students, with the administration vacillating depending on the particular issues and who happened to occupy the office of the president. More often than not though, evidence indicates that the administration supported student moves toward experiment and innovation. Under John Summerskill, president from 1966 to 1968, the college had its greatest period of innovation; some claim that this was true to a fault. Many of those on both sides of recent controversies suggested that Summerskill's inability to say no, even when he did not have the resources to deliver, contributed to campus difficulties.

Although it is true to some extent on every campus, the faculty at State is perhaps more divided than most. The cleavages seem to extend along the lines of educational philosophy (e.g., elitists vs. non-elitists), faculty organization (e.g., union vs. non-union), and perhaps to some extent racial loyalties—undoubtedly due partly to pressures by militant students on minority faculty. The net result is that while conflicts may appear to take on the broad appearance of faculty-student or student-administration contests, there are almost certain to be more than the usual number of factions out of place when the parameters of a controversy have been defined. Thus, during the strike, a portion of the faculty, including the union, were martialled behind the student cause at least for a period of time. The faculty, however, settled before the students so that the alliance was at best a tenuous one.

On another front, it is important to note that there was a conservative faculty group calling itself the Faculty Renaissance which took a strong public stand in the early stages of the strike against the demands of the students and against the student philosophy of community government. The leader of the group was S. I. Hayakawa who was appointed president of the college not long after the group took its public stand.

The fact that there are going to be factions within the major units of students, faculty, and administration is hardly a discovery of earth-shaking moment. It does not hurt, however, to return to this fact periodically because it has important political consequences for the internal operations of the institution and may well have important consequences for relations with external agencies attempting to assume regulatory power. Most of our informants, for instance, indicated that there was a time during the strike when the students had coalesced their forces successfully enough so that they could have extracted concessions from the administration. At this point the student forces were strengthened by the participation of part of the faculty led by the union (American Federation of Teachers, San Francisco State College Local). As the crisis wore on, however, forces which had been coalesced for a short period of time began to split once again, and the strategic advantage was lost. Mobilization of a cross-section of the constituencies was a fleeting event, and the leadership would have had to act quickly if it were to utilize its momentary power to bring about change. It is clear that they did not maximize their temporary advantage.

The problem of mobilizing for a confrontation with the administration or extra-institutional forces is even greater in the case of faculty than in the case of students. The interests of faculty in this regard are considerably more varied and their activities may be circumscribed by what they interpret as the consequences for their long-range career and institutional aspirations. Given that this is the case, it has been true that faculty have rarely, at State or any other campus, mobilized for even short periods of time. The difficulties become apparent when one notes the pattern of faculty participation in professional organizations which cut across departmental or disciplinary lines. Rarely, for instance do the American Association of University Professors (AAUP) or the American Federation of Teachers (AFT) have a membership representing more than a small minority of the faculty, and rarely are there issues which can appeal to the broad spectrum of faculty, especially when these issues are mediated by a broad array of peculiar individual interests which may mitigate against participation in a collective effort.[53]

Assuming for the moment that the problem of mobilizing faculty is more difficult than mobilizing students, at least where "extreme" actions are involved, then the potential for success of confrontation tactics by students is significantly reduced. The power of the student to strike was attenuated by the fact that, as President Hayakawa pointed out, "students are always at liberty to cut classes, individually or collectively." [54] In addition, the extent to which a student strike is likely to martial public support or force concessions from the administration depends largely on the percentage of students that walk out, the amount of time that they stay away, and the mass appeal of the issue. There is little evidence that either of the first two, let alone the third, has ever been large enough to bring the administration to the point of acceding to student demands. It would also seem that the likelihood of mass appeal is more remote in the public institution, where the student's education is regarded as free, than in the private institution where students pay large sums in order to purchase an education.

What this means is that the crucial element in the contest with government and trustees is the faculty. Faculty are in a strategic position if they act collectively because they are perhaps the only scarce element in the entire system [at least until recently]. One is never lacking for students, and administrators, with the possible exception of college presidents, are not in particularly short supply. Besides, the function of the latter is to carry out the policy of the regulating agency and therefore one does not expect them to be at the vanguard of radical forces on the campus. In any campaign to bring about change then, it becomes necessary to mobilize the faculty, or at least to neutralize them since it is better if faculty are disinterested than if they are resistant.

At best, the faculty is likely to be uninterested. This was true at State in the early stages of various innovative programs. During the strike a significant portion of the faculty walked out with the students and all seem to agree that this was one of the most important strengths of the strikers. One militant professor commented that the settlement of the AFT in effect broke the strike. It was his feeling that they lent an air of legitimacy to the strike and also formed a kind of buffer between students and police. The police were perhaps more hesitant to hit a professor than a student. The fact that the AFT settlement broke the strike is indeed true but only because they were the last remaining pickets at the time of the settlement. Students had abandoned picketing and other forms of active support of the strike by this time. There is also evidence that even the BSU leaders agreed with the strategy of pursuing a face-saving settlement at this point. While there are those who interpreted the AFT's involvement as opportunistic, the observation of one insider that this was probably the "greatest act of idealism and toughness by any large number of professors in recent history" is probably a much more accurate assessment. His observation is buttressed by the fact that all participating faculty without tenure were subsequently dismissed.

In any case, the absence of the professor from the classroom is likely to mean the end of the educational process, not because he is an absolutely necessary component, but because most students and certainly the administration define him as necessary to the process. The faculty's active support, then, is a most important advantage. Active support in this case though was limited primarily to members of the AFT, only a comparatively small minority of the total faculty.

What happened at State is that the faculty, which was initially slightly supportive or indifferent to the kinds of innovation that student leadership was attempting to implement, has begun to shift to a position of antagonism. Those who were initially hostile have probably become considerably more so in the ensuing period. Even in the case of those who were clearly supportive, including the union, there may have been some shift in sentiment. In this regard one informant noted: "Faculty will fall into ranks in the fall [1969, after the strike]. They want to teach . . . not deal with the problems of society." A combination of the desire to teach, an impatience with the tactical ineptitude sometimes exhibited by the students, and fears of the "radicalization of the student body" has reduced support for further conflict. The result is that the advantage has shifted to the more conservative forces, as it has on the Berkeley campus.

There is one final observation that should be made regarding the developments at San Francisco State College. Perhaps no public institution in the country had involved students in the formal decision-making apparatus as early or as extensively as did State. Given this fact, it may seem puzzling that the events at State took the course which they ultimately did for the inclusion of students in the governing process is supposed to siphon off the potential for the kinds of gross conflict that occurred during the strike. In this case at least, the effectiveness of the strategy was somewhat less than monumental. Since this is illustrative of one of the most pressing problems of university governance, we are forced to ask why this is the case.

Let us first approach the question indirectly by noting that students, too, like the faculty, have aspirations for their institution. It was noted earlier that there are indications in the statements of student leaders and in the student press that students do not like the pejorative label of second-rate any better than the faculty. But while the concern may be similar, the perceived solutions are quite different. While many of the faculty wish to emulate Berkeley, it is unlikely that many of the students have that model in mind when they think of educational alternatives. It may be that they have no model in mind but simply some vague notions that life would be better if classes were smaller and the professors spent more time relating to students on a person-to-person level. But the lack of an alternative model does not matter so much as the fact that the undergraduate student who shares the professional concern for research and publication or other professional activity is rare indeed. Rather, the student is likely to see this as a problem in an entirely different way than many of the faculty. While the faculty is thinking in terms of more time for publication and research, the student is thinking in terms of less—the kind of issue to which we refer when we speak of inherent conflicts of interest.

Speaking more directly about the question of including students in the decision-making process, one must continually keep in mind that the students' position is almost always that of the minority. This fact is no less crucial for the student than for anyone else engaging in political activity. The result of his minority position is that the student will probably lose on most, if not all, of those issues where conflicts of interest come into play. And it is the fact that he loses, not that he had a chance to play the game, that is crucial to understanding the pattern of events that subsequently develops. What happened at State is that the student had been given a voice but no substantive power which may make no difference in cases where there is consensus, but it makes a very great difference where there is not. The frustration of the student in this position is likely to be greater, not less, than if he were totally locked out of the decision-making process. Now he has been made a party to decisions with which he not only does not agree, but which he never had a real chance to influence in the first place.[55] He has, in short, been co-opted in every sense of the word. But not only has he been co-opted, he recognizes that fact, and unlike co-optation in other spheres, his does not have any consoling features. He is not a recipient of conventional patronage, and his status in having been admitted to the councils of power is somewhat ambiguous since fellow students will probably expect some tangible results.

One important consideration in the case of San Francisco State is that the continuity of pressing demands by students for participation in college governance was broken down by the lack of continuity in student leadership. Students in 1965–66 were committed to internal educational reform, to the development of student-initiated curricula, and to the educational links to the community. By the next year, while State was gaining national attention for its Experimental College and while the internal challenges to student initiatives were developing, the larger phenomenon of the hippie-dropout movement was reaching its peak. Many students at San Francisco State were caught up in despair of ever reforming existing institutions and in the quest for countercultures. What followed was a critical loss of student leadership as people dropped out, went to other universities, or left the campus entirely.[56] The leadership problems emerging in 1967 coincided with the developing resistance to student-initiated courses and student participation in governance. Although solid leadership re-emerged in 1968, and the crisis of the strike created leaders—particularly representing Third World students—a lack of continuity in leadership, goals, and tactics from the early days of the Experimental College to the post-strike era after 1969 was a source of severe difficulty. That this should be true during what were among the most tumultous years in the life of any institution or society is not surprising, but it did affect the situation at San Francisco State College.

One might argue that, at a minimum, admission to the governing process is likely to institutionalize nonviolent or parliamentary methods of resolving conflicts only where the student's power is at least equal to that of the other constituents involved in the enterprise. Of course, the extent to which this is true will vary with several situational factors, perhaps the most important of which is the interpretation of what his appropriate role should be. If he views it as advisory, then his minority position is irrelevant. But if he does not see it simply as advisory, his minority position is likely to become a source of tension. At State the definition of participation which the students advanced was one of equality not subservience. In general the result is that the inclusion of a few students on decision-making bodies, even if they are given voting privileges, will not necessarily channel student protest in constructive directions. Only on those issues where constituent interests are not defined by their unique roles would such a model of operation be likely to effectively meet the perceived needs of students. In such cases, theoretically at least, support for the student position on an issue could be martialled on the merits of the student's arguments rather than in terms of the interests of particular constituent groups.

One can argue of course that all of the foregoing considerations are mitigated by the fact that faculty do not always act in terms of faculty interests, whatever these may happen to be, but often are sympathetic to student interests. This is indeed true—in some instances. It is also sometimes true for students. But it seems likely that in the long run and over the broad range of issues this is not likely to be the mode of operation of faculty or administrative or student representatives on decision-making bodies. Under conditions of minority representation, less conventional strategies may be allayed for some time, but, eventually, it is likely that they will be employed. Not only is student participation not a panacea in its present form, it may ultimately heighten the level of conflict between constituent groups. Of course, balancing the power may help to resolve the problem, but there is no indication that faculty and administration are inclined to make such a move.[57]

After the Strike: The End of Innovation and the Death of a College

Attempting to draw conclusions about the recent experience of San Francisco State is a morbid process, made all the more so because of the exciting beginnings of the era of educational experimentation and innovation. In drawing this analysis to a close, however, we should attempt to pay particular attention to the larger thematic issues which transcend the particular consequences for State.

The initial period following the 1969 strike settlements saw simultaneously, a period of extreme polarization, suspicion, and bitterness and a mood of quiet. In particular, the distrust between the various constituencies—students, faculty, and administration—were exacerbated by the internal bitterness. There was, for example, open hostility between faculty strikers and those totally unsympathetic with what they felt was an ill-conceived action bound only to inflame reactionary forces in the general public. The college resumed a relatively normal schedule in the spring of 1969; however, the strike continued in the public eye since the courts and jails had been filled during the strife of the winter and spring months.

S. I. Hayakawa, named acting-president the day after Robert Smith's resignation in November 1968, was named permanent president of the institution, amidst massive public speculation that he would oppose Ronald Reagan for the governorship in 1970. In his early moves as permanent president, he continued to function with the moral assertiveness which characterized his conduct during the strike. First, he voided the student government elections, initially swept by an anti-Hayakawa slate. A new election under his direction was swept, interestingly enough, by a pro-Hayakawa slate. The president referred to the latter as "the first scrupulously honest elections held here in years." President Hayakawa then went on record as "consistently opposed to amnesty." [58] He indicated that he would not be bound in advance by the recommendations of the negotiating committee in regard to the discipline agreed to in the final settlement.[59] The combined show of strength by police, Governor Reagan, State College Trustees, and President Hayakawa and his supporters was thought to be sufficient to have taken control of the college. In the aftermath of the strike the administrators assumed a position which indicated no retrenchment from the posture of toughness. This has continued to define the milieu on the campus.

The developments since the strike have had several consequences and we shall touch upon each in turn. First is the area of educational innovation. In the words of one faculty member in the fall of 1970, the Experimental College is "not only dead but not even a memory anymore." While there are experimental courses approved by departments, no serious use is made of them. Supportive organizations which once exerted pressure for experimental and radical courses have dissipated. A professor in one department which formerly responded to the Community Services Institute with experimental courses said that "the political life of San Francisco State has reached such a low ebb, there is no impetus for experimental courses which would elicit a backlash." A further selective factor influencing recent curricular developments has been the exodus of supportive faculty—voluntarily or under pressure.

Although the faculty at San Francisco State has traditionally been of high calibre, the turnover rate, still low for the California State Colleges, has increased in the past two years and the percentage of faculty without doctorates has increased. Faculty have resigned for a variety of reasons. Some wished to leave as a matter of principle in order to protest political intervention in the running of the college or arbitrary administrative action. Others found the interpersonal climate, with a substantial residue of bitterness among faculty, untenable. Budget cuts and increased pressures to raise teaching loads has continued to make the institution less attractive to many faculty and potential faculty.

As a result of extreme pressures, sometimes overriding recommendations of faculty and deans, faculty who were active in the strike were denied tenure. After the AFT strike was settled, grievance procedures were set up with state-wide committee appointments to be made following designated procedures. The chancellor and the trustees abrogated these agreements. In the words of one faculty member, "the faculty has been stripped of all authority and the chancellor can initiate and be the final authority on faculty disciplinary cases." In a direct violation of commitments made in the 1969 strike settlement regarding amnesty for faculty strikers, the trustees adopted a new set of procedures for dealing with state college faculty who struck. These procedures were made retroactive in order to allow the trustees to deal with "special cases," most notably that of Jack Kurzweil of San Jose State, husband of Communist Bettina Aptheker, an early FSM activist.

In one case a San Jose State College faculty member has obtained a favorable decision challenging the trustees' action against him for "unprofessional conduct" (for striking in support of the San Francisco State strike). In the cases of several San Francisco State faculty who were terminated, court action is in process. The net effect, however, has been to demoralize San Francisco State faculty remaining after separating faculty activists from the 1969 strike. The evidence suggests that among those now departed from the faculty were a substantial number of faculty supporters of student efforts at educational innovation.

Although there is a School of Ethnic Studies headed by an Oriental-American anthropologist, the full-time Black Studies Department faculty in the year following the BSU strike were all terminated. In an attempt to pick up the slack, some of the experimental courses within departments are being used for Black and ethnic studies curricula. Current ethnic studies activities on the campus are minimal and clearly less than any of the pre-strike proposals. On balance, the events of the past three years have shown a regression in terms of ethnic studies programs and minority student admissions.

In addition to the early moves for student-initiated curricula in the Experimental College and the ethnic studies proposals, one of the features of the college which gained it some reputation in the last decade was the activist character of the institution seen in the Community Services Institute and the total-involvement ethos of the school. The consequences of the strike in this area are painfully blatant. There is an ethos of passivity approximating the dullest commuter college. Nothing happened in May 1970 during the national college and university protests over Cambodia and the Kent and Jackson State killings. One student suggested that "although no one likes [President] Hayakawa, [Chancellor Glenn] Dumke, or [Governor] Reagan, they aren't doing anything."

The pressures on the state colleges have already been discussed. The dynamic, as it has affected San Francisco State College, has been a continuing tragedy. The substantial electoral victory by Governor Reagan has only reinforced the position of reactionary forces. One State faculty member said pointedly that "Chancellor Dumke always placed himself at Governor Reagan's disposal." He suggested that the trustees, whether left or extreme right in their orientation, don't like the chancellor, but since he has a "no-nonsense attitude to students and leftist faculty, the trustees can't get rid of him" which, he indicated, was due to "the politics of California focusing not on context, but symbolism." The result is that the chancellor is supported despite general feelings of antagonism. He concluded that "the extreme polarization of California politics have preserved men like [Chancellor] Dumke" and shaped the educational climate in the state.

In the initial period of Black militancy, demands for Third World studies, and increased minority student enrollment, analysts spoke of "How to Wreck a Campus," [60] and implied that responsibility lay at the feet of the students. One cannot escape the conclusion, however, that San Francisco State College, if it is deserving of a postmortem, has been laid to rest, a victim of successful educational innovation, autocratic administration, and reactionary politics.

IV
Successful Innovation and the Challenge of Change: University of Oregon

Counterculture, Radicalism, and
Bombings: A Changing Milieu

While the University of Oregon may have once projected an image of social life and athletics, today there is another scene. Most of the nation's campuses have been transformed in the past few years by a stylistic revolution that Charles Reich refers to as the emergence of "Consciousness III." [1] Oregon showed signs of change at the same time the Bay Area was transforming into the mecca of the hip culture. Rock music, the 1967 "Love Summer" in Haight-Ashbury, and the growing drug culture proselytized by author Ken Kesey—an Oregon graduate now returned to a farm not too far from the university—all had an impact. By the summer of 1970 the highways were filled with young people coming into Oregon: some for the so-called People's Army Jamboree and the many rock festivals set up to prevent political confrontations at the national convention of the American Legion in Portland; some to join or start rural communal experiments others to escape the crowding and pollution of the East and California and to find a refuge where "free people" would not be hassled. Eugene, the community in which the university is located, became a center for the hip culture and the "New American Community" has thrived there. Among its many trappings are a number of free schools, rural and urban communes, craft enterprises, various food and service coops—wood, fuel, and so on—"people's" garages and cafes, and a range of institutions built by, for, and around the counterculture.

At the same time, the University of Oregon and the city of Eugene has perhaps experienced more bombings than any area outside a few metropolitan centers such as New York and San Francisco. There was a series of bombings during 1969 and 1970 both on and off campus. The most recent episodes occurred in the university administration building and a substantial section of the Sociology Department faculty and students' offices and research rooms. Although the annual press reviews of campuses around the country may be headlined, "After Years of Turmoil, The Nation's Campuses Are Quiet But Not Content," [2] they are filled with commentary about the bombings in Oregon. One student in Oregon was quoted as saying,

> "[Students] are just tired and frustrated; five years ago they tried petitioning. Three years ago they tried talking to the deans. Last year they tried demonstrating. They haven't been able to make a dent in the iron curtain between the administration—of college, state and nation—and the students. So what are you going to do? You can go back to reading, writing and arithmetic or you can become revolutionary. You can't go on bumping your head against a wall." [3]

The Chicago Conspiracy Trial included among the eight defendants a professor of chemistry at the University of Oregon. One professor from Oregon arrived at an international conference in Zurich, Switzerland in April 1970, prior to the Cambodian invasion demonstrations, to find the front page photograph of Oregon National Guardsmen and State Police with tear gas making mass arrests of University of Oregon students who had taken over the administration building following firebomb attacks on ROTC.

In brief, the University of Oregon and the community surrounding it are not the same as a few years ago. To talk of the change from tranquility to bombings may, however, obscure the degree of achievement in educational innovation, and we shall need to trace these developments to understand the sequence of events and to assess the character of the institution.

A University at the Crossroads

If any of the institutions studied can be said to represent the median in the range of colleges examined in this study, it is Oregon. The University of Oregon, fast approaching its centennial year, is the state's most distinguished center of higher education. It is modest in size as major state universities go, with current enrollment in the neighborhood of 15,000 students. There is much talk on the campus about growth, most of it speculating on about how long it will continue, whether it should be continued, and where it should stop. There seems to be an emerging consensus that the university is rapidly approaching, if it has not already reached, optimum size.

The university is located in Eugene, Oregon's second largest city. The metropolitan area has a population of approximately 150,000. The university's payroll is by far the largest in the area making it an important feature in the local economy, but although it is usually considered an asset to the area, the local community has mixed feelings toward it. There is a great deal of hostility toward the university in evidence, though it is probably no greater than that in other university communities, especially those which have experienced severe disorders.

Unlike many of the other institutions which we have seen, Oregon is a university at the crossroads. The course of its development is not firmly established by an overall master plan or any obvious features of its relation to the remaining state institutions. It is not irrevocably committed to a particular emphasis or mission. Although it has traditionally been the center of graduate study in the liberal arts and the pure sciences, the elevation of Portland State to university status has left at least some uncertainty about what will be the university's future role in this regard. This uncertainty is compounded by the fact that there has been a strong reaction in public and political sectors against the increasing emphasis on graduate instruction. A limitation on the enrollment of out-of-state students effected by state legislative mandate for fall 1969 has had particularly important implications for the future development of graduate study.

In many respects the University of Oregon is schizophrenic with regard to the issue of its development. In discussing the question, members of the state board and many of the distinguished faculty agreed that one of the institution's major problems has been its failure to begin thinking in terms of any long-range plan. A clear trend toward a model typified by major graduate centers such as Berkeley and Michigan has been established, but the extent of the commitment in this direction is uncertain. One faculty member, in an aside during the discussion alluded to above, suggested that "perhaps the university is afraid to think about the future." Although the comment was made only half seriously, it may not be far from the truth. Increasing political pressures, growing public hostility, more frequent student unrest, and events transpiring just a few hundred miles south may render thoughts of the future particularly distressing.

Whatever the reason, the development of the university during the past several years is probably best described as haphazard. No long-range plan or set of goals, except perhaps an elusive and undefined ambition for "excellence," has guided its transition. In the past ten years, the graduate student body has rapidly increased both in absolute numbers and as a proportion of the total enrollment. Graduates now represent about thirty per cent of the student body with an enrollment of more than 4,000 putting a severe internal strain on an institution which likes to think of itself as combining the best features of the large multiversity and the undergraduate college meeting equally well the needs of both constituencies.

Although nothing comparable to California's *Master Plan* has been developed in Oregon, some state-wide studies and planning have been done in the past year. A special university committee worked during 1969–70 and issued a *Report on the Future of the University* (Novick Report).[4] This is the initial effort to systematically evaluate the direction of the institution and suggest future plans for enrollments, admissions, level of graduate program, possible directions in university governance and the like. One specific recommendation was to continue to have a committee concerned with future planning.

Most of the departments with established graduate programs were rated relatively strong, although not distinguished, in the American Council of Education's study of the quality of graduate education.[5]

Many of the departments would like to think that they have significantly strengthened their programs since the study was conducted in 1964 and would now advance claims to a "distinguished" rating. Others feel that they are on the verge of such a rating and are pushing for the addition of new and more distinguished faculty, increased research funds, and better graduate students.

During the 1950s and early 1960s, state support for the university had been quite high contributing to the rapid increase in the institution's stature during this period. During the greater part of the sixties, however, the dependence of the institution on federal funds increased considerably. With the escalation of the Vietnam War both federal and state sources of funds have become increasingly scarce. As the nation commits an increasing portion of its resources to war and war-related activities, it has diverted increasing amounts of money previously earmarked for education. To add to its difficulties, the Oregon economy, highly dependent on the lumber industry, has been seriously affected by the scarcity of money and the cutback in home production that has accompanied these increasing military commitments. The university therefore finds itself caught in a fiscal squeeze from both directions.

The push in the area of graduate training has generated some question on the campus regarding the overall quality of education. Any suggestion that undergraduate education has suffered as a result of increased graduate enrollment will be met with a host of assurances to the contrary. But there are also many who would agree. Like other institutions in similar situations, the development of graduate study generates a variety of reactions ranging from deep concern to dismissal of the issue as the price that one pays for this kind of development. Perhaps more often than not, however, one finds concern, if for no other reason than public relations. An increasingly large segment of the public believes that undergraduate education is suffering and their sympathies are definitely in that direction. Although the Novick Report [6] suggested maintaining the graduate ratio, the state legislature is requiring a reduction, due to economy moves. Given the state's comparatively limited resources and the legislature's growing enthusiasm for economy, especially at the university, any damage to the university's public image may have repercussions in dollars and cents.[7] Since the state support is already woefully inadequate in light of the institution's ambitions, and since previous sources of federal support are rapidly disappearing, there is more worry than ever about maintaining good public relations.

Like that of San Francisco State, the situation at the University of Oregon can be characterized as one of growing ambitions and shrinking resources. Its problems along these lines may be considerably greater though, inasmuch as its resources are probably shrinking faster while its ambitions are much nearer to realization. Compounding all of these difficulties is the fact that Oregon, too, is facing increasing internal pressures from the student body on a number of fronts.

Conduct Codes: Student and Faculty

Because of its proximity to that state, much of what happens in Oregon is probably a reflection of the current problems in California. A very large proportion of the university's students are from California. In many areas, students on the Oregon campus, especially student leaders, have looked to the Bay Area institutions as sources of educational leadership. Many issues first contested in California have been developed a short time later on the Oregon campus. One of these issues appears to have been the problem revolving around the principle of *in loco parentis,* that is that the university adopts the position of a surrogate parent during the student's campus sojourn.

The issue of *in loco parentis* appears to have emerged on the Oregon campus in a serious form at approximately the same time that it did on the Berkeley campus during the Free Speech Movement. It is important here though, not because it led to the same kind of ultimately unresolved difficulties that plagued Berkeley, but because the resolution of the problem set the style that was to characterize the problem-solving process on the campus in the immediate future. This style was marked, until late in the 1968–69 school year, by a mutual trust and respect among many of the antagonists, and usually allowed the solution of problems without an outbreak of serious hostilities.

The University of Oregon's approach to the *in loco parentis* problem was the simplest possible. The institution simply abandoned the principle and turned responsibility for matters of student discipline and conduct over to the students. A committee of faculty and students, at the direction of the president, and with the consent of the faculty, developed the institution's Student Conduct Code [8] which has subsequently become a model for many other institutions around the country.

The implementation of the conduct code had two important features: first, it recognized the responsibility of students in a tangible way; and second, it extended the principle of due process to student affairs. From the student's viewpoint, the code insured adherence to the principle of due process in a way that perhaps no other action could have. This was particularly important because at the heart of many of the continuing difficulties at other institutions is the problem of disciplinary measures and how they will be handled. It should also be pointed out that while this may not seem to be a particularly progressive step now, it was a fairly radical departure from the principles in force in perhaps all public colleges and universities at the time it was instituted. It was also the first step in what was to be an increasingly greater role for students in the government of the institution in the years following.

A major shift in the climate surrounding the Student Conduct Code has emerged in the past two years. This has developed, in part, over the wider matter of legal sanctions against students and university cooperation with legal authorities over such volatile issues as dormitory student arrests for narcotics. The critical issue, however, pertains to disruptions—in the classroom, over recruiters on the campus, in the faculty and administrative meetings, and in general physical challenges to the "normal conduct of the institution."

There had been a number of demonstrations against military recruiters, Dow Chemical recruiters and others starting in 1967. By 1969 there were disruptions of some classes. The RAT Troupe (radical action) carried guerrilla theater into classes and in front of military and corporate recruiters. Developments came to a head when eighteen students were arrested for demonstrating against recruiters from Weyerhaeuser Corporation, a major local industry, a polluter, and a company with extensive overseas operations including Southeast Asia.

Faculty became increasingly disturbed over the inability of the Student Conduct Code to deal with the situation, and amended it in an attempt to curtail activities which disrupted the normal functioning of the university. The Weyerhaeuser demonstrators, however, have had charges dismissed over technicalities (the issue was raised whether or not corporate and military recruiting is part of the educational function of the university). Some anti-ROTC demonstrators in 1970 were convicted by the Student Conduct Code and a number of other cases are pending. The addition to the code has not proven a deterrent to disruptions as some have argued, although there have been fewer disruptions in the 1970–71 academic year. On the other hand, there have also been more bombings.

The most critical developments have been for faculty. First, a postdoctoral scientist was charged with disruptive activities—against ROTC and military and corporate recruiters—and his federal research grant was administratively rescinded. A challenge is now pending in the civil courts.

The controversy surrounding Professor John Froines, on leave of absence during the Chicago Conspiracy Trial 1969–70, assumed significant statewide proportions. This was coupled with a substantial increase in demonstrations and activism on the campus and massive joint faculty-student participation in anti-war activities in May 1970 which included open support of Oregon Senator Mark Hatfield's bill, co-sponsored with Senator George McGovern, to legislate an end to the Vietnam War. This culminated in action by the State Board of Higher Education making a faculty conduct code part of the administrative manual. The new code included several provisions on incitement to riot, disruption of university activities, and obstruction of persons or occupancy of buildings in the face of orders by appropriate administrative officials.[9] A non-legislated section of opinion discusses professional roles and outlines the expectations such as one that faculty will not propagandize in the classroom.

The matter of conduct codes which might affect all university persons —faculty, staff, and students—has been discussed as one of the matters by the Committee on University Governance, about which more will be said later.

The Student and the University Government

As appears to have been the case at most major universities during the past few years, the student government at Oregon has been pressing for a progressively greater role in the overall decision-making apparatus. At Oregon, unlike most other major state institutions, progress toward the attainment of student goals in this area has been quite rapid. With the exception of the Advisory Council, where recommendations concerning promotion and tenure are formulated, students participate actively on most of the relevant faculty and administrative committees.[10]

While participation varies from floor privileges and minor representation on the one extreme, to full voting participation in equal numbers on the other, the pattern is rapidly moving toward a mode of participation which incorporates students as voting participants with an increasingly significant but still minority voice.

The first real move toward student participation was made in 1965 with the appointment of the first Faculty-Student Council.[11] The council was a faculty committee and as such was the first faculty committee which had regular student membership. The original charge to the committee was to serve as a kind of liaison between the faculty and the student body. In the course of its operation, it rapidly became the vehicle by which students could initiate motions and legislation to be acted upon by the regular faculty. Since the committee provided a direct mechanism for affecting faculty decisions, or at least getting the faculty to consider student-initiated proposals, it rapidly became the focal point for student efforts to implement innovative or experimental programs and for the push for wider student participation.

Shortly after the formation of the Faculty-Student Council, the question of student participation in the faculty meetings was raised. Until this time, the meetings had been closed to all but the faculty. At issue was the admittance of two students, the student body president and one other representative of the student government. The strength of student feeling regarding the issue was indicated by a series of rallies held before the faculty meeting where the issue was to be decided. The largest and most dramatic of these, in the spring of 1966, featured several student and faculty speakers and threats of a blockade at the entrance to the building where the meeting was to be held the next day. The rhetoric was heavy with allusions to Berkeley and the FSM and the potential for a similar incident at Oregon. Approximately five hundred students attended the rally and participated with at least a modest show of enthusiasm.

For a campus characterized by relative quiescence it was an imposing demonstration. There was serious commentary from many parts of the campus about the "potential for an explosion." Although there were mixed feelings about the extent to which it was really a threat at the time, there is no question that many of the faculty and students entertained the idea as a serious possibility. The faculty voted to open its meetings. The two student representatives would be admitted and given floor privileges. The situation calmed for the rest of the year.

Innovation and Challenge of Change: University of Oregon 123

The next academic year, 1966–67, students showed more interest in the idea of participatory democracy and the development of innovative educational programs. In terms of the time of the development of student activism on these issues, Oregon might be said to have been somewhere between California's Bay Area campuses and Western Washington State College. Students in Oregon were clearly attuned to what was happening in California. On the other hand, this did not mean a simple attempt to transplant the issues and the tactics of the California schools to Oregon without any adaptation to local interests and idiosyncrasies. While the fundamental issues were very similar, the form of educational reform and the tactics used differed considerably.

The reason for the difference was no doubt due in no small measure to the personal style of the individual who was president of the university during this period. Arthur Flemming, United States Secretary of Health, Education and Welfare in the Eisenhower administration, enjoyed a truly unusual rapport with students at the university. There appears to have been a genuine feeling of admiration and respect from every sector of the student body, including student radicals and conservatives, Black militants and white moderates, graduates and undergraduates. In ways that few college presidents are able to do, Flemming articulated and shared the concerns of today's activist student for problems of racism, war, poverty, and exploitation. His views in these areas were not silent either. He was a vocal critic of the Vietnam policy and a national leader in other areas, speaking out frequently on the compelling issues of the day. In addition, he met regularly with student leaders and made it possible for any student on campus to have access to the presidential office by holding regular open office hours. Finally, his was usually a position in favor of expanding student participation, and students interpreted his leadership in this area as most important in continuing the expansion of their role. During a time of growing hostility between students and other campus constituencies, his influence was an important force in maintaining the level of conflict within limits which permitted solution.

Despite Flemming's leadership and influence, however, student rancor continued to increase over the issue of educational reform and the associated issues of more important roles for students in deliberative and decision-making process. The two issues have developed along parallel lines during most of the period since 1964.

An example of the way in which the issues were dovetailing in

1965–66 came with the introduction to the state legislature of the Mosser Plan. The plan, named after its author John Mosser, a young state representative at the time and the governor's most recent appointment to the State Board of Higher Education, was based on the assumption that undergraduate education was being slighted in the state system, especially in those institutions where there had been a rapid increase in the commitment to graduate training. It applied especially to the University of Oregon but also to Oregon State University. The idea behind the plan was to set aside a sum of money that would be used to give yearly awards of $1,000 to encourage outstanding undergraduate teaching. The recipients of the awards were to be chosen by the individual institutions, in a manner which they designed, with the proviso, however, that students were to be involved in some "significant way" in making the selection. There was an additional requirement that, during the year's three teaching terms, recipients must have taught at least two courses per term in two of the terms.

Student reaction to the proposal was generally enthusiastic. From their point of view it provided a double opportunity. It would be a positive move to encourage excellence in undergraduate instruction, and it would force the administration and the faculty to give them some formally recognized role in the evaluation of faculty. The Student Senate adopted a proposal for implementing the Mosser Plan and presented it to the Faculty Advisory Council.

In the faculty camp, the reaction was mixed. There was an immediate negative response among those who were opposed to the idea of student evaluation of the faculty for any reason. This contingent was apparently represented in the Faculty Senate where the level of student involvement proposed by the Faculty Advisory Council is reported to have been cut back.[12] It is of significance that the Advisory Council's recommendations in this regard are reputed to coincide to a significant degree with the Associated Students of the University of Oregon's (ASUO) plan.[13]

When the proposal of the Faculty Senate, already somewhat changed from what students had requested, finally came before the full faculty for a vote, there was opposition for a variety of reasons. As it turned out, as least three of the largest departments in the university had no professors who could have met the teaching load qualifications specified by Mosser. According to the editor of the student newspaper, only 342 of the 890 university faculty would have qualified for competition for the award on the basis of teaching loads.[14] The faculty finally rejected participation in the plan by more than a two-to-one margin. The decision was received bitterly by a number of student leaders who saw the plan as a progressive step in the direction of improving undergraduate teaching.

During the next academic year, 1966–67, several resolutions which encompassed most of the major concerns of the students were introduced through the Faculty-Student Council. Foremost among these were the development of a program of student-initiated courses and the introduction of a pass/no-pass grading option. The first was aimed primarily at the issue of relevance and the second was intended to reduce some of the pressures of academic competition as well as to serve as a possible alternative model for the total academic evaluation system in the future.

The first of the issues introduced to the faculty was the pass/no-pass grading option. A motion was entered in the faculty by the chairman of the Faculty-Student Council at the direction of the Council members to the effect that a thirty-six hour pass/no-pass option should be adopted by the faculty for a trial period. Although the matter was the subject of some extended debate in the Faculty-Student Council, it was passed with relatively little debate by the faculty. It is interesting though to note some of the debate that took place in the council in order to get some feel for where student leaders were in their thinking at the time the issue was raised.

Faculty members on the council were in general agreement that the idea was a good one. Their debate centered primarily on mechanical questions such as whether the limitation should be thirty instead of thirty-six hours. Undergraduate members of the council were divided, however, on the question of whether or not graduate students should be included in the option. The division was not on a matter of principle, but over the question of strategies. For some reason, the student who introduced the resolution, an undergraduate and a central figure in student government activities, felt that the possibility of adoption of the proposal would be jeopardized if graduate students were included. As a matter of expedience, therefore, he wanted graduates specifically excluded from the program. After an extended debate, the chairman was directed to enter in the next faculty meeting the motion that the pass/no-pass option be adopted for a trial period for the entire student body. The episode is of interest, not because of the merits of the issue, but because the individuals who adopted the position of exclusion of graduate students were generally considered to be on the left among student groups with regard to their position on campus issues. However, they were not the type of student who was likely to lead a march on the administration building in the event of a disagreement.

Yet, the character of student leadership at Oregon has been critical in shaping the political life of the campus both on university government and on broader issues. The student body president in 1967, who was the first to participate in faculty meetings, became a critic of the war in Vietnam and the inequities of the draft and allowed himself to be drafted six weeks prior to graduation by declining his student deferment. This was the beginning of continuing bold leadership. The 1969 student body president has a case currently pending before the United States Supreme Court. He is appealing his conviction for disrupting local draft boards by performing guerrilla theater war crimes trials. The then vice-president of the student body took over leadership and pushed hard for the extension of student power, participation in decision making, and on issues such as the conversion of the faculty club into a day-care center.

The student body president elected in 1970 won with strong radical and minority student support. He had been actively leftist in his position as editor of the *Daily Emerald*. In the fall of 1970 he joined ten student body presidents under the auspices of the National Student Association and travelled to Paris and North and South Vietnam to sign a "People's Peace Treaty" with the Vietnamese people. The student government has become increasingly identified with radical and left liberal components of the student body and as such has pushed not only for increasing student participation in university governance but on the wider issues of racism and militarism within the university and the broader community.

A convocation was held in the spring of 1969 designed to open dialogue between students and faculty in schools and departments, to deal largely with student grievances and demands for change. Some governmental shifts did emerge at the time and in the subsequent period. A number of departments and schools in the university have provided for active and full participation by students, generally in a minority status. Some parity on committees has been developed, both within departments and on university-wide committees. Nevertheless, the quest for increased student participation has continued.

Innovation and Challenge of Change: University of Oregon

During spring 1970 the campus was in constant turmoil with massive demonstrations related to ROTC. The faculty very nearly passed a motion to abolish ROTC, and the meetings included substantial student participation with hundreds of student demonstrators and observers. In the meantime ROTC had been assaulted, there were arrests, sit-ins, and related issues emerged—notably the closing of a street running through the campus.

This last issue took on the character of a "People's Park" a la Berkeley. Students and some street people barricaded a campus street, claimed it as a liberated people's zone, held art and music fairs, and increasingly identified its closing as a *fait accompli* although the City Council had not made a legal decision. The action precipitated a substantial community backlash accompanied by charges of flagrant disregard for the law. Vigilante groups from the community threatened and physically confronted those at the street barricades. In the course of confrontation, the climate of polarization was further heightened in the community and on the campus.

A large teach-in on the war, racism, and related issues was held immediately before an emergency meeting of the faculty following the initial ROTC vote. The visitors gallery, normally holding 200 was jammed, and thousands of others were packed into the hall and outside until the president moved the meeting to the basketball arena. Thousands of students followed. The climate on the campus was one of constant demonstrations, activism, and student concern prior to the Cambodian invasions and the Kent and Jackson State killings.

During this same period, ad hoc student-faculty groups were urging the creation of a special governance commission. The Student-Faculty Coalition, an outgrowth of the ROTC demonstrations, sit-ins, and the Cambodian crisis, began to talk about alternate joint approaches to decision-making in the university. In addition, the coalition was successful in campaigning for the election of a slate of faculty liberals to the Advisory Council and Senate. Students interviewed candidates, printed results, and worked openly on the election. The Committee on the Future of the University issued its report and recommended a university forum of students and faculty, a joint student-faculty senate for legislative purposes, and the creation of a committee on governance.

In the fall of 1970, months after the crisis period, the president appointed a student-faculty Committee on University Governance which is to make a report in the spring of 1971. This committee is addressing the total range of concerns from the student conduct code to modes of student-faculty cooperation in decision-making on curriculum, personnel matters, and the like. While the direction continues to reflect the national mood of increasing student participation in decision-making, there is little evidence to suggest that Oregon will lead the way in terms of community government in the way that it did in the area of its student conduct code almost a decade earlier.

The Student and the Curriculum: SEARCH

The most important development in the area of educational reform in terms of student-initiated curriculum has been an Associated Students program labeled SEARCH—Students' Exploratory Actions Regarding Curricular Heterodoxy. The mechanics of the SEARCH program are quite simple. Any student who is interested in getting a course offered for credit can do so if he can convince a faculty member to assume responsibility for the course and the appropriate department chairman to approve. The SEARCH office enters into the procedure primarily as an agency for facilitating the development of courses and publicizing their availability. In addition they might provide small allowances for bringing guest lecturers to class, renting films, and so on. They do not, however, have a budget for picking up the professor's time. If the professor is to be paid for teaching a SEARCH course, that is something that must be worked out with the department in question. With only rare exceptions, the participation of the professor has been voluntary and without remuneration.

The initial source of the idea for the SEARCH program is uncertain. Although students had exhibited some interest in educational reform prior to the proposal for the SEARCH program, the expression was primarily in the form of criticism of current structures and attempts to begin some sort of faculty evaluation. The actual initiation of the SEARCH program seems to have been an indirect outgrowth of this early student criticism of course quality and content. Implementation of the program was begun, not by students, but by an employee of the Associated Students, the program director, who had been hired to coordinate the organization's various extra-curricular educational activities. Initial inquiries and investigations into programs designed to meet the same kinds of objectives addressed in student criticisms of their education was begun by the program director and actively supported at the time by the dean of men who seems to have been genuinely interested in the educational issues involved and was also very much worried by the possible political implications of the development of a free university. In a memo to President Flemming in early fall 1966, he outlines his fears:

> It is very likely that the University will soon encounter organized student drives to establish a "free university" within the University of Oregon. If patterned after the "free university" in New York City—and this seems to be the early indication—such a movement might well prove seriously devisive and detrimental to the educational tasks of the University of Oregon. This particularly [sic] so if the movement leaders are not strongly encouraged to use existing University means to achieve their goal of developing special educational offerings they feel are now lacking.[15]

The dean went on to point out that there were many positive benefits to be derived from a program supported and encouraged by the university using the unstructured 407 seminars already available and in use among all of the departments. This number had been set aside to allow individuals to teach in their special areas or to readily expand the curriculum to an area of special interest without going through the lengthy and complicated procedure of having a course established as a part of the regular curriculum. He pointed out that the program could be a positive force in inducing "curricular change through faculty guided experimentation,"[16] but even in listing the educational advantages of the program, he dwelt on its potential for offsetting what the possible negative consequences of a free university structure might be. Among these advantages were:

> Involving members of the faculty rather than by default forcing those students to call upon "outside" personnel who might be recruited to teach in a "free university;"

> Encouraging a true *community* approach in resolving differences between students and faculty, and thus blunting the efforts of those few individuals who seem intent on furthering dissension and division; and

> Reinforcing and making manifest the University's determination to provide the intellectual atmosphere and means for the pursuit of truth through free inquiry *within the University structure*.[17]

At this point his emphasis on the appealing political aspects of the program has become clearer. By the end of the memo, he raised what appeared to be his major objection to the idea of a free university, the involvement of SDS:

> In addition, the apparent direction of the Students for a Democratic Society (SDS) is to create a "free university," either within the University of Oregon or in the vicinity of the University of Oregon. This group seems to have little interest in intellectually exploring problems, and instead devotes its efforts to promoting its answers as the only possible answers. Should it capture the latent interest of the student body in promoting its idea of a "free university" I believe it is fair to say that such a "free university" would not be consonant with the intellectual ideal of the University of Oregon.
>
> I suggest that department heads be advised of this movement and of the likely approach by student delegations who may wish to establish such "courses." [18]

What impact this memo may have had on the thinking of the president of the university is difficult to estimate inasmuch as there is every reason to believe that he would have been supportive of the idea, even without the added incentive that it might be used to successfully counter a plot of radical students and assorted leftist "outsiders." It is interesting though that Oregon is the only case in which this source of support for such a program was apparent. If a similar rationale was entertained on other campuses, and it conceivably could have been, it was not obvious.

In order to arouse enthusiasm, the idea for the SEARCH program was publicized in the student newspaper. The first news release was published in the December 8, 1966 *Emerald* and drew immediate negative response from the Faculty Curriculum Committee which at the time, due to its composition, was among the most reactionary groups on campus. It had taken a consistent stand against the introduction of innovative courses into the curriculum. The committee continued to adopt a conservative position throughout the following year, 1967–68, opposing many of the courses proposed by the new School of Community Service and Public Affairs and SEARCH courses taught by controversial campus professors. In a memo issued within four days of the publication of the *Emerald* article describing SEARCH, the committee announced its findings that courses listed in the article to be offered the following term were not approved by appropriate deans or division heads. The members of the committee went on to point out that:

the inauguration of programs such as the SEARCH proposal, if planned for University credit, obviously raises a major question of academic policy, which can be answered only by the faculty of the University—not by students, individual faculty members, or the several schools and departments: Will the University grant credit for instruction defined, organized, and administered by nonfaculty agencies? [19]

Not only did the committee raise the issue, it noted that discretion on the use of seminars had been delegated to the various departments, but that "basic jurisdiction of the committee, as an agent of the faculty, covers instruction under 400–410 and 500–510 numbers, as well as in formally organized courses." [20] The intent of the committee was clearly to inhibit the use of the open course numbers of the SEARCH program, at least until it had had the chance to satisfy itself that "appropriate" personnel would be in charge.

The warning of the Curriculum Committee notwithstanding, the first two courses labeled as SEARCH courses were offered during the winter term of 1967. One was entitled Student Political Movements and taught by a political scientist; the other was a course called Seminar on Drug Use and offered by the Department of Health Education. Although there was apparently some negative reaction on the part of the Chairman of the Curriculum Committee, no real action could be taken. Traditionally such courses were left to the discretion of department chairmen and intervention would have been difficult. It may also be that there was some confusion about whether or not the courses were really offered under the auspices of SEARCH since the program had not been formally established. What had in fact happened was that students interested in the issue had asked two professors to offer courses that were clearly within the legitimate purview of their disciplines. Given the nature of the courses and the lack of publicity surrounding them, it may well have been that they were considered more or less irrelevant to the problem at hand.

In any event, the administrators and students interested in pushing the program continued preparatory activities. That spring the students convened a major conference to discuss the whole question of educational innovation and the student's role in curricular reform. The conference was intended to highlight the proposed SEARCH program and to serve as a source of ideas to be included in the final deliberations before the program was finally launched. It was also to be a catalyst for educational innovation on the campus. A variety of local notables from administration, faculty, and student leadership positions participated in the conference. Leading educators and student activists from other West Coast campuses were brought to the campus to speak. The major address of the conference, "Student Confrontations of the Curriculum: Crisis and Opportunity," was delivered by President John Summerskill of San Francisco State College, then at the peak of his notoriety as an educational innovator. The conference lasted a full two days and included more than forty participants and three major addresses. It was a flop! No one came, or perhaps more correctly, very few came. The major address by Summerskill attracted an audience of approximately one hundred including students, faculty, citizens, and administrators forced to attend as a matter of protocol. According to the program director and the student organizer, the conference had fallen far short of its original objectives.

In spite of the failure of the conference to capture the imagination of the campus community, it did serve a useful purpose as a source of ideas. Perhaps even more important, though, was the fact that it added a dimension of legitimacy to the student effort by indicating an interest in constructive innovation.

In the meantime, the Faculty Curriculum Committee had prepared a report on the use of the special course numbers historically and guidelines that should be used in implementing particular courses in the various departments. The new report was released just as the Conference on the Curriculum ended. This second memo regarding the use of special numbers represented a substantial retrenchment from the earlier position assumed by the Curriculum Committee. This time there was no talk of the committee's jurisdiction, rather suggestions about precautions which might be taken to insure the integrity of the courses. In referring to the use of the courses in the past the committee commented:

> The overall impression . . . is that the course numbers involved serve a particularly valuable and useful purpose. Although there are some inconsistencies and lack of uniformity, it seems obvious that the numbers satisfy a clear need for flexibility in the development and expansion of the curriculum. Possibly, in one or two cases, the present uses may be opened to question, but this is a minor matter compared to the obvious benefits to the faculty and departments provided by the judicious application of these numbers.[21]

It is rumored that after the release of the first report, the committee was upbraided by members of the faculty who were sympathetic to the program for overstepping the bounds of their authority. Furthermore, in the investigation, it apparently became clear that the Curriculum Committee did not have authority over the courses in question. The numbers used for the courses had not been established by faculty action but had been set aside by interinstitutional administrative action in 1932, which had established a uniform policy throughout the state system of higher education reserving these courses for special purposes.[22] This apparently eliminated the courses from the jurisdiction of the committee, and the issue of their prerogatives as an "agent of the faculty" became an irrelevant question. The committee, in fact, appears to have addressed this issue, at least indirectly. Commenting with reference to the guidelines that they suggested, they say:

> When these conditions are fulfilled, no criticism can be levelled at the course either by the faculty, a university committee, or an outside accreditation agency.
>
> Some concern has been expressed about the so-called seminars initiated by undergraduate students. To the extent that the University might find itself granting University credit for informal "bull sessions," this concern would have some real basis. The point of initiation, however, is not the basic question. If the student initiation is responsible and mature, if the division concerned is able and willing to undertake the proposed instruction and to insure that it meets the standards of University work outlined above—then no serious problems are anticipated by the Committee on the Curriculum.[23]

The Curriculum Committee had, in effect, given its stamp of approval at this point. With these major hurdles cleared, the program director and student leaders began to prepare for the first term of full-scale operation.

The first term, fall 1967, SEARCH sponsored eight courses. Of the eight, only two or three were truly student organized. The remaining courses had been initiated by faculty interested in teaching a particular course, or who had used the SEARCH bulletin in order to get enough students to justify offering a course in a particular interest area. During the second term, the number of student-initiated courses grew by two or three and a few more special interest courses were added by the faculty. By the third term a total of twenty-two courses was being offered. Of these, thirteen were listed as student-initiated, nine as faculty-initiated. The number of courses was inflated by the fact that there were several sections of some courses, especially a follow-up on *The Kerner Report* in spring 1968.

By the second year in operation, the idea of the SEARCH program had become firmly entrenched and the program leveled off at approximately fifteen to twenty courses per term. The program was never what it might have been, however, because of the lack of a budget for faculty. When the courses were initiated by faculty, the instructor was on rare occasion given released time by the department, but this was never the case in student-initiated courses. Some instructors who had attempted to remove any element of coercion from the classroom were disappointed at the student response. One commented "there has to be some way to get the work out of them." In another case where a course had been listed in the bulletin as being offered on a pass/no-pass basis only, three-quarters of the students registered for a letter grade.[24]

The result appears to have been a slackening of enthusiasm among many of the regular faculty who had earlier offered courses in the program. More than one faculty member became disenchanted because of what he interpreted as a failure of many of the students to take the courses seriously enough to warrant the extra effort on their part. As their enthusiasm began to wane, the slack was picked up somewhat by graduate students who would step in occasionally to teach a special course. Finally, a few undergraduates were allowed to teach courses under the direction of a faculty sponsor.

The general response of the faculty to the program had been one of approval or disinterest during most of the first two years. Department chairmen whose aid had been solicited in promoting the program generally responded with a show of moral support but a lack of enthusiasm for allocating department resources to the program. Probably because of the inability to secure any major funding and the failure to pursue this goal by the ASUO, faculty participation appears to have become more difficult to secure. Student participation continued to grow, however. In the first term of official operation in the fall of 1967 there were 212 students listed in SEARCH courses. By the winter the number increased to nearly 1,100 and in the spring of 1968 the program hit a peak enrollment of more than 1,700 students. The next year, 1968–69, detailed records were not kept, but a survey of course enrollments by the SEARCH director indicated an enrollment which fluctuated between 600 and 1,000 students per term. It was also during this year that more controversial courses were being added to the curriculum. As a result, the first official negative reaction against the program came in the summer of 1969 at the end of two full years of operation. In a memo from the dean of faculties, concern was expressed over the direction that some of the courses offered under SEARCH auspices were taking. The memo states:

> It is apparent that in our SEARCH course offerings there has been considerable drift away from the original concept, both in the development and in the teaching of such offerings.
>
> Questions raised by many faculty members and administrators concerning SEARCH courses over the past few months—particularly with respect to the current Summer Session offerings—point to the need for a thorough review of the program with recommendations for appropriate procedures and adequate safeguards.
>
> Pending such a review . . . all deans and department heads under whose jurisdiction SEARCH courses are presently being offered, or are likely to be offered in Fall term, are asked immediately to scrutinize these offerings, or proposed offerings, with a view to seeing that they comply with the principles set forth by the Committee on the Curriculum in May, 1967. . . .
>
> It is generally recognized that the SEARCH program is inherently experimental, innovative and unconventional, but it is beyond question that the faculty, in lending its support to this undertaking, had no intention of doing violence to the principle that courses carrying academic credit at the University of Oregon must be given by duly qualified members of the faculty, or in exceptional cases and for demonstrably valid reasons under the direct supervision and guidance of a faculty member. Casual "sponsorship" of a SEARCH course by a member of the faculty is not consistent with this policy.[25]

The distribution of the memo brought an immediate reaction from student leaders who interpreted the action as an attempt to control the content of courses and to eliminate controversial material. The dean responded in an interview in the student newspaper that the purpose of his memo was misunderstood. He was quoted as saying that he "did not want to see the program damaged by what some might consider abuses." He also added that he felt the SEARCH procedures should be examined by a standing committee of the university on which students were represented, perhaps the curriculum committee.[26]

What initiated the memo, according to the dean, was a complaint registered by the director of the summer session after he had received letters from students' parents which had apparently complained about the content of courses being offered by graduate students. He also noted though that individual faculty members had expressed concern informally on several occasions. Although parental complaints did not allude to all courses taught by students, apparently the complaint of the director of the summer session did. It is probable that he registered the complaint against all student-taught courses because these were by far the most controversial in their content, but also importantly, because they were among the largest enrollments in the summer session.

Pressure had also come from the dean of students office because courses were being taught in part by students who did not meet the "necessary qualifications for teaching in the university." It is also alleged that the dean had registered several charges against a course on American Imperialism which were patently false. Among these were that one of the student-teachers who had had an A average for the preceding term was flunking out, that the professor who was sponsoring the course had not been supervising it, and that "unqualified" persons were being used as guest lecturers. On the latter two counts it was pointed out that the faculty sponsor was in regular attendance and that guest lecturers had been faculty members at the university and at other institutions, among them one of the nation's most distinguished historians. Not surprisingly, the students in question were all political leftists. Some were members of SDS, a fact which undoubtedly confirmed the worst fears of infiltration expressed earlier in the memo to the president from the dean of men.

Again, as it had at San Francisco State and at Berkeley, the student-organized curriculum had begun to pose a threat to the regular curriculum and therefore to faculty and administrative interests. Given the experience at these other institutions, the eventual reaction at the University of Oregon was predictable. The rationale developed to cope with the students' arguments for SEARCH courses having the largest enrollments was that the university should not be an agent of social action, but should remain detached in order to maintain an objective perspective. The paradox, of course, is that many, perhaps most, university administrators argue that community service is appropriate while community action is inappropriate for the university, even though there are clear-cut value and political commitments entailed in any service program. The crucial difference and what bothers university and college authorities is that while "service" generally implies support of existing institutions and a buttressing of the status quo, "action" implies a commitment to radical change and reorganization of the society. Such a radical stance is clearly the antithesis of the political ideology of most college and university administrators.

The stand for community service and against community action is one that has been taken by the chief executive officers of both Berkeley and San Francisco State College. The results in both cases, as we have already seen, have been disastrous. As he was about to assume office, the President of the University of Oregon adopted the same position. He argued that the "enlistment of education in the interest of change . . . is a dangerous tenet, one that could transform the lecture into a pulpit, transmute the scholar into a demagogue. . . ." A few moments later, however, he noted that "from the outset, the public university has served the nation as an instrument of socialization." [27] He did not, however, note that elements of the pulpit and demagogue are as much a danger in the process of socialization as in the pursuit of change. The activist student, however, sensitive to the enlistment of the university in the baser interests of the society (e.g., political manipulation and biochemical and other types of war research) does not fail to make this observation.

The conflict over the Oregon SEARCH program presents an interesting dilemma because the events are so very much parallel to those surrounding the difficulties at Berkeley and San Francisco State. Some members of the faculty and administration may be willing to ignore the parallels and simply abolish the program. This would not appear to be the majority sentiment, however. Faculty sentiment, to the extent that it can be tapped, probably favors the more moderate course of action proposed by the dean of faculties.

The controversy has carried over since the 1969 administrative response which seemed as though it would prompt an immediate shift in the SEARCH program. The program has continued and there has been a substantial enrollment in its courses. A number of controversial courses—ranging from Human Sexuality, which included the use of films and lectures from the Gay Liberation Movement, to courses which included analyses of revolutionary efforts in which it was alleged that target practice was one activity—have generated considerable reaction. There were pressures from the public particularly when SDS and student activists were involved in several labor strikes along with students in SEARCH courses who worked with the SDS Labor Committee. The strikes were tense and involved arrests of both unionists and students. Courses continue to be controversial, and expressions of public concern are transmitted via the administration to the university community in the form of periodic appeals for scrutiny of content and faculty. Nevertheless, the program is viable, popular with students, and apparently in no immediate danger of termination. There has been a reduction of offerings, and some departments have developed procedures which put student instructors and faculty sponsors under more formal obligations in developing courses, student evaluations, and other aspects of the SEARCH curriculum. In contrast to the experience at many other campuses, however, the structure for student-initiated courses at the University of Oregon remains. The program is run by students and offers courses in Chicano studies, militarism, nonviolence, social change, and a variety of topics which augment the traditional curriculum. In some cases SEARCH courses have influenced permanent departmental curricula and have been introduced into the regular university catalog. At the present time it seems possible that the ethnic studies courses now in SEARCH will develop into regular departmental offerings.

Although not directly related to SEARCH, one further recent development might be mentioned. In 1970 an ad hoc group of faculty met, with the encouragement of the president, to discuss an experimental college. The concept is like the Tussman experiment at Berkeley to the extent that it would be innovative, interdisciplinary, and would attempt to structure a teaching-learning model substantially different from that which currently characterizes the Oregon campus. Unlike the Berkeley experiment, however, the proposed Oregon experiment would be less rigidly structured and would include students in planning and development. The planning is only at a very preliminary stage, and is conceived as something unrelated to SEARCH or other current activities.

One final note should be introduced: namely, the existence of a Free School in the community which offers some of the more esoteric courses, including sensitivity training. There was also a growth center fashioned after Esalen and Topanga and the better-known centers, but it did not survive. Students at the university who wanted "touchy-feely" experiences took them off-campus. Hip community people who want a course in astrology, auto repair, or organic gardening have the Free School. In contrast to the experience at San Francisco State and Berkeley where students went off-campus and experimental efforts died, the SEARCH program at Oregon continues to be part of the academic offering of the university. The Free School complements SEARCH and is available for students and community people who want to involve themselves in a less conventional learning opportunity.

Addressing the Problem of Racism

As a former Secretary of Health, Education and Welfare, President of the National Council of Churches and the National Association of Social Welfare, and a member of the Urban Coalition, the former President of the University of Oregon, Arthur Flemming, was perhaps more sensitive to the pressing social and moral issues of the time than is often true of college administrators. Because of his sensitivity to these kinds of issues and his leadership in these areas, the University of Oregon was changed considerably during his tenure. Along with the acceptance of responsibility for the Tongue Point Job Corps center in Astoria, Oregon, the university began to involve itself in other programs for the disadvantaged such as Upward Bound, a High School Equivalency Program, the School Desegregation Institute, and so on. Not only did the programs alter the character of the campus considerably, they met with a fair amount of criticism both inside the university and in the outside community.

The state of Oregon is among the most "lily-white" in the nation. Non-white minorities comprise less than two per cent of the state's population. The Black community in the state, such as it is, is concentrated in Portland. It is no exaggeration to say that there are freshmen students who have rarely seen a Black man. Before the introduction of special programs for the disadvantaged, the percentage of non-whites on the campus (excluding foreign students) was less than it was for the state as a whole. Almost without exception, Black students were athletes who had been brought in to compete on scholarships.

The first significant change from the all-white character of the campus was brought about with the introduction of the Upward Bound program in 1965. According to participants and individuals teaching in the program, the reaction from many sectors was antagonistic. Faculty were not interested in giving special attention to students who had a need for remedial or other kinds of help. The attitudes seemed to be a mixture of sympathy and antipathy and the early attrition rate in the program was quite high. Many individuals who were instrumental in adding or enlarging such programs felt that the feelings of antipathy, if not increased by the programs' growth, at least became more evident.

Ill will toward programs for ethnic minorities reached a new plateau in the spring of 1968 when, in the wake of the assassination of Martin Luther King, President Flemming appointed the University President's Committee on Racism.

After the King assassination, the Black Students Union had presented the president a memorandum charging widespread racism on the campus and demanding that steps be taken to address the problem and to move toward implementing a list of demands contained in the memo. The president's first move was to appoint the Committee on Racism under the chairmanship of a professor of political science known for his activism in the area of radical and political matters. Compounding the antipathy toward the committee was the fact that its chairman was disliked by many of the moderate members of the campus community. In the memo announcing the formation of the Committee on Racism, the president pointed out that he considered the problem a serious one and that the committee was to have his full support. He noted:

> I am looking forward to the groups' recommendations as to programs and policies designed to eliminate any present, or prevent any future, manifestations of racism on our campus.
>
> The full support and resources of my office stand beind the committee in its endeavors. In order to implement the charge to the committee, it should be understood by all University personnel that this committee will have:
>
>   a. The responsibility of initiating relations and actions in connection with any segment of the University in their inquiry and development of policy and programs of action where it perceives problems to exist.
>
>   b. Direct access to, and communication with, the total University Community, through public statements, memorandums, etc.
>
>   c. The responsibility of transmitting and discussing with me the committee's recommendations.
>
> I anticipate the full cooperation from all areas of the University in the implementation of the work of this committee. Just as there can be no higher priority for this nation than healing racial bias and

cleaning up city slums, there can be no higher priority for the University of Oregon community than eliminating and preventing any racism which may exist on this campus.[28]

The appointment of the committee and the nature of the charge were offensive to many members of the faculty. Some were antagonistic because the president had lent credence to the charge of racism by appointing the committee. They felt that the charge was overstated at least, if not completely false. Others charged that the president had usurped the authority of the faculty by establishing and appointing a university-wide committee without first consulting them. The charge was undoubtedly more than a simple procedural issue. Questions of faculty versus administrative powers, possible extension of minority programs, and costs, among others, must have entered into considerations of this group. The events that followed revealed a serious rift that had developed in the campus community between those generally supportive of the policy direction which Flemming had given to the university and those who were not. The cleavages were described by one faculty member as being between the "old and the new guard," but the reference here is not to age. Supporters of both sides of the issue ran the gamut from very young to very old, and from junior to senior faculty. Each group represented, to some extent, a cross section of the faculty community and were represented by existing organized or quasi-organized conservative and liberal caucuses.

In the course of the work of the committee that spring, a move was made among the faculty to introduce a motion of censure of the president over the issue of the Committee on Racism. This move was countered by a proposed motion commending the president and the committee. It was a standoff. Neither motion was introduced since the contending parties reached agreement but this did not mean that the ill will generated by the issue subsided. The activities of the committee, especially the expansion of special programs with Project 75 maintained the antagonism of the opposition at a relatively high level.

Project 75 was a program to bring to the campus an additional seventy-five minority students who otherwise would not have come through a program of active recruiting and the provision of special scholarship and loan funds. Distaste for the program was voiced on two grounds: first, that the program was committing the university to a program which its already strained resources could not sustain; and, second, that bringing in students under special academic provisions threatened to lower standards and therefore jeopardized the interests of the entire university community. The lowered standards argument was articulated by some members of the State Board of Higher Education as well as by members of the faculty and administration.

Although the first argument, that Project 75 would strain the resources of the university was in fact true, it was rejected in favor of the more important considerations of priorities in the event that the university had to bear the brunt of the costs. Outside sources of funds were successfully cultivated and the university's initial contribution proved to be minimal. There has been, however, a persistent worry that as such outside funds have become more scarce the university might be required to use its own resources to continue the program. University support for Project 75 was not high on the list of priorities for many of the faculty.

An additional issue resulting from the proposed program arose in the area of curriculum. In addition to the extra resources required to support the students, it would be necessary to provide at least a minimal special curriculum in order to prepare these students for competition in regular university classes. The idea was to build what were labeled as "curriculum bridges," which would help the student to make the transition successfully. In addition to these kinds of special courses, there was also the obvious fact that the introduction of greater numbers of minority students to the campus would require the university to face up to the issue of introducing into the curriculum courses relevant to the minority experience.

While the enthusiasm for the new curricular obligations was certainly not uniformly high, it was interesting that the greatest commitment in the area of curriculum revision came from some of the departments which had traditionally been considered the most conservative. Many of those which had been considered liberal adopted comparatively rigid stands against any such curriculum revisions. When the obligation to actually do something was imposed, liberal rhetoric was often found lacking in substantive commitment. In the face of a relatively severe opposition, the Project 75 program was implemented. While the opposition reconciled itself to the decision, it can hardly be said that a sense of amicability was restored to the campus. The cleavages that appeared during this particular issue seemed evident almost immediately in the development of other issues.

It was in a setting of hostility on a number of fronts, both inside

Innovation and Challenge of Change: University of Oregon 143

and outside the university, that the president announced his resignation to accept a similar position at another college. The announcement was only coincidentally issued shortly after the convening of the Committee on Racism, but it added fuel to the fires of internal hostility. Those who had been incensed by the appointment of the committee and worried by its implications intimated that the actions were inappropriate for someone who was not going to be held responsible for delivering in the end. The president rejected these arguments and held fast to his original position of firm support for the committee.

While there were no major confrontations over such issues, Black student leaders have been generally unhappy with progress. Among the major recommendations of the Committee on Racism had been the beginning of special ethnic studies programs and the recruitment of appropriate minority faculty.[29] Not only has there been no progress on the implementation of an ethnic studies program, the result of recruitment efforts in securing minority faculty resulted in a standoff. Two Black faculty resigned from the university while two were added. It is rumored that the Black Studies Program appeared far from the top of the list of university priorities contained in the budget request submitted to the state board for transmittal to the legislature. Black Student Union leaders contend that the state board rearranged the priorities so that the Black studies item no longer appeared.

In addition to these problems in implementing the suggestions of the Committee on Racism, the chief program emanating from the activities of the committee has been in jeopardy. By midsummer 1969, it had not been determined whether funds would be available to continue commitments to students brought in under the program during the previous year, much less to expand the program as initially planned by the BSU. The financial restrictions affecting minority student enrollments and programs has continued. One presidential assistant in 1969 described the situation as, "not a lack of commitment, but a lack of ability." He believed that the university administration's commitment in this area was genuine, but that their resources were so severely limited that federal and foundation money was the only possible way that such commitments could be met. "Unfortunately," he said, "all of these programs were begun in a period of increasing federal involvement. We are now in a period of federal withdrawal, and the programs are coming home to roost."

Late in the spring of 1969, the whole issue of programs for the disadvantaged blossomed when a popular professor who is a leader in this area announced that he was considering leaving the university because of its lack of commitment to programs for the disadvantaged. After a series of confrontations with members of the administration, it was decided to hold a week-long convocation "Time Out for University-Wide Evaluation" in which this and other related and unrelated issues could be discussed, debated, and resolved. The theme of the convocation was "the role of the university in survival in 20th Century America." During this week, classes were suspended for a day and a half so that the various departments could hold departmental meetings of students and faculty in order to address problems at this basic level.

The results of the convocation were uncertain at the time. Student response ranged from enthusiasm to apathy. Few departments were overwhelmed by the level of student interest in the convocation, but many engaged in serious discussion of issues with student groups for the first time. In some departments important agreements were reached. Interestingly enough, it appears that these agreements rarely had anything to do with programs for the disadvantaged or with issues otherwise relevant to the education of the disadvantaged. The whole thrust of the convocation shifted rather abruptly to questions of decision making and student participation at the department level. In this regard, there were apparently great strides forward as several departments agreed to admit student representatives to faculty meetings in the departments, in many cases with voting privileges.

What had started out as a program to address the issue of the university's programs for the disadvantaged, however, wound up addressing another issue which, from the standpoint of the minority student community, was of only peripheral interest. Insofar as the extended student participation might help to secure more extensive commitments to minority programs, the results could be taken as positive. Many Black students did not feel, however, that this effect was probable, and they continued to push for commitments to minority programs independent of efforts to increase student participation in governance of the university.

The period following the appointment of the President's Committee on Racism was one of considerable white awareness of racism. This awareness was developed in part by the *Kerner Report,* which was assigned reading on the Oregon campus for an estimated 3,000 students during spring 1968. In addition to new programs such as Project 75, there was a resurgence of discussions concerning proposals for ethnic studies programs, one which had been drafted by the Black Student Union. In addition, some minor but serious efforts were developed during the next year to recruit minority faculty, which met with only a modicum of success.

By 1969–70, however, there was a Committee on Ethnic Studies developed. The committee released a report based on discussions and a special conference convened to plan ethnic programs. No commitments were made to recruit faculty or to develop departmental curricula or ethnic studies programs. The 1970–71 year again began with the University of Oregon being the only institution included in this study which did not have a formal program in ethnic studies. Despite such failures, there were some substantial gains in minority student enrollments, especially American Indians and Chicanos. In both cases active student organizations were developed which played a key role in additional recruiting and in assisting minority students in their curricular and extra-curricular needs. Furthermore, these students provided the major impetus in pushing for SEARCH courses in ethnic studies, regular departmental development of such offerings, and recruitment of minority faculty.

Although a few minority faculty have been added to the staff, the overall growth has been minimal and the university has lagged behind comparable institutions. The growth in minority students has been accompanied neither by recruitment of minority faculty nor development of ethnic studies programs or curricular offerings. This is true despite the fact that there has been an important history of white community support for ethnic studies and minority community organization. In the fall of 1970 the student government had a week-long conference on racism which precipitated a massive controversy when the student group which controlled ASUO conference funds overexpended the entire year's budget on the one conference. Although the conference committee did attract major leadership from the ethnic, largely militant, organizations across the country, it also paid substantial fees to local minority persons. The student body president then fired the student program leadership, an act which cost him most of the radical and minority student support which had helped him win the office.

The community of Eugene has a very small minority population. It had an active CORE (Congress of Racial Equality) chapter in the early and middle 1960s, and a Black faculty member was CORE Western Regional Director after the organizational leadership was assumed by Stokely Carmichael. By 1968 there was a chapter of the Black Panther Party, including original members from Oakland who had worked with Eldridge Cleaver. The Party suffered continuous harassment by the police and arrests, confrontations, and near shoot-outs were regular events. Eventually the chapter was closed down although many of its members remained at the university. The presence of militant Blacks actively recruiting, raising funds, holding public rallies, selling the Black Panther Party Paper, and engaging in public paramilitary training made a significant impact on white awareness of Blacks in the community and on the campus.

At the same time one of the early chapters of the Patriot Party emerged in Eugene, organized along principles parallel to the Black Panthers. The Patriots took over the Panthers' breakfast program and some community organizing and education efforts. The local head of the Patriots was arrested in Eugene and with national Patriot Party leadership in New York on gun law violations. He is now appealing his maximum ten-year federal sentences from a federal penitentiary. The Patriots have continued to support the Panthers, worked in the community, and have attempted to put pressure on the university to respond to community needs and deal with racism within the institution.

Other organizations both on and off the campus have supported the call for ethnic studies and minority student charges of racism. Most recently the Radical Collectives Union and other activist community groups backed the demand by the university Black Students Union that the president intervene to stop police harassment of Blacks. In their efforts white radicals have maintained defense of the Black Panther Party including Angela Davis and Bobby Seale (one of the Chicago Eight along with ex-Oregon professor John Froines).

The Presidential Search: Pushing the Issue of Student Participation

Among the students, the announcement of the resignation of President Flemming was met with a combination of disappointment and apprehension, the disappointment of losing a respected leader and apprehension over the possible kind of man who might be appointed to the new position. The student body president immediately issued a statement insisting that there should be student representation on the

Presidential Search Committee. The chancellor's office responded with a quick assurance that there would be student representation but with no immediate reference to numbers or the proportion of the committee that would be students.

When a tentative announcement of the makeup of the committee was issued, the formula called for approximately seven faculty and two students. The numbers were not firmly established yet, but it appeared, to the students at least, to be a more or less final decision. Reaction of the student body, as it is to any issue, was mixed. Many thought that the idea of two students was a tremendous concession from the chancellor. A few thought it was two too many. Radicals and student activists were unhappy. While there was no way to tap campus opinion accurately, it would probably be safe to say that a majority of students would have been happy if the original formula of seven faculty and two students had prevailed. A coalition of radical and activist students, however, announced their intention to take over Johnson Hall, the administration building. Oregon was to experience its most serious student siege to that date.

The students who led the takeover of the administration building were prompted by a variety of apprehensions and fears, as well as by ideological considerations of equity in the composition of the search committee. One of the leaders of the sit-in, who was later elected student body president, articulated most of the fears. He was worried that someone would be chosen who "would not be sympathetic to the idea of student participation, to curricular reform, and to minority programs." Even worse than lack of sympathy, he felt the committee might even choose someone who would retreat from the position already taken with regard to student participation on faculty committees and in curricular matters through the SEARCH program. He and the students who shared his perspective were interested in increasing the student power on the committee to assure that such a bad choice was not made.

The more radical contingent among the building's "liberators" were arguing for equal representation for students. The rationale for the demand was an appeal to the principle of community government.[30] The principle had been introduced to the politics of the campus earlier in the year when an ad hoc group of students, primarily graduates, issued a declaration of "revolt on campus." The declaration was prompted by what they felt was a failure of the university to move in the area of educational reform or even to show any inclination to address legitimate student grievances. As it turned out, the declaration was far more dramatic than the revolt, and nothing in the way of a mass movement ever materialized.

The declaration did, however, prompt some interest among six distinguished members of the faculty who asked the students involved in the revolt to discuss the nature of their grievances and possible solutions. The result of the meeting and a series of discussions which followed was the publication of a plan for a new university government, manned by equal numbers of faculty and students and incorporating many of the basic principles of the more generalized concept of community government. The plan was presented to the university president in late fall 1967. He reacted quite favorably and characterized it as a "most responsible approach to the difficult question of university government." He went on to express his general support for the concept and to encourage distribution of the plan to the entire university community. The plan was published by the student newspaper under the title "Guidelines for Faculty-Student Participation."[31] There was virtually no reaction from the university community. No one attacked the plan, and no one waxed ecstatic over its substance. It apparently did have some impact though, inasmuch as the concept of community government began to creep into the vocabulary of student leaders of several political perspectives. Official study of university governance, however, was to await the appointment of the post-crisis student-faculty committee in 1970. In any case, as the events at the sit-in transpired, the idea of community government was invoked as the guiding principle of the students' negotiating position.

As the sit-in went into its third day, the chancellor was refusing to budge from his first offer, and students continued to demand equal representation. Late the third day, student negotiators emerged from a meeting with the chancellor, announced a settlement, and issued a declaration of victory. The settlement involved the appointment of three faculty, three administrators, and three students. Later two members of the State Board of Higher Education and a member of the Alumni Association were added. During the course of the negotiations, the principle of equal participation had been redefined to include administrators as a separate element. In this case, however, the "administrators" were the dean of the School of Journalism (who had announced his resignation from the deanship six months before) and two department

Innovation and Challenge of Change: University of Oregon 149

chairmen, both of whom bridled at the thought of being labeled a part of the administration.

What followed was inevitable. Although the students withdrew from the building, the student negotiators were charged with selling out, or having been co-opted, or having failed in a variety of similar ways. The negotiators countered in some cases by defending the principles of the settlement or in others by arguing that if they had not settled, the police would have been called that afternoon. While there was some talk of reoccupying the building, enthusiasm for the sit-in had obviously dissipated. Students were satisfied to declare the settlement a victory and prepare for final examinations which were fast approaching.

The gains from the sit-in, even calculated in terms of their implications for the principle of student power, were at best negligible. Arguments to the contrary by some students were specious. There is good reason to believe that had the sit-in never occurred the chancellor could have been persuaded to add a third student to the committee.

The negative consequences of the sit-in, however, were anything but negligible. The press in the state was overwhelmingly hostile. The fact that the students had been orderly and had confined the sit-in to the halls and corridors of the building without disrupting business was of little consequence. The action was condemned from one end of the state to the other. The bad press probably confirmed the suspicions of the already hostile public and added an indeterminable number to their ranks.

Members of the faculty who were opposed to the idea of student participation pointed to the incident as a confirmation of their lack of faith in the maturity and responsibility of the students. Other faculty who had been vacillating on the whole idea began to move in the direction of the conservatives and introduced a motion to the effect that the principle of negotiation should not be used in further disagreements with the students. The motion was passed by a substantial majority.

In yet another and perhaps the most important sector, the student action invited reaction. The State Board of Higher Education was meeting on the campus during the sit-in and opinions of its members regarding the activities were uniformly negative. One member of the board later summed up the position of its members in a comment to student members of the search committee when she said that "the student grievance was legitimate, but the tactics were intolerable." This tactical error no doubt partially caused the legislature to adopt the next year a policy restricting the number of out-of-state students admitted to the university. Its more conservative members saw this as one way of limiting the number of "outside agitators."

The push for parity, or as least increased student participation was extended into additional areas after this sit-in. Aside from the fact that students recognized their relative impotence in the selection of the president—a decision clearly in the hands of the State Board of Higher Education—they did achieve increasing participation in other personnel selection committees, ranging from the choice for deanships to regular faculty recruitment.

The Wider Context of Educational Innovation

As is the case for all institutions, one has to appreciate the external pressures and the community context which impinge on their operation. This is of profound importance in the case of a public institution, especially given the controversial character of events which have taken place on most campuses. At Oregon the 1968-69 academic year was filled with dramatic events. It was a politically important year in the aftermath of national events which included the "children's campaigns" of Eugene McCarthy and Robert Kennedy, the disillusionment over the conventions (especially the Chicago Democratic Convention), the election of Richard Nixon on a pledge to end the war in Vietnam, the racial tensions which continued to mount following the assassination of Martin Luther King, and the substantial number of student demonstrations on the nation's campuses.

After the resignation of President Flemming, Charles Johnson, the Dean of Liberal Arts, became acting president. His tenure was marked by a range of issues: the public furor over his reversal of a coach's decision regarding the hair style of a black athlete; a decision to stop buying California grapes (during the Farm Workers boycott); and the public outcry over political flyers and the publication of *the* "dirty word" in the student newspaper. The incredible impact of cross-pressures from student militants and an increasingly hostile public can be measured to some extent in the untimely death of the acting president. Under a physician's care and suffering from acute exhaustion and depression, President Johnson was killed in an automobile accident on the day following the university's commencement. Although his position might have been made more difficult by the limitations imposed by the role of acting president, the consequences of the year's events give some indication of the intensity of pressure. Johnson is quoted, in his last public interview, as feeling that he "had accomplished nothing and that he had failed on his promise 'to keep the University moving ahead.' "[32]

Into this milieu came the new president, Robert Clark, former Oregon Dean of Faculties and most recently President of San Jose State College where he maintained leadership in the face of pressures from Black militants on the one hand and the encroachment of Governor Reagan and the chancellor on the other. He came to Oregon at a time of clear escalation of public hostility to the university, growing financial restrictions from federal sources, and heightened polarization on the campus which stemmed primarily from demands for student participation and shifts in university activities and priorities. As indicated earlier, the new president's initial pronouncements on the function of a university were not congenial to those championing the cry for change in the institution and the use of knowledge for societal change. It was also widely known that he was the nominee of conservative faculty at the university and that his positions on divisive campus issues in support of ROTC, for instance, were substantially at odds with campus militants. More important, the new president came at a time of substantial change in the political climate of the state, especially as it concerned higher education. The shifts in political winds became a major factor in shaping recent developments.

In the area of student participation, a late 1968 policy statement of the state board, although officially supportive of "responsible student participation," reflected the deepest fears of the larger community of the radical student population, especially SDS.[33]

Although the university moved ahead in the area of student participation during the 1968–69 year adding students to an increasing number of faculty and administrative committees, the pressures for a more important role for students continued. While the policy gave tacit recognition to the legitimacy of student participation, it is uncertain whether the adoption of the policy was prompted more by an interest in furthering the student role or in suggesting, in a circuitous fashion, that the university get tough when students adopt tactics defined in the policy as illegitimate.

The new state board policy reaffirmed the power of the institutional president (absolute), while recognizing his reliance on faculty, and the need to involve students in "deliberative and decision-making processes affecting students." [34] With regard to student involvement, the policy states:

> Students should be involved in the formulation of institutional policies, rules, and regulations governing student conduct and student participation in the affairs of the academic community. They have much to contribute to the deliberative process in many areas affecting their academic lives. And quite understandably, their commitment to the resulting policies, rules and regulations may be expected to be more meaningful if students have participated in their formulation. . . .
>
> The extent and the range of the areas of the academic world to be subjected to student-faculty-administration deliberation and decision-making, and the mechanism through which such joint activities should be carried on, are matters best left in the hands of the individual institutions. But the board ventures to suggest that the wider the range of shared concerns within the institution, the greater the sense of community which is likely to develop.[35]

While this would appear to be a positive step in the direction of student participation, only two lines later the tone of the policy switches to a coercive one.

> A range of sanctions of varying gravity is necessary to the administration of effective institutional rules and regulations. Sanctions may range from *warning* (notice to the student that continuation or repetition of specified conduct may be cause for other disciplinary action) to *expulsion from the institution*. [Emphasis theirs.] [36]

This commentary, coupled with an introduction stressing the need for the preservation of order and tranquility on the campus, suggest somewhat mixed motives on the part of the state board. Furthermore, just prior to adoption of the policy several members of the board had referred to increasing pressures from the legislature.

The suspicion that the policy may have been offered more as a suggestion to crack down on student dissidents than to extend student participation is given further credence by the "Discussion of Student Unrest," which was offered by the board's Committee on Academic Affairs as support for adopting the policy.[37] The "discussion," a lengthy combination of fact and fantasy, covers a number of issues but dwells

Innovation and Challenge of Change: University of Oregon 153

for the most part on the threat of student revolutionaries to the university and, perhaps, the nation. The opening page alludes, in order, to the role of student revolutionaries in: "the revolutions of 1848 in Germany and Austria; the toppling of the Imperial Chinese dynasty in 1911; in Czarist Russia . . . the overthrow of the Romanov dynasty"; and assorted disorders in Latin America, Japan, Korea, Indonesia, and finally, the United States.[38] Following this opening, the report draws extensively and selectively from the writings of national leaders of SDS and others in order to outline in detail "the threat posed by social revolutionaries (New Left)." [39]

As was pointed out earlier, the fears expressed reflect some of the misgivings of the outside community. The same may be said for some members of the university community. While these fears may be more general and more virulent on the outside, the pressures which they engender wield a strong influence on many university personnel. It is clear that many individuals have neither the capacity nor the will to withstand such pressures. Finally, what is true of many in the university may be equally true of the state board. Given their fears and those of the state along with the political pressures from the office of the governor or other elected officials, the evasion of their previous policy of noninterference in the internal affairs of the university was predictable. In addition, there has been a growing threat of direct intervention in the affairs of higher education by the state legislature, and legislative action has severely affected higher education in Oregon during the past few years. With regard to the potential for interference from the legislature, the faculty of the university adopted a resolution at its May 1969 meeting expressing concern over the trend toward "political intervention in the organization and administration of higher education in Oregon." [40]

The apprehensions of the faculty in this regard were prompted by actions of the legislature earlier in the 1968–69 year. In November of 1968, the legislature appointed the House Task Force on Higher Education. The stated purpose of the task force was "to give the Legislature a first-hand, on-the-spot assessment of the policies and programs in all our institutions of higher learning." [41] During February of 1969, the task force held hearings on five of the state's college campuses, including the University of Oregon. The hearings were unstructured and anyone who wished to do so could speak. The result was a seventy-page *Report* issued in April 1969. Not surprisingly, the bulk of the *Report* dealt with the issue of student dissidence and unrest. In those few chapters which were not directed specifically to this issue, there was an indirect focus on the problem of possible disorder. On more than one occasion, it issued warnings like the following:

> Legislative intervention is neither desirable nor necessary at this time and the action of the administration will make it unnecessary in the future. The Committee hopes that the day will not come in Oregon, as it has in many other states when legislative response is required to govern the conduct of students in our colleges and universities. . . . this necessity shall not arise unless the State Board of Higher Education and the college and university administrators fail in their responsibility to enforce existing policies.[42]

The fears of the faculty regarding legislative interference were warranted. Some of the actions growing out of the recommendations of the Task Force of Higher Education were clearly reprisals against the university. Among these were curbs on graduate enrollment and a limitation of out-of-state students. In addition to the direct reprisals, there was a general cut in the budget for higher education, and, perhaps most ominous, the passage of a law to give the governor emergency powers, including the right to declare a state of emergency, in the case of campus disorders. The law is similar to one in California which has been used to mobilize national guard and police on a number of occasions.

Events during the 1969–70 year substantially increased intervention by the state board in the internal affairs of the university. A number of issues precipitated the growing loss of autonomy. Among the most notable was the case of John Froines, Chicago Conspiracy defendant, and other faculty activists. State legislators and state board members publicly stated that the administration of the university seemed unable to make wise personnel choices and that they should see to it directly that controversial faculty members were removed.

The public image of the university continued to deteriorate in the press of the state during the year, and pressures to toughen the policy regarding student activists became more overt. By spring 1970 events on the campus elicited the ultimate response. Student demonstrations against ROTC and military and corporate recruitment were one thing, but allowing national leaders of the Black Panther Party and Chicago Conspiracy to hold rallies on the campus was quite another. The decisive events, however, were the massive sit-ins in the administration building. These were interpreted as the final challenge to the authorities. The governor intervened personally, and, under severe pressure, the president allowed the use of local and state police and national guard to forcefully take demonstrators out of the building.

The demonstrations had already gone on for three weeks continuously as the United States invaded Cambodia and students were murdered on the Jackson State and Kent State campuses. As did most campuses throughout the nation, Oregon terminated "business as usual." Substantial redirection of the university occurred, with whole departments recommitting faculty and student time and efforts to education on the issues of the war, militarism, and racism. In addition, there was massive political action including statewide efforts to sign End the War Amendment petitions.

The public again called for intervention in the university to insist that it stop functioning as a political action center. The result of some of this pressure was the state board's faculty conduct code discussed earlier. It was designed to control political propagandizing and disruptions of the normal educational functions of the university. The code was adopted even though the university president testified and urged its defeat. The adoption of the code underscored the conservative thrust of what was happening to higher education in Oregon. Universities were coming more directly under the control of the state board—appointees of the governor who won re-election in 1970—and the state legislature. While there was no constitutional decree, direct intervention in the affairs of the university was increasing as a precipitous rate.

The state legislature has continued a policy of selective allocation of funds for the university. Such a procedure gives it a lever for direct control of internal operations of the institution. The enrollment of out-of-state and foreign students is being restricted and graduate enrollments are to be cut starting in 1971. Faculty salaries are to be raised only slightly and lag behind the national increase in cost of living.

The recent history of the University of Oregon includes many of the difficulties and disasters of other state universities. Budgetary cutbacks by the state legislature and the drying up of federal funds has created a financial crisis. Political forces impinging on the university have moved in an attempt to curb faculty activities and to make the administration more cautious about hiring controversial professors. The university is undergoing a period of defensive reappraisal of institutional priorities, comparable to colleges and universities all over the country. After an impressive beginning, the university has joined the retreat in the face of intensified community pressure.

V
Alternative Models for Excellence: Western Washington State College

Of all the institutions discussed, Western Washington departs the farthest from the group norm. Located in a nominally rural area in Bellingham, a city of approximately 36,000 in the northwest corner of Washington state, the college is approximately a hundred miles north of Seattle and fifty miles south of Vancouver, British Columbia. The campus itself is set high on a hill overlooking Bellingham Bay and the San Juan Islands. The integrated blend of turn-of-the-century and modern architecture is uniquely suited to the magnificent natural setting in which Western is located.

In addition to the fact that it is located in a comparatively small city, Western differs from the other colleges we have discussed in a number of ways. It is the smallest with a total enrollment of 9,590 students. Its graduate enrollment is token, representing only about five per cent of the total. Of these graduate students, the vast majority are in education programs where the college has long excelled. Although they are growing, graduate programs at Western present no threat of overwhelming the institution in the way that they may in colleges where they are rapidly approaching a majority of the enrollment.

Western was originally founded as a two year normal school. Later it became a teachers college and in 1961 was designated a state college which changed its character to a more general purpose campus and reduced somewhat the emphasis on teacher training although it has not yet escaped its heritage. A large proportion of its students are still oriented toward teaching careers and its teacher training program is one which has long been a source of pride for the institution. According to Western's president and many others with whom we talked, the college has for a long time enjoyed a national reputation as an outstanding teacher-training institution. Now the faculty and administration are interested in extending that reputation to include excellence as a liberal arts college. Initial moves in this direction have apparently been successful inasmuch as the institution was one of the eighteen chosen nationally by a Columbia University research project to be studied because it had exhibited outstanding vitality in its development.

Institutional Growth and
Alternatives to the Multiversity

As is the case with almost all institutions of higher learning in this country, Western Washington is growing rapidly. Despite its growth, however, and despite the fact that it has begun to develop a graduate program outside of the area of education, its primary commitment has not been one that will lead it to try to emulate the model of the multiversity. The current emphasis is, and will continue to be, on undergraduate education.[1] Although the college has been authorized to offer the doctorate in education, it will not begin its doctoral program until 1974. A similar restraint exists in other areas regarding the development of graduate programs.

This restraint should not be taken as an indication of a lack of interest or commitment on the part of faculty and administration. Rather it indicates a realistic understanding of the resources necessary for graduate education and Western's potential for securing them. With two major state universities, both having extensive graduate programs, it is unlikely that Western would be singled out for rapid development in the area of graduate training.

Although its graduate program will not expand rapidly, its faculty, like that of many similar institutions, has shown an increasing interest in research and other scholarly activities. While the faculty had approximately doubled between 1954 and 1969, for instance, the number of publications reported by faculty during the 1968–69 academic year was greater than for the entire decade from 1954 to 1964. But while its faculty are not unambitious in the conventional sense, their ambitions are tempered by an interest in excellence within the framework of the limitations and goals imposed by its place in the overall educational plan of the state of Washington.

In the effort to make its mark as an undergraduate liberal arts college, Western has earned a reputation in the Northwest and nationally as an innovative and creative institution. Its commitment in this regard is articulated in a statement of purpose included in one of the planning documents issued by the college. The plan's authors note that:

> Great institutions do not remain static. They move, change, and progress as an organism, instilling within the individuals who are associated with them a sense of dynamism and purpose. . . . Accompanying this human force and achievement is a creative momentum, compelling new dimensions, fostered by the demands of students for enrichment of programs, and for more sophistication in subject matter.[2]

The reputation enjoyed by Western is relatively unique given its recent status as a teachers college and its unlikely setting in a comparatively isolated region of the rural Northwest. For this reason, its immediate past history is particularly interesting as it relates to the issues that are of concern here.

It was widely contended among those interviewed that the faculty at Western has always been better than one would expect given the character and mission of the institution. Whether or not this is true might well be questioned, especially given the well-known disposition of faculty and administration to overrate their own institution relative to others. Assessing such claims is made even more difficult by the generally obtuse criteria that one is forced to use. We can say though that there is every indication that on the usual measures there seems to be a continuing improvement of the Western faculty. A growing percentage of the faculty has the doctorate and virtually all of the nation's distinguished graduate institutions are represented. As noted earlier, scholarly activity is increasing rapidly. Furthermore, Western's attraction for better than average faculty members is not hard to understand once one has visited the campus. The natural setting and the aesthetic qualities of the campus, plus easy access to two major urban centers undoubtedly make Bellingham an attractive place to live and work. It may well be, then, that one can take the modest claims of our informants at face value.

According to the current president Charles Flora who has been at Western as a faculty member since 1957, the student body was fairly inert when he came. In a sense, it was what one could expect at a good "teachers college." But while this may have been true of the student body, he contends that it was not true of the faculty. He characterizes them as lively and imaginative and a source of stimulation for one another. An early president (circa 1940), finally fired for what was then considered radicalism, appears to have been the initial source of this active faculty. Though he left, the nucleus of faculty that he had attracted remained and continued to be a positive force. Interestingly enough, Flora feels that the continuation of faculty activity was the consequence of a most unlikely source—a president who was somewhat a tyrant—President Haggard. Among the more objectionable regulations enforced by the "old despot" was a ban on smoking and drinking. The current president believes, though, that these regulations had the unintended consequence of driving together diverse segments of the faculty in ways that ultimately proved uncommonly healthy.

When Flora arrived on the campus, smoking was confined to a special faculty smoking room. Since those who smoked at Western in that period were in a sense the renegades, the regulation had the effect of bringing these elements together from diverse sectors of the campus, and the room became a center of faculty power. Here, a coalition of what were then the most progressive forces on the campus could discuss issues, plan strategies, and work collectively to move the college in a progressive direction. Until the retirement of President Haggard, whom one administrator described as imbued with the "teachers college mentality," the ban remained in force, and the faculty smoking room continued as a center for faculty politics and interdepartmental exchange in ways that have subsequently disappeared.

In 1959 with the accession of James Jarrett to the presidency, the ban on smoking was immediately repealed and the institution of smoking room, once a lively source of faculty interaction and exchange, quickly dissipated. While this was no tragedy, the president feels that it had a kind of stultifying effect since it eliminated the kind of interaction across disciplines that is such a healthy force on any campus. On the other hand, this was balanced in part by the fact that Jarrett was apparently an innovative, student-oriented president and played an important role in the development of Western's current reputation. During Jarrett's presidency, the faculty is reported to have remained an innovative force, but innovation on the campus is said to have lost its "collaborative character." During that period, individual faculty assumed the initiative for a variety of innovative projects, but it was suggested that the potential impact of such efforts may have been reduced because of their peculiarly individual nature. Had such programs been thrashed about among a number of the faculty as they once had been in the smoking room, general receptivity might have been considerably greater.

The impetus for change has only recently swung, to some extent, to the students. One dean observed that, comparing Western with schools in other parts of the country, there was perhaps a three to four year lag in student initiatives for change. This is not to suggest, however, that Western students can be said to be "out of it," when compared with their counterparts in other sections of the state or in this area of the country. Quite the opposite is the case. The news media has often cast Western in the role of being the center of radicalism in the state, a role usually reserved for major state universities. To the extent that any student body in the state of Washington can be said to have an activist character, it is perhaps as true of Western as it is of any other.

The faculty, the growth and change in the nature of the college's mission, the new demands of students, the progressive administration of the recent past, and the recognition of the limitations inherent in the college's current situation with respect to location and its role in the state system have combined to move Western in new directions in an effort to meet its obligations to its students and the state. In this respect Western has been forced to develop unique alternatives which will allow it to be something more than an inadequate and disadvantaged replica of the state multiversity. The best known of these alternatives has been the development of the cluster or satellite colleges of which Fairhaven College was the first.

Fairhaven College

At the time that Western Washington became a general purpose state college in 1961, the decision had already been made that the college should make its mark as a first-rate liberal arts college. The decision was undoubtedly due, in no small measure, to the leadership of Paul Woodring, one of the college's most distinguished faculty members. Woodring achieved a national reputation as the Education Editor of *Saturday Review* from 1960 to 1966 and as the author of a number of books on American education. One in particular *The Higher Learning in America: A Reassessment*[3] contains the educational philosophy which was the guiding force in the development of Fairhaven College. The essence of this philosophy is contained in a brilliant argument for broad liberal education and against increasingly early specialization and the segmentation of learning into narrow disciplinary foci. Here he also characterizes the satellite college as one which combines the best features of a large university in allowing wider sharing of important resources (e.g., libraries, labs, and gymnasia) with those of the small college which develops a particular style and character of its own and which allows close faculty-student interaction in a comparatively intimate setting.

Fairhaven is the first of what are, as yet, an undesignated number of cluster or satellite colleges which will be a part of Western. According to its founders, the idea of the cluster college grew out of the pressures and problems which have come about largely as a feature of the massive growth in American higher education. Fairhaven, in particular, was established with a fourfold purpose to:

Recapture the best features of a small college while making full use of the facilities of a much larger institution. According to this first criterion, Fairhaven's enrollment will not exceed 600 students.

Provide a superior quality of liberal education at a cost no higher to either students or taxpayers than that of a conventional education in a state institution.

Create an atmosphere conducive to experimentation with curricula, teaching procedures, staffing arrangements, group and independent study off campus as well as on, and the new educational technology. Imagination and innovation are high-priority qualities at Fairhaven.

Enable students to make a greater contribution to educational planning, and give them a greater sense of participation. A number of them are continually involved in planning the curriculum and other features of Fairhaven.[4]

Neither the idea of such cluster colleges nor the purposes listed are new, yet the idea is unique to the educational system of the state of Washington and is not one that is particularly widespread in public higher education.

The idea for the cluster college at Western was first advanced in 1964 by Professor Woodring, then a member of the Long Range Planning Committee. The response of the committee was favorable and the idea was carried to the administration early in 1965. The reception of the administration, like that of the planning committee, was positive. The current president commented that, at the time, the administration "took the idea to heart in order to make its mark." Whatever the reason, the development of Fairhaven from that point was relatively rapid, especially for the academic community which is notorious for its inability to respond to an idea with anything resembling dispatch. The speed with which the program was developed was undoubtedly due in great measure to the strong administrative support for Fairhaven. One administrator noted such support was absolutely necessary if Fairhaven was to succeed.

In addition to the strong administrative support given to Fairhaven, it enjoyed an autonomy which has been both a source of strength and difficulty during the course of the college's development. It has been a source of strength inasmuch as it has given the college's administration and faculty the widest possible latitude for the structure and content of the curriculum, the rules governing the college, and the development of faculty. It has been a source of difficulty in that many of the faculty have shown signs of resentment over the fact that regular institutional controls have not been applicable to Fairhaven. This has the combined effect of placing Fairhaven in what is interpreted as a position of excessive privilege vis-a-vis the remainder of the Western community and of threatening the status of the institution with the possibility of diminution of standards, especially with regard to faculty whose employment and advancement will be strictly on the basis of interest in teaching and classroom performance which is of course always threatening where the character of the institution is changing from one emphasizing its undergraduate teaching mission to one more interested in

Models for Excellence: Western Washington State College 163

the development of scholarly activity, research, and perhaps, ultimately, graduate training. While such pressures have not been decisive in shaping the character of Western, they have not been without impact.

Despite some pressure, the commitment to innovation and freedom in Fairhaven has, if anything, increased during its first two years. From the beginning the student at Fairhaven has been required to take about two-thirds of his work in the college. Initially this was divided between area requirements in the sciences, social sciences, humanities, composition (credit was given the students' tutors when evidence was presented by other faculty), and Fairhaven elective seminars and independent study programs.[5] During the second full year of operation, however, there was a switch in which area requirements were abandoned altogether. The only requirement retained was that each student must have a course in the history and philosophy of science. The elimination of requirements was to allow the student more freedom in the development of his or her own individual educational program and to increase opportunities to participate in the seminar program.[6]

The determination of the curriculum of the college is also one of its more interesting features. Each faculty member determines for himself what his teaching load will be and how he will divide his time between seminars and traditional courses. In order to offer a course though, he must have approval of the faculty-student committee on the curriculum. The result of this arrangement has been that most of the faculty take responsibility for a much greater teaching load than they would in the regular college. Such commitment enhances their position within the college, however, as the primary determinant for promotion and tenure is a commitment to and excellence in teaching.[7]

The seminars are of interest because of their scope and the fact that students may organize and run their own with a minimum of faculty direction. Sixty-nine seminars, fifty-four run by faculty, were offered in 1968–69. During the second year of operation, there were 128 elective seminars offered. They included:

American Indian History	Drugs
Ballet	Dylan Thomas
Beginning Piano	Ecological Action
Chamber Music	Economics and the Novel
Computer Programs	The Good
Creative Writing	Human Ecology
Dance Workshop	Human Sexual Behavior

Life and Thought of William O. Douglas	The Political Boss
	Psychic Phenomena
Logic	Revolution and Violence
New Ballad Poets	Sense of Self
Organized Crime	Vista Tutoring [8]

Each quarter there appears to be an expansion of the program. The keynote throughout has been on maximizing flexibility and student participation, and what few restrictions existed initially have been progressively eliminated.

Although there is now some faculty antagonism, it was not apparent at the time of the founding of Fairhaven, though some contend it may have been present even then. When the initial plan was proposed to the Academic Council, the institution's most important governing committee, it was with the proviso that the council would retain control over Fairhaven's curriculum. According to both the president and the Dean for Academic Affairs, this would have been self-defeating and the administration granted the college autonomy. Its dean was to report directly to the president and none of the conventional relationships between departments and the various faculty and administrative control committees would apply to Fairhaven. When the trustees approved the development of Fairhaven in November 1966, they made it autonomous in curriculum matters, confirming the administration's decision. At this point the dean was appointed and the development of plans for the college was begun with state funds and a small planning grant from the Carnegie Foundation.

One of the features of Fairhaven which distinguishes it from many other similar enterprises is the extent of student participation in the development of policy and in the overall direction and planning of the college. After the necessary approvals had been obtained and the planning activities for Fairhaven were begun, five students were immediately added to the planning committee. Very shortly thereafter according to the late Charles Harwood, Fairhaven's first dean, it was decided that the planning activities would be facilitated considerably if they were Fairhaven students, so thirteen students were recruited for the 1967–68 academic year to comprise Fairhaven's first class. Ten of the thirteen remained during the second year of operation (1968–69) in which a freshman class of two hundred students was admitted, and nine of the first class continued through the third year.[9]

With the admission of the two hundred new students, the planning of the college had not been completed. In a sense, the first regular class is helping to determine what the character of the college will be. In this regard, a considerable amount of freedom can be exercised since the only two decisions about the college that are unalterable are that it will stress the liberal arts and that it shall be residential. Within these two confining limits almost anything is possible, and it has been the intention of the first planners to maintain maximum flexibility.

Among the major orders of business during the first year was the development of a constitution specifying the nature of the government of Fairhaven. In the constitution the college departed radically from the traditional government of public institutions. In addition, it is quite a contrast to the operating principles governing the Experimental College at Berkeley which was discussed earlier. The guiding principle that best describes the constitution is one of community government in the fullest sense. Included in the Fairhaven community are all of the following: Fairhaven students, the dean and the administrative staff (full- and part-time), the faculty (full- and part-time), and the regular custodial staff.[10] Each has one vote. Joint membership is a feature of all committees of the Fairhaven Community Government. The original composition of committees varied with the nature of the committee and its particular relevance to the several community factions. The Faculty Hiring Committee, for example, was composed of equal numbers of students and faculty. Curriculum committees, on the other hand, were dominated by students. There were seven students and three faculty on each of the two curriculum committees. The Faculty Re-Hiring, Promotion, and Tenure Board was composed of five faculty and two students. And so it went. It should be noted, though, that there had been no a priori decision that faculty would have the dominant voice in recommendations for promotion and tenure. The format of this board was the recommendation of the constitutional convention held to develop the provisional document and in which students had the potentially dominant voice. Students maintain this potential inasmuch as the document can be altered by the Fairhaven community at will. The important fact is not the final form that the constitution takes but the nature of the governing procedure. Here is an attempt to implement the basic features of the participatory democracy model that is at the heart of a great deal of contemporary student rhetoric. It is also important to recognize that, in this case at least, the development of the Fairhaven government along these lines was not a function of student demands but was envisioned as a basic feature of the college from the beginning. Support for this model comes not only from the students and faculty, but from the administration—both within and outside of Fairhaven.

Since the adoption of the provisional constitution, there has been a change in the document which further strengthens the commitment to a participatory government. The composition of all committees is no longer a matter determined by constitutional mandate. Committees now consist of "those who attend the first two meetings of each quarter." [11] The dean is responsible for calling the first meeting, and membership on the committees is open to all those with sufficient interest to participate. The effect of this change is of course to give students the potential for control of all facts of the direction of the college. This possibility apparently has not generated any substantial fear or reaction among the faculty of the college who appear committed to such ideals.

At the end of two years of operation, Fairhaven had what appears to be a record of successes, although more time will be required to really assess this. There are presently six hundred students, and full strength will be reached in another year. In spite of its apparent internal success, however, the operation of Fairhaven has not been without its difficulties, especially in the larger campus community. As noted earlier, a part of this difficulty has been as a consequence of the autonomy granted to Fairhaven. One observer commented that "no one objected to the idea of Fairhaven until it was clear that they were going to do something different." According to one faculty member, some of his colleagues have a disdain for Fairhaven. They see it as "a far-out place with freaky students."

Incidentally, we noted that there was a question about the different criteria for faculty selection and promotion. Although this might have been a source of real difficulty in theory, it has not been in fact, primarily because the Fairhaven administration has asked the appropriate department chairmen to assess the credentials of potential faculty recruited from outside of Western. As the dean points out in a memo to the president, "Although all of our faculty have been selected primarily because of their interest in and ability to teach, several are active specialists as measured by research and publication." [12] This kind of interaction with department chairmen has served to allay, to some extent, some critics' fears of "diluting the quality of the institution's faculty." The move of the Fairhaven administration in this regard was, however, pragmatic as well as diplomatic. As we were reminded by the

Academic Dean, the institution would be obligated to absorb tenured faculty from Fairhaven in the event that Fairhaven ever folded; therefore totally disregarding departmental interests would have been potentially disastrous.

The fact that Fairhaven faculty meet the traditional standards of Western's regular departments should not be interpreted as undermining the commitment of the college to undergraduate teaching, the strength of which is obvious in the rather remarkable policy which was unanimously recommended by the faculty and Policy Board of Fairhaven. They suggested that:

> Where, on the basis of the evaluation of a *tenured* member of the faculty, there is strong evidence that the teaching performance of the individual has materially deteriorated, an intensive investigation shall be made to determine the nature and cause thereof. If appropriate, the faculty member may then be warned that his service to the college is unsatisfactory and a written statement of the basis for this judgement shall be provided to him. The faculty member will then be given a period not to exceed two academic years to re-establish himself, during which period he will not be entitled to promotion and/or any increase in salary. Near the close of the warning period the faculty member will again be evaluated, on the basis of which either he will be reinstated without prejudice or under academic due process, proceedings leading to the termination of his appointment will be initiated.[13]

The creation of Fairhaven has also created some anxieties on a rather unexpected front—the student government. Although members of the student government feel that the Fairhaven students are highly regarded by the rest of the student body, some are bothered by what they see as a kind of exclusivity among the Fairhaven group. One woman student characterized it as a "break between the two student bodies." The extent to which this is the case is hard to ascertain, but, given the nature of Fairhaven, the charge undoubtedly carries some weight. Two-thirds of a Fairhaven student's coursework is taken within Fairhaven, and since it provides at least some extra-curricular program of its own and requires residence of all of its students, there are powerful forces fostering some degree of exclusivity. The development of its own sub-campus in a remote area of the larger campus may compound such feelings. The reason for fearing exclusivity appears to have to do with the fact that it is interpreted by some as weakening the position of the larger student body with regard to advancing student political interests in the governing of the larger institution.

Although it does not have higher entrance requirements than the rest of the institution, it has not escaped the student government that Fairhaven has attracted a group of students who perform at a level that exceeds by quite a large margin that of the remainder of the student body and that as an aggregate they seem to lean slightly more toward the political left than does the average student.[14] The interpretation of these facts varies, however, and there is certainly no consensus that they have important consequences for the aspirations and goals of the student body officers.

Despite these sources of friction, relations between Fairhaven and the rest of the college appear to have been quite amicable. This observation is reflected in the fact that the second and third satellite colleges are now being developed. Although there is no plan for the entire campus to eventually evolve into a series of cluster colleges, their role in the future of Western is undoubtedly to be an important one.

Expanding the Satellite Concept: Huxley College and the College of Ethnic Studies

After only two full years of operation, it is still too early to realistically assess the successes and failures of Fairhaven. The President of Western Washington commented pointedly that, "Fairhaven has to be exciting and dramatic right now because it is new. The problem is, how will it be after five or ten years?" But in spite of the fact that Fairhaven's success is still open to question, the Western community and the trustees had enough faith in the basic concept of the cluster college that they approved two additional colleges. The first of these Huxley College opened during the 1969–70 academic year.

Although it falls within the framework of the general concept of the satellite college, Huxley is hardly a carbon copy of Fairhaven. As opposed to liberal arts, Huxley is a college of environmental studies concentrating on an interdisciplinary program in the natural and social sciences. A combination of biologists and political scientists, physicists and sociologists, chemists and anthropologists, and assorted others will eventually bring their combined talents to bear on the problems peculiar to the human environment. Given the nature of the enterprise, it is obvious that the program will not be limited to undergraduate studies as in the case of Fairhaven. Nor will Huxley be residential. It will have only upper division and graduate students, and living arrangements will be the same as those of the larger college community.[15]

Only in its most basic aspects will Huxley parallel Fairhaven. It will enjoy relative autonomy, have a small student body, and tend toward exclusivity in much the same way that Fairhaven has. Like Fairhaven also, it will have a faculty which encompasses a variety of disciplines and will therefore avoid, to some extent, the problem of excessively narrow specialization and failure to communicate across disciplinary boundaries. As at Fairhaven, the accent at Huxley is on maximizing flexibility. Students are provided with a great deal of latitude in determining the course of their studies. The degree of flexibility is not as great as at Fairhaven, however, inasmuch as the nature of the focus, environmental studies, obviously dictates some restrictions.

Given the current public interest in environmental problems, moral support for Huxley has not been lacking. In addition, faculty recruitment has apparently been very successful. There are reputed to have been more than one thousand applications for faculty positions this year (1970-71). Like virtually every other institution in the country, however, Western has been experiencing a financial cutback during the last few years. Huxley is apparently feeling the pinch, and they feel they must be supported to hire seven new faculty in the next year (1971-72) if they are to really get off of the ground. Whether they will get the support which they feel is required is questionable in the face of Washington's lagging economy. The dependence of the state economy on Boeing, particularly hard hit by the collapse in the defense industry, and on the wood products industries, an early casualty of war-related economic disasters, makes the outlook bleak. Despite the state's financial hardships, however, the satellite colleges have at least been able to remain viable and to move forward at a modest pace.

The third in the series of satellite colleges the College of Ethnic Studies represents yet another departure from the model established by Fairhaven, although it, too, shares many of Fairhaven's basic characteristics. Again there is a separate program, a multidisciplinary framework, and a measure of autonomy from the larger college. Although it was ultimately approved, the College of Ethnic Studies had a more difficult time securing approval than did either Fairhaven or Huxley.

The chairman of the original Ad Hoc Committee for Programs on Minority Cultures, outlined some of the problems in securing approval for the new college. He first noted that there is a good general atmosphere at Western. While it does not have the resources that the big schools have, he feels that it is moving well now and getting good people. But while this is the case, it has not meant clear sailing for the idea of an ethnic studies college. This professor felt that the idea of the cluster college was ultimately a benefit to the ethnic studies program because it provided a precedent for initiating a degree-granting credit unit like ethnic studies. Nevertheless, he argues that there was a political backlash which imposed more stringent requirements on the College of Ethnic Studies than on Fairhaven or Huxley. In any case, the college began its regular program in the 1969–70 academic year. By the second year of operation it enrolled eighty students and had begun to develop its own faculty. Although the first dean has resigned, the college is clearly viable. While it faces the same budget restraints as Huxley, there is every indication that it will continue to grow, if modestly.

Hostility toward the idea of an autonomous ethnic studies unit was initially present at Western just as it has been at every institution which we have examined. Here the opposition may have been due in part to the militancy of the Black Student Union (BSU) in pushing for the program. The impact of the hostility was undercut, however, by the fact that such programs had already been established in other areas. In contrast to Berkeley, for instance, objections could not be raised effectively concerning the issue of autonomy. They would have to be leveled on other grounds. This, in effect, took the wind out of the opposition's sails, inasmuch as strident opposition might have made them vulnerable to the charges of racism or bigotry.

In spite of opposition greater than that faced by Fairhaven or Huxley, approval for the ethnic studies college passed the Academic Council with eleven for, five opposed. The faculty and administrators actually split their vote, seven for and five against. Then the students voted four to zero in favor of the new unit. While administrative backing had not been as vocal as for the other two satellite colleges, the Chairman of the Ad Hoc Committee felt that the administration was supportive. Legislative support was not entirely lacking either, and the new college was allocated $75,000 over the first two years for planning and development. While it is a modest amount to be sure, it represents a somewhat greater commitment for this type of program than has been forthcoming from other states with similar needs.

Western's president suggested that the legislature is supportive of educational programs for the disadvantaged. The commitment at Western Washington is the more surprising because as late as 1965, there were virtually no minority students. The impetus for minority programs came when the college became one of the first in the nation to participate in the Upward Bound Program, a federally sponsored project to bring to the campus high potential minority youth who did not meet the conventional college entrance qualifications and to prepare them to enter college with the eventual goal of obtaining a degree. The program flourished so well at Western Washington that its director was later named National Director for Upward Bound.

Enhancing the program of the College of Ethnic Studies is the fact that there is an assistant to the Dean of Students working full time on minority recruitment. Admission to the ethnic studies program is determined by an interview with an admissions committee made up of two faculty members and three students, one Black, one Chicano, and one Indian, all with equal voting rights. Although conventional entrance criteria such as grades are considered, they are not a paramount consideration in determining admission. The result of the policy of active recruitment and alternate admissions criteria has been some growth of the minority student body, but it has not been extremely rapid. It appears especially important though, that Indian students from local tribes, never a part of the student body in the past, have begun to come to the campus.[16]

It is interesting to note that in the public institutions of higher education (four-year) on the West Coast, the only autonomous "colleges" of ethnic studies are on campuses where there are cluster college arrangements, Western Washington and the University of California at Santa Cruz. Whether this will continue to be the case is questionable, but initially at least, the idea of an autonomous college of ethnic studies appears to be much easier to establish in such an ethos. Here different principles govern the arrangements of institutional governance and autonomous units have already been established. In such a setting, it appears that the idea fails to generate the kinds of fears that it does in other types of institutions.

Reforming the Remainder: Northwest Free University

As all of these events transpired in developing the satellite colleges and similarly exotic programs, the students at Western, most of whom are not involved in Fairhaven, Huxley, or ethnic studies, were not hibernating. Like college students everywhere, they have been more active in the past few years than at any other time within the memory of most of those on the faculty or administration. One professor, for instance, argues that leadership for innovation on the campus has shifted dramatically with the past few years from the administration to the students. Paul Woodring, a champion of educational innovation, stated that Western's students "are prone to work within the system." [17] Others tend to not see them in such a position of leadership, although they all recognize a change in the temper of the student body. One dean who was having special problems with the students and who resigned as a consequence puts it this way: "The type of student body president elected [1969–70] must indicate some dissatisfaction on the part of the students, but I'm not sure what it is."

The type of student body president elected was not unique. He was highly supportive of the student-developed Northwest Free University and fell into the general, if somewhat vague, category of student activist. He was the type of student who, when referring to the internal machinations of faculty and administration, talked in terms of "power blocs" and "authoritarian structures." He was obviously interested in seeing some fundamental changes in the nature of the educational system in general and in Western Washington in particular. In short, he is the type of individual who speaks for increasing numbers of Western students, at least insofar as he articulates their anxieties, their fears, and their distress, if not, perhaps, their solutions to the problems which they see in higher education.

The Northwest Free University was established by the 1968–69 student body president and other student leaders so that students could, according to one student body president, "express freedom—be totally free from the compulsion of the regular college." He personally hoped that the Free University would bring students to accept some responsibility for their own education, a hope that was shared by several other active students who were present during the interview. The Free University was to be a vehicle for educational reform similar to those at San Francisco State, UCLA, and Stanford. Courses would be organized by anyone with enough interest and ambition to make the effort. There would be no instructor in the conventional sense. The emphasis, as in other similar experiments, would be on the sharing of experience and knowledge and on learning together. There were no provisions for credit, and the operation would be administered primarily by students through the Associated Students organization. If all went as planned, the Free University would change the character of the college by providing a model for educational innovation. The consensus among those present was that it was a failure in this respect.

While no one could specify exactly why the Free University was a failure in educational reform, most seemed to agree on at least one point: that it was the type of student that the Free University attracted. The adjectives used to describe him ranged from "freaky" to "irresponsible" and commonly referred to disinterest in discipline. This led to the observation by one of the students, a woman who had been secretary-treasurer for the Free University during its first year of operation, that "any influence [on Western] coming from the Free U. is from the least Free U. things." She argued that it was the classes that were most rigid in their design and that relied on some sort of compulsion or fee, but not on the general responsibility of the participants, that were the only ones which were affecting the college. Her view, after a year of experience, was decidedly skeptical. Most of the other students vacillated between her position and one of cautious optimism that the Free University might be having some limited impact on the larger college. Whatever the extent of the impact, all seemed to agree that it had been in terms of individual courses, the most important of which was probably Reality of the Ghetto, taught by a team of Black faculty and students. They pointed out that this was one course that attracted several faculty and administrators, as well as the usual array of students and townspeople, and may well have had some positive effect on the development of the ethnic studies program.

Initially one of the guiding lights of the Northwest Free University was a former political science professor from Western Washington State College, a man whose separation from the college was itself a matter of considerable controversy. The thrust of the Free U. was considerably political, and there was concern about generating change in the college as a whole. Some shift has occurred over time. Bellingham has become one of the centers of a substantial counterculture and the "freaky" or hip types have increased in numbers and have shaped the Free U. offerings. It has become increasingly dependent on people only loosely connected with the college, and student interest seems to have deteriorated somewhat. In part this may be due to the impact of the cluster colleges which serve as outlets for many of the interests which once might have attracted students to the Free University. The Free U. is still viable and offers a range of courses and workshops and reflects the strong interests in the community which have made the Bellingham *Northwest Passage* the first underground newspaper committed to environmental and eco-action concerns. Whether or not the Free University has any impact on the larger institution, it may continue to operate, though on a reduced scale, much like the Experimental College at UCLA inasmuch as it still meets the extra-curricular needs of some members of the college as well as the community. This does not mean, however, that the students are an impotent force in affecting the overall policy of the institution.

Students and Institutional Policy

In regard to the whole question of student participation, Western is certainly among the most progressive institutions we have examined. Since students were admitted to the Curriculum Committee in the fall of 1966, the participation of students in the formal decision-making structure of the institution has been extended rapidly. While they do not participate in faculty meetings, students were admitted to membership on the Academic Council, the most powerful deliberative body in the institution, in 1968–69. The council consists of sixteen members. Eight of these are chosen by the Faculty Council. They nominate two candidates for each of the eight positions and the president chooses in each case. Four members are similarly chosen from the Council of Department Chairmen. The remaining four members are selected by the student government. In addition, students are active participants on many departmental committees. While there is currently no provision for student-initiated courses, this does not appear to be an issue here as it is at many campuses. Part of the reason may lie in the fact that such pressures are largely taken care of through student participation on departmental curriculum committees and also through the numerous opportunities for such activities in the satellite colleges.

Response to the student participation has been generally positive although not uniformly so. One dean who left, for instance, believes that students were admitted to the Academic Council because the administration was afraid to say no. It is his contention that the quality of decisions by the council has deteriorated with the ascendancy of the students. His opinion was not shared by most of the others with whom we spoke. The president, in fact, was unusually progressive in regard to the whole issue of institutional government. It was his stated belief that the institutional government had to be renovated:

> The size of the institution, and new forces have rendered it [the government] obsolete. Western is a community—not necessarily of scholars—including faculty, students, administration and staff. We need a community government recognizing the elements and each one's legitimacy. This will eliminate the Academic Council, the Associated Students, Administrative Council, and the Staff Council.

In spite of the progressivism of the president, which the students concede is genuine, they are not entirely happy with the progress of student influence on the affairs of the college. There was consensus that the real block to meaningful academic reform was in the office of one of the deans. Student leaders contended that it is not any structural barrier that prevents progress, but a personality in a strategic position. They felt that if they could either loosen up this particular individual by bringing pressure to bear through established mechanisms or get rid of him the major impediments to educational reform would be overcome.

The primary reason for student dissatisfaction with the office of the dean in question is in the area of personnel matters. It is in this office that the important decisions are made with regard to rehiring, promotion, and tenure. This is unquestionably the most sensitive area with regard to student-administration relations on most campuses, and Western is no exception. Interestingly, were it not for issues relating directly to the matter of re-hiring of faculty, one would be hard-pressed to find major points of dissension among the various campus factions. But in this area, Western students have very deep feelings of dissatisfaction with the way things have been handled during the past few years.

Some indication of the magnitude of the friction over personnel issues comes from students' observing that eight of the top ten professors, according to the student course survey published in 1968–69, were released. Needless to say, the students were incensed by this action. Considering the strong feelings of students regarding classroom instruction, it is not surprising that reasons like insufficient scholarly activity or research are not particularly soothing. The situation may have been somewhat mitigated by the fact that the survey was taken in the winter quarter and results were probably released after action had been taken on the contracts of the professors in question. In this regard, however, the students felt that those making the decision had not really paid attention to the teaching ability of the professors or had, perhaps, not renewed the contracts for political reasons. All of this, in itself, would have been bad enough from the student viewpoint, but the level of acrimony was raised by the fact that this action came after the Teacher of the Year had not been rehired, provoking an extended student protest and resulting in the resignation of the department chairman involved. The students' ire was somewhat salved by the fact that they considered it a "pretty good trade off" since they felt the new chairman to be one of the best on campus. Also, the students hired the teacher in question to be the director of the Free University.

Despite the fact that the first issue of the "Course Critique" did not have the desired effect, the students were optimistic about its use in the future. Even if the administration refused to consider the material in decisions regarding promotion and tenure, they hoped that a consistently bad critique would "leave lousy instructors without students. If he has no students," they said, "there won't be any room for him."

Protecting Institutional Freedom

Although it has had its share of sit-ins, nonnegotiable demands, and public hostility, Western Washington appears to have maintained an atmosphere of freedom to operate internally and has enjoyed relative immunity from outside interference. With regard to its internal operations, every indication is that a kind of administrative permissiveness prevails. The institution was described by one informant as "always having been underadministered and very fluid compared with other institutions." This fluidity seems to have served it well. Both in its ability to respond to the pressures brought on by population growth and the demands for increased education for the masses and in its facility to address internal problems, Western has an enviable record. Its vitality is perhaps a reflection of the youth of the president and its faculty, more than sixty per cent of whom have come in the past five years.[18]

The relative internal freedom is such that anyone who visits the campus cannot help but be impressed. But perhaps more impressive in this era is the freedom from outside interference which the institution has enjoyed to date. This freedom has been maintained in spite of the fact that, as the president pointed out, relations with the local community had been deteriorating. He characterized the state as fairly conservative and the colleges as fairly liberal, so that some friction is to be expected. In addition to the normal problems, the problems of institutional growth have led to some contests with the community over such issues as closing the campus to through traffic, building a temporary trailer village, housing, and so on. More important than these though, are the problems associated with the image of the college in the minds of the community. In this area, hair, political activism, and marijuana have been a source of displeasure to the townspeople. The addition of Fairhaven might have increased the hostility because the students have, perhaps, a little more hair and lean a little further to the left. A growing hip community, which many associate with the college, is also a source of antagonism. Despite the growing friction, however, and despite the fact that most of the trustees are members of the local community, there has been a surprising lack of trustee interference.

The arrangement of governing boards in the state of Washington is unique in the three states we have discussed and seems relatively unusual at a national level. Here each institution has a separate governing board of trustees. There is a coordinating council at the state level, but it does not have the power to make decisions with regard to particular institutions. Unlike California and Oregon, there are no central agencies which control activities at all of the state institutions. This fact in itself may be of singular importance in understanding the relative tranquility that has been maintained, even in the wake of serious disagreements and controversy. Given simple logistical problems, the governor or any other state official may find it difficult to inject himself directly into the affairs of individual institutions. In each case one would have to deal with a separate board presenting separate kinds of problems. The built-in limitations are obvious. While politicos could conceivably single out individual institutions for sanctions through the use of their funding power, they have not, to date, used such strategies. The result of existing barriers to interference has been that the administration has maximum latitude to handle difficult issues. No directives have been forthcoming at the demand of an insistent governor or legislator. Nor are such demands, even if issued, going to carry the weight that they might elsewhere. The separation of boards has prevented an arrangement where the governor is an ex officio member and officer, and perhaps serious escalations in hostilities have been avoided as a result.

Another possible reason for the lack of outside interference may be that the nature of the governing boards serves as an inducement for each board to adopt a protective role vis-a-vis the institution. The separate board arrangement may have set in motion a kind of healthy competition in which each board looks out for the interests of its own institution. Such is clearly not the case in many other states where particular institutions are frequently singled out for sanctions because the overall board did not think that their behavior was as good as that of other institutions falling under their control. If this is the case, it might be argued that the arrangement has combined the best features of cooperative and competitive arrangements. While there is a group for mediating and accommodating different needs and aspirations, each board is induced to promote institutional excellence and to protect its institution from outside interference, rather than to act as a source of such interference.

Of course all of this might be overcome if a particularly hostile group of trustees were appointed. In such an eventuality, the healthy aspects of competition might be seriously undermined by an emphasis on discipline and order to the exclusion of creativity and institutional development. The problem, then, is not entirely structural in nature. Structural factors can accommodate a healthy atmosphere, but they do not insure it. It may be, though, that the relatively good record of institutions like Western in dealing with the challenges and difficulties of the decade, will mitigate against an overwhelmingly hostile public and political reaction and a rearrangement of governing procedures. Whether or not this will be the case may be unrelated to what happens in the individual institutions. It may simply be a matter of political developments at the state and national level within the next few years. It is certain that Washington will not be unaffected by what happens in California and other states, but just what this effect will be is difficult to foresee. Two of the institution's administrators, for instance, interpreted the repressive actions of the 1969 Oregon legislature (see Chapter 8) as having acted as a buffer to the events in California and as having positive benefits for Washington. Apparently, they felt that that the Oregon actions had been interpreted as a reaction to the events in California by the Washington legislature, which had taken note and acted with greater restraint and rationality. Whether Oregon will continue to act as a buffer is a moot question. Perhaps the optimism of these observers is unwarranted, perhaps not. Given the success of Western Washington in adapting to the current needs of both the students and the state, however, anything that would limit institutional freedom could only be interpreted as a step backward.

VI
Exploring the Possibilities of Freedom: University of California at Los Angeles

The Multiversity in the South

The University of California at Los Angeles campus is in many ways a reflection of the community which it serves. Established in 1919, it is relatively new as major universities go, and its growth in the last two decades has been phenomenal. It has more than doubled in size to nearly 30,000 students making it the largest of the University of California's several campuses. The campus itself is a beautiful one with attractive landscaping, wide malls, and an impressive variety of buildings of both recent and early nineteen-twenties vintage. Even though the campus life style is seductively pleasant, there is an air of massiveness and impersonality which permeates the campus. This is due in part to the fact that the university is huge in terms of its student enrollment. In addition there are a number of features which combine to give the impression of even larger size.

Given the number of students which it accommodates, the campus is relatively small. There are only a little more than four hundred acres to accommodate facilities for the daily activities of some 60,000 people (including faculty, staff, visitors and one of the nation's largest extension programs). Further strengthening the feeling of immensity is the fact that most of the educational facilities are relatively centralized so that the bulk of activity takes place on only about half of the actual campus. In addition to the students, faculty, and staff of the institution, there are large numbers of people on campus daily for a variety of special conferences and institutes, many sponsored by the university extension, and a number of clients who visit the campus seeking professional services from the many centers and outstanding professional schools.

When one steps aside and observes momentarily the students and others of the campus community going resolutely about their business, rarely stopping to pass the time of day and rarely showing any sign of recognition of other community members one begins to understand the frequent comments about the lack of any sense of community that one finds on some campuses.

UCLA students are primarily commuters and they often come great distances to get to the campus which lies on the west edge of the sprawling city of Los Angeles. Further limiting the possibilities for the establishment of a traditional college community of any size is the fact that the university is located in the center of one of the more opulent Los Angeles residential areas, and there is no cheap student housing readily available. Those who do not live at home, in one of the fraternity or sorority houses, or in the dormitories are forced to look for more modestly priced housing at some distance from the campus.

Another feature of the campus that distinguishes it from its sister institution at Berkeley is what appears to be a difference in the general character of the student body. The most frequently heard adjective used to characterize the students is "apathetic," whether one is talking to faculty, students, or administrators. The organized radical contingent on the campus is very small both in absolute numbers and as a percentage of the university population. The appearance of the students is almost uniformly middle class, and the level of organized student political activity is relatively small compared to other major institutions.

In other ways, too, the students are a "mixed bag." Approximately one-third are graduate or professional students. At the undergraduate level, the school provides, along with the conventional liberal arts programs, a full gamut of professional and preprofessional training.

Ethnically, UCLA has the largest percentage of minority students of any major West Coast university. This is not to say that the Black and Mexican-American students are even nearly represented in percentages equal to their percentage in the community at large, but only to point out that by comparison with the other elite institutions in the state and on the coast, one finds greater representation. In addition to these two groups, there is a very large number of Oriental-American students, primarily Japanese, drawn from local Oriental subcommunities. Finally, the foreign student population of the university is one of the largest in the country.

The image of the campus as a refuge for apathetic middle class commuters is one that extends beyond the bounds of the campus itself. Students and faculty of other campuses often refer to it in such terms while also characterizing it as a "jock factory," referring to its athletic emphasis. In the eyes of the public it is often held up as an exemplar of academic virtue (that is, it's quiet) to be contrasted with that model of disorder to the north, Berkeley. In *The Academic Revolution,* Jencks and Riesman refer specifically to UCLA as an example of what they call "safe" colleges,[1] which fall into two categories: the church-controlled, closely regulated, residential college and the publicly controlled commuter college. The "safe" label is one that is taken from the perspective of an adult backlash reacting against perceived campus radicalism and disorder. The safe schools are characterized by their distinct lack of radical activism and what, from the perspective of the jaundiced-eyed outsider, is an appropriate seriousness of purpose. The authors point out that the apparent safeness derives from the fact that most of the students spend all of their time on campus in the classroom and have little time to become involved in extra-curricular activities. The time in the classroom "gives the adult faculty an almost completely effective veto over what the students do while on the campus."[2] The net result is an environment which does not lend itself to the formation of a cohesive university subculture of an apparently subversive character. It should be added parenthetically that Jencks and Riesman point out that the safe label may be very deceptive, as in the case of San Francisco State College.

While the preceding is the image that is projected to the public, it would not be fair to let this commentary pass without looking to some of the institution's more distinguished features. To begin with, its students are among the brightest (or most competitive) in the country by all of the conventional measures, and they distinguish themselves both at the undergraduate and graduate levels. The campus also has a number of the distinguished faculty and an overall graduate program ranking with many of the nation's finest.[3] In addition, it has a complete repertoire of professional schools, many of which are among the best in the country, and some of which are at the vanguard of curricular innovation for professional training.

The sense of apathy which is so pervasive on the campus may be, in part, a reflection of the whole southern California ethos where a fantastic growth in the general level of affluence, and continuing emphasis on economic mobility, have more or less keynoted the area's development. Without any hard data to prove it, it is probably reasonable to speculate that the student at UCLA tends generally to be more pragmatic in his outlook and is probably considerably more job-oriented than the student at Berkeley. In addition to the local ethos, there is undoubtedly a selective factor working which tends to attract the active student to Berkeley and away from UCLA. This selective factor includes both Berkeley's reputation as a center of activism and its place as the most distinguished of the state's universities. Its distinction often makes it the number one choice of the high school student who thinks of himself as a budding intellectual. This attraction is reflected in the fact that Berkeley must often redirect many of its applicants to one of the other university branches while UCLA, according to one of the vice chancellors, has not had to turn away qualified applicants.

Given this kind of an environment, it may seem peculiar to find that UCLA, among the established major institutions in the state, is at the front of the forces for educational innovation and change. But the fact is that UCLA's record in this regard, both in the variety of programs and in their general level of success and overall quality, is probably unmatched. In addition, the level and quality of student participation in the planning and development of experimental and innovational programs is equally impressive. Despite its record, however, UCLA, like each of the other institutions has been faced with virtually insurmountable barriers to progress. Even with a committed administration and a more constructive approach to vital educational problems than most, the battle to move forward has been a losing one. At best perhaps,

Exploring the Possibilities of Freedom: UCLA 183

UCLA has managed to creep forward on some fronts and has not regressed as far on others as have some campuses we have examined.

Combatting Alienation and Apathy:
Development of Educational Innovations

Innovational and experimental programs at UCLA can be divided into roughly four categories: 1) special educational programs directed toward the needs of the disadvantaged, who in this case are predominately minority youth; 2) ethnic studies programs designed to fill the gap in what is often criticized as a "lily white" curiculum; 3) programs designed to cope with the more general problem of curricular relevance; and 4) community action projects. The distinctive features of each of these areas and of the several programs and their development will be discussed in turn, but first we should make some general observations about the climate for innovation at UCLA.

As nearly as could be discovered from interviews with faculty, administration, and students who have been around long enough to provide a perspective, UCLA was not significantly different a few years ago from the rest of the nation's colleges and universities. Like most institutions, it conceived of its mission in relatively pedestrian terms, and the emphasis seems to have been on the usual improvement of faculty, facilities, and general academic program. The administration, while demonstrating no animosity toward the idea of innovation, appears to have lent little if any leadership along this line. In short, UCLA was little different than anyplace else—they simply had not given much thought to the issues that seem to be the most compelling currently. Curricular relevance, minority education, and the urban crisis were simply not central issues on the campus.

Unlike many other institutions, however, the initial involvement of the university in some of these issues was not the product of a massive upheaval in either the university or the local community, but rather seems to have been the result of a more general impetus of the civil rights movement in the early 1960s.

Beginnings of Special Education

The origins of involvement with the minority community were not, as is often the case, in the form of extra-curricular programs, but came through the rather unlikely channel of the university extension. It began, according to the Coordinator of Special Educational Programs, in 1961 with the idea of the extension sponsoring a series of cultural events or centers in the outlying ghetto areas of the city of Los Angeles. One of the unique features of the program for that period in history was the fact that ethnic community leaders were invited to participate in the planning at an Arrowhead Conference.[4] There the needs of the particular communities could be explored and alternative strategies discussed. Following the conference a series of exhibits, workshops, and performances were held, but the program began to wither until outside funds were found to revitalize it in 1964. At this time, a Ford Foundation grant allowed the program to expand into a series of programs for the various communities such as "The Negro and the Arts" and "Mexican Culture." Chancellor Franklin Murphy, who happened to be especially interested in the arts, gave the program much support.

About the same time as the Ford Foundation grant was procured for the Community Arts Program, the faculty began a Saturday tutorial program for minority youth. In this program students were brought from the Watts-Compton area to the campus with money raised from the faculty by passing the hat at a faculty meeting. A Black informant observed that the initial program was quite altruistic, and its intent was to upgrade the skills of the participants so that they could successfully enter college.

As a consequence of the Saturday tutorial program, UCLA was invited to be among the first participants on the Upward Bound program in 1965. After a contract was written and funded, "as soon as there was money," the Special Education Coordinator commented, "the game changed." The initial altruism disappeared and this activity entered the realm of the university political arena. In this context, the program's relationship to the rest of the university community changed somewhat since it was now officially a part of the university structure and therefore could not be readily ignored by previously disinterested parties. In entering into a contract of this sort, the university had formally committed itself to a kind of educational enterprise which would previously have been considered inappropriate for an institution geared to the intellectual elite. This departure from tradition was not met by uniform enthusiasm from the university community, although the implications of the program from the larger institution were not clear at the time of initial involvement. Most of the previous involvement of the university with the minority community had been through the extension division or through research projects like the Watts riot studies [5] in which the community had been the subject of study. These new programs added an entirely different dimension to the university's involvement. The impact of this particular kind of program is a point that we shall return to later in discussing the expansion of minority programs at UCLA. At this point, however, we should turn to another front where there were simultaneous developments of experimental programs.

University Response to the Cry for Relevance

By the fall of 1966 UCLA like every other major college and university was being subjected to increasing pressures from students or student factions to take positive steps toward undergraduate educational reform. The reforms demanded centered on the content of courses and their relevance and less critically, though not unimportantly, on pedagogical technique. Concomitantly there were moves within and without student government to give the student a more strategic role in the governance of the university community. The issues are linked rather critically because the students, at least the student leaders, were of the opinion that changes simply would not occur if the faculty and administration were left to their own devices. Therefore it became necessary to introduce a meaningful student participation in decision making at various levels.

At this point, in October of 1966 the first Convocation on Undergraduate Education was held at UCLA. The convocation, a two day meeting of faculty, students, and administrators, was held before the beginning of the semester to discuss potential solutions to the problems of the undergraduate educational process. The ideas discussed were fairly conventional, running to such things as small freshman seminars, independent studies, comprehensive examinations for the breadth requirements, nondirected majors, and facilities for campus political organizations. What is more interesting than the content of the conference is the fact that such a conference took place and that, at least according to local observations, an encouraging number were interested enough to participate. The reaction to the ideas did not appear to be particularly positive, but the convocation was generally seen as a breakthrough of sorts in faculty-student-administration relationships. Momentarily at least, the adversary roles of the various contingents represented appear to have been reduced in their intensity. In addition, the convocation appears to have set the tone for the implementation of a variety of novel enterprises during the year that followed. The most important of these programs were the Experimental College and the Committee for the Study of Education and Society (CSES).

Experimental College

One of the first attempts to create a special program dealing with the problem of educational reform was the Experimental College. The initial intent of the college, according to one of the co-founders, was that it could be a kind of "constructive activism" which could be used as a means for educational change. The idea that students could and should take responsibility for their own education was one of the driving forces behind the idea.

The suggestion to begin the Experimental College arose in the convocation earlier in the year but nothing came of it immediately. Meanwhile, similar experiments at Stanford and San Francisco State were given considerable coverage in the student newspaper the *Daily Bruin* and informal groups were meeting to discuss the possibility of such an enterprise at UCLA. The first attempts to do anything came in the form of ad hoc groups which met to discuss current issues of particular interest. The first of these ad hoc groups was led by a professor from the Political Science Department. The topic was leadership problems in Watts.

The groups continued to meet and then sought the support of a student group calling themselves VOICE which was described as "a front group to help people with ideas gain the use of facilities, etc." A meeting place was arranged and an organizational meeting was held. At the initial meeting approximately thirty students and one faculty member gathered and developed a tentative list for courses which was subsequently published. The Experimental College was launched in the winter 1967 term.

Although attendance and participation were relatively high during the first term, there were certain respects in which the program fell far short of the hopes of the organizers. The most important of these was the level of faculty participation. Although the college was to demonstrate the student's ability to assume educational responsibility, the lack of faculty participation severely limited the possibilities. What was needed in fact, were a group of faculty who, while having no formal authority, could nevertheless evaluate on an informal basis and in turn champion the cause of the Experimental College with the faculty as a whole. In addition, it was hoped that students and faculty could interact in a peer relationship rather than within the conventional authority framework. This would give both the opportunity for mutual exchange and exposure that was impossible in a university of some 30,000 students. In these respects the college was a failure.

One of the college's founders was quoted in the *Bruin* as having said, "We will show the University what kind of education we want by going ahead and doing it. In that sense the Experimental College will be a model for education that the University administrators will be able to refer to in determining curriculum changes." [6] After the initial experiences, however, it appeared that what was actually happening was that the university community simply was not paying any attention. According to the student body president, there was no administrative response —either positive or negative. This led to an attempt to solicit more participation by faculty and administration, primarily through appeals in the *Bruin* but also through direct contacts. The appeal used was that the Experimental College provided a kind of educational experience which was not available within conventional multiversity arrangements.

Despite relatively intensive efforts, the kind of support sought for the Experimental College never did materialize. Although the college asked for financial support and credit from the administration at one point, it was not authorized. One reason for this, according to a vice chancellor, was the fact that many of the courses were outside of the bounds of what the university considered legitimate academic concerns. Many of the courses which were not, were "simply repetitions of something already in the regular curriculum, but with less rigor." In addition, there was again the fact that most faculty were not willing to voluntarily assume additional duties along with their regular loads.

Despite the failures to meet many of the original objectives, however, the Experimental College continues to function. In part, this is probably because alternative types of programs, most notably the Committee for the Study of Education and Society (discussed later), while providing a mechanism for student-initiated curricula, are comparatively limited in their scope. Also important, according to a former student body president, is the fact that the type of people who were most attracted to the Experimental College were not motivated by the conventional pay off of credit hours and grades. Their interest was primarily in finding others with whom they could, in effect, "do their thing." Since the Experimental College served this function nicely, they were content to change the thrust of the program from one of a conscious attempt at educational reform to one that is probably best described as an unconventional interest group program. This may not have been true initially, but the establishment of CSES probably contributed to a sorting out of the different types of students.

Although supported by funds from the Associated Students, the Experimental College is not bound by any academic conventions. It has become an effective mechanism for "doing your thing." Like Western Washington, the unique feature of the continuation of the EC in this fashion is that it has adopted the form of the off-campus free universities in other cities without abandoning the campus. It is in better shape than many of these in that it receives some operating funds from the Associated Students thereby freeing it from one of the chief problems facing most free universities, that of money. While serving exactly the same function as the free universities now, it operates as a service to the student body in much the same way as any other extra-curricular activity.

Committee for the Study of Education and Society

At approximately the same time as the student group was planning the beginning of the Experimental College, another enterprise aimed at almost exactly the same problems was being planned. The Committee for the Study of Education and Society or CSES emerged out of a discussion between a dean of the Graduate School and a professor in the Physics Department. Local credit for the establishment of CSES is given primarily to the physics professor whom another professor described as "a sweetly opinionated and tenacious faculty member." The plan itself was very simple. They wished to set up a joint faculty-student-administration committee which would sponsor courses and seminars for credit studying "the current social problems of our society." The accent was on relevance and the topics were those which would not ordinarily fit within the curriculum of a particular department. According to one of the two initiators, they also wanted to see whether the student concern over relevance was justified.

The criteria for selecting a course were the following:

Exploring the Possibilities of Freedom: UCLA 189

1) They freely cross departmental lines; 2) They provide a mechanism for making University education relevant to our society; 3) They be innovative in format and subject material; 4) They possess a high degree of intellectual challenge; and 5) They be constructed and run by students and instructors in a close working relationship.[7]

Before submitting the CSES proposal, there were a series of meetings with sympathetic faculty members, but there were no formal discussions. Conventional faculty channels in the Academic Senate were assiduously avoided. Finally, the proposal was worked out between the physics professor, the Dean of the Graduate Division, and the Assistant Dean of Student Activities.

At this point the proposal was taken directly to the chancellor who indicated his support. In addition to moral support, there was a more tangible support in the form of an allotted maximum of five FTEs (full-time equivalencies) per quarter, thus providing faculty time. This meant that they would be able to sponsor a maximum of ten courses in any one quarter given the formula of one-half an FTE per course. Although they have never used the maximum allotted, the CSES has sponsored courses during each quarter since its inception in fall 1967.

Most of the political intrigue associated with CSES revolved around the establishment of the first course. Since that time, the Academic Senate appears to have more or less ignored them. The establishment of a course entitled Corruption did, however, generate some negative feeling in the Academic Senate. The course, developed by five faculty and five students, was approved by the Dean of Letters and Science and the Undergraduate Course Committee and then offered under the auspices of the College of Letters and Science.[8] When the Academic Senate was finally asked for approval of CSES, however, they were not happy, says one of the CSES founders, "because no one in CSES could be identified as responsible for what went on." This is a result of the fact that CSES continued to operate without any formal organization. It had no chairman, although one founder was generally unofficially cast in that role, and there was no formal membership. Anyone, faculty, student, or administrator. who wanted to participate could do so simply by attending the weekly luncheon meetings where course proposals and new course ideas were discussed. The result of this apparent lack of organization in terms of their official relationship to the Academic Senate was simply that they never received its official sanction. Also, there was a point of minor contention with the Academic Senate's Committee on Educational Policy. It was necessary, according to a faculty member, "to demonstrate [to the Committee] that a course could be both relevant and have content." Aside from such minor skirmishes with the Academic Senate, there was little in the way of any negative reaction. As much can also be said for positive reaction. One founder noted that their chief problem has been apathy.

One minor change that did occur within the Academic Senate that had an effect of sorts on the CSES was the formation of a Committtee on Educational Development (CED) which was an outgrowth of the "Kneller Report" (which we will discuss in another context) and was apparently intended to be something of a counterpart to Berkeley's Board of Educational Development although its mandate is not altogether clear. In any case one of the CED's chief functions is to approve CSES courses which formerly had gone to the Undergraduate Course Committee. It was suggested that this approval is pro forma, however, primarily because CSES has been very careful with its own approval. No CSES approved course has ever been turned down by CED.

Assessing the impact of an organization likes CSES on an institution the size of UCLA is a difficult task at best, but there are some interesting and plausible kinds of consequences of the organization's existence. Perhaps the most immediate is that it has probably been one of the chief reasons for the shift in emphasis of the Experimental College to non-curricular or extra-curricular matters. While the Experimental College began two terms earlier, both programs were, whether by intention or by accident, competing with one another in a very real sense. As a result, CSES probably siphoned off a great deal of potential interest in the Experimental College. Much of what the two organizations were attempting to do was identical insofar as they focused on the curriculum of the university. The strategic advantage of CSES in this regard is obvious. Not only were there a respected faculty member and dean at the head of the organization giving them an advantage in terms of their academic legitimacy and therefore access to academic credit, they had an inside track in their access to university decision makers and their resources. Subsequently, for this and for other reasons mentioned earlier, the Experimental College changed its focus and dropped out of the picture as a serious influence in the sphere of curricular reform. As one vice chancellor put it, students interested in the UCLA curriculum do not deal with the Experimental College any more.

Aside from its general impact on the Experimental College, there seem to be a number of areas in which CSES has had some effect. One of these is that it was one of the earliest enterprises dealing with curricular problems which found a place for full-fledged student participation. Full-fledged here means equal status, with student votes carrying as much weight as faculty votes. In this respect it appears to have been a force for countering resistance to student participation in other areas where arguments of irresponsibility or lack of suitable expertise might have been advanced.

On another front the organization may have had an impact as a catalyst for student action. One of the founders suggests that CSES played an important role in creating an "aware student body." Publicity surrounding the committee had been extensive, he said, and while "it really hasn't revolutionized course offerings in departments, nor even acted as a catalyst for change, nor even spurred faculty interest, it has provided a model of relevance for a number of student action groups." Such groups, operating at the departmental level have articulated demands for participation and curricular innovation in terms of departmental formats paralleling that of CSES.

As well as acting as a catalyst for action among certain student groups, CSES has had a strategic value for the university in that it can be an effective palliative for militant student groups seeking specific kinds of curricular changes which do not require the restructuring of the entire university. The classic example of this type of curricular demand is, of course, the ethnic studies program.

One of the first courses sponsored by CSES was The Black Man in a Changing American Context. The fact that there was an agency available which could and would sponsor such a course probably reduced significantly the possibility of the kinds of confrontations which have arisen in situations where there were no mechanisms for the immediate introduction of such courses into the curriculum. But over and above this kind of palliative effect, CSES's informal director felt that this first course in particular may have cooled off the situation with regard to distress over the speed with which a full scale Black Studies Program was being implemented.

The course was designed and run almost entirely by members of the Black Student Union (BSU), a fact that was corroborated by the official faculty sponsor, a professor in the English Department. It was only, according to him, when the course "had been sketched out and quite firmly shaped . . . when things were in penultimate form at least . . .

that [he] was involved as an 'authority figure,' " a title which he claims to have rejected on several grounds, "preferring the more appropriate designation of 'O.B.'—'Old Bahstud,' " a title which he considered more honest if somewhat less dignified.[9] The point that all agreed on is that the course required a monumental effort on the part of the students who planned it. While it was apparently a tremendous success, it did demonstrate to the students the kinds of effort required to develop a first-rate curriculum so that their expectations for an immediate full-scale program may have been somewhat mollified.

In addition to its other consequences, it is quite clear that CSES was responsible for generating a self-conscious student group among the Oriental students. Although, according to students working in the Oriental-American Cultural Center, there had always been a tendency for Oriental students to be isolated socially and intellectually from the rest of the campus, there was no conscious awareness of this fact by the students themselves. The result of a course sponsored by the CSES on the Japanese-American was the generation of a self-conscious nucleus of Oriental students who wished to cultivate an awareness of the historic and cultural heritage of the Oriental-American.

With regard to the university community's reaction to the program, it was pointed out that departments had never failed to give support for the program by releasing instructors. It was cautioned, however, that this probably did not indicate support, only that CSES had the money to pay for released time. As of this writing, the CSES continues to operate, apparently quite effectively, within its original framework of an informal, highly unstructured participatory democracy. Despite the past success though, there has been a persistent apprehension that outside interference in the form of political pressure to eliminate such programs, or in the form of tampering by the University of California Regents, may affect future activities. Participants have remained optimistic, however, because of the relative success of the local administration in providing a climate for educational reform while keeping the state's conservative political forces at bay.

While initial fears about possible legislative or regent interference with CSES may have been warranted, affairs took a positive turn in the 1970 academic year. The originator of CSES has now been appointed Vice Chancellor for Academic Innovation. While the academic community doesn't appear to be any more enthusiastic for the program now than it was in the early days, the pressures from the public for the reform of undergraduate instruction may have generated some unexpected outside support for certain types of innovation—which, of course, are those which address primarily the problems of undergraduate teaching quality and content without abandoning altogether the conventional academic format. In this regard, the tide may well have turned for programs such as CSES as long as the courses generated do not depart too radically from accepted conventions. In any case, as one informant put it, "the University of California is under pressure to work on undergraduate teaching [and] the Chancellor goddamned well will work to improve undergraduate instruction" as a result.

Summer Task Forces and the Further Development of New Programs

When Charles Hitch was inaugurated as President of the University of California in the spring of 1968, he appealed to the university community to address its resources to the resolution of the immense problems in the areas of race relations and poverty which were threatening to generate continuing massive conflicts between the affluent white majority and the predominately non-white poor minorities in the nation's cities. The appeal to do something about what he labelled as the "urban crisis," came at a time when both minority and white students were making the same appeal, often in more strident fashion, on all of the university's campuses. Although he outlined a "four-point program of research, public service, employment and student recruitment,"[10] the exact nature of the program or the thrust of its energies was not clear. To some extent it has remained unclear at the university-wide level, although individual campuses have begun some programs on their own which purport to meet this challenge in significant ways.

Among those which have begun to move, UCLA is probably the most active. During the summer of 1968 the new Chancellor, Charles Young, took the initiative at UCLA by appointing a Summer Task Force which was to examine ways the university could begin to meet the "social responsibilities" Hitch had referred to earlier. The task force consisted of a steering committee made up of members of the faculty, students, and administrators. The committee was asked to focus specifically on the following:

1. Development of special educational programs which, by intensive recruitment, special entrance criteria and extensive financial and academic support, would drastically increase the number of people from minority groups educated at UCLA.

2. Modification and extension of the curriculum to insure that . . . [the] academic program fully and accurately takes into account the special contributions of, as well as problems confronted by, the members of these groups in our society.

3. Examination and where necessary modification of the University's contractual and personnel policies (academic as well as nonacademic) to see to it that we are making the fullest utilization possible of the relatively untapped manpower potential which exists within these minority groups.

4. Organization of our resources to insure that we are making the fullest possible contribution, commensurate with the University's total mission, to action programs undertaken within the community to improve the quality of life and future prospects of members of minority groups residing therein.[11]

The Steering Committee was chaired by the top Black administrator at UCLA, an assistant vice chancellor, and included among others the Chairman of the Academic Senate, the Chairman of the Budget Committee, the Chairman of the Committee on Educational Policy, the Vice Chancellor for Educational Planning, and student representatives from the United Mexican-American Students (UMAS), Black Student Union (BSU), and the two student legislative councils (ASUCLA and GSA).

After they had met as a group, the steering committee broke down into smaller task force units each chaired by one of the student members on the steering committee. These smaller groups included a Task Force on Student Entry, one on Curricular Development, and a third on Urban Research and Action.

The Task Force on Student Entry's major contribution was the development of the High Potential Program, originally called the "high risk" program, but the name was apparently changed as a strategic measure somewhere along the line. In any case, the aim of the program was to identify potential students who had a record of poor academic performance but whose behavior in other spheres suggested a high potential for successful college work. These students were to be identified by other minority students already at UCLA and were chosen on the basis of such criteria as sustained motivation (successful job or career commitments or self-initiated efforts to secure advanced education), originality, creativity, inventiveness, initiative and leadership, sophisticated humor, poise, autonomy and self-directedness, and uniqueness.[12] No one individual was expected to contain all or even several of these qualities to be sure but these were the kinds of guidelines that student recruiters were to use.

The High Potential Program was initiated immediately and 100 students, fifty Black and fifty Mexican-American, were admitted, under the program in the fall of 1968. In addition to a special curriculum designed by the Task Force on Curricular Development to upgrade the necessary skills of the entrants, a special staff was provided for the program.[13] The program also included such features as peer counseling and tutorial assistance, and the instructional staff was composed of seven instructional specialists from local minority communities.

The longevity of the High Potential Program was not, however, what its developers had hoped. By the beginning of the 1970-71 academic year, High Potential had become one of the foci for suspicion, in part the result of the governor and other regents' assaults on such efforts by the university. In the continuing series of controversies over ethnic studies programs and more generalized attempts at curricular innovation, programs such as High Potential became the center of hostility. Such programs were singled out apparently because they were most vulnerable to the charge of erosion of university standards as a result of their unconventional admission procedures.

While High Potential seems to be on the way out, however, UCLA has not entirely abandoned its efforts in the area of minority education. The Educational Opportunities Program, of which High Potential is a part, has altered its recruitment criteria in order to reduce the risk of failure by incoming recruits. While EOP did recruit 150 new students for 1970-71, this represents a severe cut in the budget that had at one time been projected for such programs. The new recruiting procedure is also a significant departure in philosophy from programs such as High Potential. To the extent that the latter departure remains the norm, it should be noted that the potential of such programs for meeting the aspirations and long range educational needs of the minority community will be severely impaired.

The Curricular Development group, which designed the curriculum for the High Potential Program, devoted its major efforts to the planning of an Institute for the Study of American Cultures which was to become the eventual home for the various ethnic studies programs.

Included in the Institute are Centers for the study of Afro-American History and Culture, Mexican-American History and Culture, Oriental-American History and Culture, and a Center for American Indian Research. These will be discussed later in greater detail.

Initially devoting itself to the planning of the Center for the Study for Afro-American History and Culture as an "action-oriented" unit, the Urban Research and Action Task Force turned its energies to the development of a Board of Urban Research and Development (BURD) as a more appropriate organization for this particular mission.[14] BURD's chief mission was to be a mobilization and coordinating agency for action projects covering a broad spectrum of possibilities. Among these were such things as the already established Compton Project in which students from UCLA and Compton College work in the offices of the Compton city government in order to participate in community development and educational programs. The idea behind the project is a reciprocal benefit between the university and the community. The experience serves as a type of internship out of which emerge potential city employees, better qualified to address critical urban problems than is usually the case. On the opposite side of the coin, many of these interns have some ability to generate creative solutions to some of the area's problems by focusing the appropriate university resources on these problems and through the medium of collective approaches to the problems which are a part of the educational program.

In the area of research BURD was intended to involve itself primarily with mission-oriented research servicing the needs of minority and low-income communities. This kind of research although undertaken in the past was to be significantly increased under the new board. Although it is in certain ways the program most directly relevant to challenges posed by the urban crisis, BURD floundered and has never really gotten off the ground. One administrator summed it up succinctly—"BURD was designed and it sat on its ass!"

The problems faced by BURD are, in a sense, the problems faced by any massive or even moderately ambitious program which must mobilize a variety of interest groups and which has a governing constituency reflecting this wide range of interests. In the first place, the original governing board had thirty-five members chosen from among the faculty, students, and the administration. This in itself probably posed serious problems of consensus and ability to reach decisions within a reasonable time period. There was also the fact that each of these groups represented what were, in fact, interest constituencies in the university community and within each of these were subconstituencies. The result in such a setting is that consensus becomes an elusive if not impossible goal. Furthermore, there was apparently some concern among existing institutes and programs about BURD's effect on each of them. Such programs were not required to come under the BURD umbrella when it was finally established, but they were invited to share their autonomy at the "operation and policy-making level" in exchange for funding the organizational support.[15] Many, however, apparently saw BURD as a threat rather than a positive force. The attempt to organize and coordinate individual efforts was apparently interpreted by many as a violation of a laissez-faire policy which consensus indicates had served the university well until that time.

The original Summer Task Forces set in motion a greater array of new or innovative programs than had ever before been launched simultaneously. Along with the prodding at the hands of students, especially the BSU, the change of local administration and the expressed commitment of the entire university to commit its resources to the urban crisis seemed to be critical, catalytic events.[16] In addition, administrators at UCLA do not hesitate to note that they had their eyes on a number of other institutions which had experienced violent confrontations over many of the same kinds of programs which they have established. They all agreed that the situation has not been as volatile at UCLA as it has on many campuses, nevertheless, the potential for confrontation and violence always exists. The general feeling that seemed to prevail is that, if a request was legitimate, and in the case of minority programs there was uniform agreement in the administrative ranks, then the university had the wherewithal to produce the resources. Although financing has been a major point which many have used to claim an inability to implement such programs, the philosophy that seemed to hold forth in this case was that priorities could be reordered, and unallocated resources could be earmarked for these programs, without doing damage to the rest of the university community.

At the time that the new minority programs were initiated, funding was a relatively simple matter inasmuch as the chancellor had a great deal of money, in the form of overhead from various projects, which could be allocated as he saw the need. With cutbacks in 1970 and following, however, not only in the overall University of California budget, but in the crisis in funding on virtually every front, such funds shrank considerably. As a result, recruitment of minority faculty has not gone as well as many would have liked, nor have programs developed at the expected pace. The institutes remain funded, however, and their progress has been quite good compared to other institutions.

While many of those interviewed suggested faculty resistance to some of the minority programs, the consensus was that most of the faculty were not inclined to register a comment one way or the other, as long as they were not affected. In a university the size of UCLA, it appears that very few feel any direct impact, even from the implementation of "major" new programs. Probably the greatest ill will was toward High Potential and similar programs which some informants indicated were criticized because they bring in "strange" students, e.g., militants or troublemakers. To what extent this was true is certainly debatable, but there is probably no question that any program adding minority students yields a percentage of activists. From the administration's viewpoint, however, this was an irrelevant concern. The more important issue was the consequence of not bringing such students to the campus. Even though two students in the High Potential Program were assassinated on campus in January 1969, the negative reaction from faculty was minimal.[17]

In the summers since the original task forces were organized, new efforts along these same lines have been attempted. Most recently, in the summer of 1970, there was a Task Force on Financial Aid to consider such problems as housing, campus employment, and, generally, how the 8.9 million dollars in UCLA student fees get distributed in terms of financial aid. After the initial series of successes, however, the enthusiasm for the task force efforts appears to have dwindled, perhaps as a result of cutbacks in the areas of support for programs. In addition to the shrinkage in support on virtually every front outside of the university, it is reported that President Hitch, who had originally articulated the university's commitment to racial and urban problems, announced plans to go along with the austerity plans of Governor Reagan. For UCLA this meant a cut on maintenance and that all faculty positions vacated will go unfilled for the time being. This not only means a lack of wherewithal to move forward, but a potential move backward in the event that any faculty should abandon existing programs. Under the circumstances, the declining enthusiasm of almost all of those involved in the initial efforts is not difficult to understand.

Institute for the Study of American Cultures

As was already mentioned, one of the key actions of the Summer Task Force was to establish the Institute for the Study of American Cultures. This houses the four ethnic studies programs within a series of interdisciplinary research units. Although the idea of research institutes rather than full-fledged departments or schools might seem to some to violate the principle of the legitimacy of the programs, there was a well conceived rationale underlying the institute approach.

In the first place, the administration argued, and most students and faculty involved seemed to agree, the normal procedural sequence for establishing a new department in an unrecognized or nascent discipline is the development of such an institute with a later transition to a full-fledged department. Although the institutes cannot technically offer courses, the staff, whose appointments are in an academic department as well as in the institute, are able to teach courses relevant to the substantive area, such as Afro-American studies.[18] In addition, the possibilities for interdisciplinary degrees are such that there is in reality little that a department can do that cannot be done within the framework of a research institute. Following this procedural convention had the additional advantages of reducing serious faculty resistance in the developmental stages and of negating the legitimacy of any serious attempt to retard or stop program development altogether.

Secondly, and perhaps more important than the procedural question, is the fact that the possibility of appointment in a traditional academic department probably facilitates faculty recruitment. It is clear, according to those who have been involved in recruiting, that the shift from a traditional discipline such as economics, sociology, or history into Black studies, is not one which faculty who meet the conventional qualifications are willing or able to make without some misgivings. The establishment of ethnic studies programs in ways which allow a dual identification, or even a major identification with one's academic discipline, while allowing faculty to bring research efforts to bear on problems relevant to the particular ethnic studies area, is an important drawing card for faculty, especially minority faculty who are being pursued most vigorously for positions in these kinds of programs.

Aside from the comparatively well thought out strategies of organization to facilitate recruitment and to avoid the kind of internal political feuding seen at some other institutions, the most remarkable feature of the various institutes is the extent of student involvement in both the planning and the general administration. In each case the students have played at least an equal role with faculty and administration in the initial planning, and in some cases they have assumed primary responsibility. The Afro-American Cultural Center is a case in point. The BSU was responsible for a very large share of the significant creative work in the development of the program; and, according to all those in the administration who were in a position to evaluate it, the program was first rate. Commenting on the students' work, one vice chancellor noted that the students focused in really creative ways on the issue of academic legitimacy, which had been a continuous point of criticism. The result was a significant reduction in this criticism.

In the current phases of institute development, students continue to assume key roles. Most of the institutes are now run by steering committees consisting of faculty, students, and institute administrators. In each case, search committees for directors have had student members, usually equal in number to faculty and administrators. Student pressures have seen the addition of black and brown associate deans to recruit minority students. Furthermore, there is no question that students will continue to be represented on the governing bodies of the centers. The extent and intensity of student participation in all of these matters has kept things moving ahead with a minimum of disruption, despite the continuing sensitivity of the student to the possibilities of being co-opted by the administration.

Aside from the substantial successes, at least comparatively, the experience with the development of the ethnic studies programs has not been uniformly positive. Perhaps the biggest disappointment has been in the area of recruitment of minority faculty. Although there was an initial push which was probably comparable to any in the country, one informant characterized the current mood on this crucial issue as "we did it once," with no enthusiasm for continuing the effort. He sensed a "mood of suspicion and sullen resentment and none of the earlier élan" and suggested that, as far as support for minority programs is concerned, "crumbling of the wings is more dangerous than some forging ahead." There is an immediate problem, of course, in the restrictions imposed by the governor and the university president, but that has not salved the hurt of those who had hoped for something considerably better. Even though UCLA's success in recruiting minority faculty was probably better than most, it was not particularly impressive in an absolute sense. The bigger problem than past failures in the recruiting area, however, may lie in the future ability to build minority faculty through continuing recruitment and development through campus programs. The overall impact of this area will probably depend on the length of time the governor's austerity program remains in effect. A prolonged drought for the minority programs, more vulnerable than well established departments, could have disastrous consequences.

Faculty Participation in the Innovative Process

As appears to be true in most university communities, the faculty at UCLA seems least concerned with the issue of curricular innovation. In addition they appear far less receptive to the principle of student participation in the decision-making process than is the administration. Nevertheless, the UCLA faculty has not, as it has in other institutions, been an active reactionary force. Rather, insofar as any position can be said to be characteristic, it has appeared disinterested or only mildly receptive. However, most of the reflection of faculty sentiment comes from the faculty politicians who actively participate in the institutional governmental process and who are only a very small minority of the faculty. According to one administrative staff member, probably only 30–40 faculty members out of approximately 2,000 come to the faculty Legislative Assembly, and while more come to the Academic Senate meetings, they are still only a small fraction of the campus community.

While it has not assumed leadership, the faculty has not been entirely inactive. In the spreading fever over the questions of relevance and innovation, they constituted a Faculty Committee on Academic Innovation. The committee was charged, according to its first chairman, with proposing "ways of guiding the continuing growth of the University." Just exactly what this was to mean was left to the discretion of the committee and, according to the chairman and other members, a consensus about just what this charge entailed was never reached.

Internal problems notwithstanding, the committee published a report approximately a year and a half after its genesis.[19] The report, generally referred to as the "Kneller Report," came to be seen as a counterpart to the much more widely publicized Muscatine Report, *Education at Berkeley*. While the Kneller document was comparatively short, omitting much of the discussion and rationale included in the Muscatine Report, the two were very similar in both their format and substance.

The report contains a list of fifty-one recommendations covering a range from a request that the administration's Committee on Educational Policy address itself to the task of preparing "a document clarifying and redefining the purposes of the University," to the establishment of an undergraduate University College somewhat along the lines of Tussman's Experimental College at Berkeley, to strengthening the effectiveness of teaching, and to broadening student participation in governance.[20]

Even a cursory examination of the report reveals what a member of the committee called its "hortatory nature." He suggested that it had to be hortatory rather than a detailed substantive plan, because of the relative lack of consensus on the committee. This informant, who was later the committee's chairman, also went on to point out that the administration greeted the report with only lukewarm enthusiasm. According to him, the report fit in with administrative intentions insofar as they wanted a counterpart of the Muscatine Report and nothing more. It might be added parenthetically, that the report suffered from the same vices (or virtues depending on your position) as the Muscatine Report in that it too could be easily ignored by anyone who chose to do so.

It would be incorrect to suggest, however, that the *Kneller Report* has been totally without impact. Some of its recommendations were adopted. Perhaps the most important of these was the establishment of a Council for Educational Development (CED) which acts as an implementing agency for educational innovation and experimentation. According to the first chairman of the committee, things were moving along "pleasantly fast" with regard to implementing the recommendations. This is especially true with regard to the recommendations for expanded student participation in decision making, he contends. He adds, however, that student participation is proceeding much more rapidly at the administrative level than in the Academic Senate. In this respect it may be difficult to suggest that the *Kneller Report* was a significant factor inasmuch as student participation at the administrative level had been moving ahead for some time in advance of the release of the report. Students had long been full-fledged voting members of a number of administrative committees, but had only recently been invited to have one graduate and one undergraduate sit in advisory capacities on Academic Senate Committees. It should be noted too that they were excluded from personnel committees. Faculty resistance on this point can be seen in their reaction to two proposals advanced in February of 1970. It was moved that students be allowed to attend meetings of the Academic Senate and, further, that some students become voting members of the Senate. The attendance proposal was defeated 597–467 while the membership proposal was rejected even more decisively, 692–370. One administrator characterized the faculty as seeing themselves as a dam to the tide of student pressure. He observed that faculty appointments to study committees were older and more conservative. Referring to increased student participation, he noted, "that door's shut and students will have to bang it open."

Both of the committee's two chairmen were agreed on the fact that the CED had not been the most vigorous committee on the campus since its inception. One traces the problem again to the fact that there was a lack of a clear mandate. The powers which this committee has or does not have are not explicit anywhere in the legislation creating it. The result has been a time in which the committee had thrashed about primarily trying to decide what its mandate is. One chairman observed that it had been timorous because of the Cleaver incident at Berkeley. This, he believed, was a blow to its potential effectiveness. Regarding its performance to date, there was uniform agreement that the council had not made a major contribution in a way that the Committee on Innovation had intended, but the creation of the new post of Vice Chancellor for Academic Innovation may increase the vigor of such efforts.

Students as Agents of Innovation and Change

During all of this students were not just passive agents watching the machinations of faculty and administration. Despite their reputation for apathy, certain segments of the student community played active roles in almost all phases of the development. It is clear for instance, that the move of the administration in the area of ethnic studies and minority programs was as much a function of pressure by student groups as it was a response to the challenges of the president of the university and the demands of the larger community. Also, despite the widespread criticism of student governments as powerless or administration flunkies, the student government at UCLA has probably been given a more important role in policy decisions than is true of a number of other major universities.[21]

Part of the reason for the relatively important role of the student government is probably the fact that there is a well developed graduate student government which is particularly involved in the university's internal affairs at all levels. Because of the active role the Graduate Student Association (GSA) plays, the role of the Associated Students (ASUCLA) has probably been strengthened. In most universities, the graduate students are usually unorganized or nonparticipants. This fact often robs the student government of some of its legitimacy in that it does not represent a significant portion of the student body which has comparatively close relations with faculty and administration. Here, however, representation covers major constituencies better and participation is facilitated.

In addition to their sponsorship of such programs as the Experimental College, ASUCLA has been working actively to extend the impact of the undergraduate student in curricular and other policy matters through its Commission on Educational Policy.[22] Among other things, this commission is directing itself to the task of organizing undergraduate students at the departmental level so that they can have some impact on departmental decision making. Moving in this direction, they are adopting a mode of operation found quite effective by the Graduate Student Association. In addition to acting strictly at the departmental level, the head of the commision sees these groups acting collectively to affect university-wide policy once they have been established.

On a smaller scale, the Committee on Educational Policy initiated a program for professional idea-sharing about such problems as classroom techniques and course surveys to help improve undergraduate instruction. An extension of this kind of activity, but with a more radical procedure, is a student group calling themselves the Community for Awareness and Social Education (CASE). CASE developed in the immediate aftermath of the Martin Luther King assassination as an organization attempting to do something about white racism. Their primary effort in this regard was a Kerner Commission Follow-Up course sponsored by CSES. After that course the organization's emphasis shifted to educational reform. Their opinion of CSES was that it was new content in the same package. It was the package on which they decided to focus. Because their techniques were more radical departures from the conventional than those of other groups, they have had a hard time getting course sponsorship through such agencies as CSES.[23] The result has been that they have had to explore the possibility of exploiting the independent studies option to do what they wanted. This has been unsatisfactory, however, inasmuch as it requires a manipulation of the intent of the independent studies program which breeds reaction, especially from the regents. The issue of the use of independent studies is especially sensitive in the continuing conflict over the Cleaver course and later episodes at Berkeley.

Another CASE program initiated in the spring 1969 term with involvement in two courses was called the "critical university" and involved students enrolling in courses and then acting as continuing course critics. The students were supposed to ask questions which challenged the basic assumptions of the professor and to act as a continual source of feedback to him about where he stood in their eyes. How widespread use of this technique would be greeted in the university is a little hard to predict, but one suspects that it might not generate tremendous enthusiasm—at least among faculty. While the CASE students believed that the program had great potential, there was a continuing problem of recruiting new students into it, a problem facing all student organizations, even those with the greatest stake in educational change such as the BSU and UMAS.

Some of our informants have noted that the organizations have ceased to function as soon as they achieve their basic objectives, and this is, in some sense, true. What appears to have happened is that, in the aftermath of a victory, interest shifts from the particular organization to the new program which it sponsored. BSU students therefore became more active in the Afro-American Cultural Center and less active in the BSU. It may be that in the long run, this refocus of energies will have the effect of slowing down the pace of change after an initial period of relatively rapid development. Whether or not this is important depends, of course, on the long term objectives of the organization. If these objectives do not go beyond the establishment of a legitimate addition to the existing curriculum, then the organizations may continue to decline as important agents for change. If, on the other hand, the objectives are more general, there is likely to be a revitalizing of the organization after the initial work of establishing the new program is finished and new issues arise which arouse fresh interest and enthusiasm.

Innovation Without Confrontation

Almost invariably, the first question observers ask about UCLA is what is it about the place that has kept it from experiencing the kind of massive internal disorders of a San Francisco State or Berkeley. Although it has had some internal problems including a 1969 demonstration which broke up a Board of Regents meeting, the 1969 assassination of two Black students, and encounters in the Westwood community following the Trial of the Chicago Eight in 1970, the ethos which has prevailed has generally been one of progress without confrontation. This is somewhat surprising because with its huge size and some of its other features, it is very much like those institutions which have had continuing major difficulties. It does have some unique features though which have perhaps allowed it to steer a happier course than less fortunate institutions.

One of the features that distinguishes UCLA immediately is the fact that internal relations between the various constituencies, faculty, students, and administration, have not been characterized by the hostility which has been apparent at other California institutions. No doubt part of the reason for the tranquility lies in the fact pointed out earlier, that the university does not attract a large radical contingent to its student body. This cannot, however, explain entirely the maintenance of conflict within limits short of major upheavals or violent confrontation. Looking at the history of the various institutions, there is no question that the administration at UCLA has been more flexible and responsive to student concerns than at many of the other institutions. But more than this, the administration has assumed leadership in ways that are not often seen in university communities. At least equally, and perhaps more than any of the other institutions studied, there has been a history of anticipatory response to potentially difficult situations. Chancellor Charles Young has shown great skill at cooling out and dealing with student concerns. This kind of administrative action has resulted in a number of programs aimed at resolving some of the problems which university students find especially pressing. Even more important than the fact that such an anticipatory response pattern has been more characteristic at UCLA than other places, is the fact that concrete actions, which visibly address the grievances of the campus's many constituencies, have created an atmosphere of trust that one will be treated with honesty and candor, and that, if one's requests are reasonable, the university will make an honest effort to find the needed resources.

In addition to its apparent willingness to respond to initiatives, the administration has been highly accessible to the student which is particularly disarming in a university the size of UCLA. Given the immensity of the administrative work load, including an extensive travel schedule, this accessibility has meant, according to one administrator, a taxing schedule which many of the staff may be hard pressed to maintain simply because of the physical demands. On the other hand, the maintenance of an open door policy which may impose immense time constraints, appears to have more than paid for itself in preventing students, faculty, and administration from adopting a system of adversary roles where everyone outside of one's own constituency is seen as an enemy. Although it is true that the faculty have shown the usual conservatism regarding the issue of student participation in their decisions, the impact of this conservatism is probably offset, in part at least, by extensive student participation in the decision-making machinery at the administrative level. To be sure, there is some hostility among the various interest groups on campus, but the level of antipathy falls far short of what it has been on other campuses. In addition, students, administration, and faculty with an interest in innovation and academic reform have shown an unusual degree of creativity in finding ways to bypass the barriers to progress existing on most campuses.

The problems resulting from the assumption of adversary roles are no less trying for an institution when the opponents are administration and faculty than when combinations including students are involved. At UCLA administrative-faculty relations seem relatively cordial. Here one does not find the history of warring between these two constituencies that one finds at Berkeley and San Francisco State. Their cordial relationship at UCLA increases the potential for the successful resolution of difficult issues. When a serious issue develops in places where faculty-administration antagonisms have been institutionalized, students often find themselves used as pawns in the continuing battle of the other two factions. It is not surprising that student response to such a state of affairs is to adopt a position of universal skepticism and mistrust which may be one of the few rational ways of dealing with groups which are not likely to address the issue on its merits but rather are likely to consider an issue in terms of its strategic implications for the prior conflict.

In Search of Excellence

Interestingly enough, the facts that UCLA is comparatively new as major universities go and that it has labored from the beginning in the shadow of Berkeley may have been positive advantages. Its continuing growth may have built in a potential for flexibility which is nonexistent in universities with long-established traditions and internal political structures which have long since passed the point of optimum utility for institutional needs. But beyond this question of the internal structure of the institution, is perhaps a more basic issue alluded to earlier in the case of Berkeley—the issue of the image which an institution has developed of itself.

In the case of UCLA, there was never any question of its position in the academic world when compared to Berkeley. In the eyes of the national educational community and of anyone else who was interested, UCLA has occupied a position of distinct inferiority. This position may, however, be one of its greatest assets. It seems that being in a position among the finest in the country acts as a distinctly conservatizing force for an educational institution. When one occupies such a position, one does not characteristically spend a great deal of time in self-examination or considering what one can do to improve. Rather one assumes a posture of trying to maintain the position of eminence already established. Such a posture usually implies a program calling for more of the same. The rationale that prevails is, "if we hadn't been doing what we should have, we wouldn't be where we are." Occupying the position of the inferior, however, leaves more alternatives open. One can emulate the prestige institution and attempt to beat it at its own game or one can search for alternatives which will preempt the competitor by establishing new or creative bases on which to be judged.

In the case of UCLA, there is no question that it has attempted to emulate Berkeley in some respects. Historically, pressures for increased scholarly activity have grown rapidly as they have at all prestige institutions. On the other hand, however, the UCLA has given more of its time and energies to programs which might have far greater difficulty getting off of the ground in the more prestigious Berkeley because of their potential for tarnishing its image. In this respect, the institution with less prestige has less to lose and infinitely more to gain by engaging in an innovative gamble.

Another feature of the UCLA community which distinguishes it from the Berkeley campus, and perhaps from others, is the comparative weakness of the Academic Senate. This does not mean that it does not have technically the same power as at Berkeley, but only means that it does not appear to exercise it as vigorously. In this respect, there is an atmosphere of letting the other do as he will "as long as he doesn't bother me" that is not characteristic of many institutions. This again may stem from the fact that the collective faculty may not see its role so clearly as protecting the prestige of the institution by watching what is going on with a relatively careful eye. It would appear that the emphasis is more strictly on building one's own department, school, or research unit so that an entrenched, relatively powerful faculty political establishment has not had time to develop and to successfully implant itself as a conservative force vis-a-vis general university policy.

Relations with the Outside Community

As we have pointed out repeatedly in the preceding chapters, no university functions independent of the interests, pressures, needs, fears, and phantasies of the outside community. The impact of the larger community, both the local citizenry and the political community, is likely to be somewhat greater on the public institution than on the private. Given this fact and the state of affairs in California, UCLA has been remarkably free of internal tampering by outside community and political forces. While they have by no means completely escaped attempts at interference, they have existed in a state of relative immunity compared to the public institutions in the north. Part of the reason is undoubtedly that some of the political forces are located closer to other institutions, but this is certainly not the complete explanation. The fact that the administration of the University of California system is housed on the Berkeley campus is unquestionably a constraint on the freedom of the Berkeley administration to operate flexibly in the face of difficulty. There are other factors, however, which contribute to the comparatively cordial relationship of UCLA to the larger community among which are the lack of a history of radicalism, the position of the university as a cultural center for the city, the operation of the very comprehensive extension program, and the absence of an identifiable university community given the commuter nature of the institution.

The fact that UCLA has not had a history of radical activity, at least not activity that is visible, has put it in a sort of position of beneficiary from the difficulties at Berkeley. Despite periodic episodes at UCLA like the student assassinations in 1969 and the Angela Davis controversy, the northern campus remains the focal point for public and political antipathy. There have been no events comparable to the HUAC demonstration, the sit-ins at the Sheraton Palace, the Free Speech Movement, or even the hostilities arising out of demands for new university programs. Perhaps the most closely comparable episode at UCLA was the controversy arising out of the employment of Angela Davis, an apparently brilliant young philosophy instructor, who also happened to be Black and a member of the Communist Party.

To anyone familiar with the history of politics in this country generally but in Southern California in particular, the resulting display of outrage by California politicians and some sectors of the citizenry, was not surprising. Despite the demands for an immediate public exorcism and the regents' invocation of a law barring public employment of members of the Communist Party, both the administration and faculty at UCLA responded with a display of courage that is rare for any public institution. The regents, violating normal faculty review procedure, appointed a review committee in this case at the end of her first year. After administrative attempts to retain Davis failed, the faculty raised the money to maintain her salary, and she continued to lecture pending a court battle over the legality of California's anti-Communist employment policy.

The controversy reached its zenith with the implication of Davis in an attempted prisoner escape at the Marin County Courthouse which resulted in the death of a judge and three others. In the ensuing search for Davis, however, the issue dissipated as far as its implications for the campus were concerned. Interestingly, too, one observer noted a reaction which he described as relief that the issue had been taken off-campus. Perhaps like Berkeley, the faculty was willing to defend the issues of academic freedom and autonomy of the university inherent in the Angela Davis case but were not terribly enthusiastic about the particulars of the case which they found themselves defending.

In spite of the Davis case and other difficulties though, the variables mentioned earlier appear to have mitigated public antipathy. There is no question that the public has always made comparisons between Berkeley and UCLA and that UCLA has most often been viewed with positive sentiment compared with her sister institution.

Contributing to the comparatively good relationship with the outside community is the fact that for many years UCLA was a center for a very large proportion of the city's cultural activities. It is only recently that Los Angeles built its new county art museum and a center for performing arts. Up to this time then, the university served a useful function for the larger community, as well as for many influential community members, in providing a variety of these types of programs. At Berkeley, on the other hand, the contrasts are obvious. San Francisco has always had a rich array of cultural resources so that the university has not served the larger community in this sense. In the same way as it served as a cultural center, UCLA's large extension program reached many of the city's residents in every area, including the various minority communities, and it has continued such a relationship. It has also engaged in a relatively large number of social action programs which have great public relations value.

Finally, its location and the fact that it is not a residence institution have been key factors. Because it is in an affluent area, it has not impinged on the ghetto or minority communities in the way that many other major institutions have. Furthermore, the fact that the students are dispersed throughout the city means that there is probably a greater identification with the institution than is the case where the university community is relatively isolated from the remainder of the city.

The net result has been a university that has been able to move on a number of fronts without disastrous consequences. It has expended a greater effort for innovation than most institutions. Progress on the ethnic studies programs is probably as good as at any institution in the country. The number and significance of community action programs is increasing continually. We should add parenthetically that along with these developments, the prestige of the university as an educational institution has been growing by leaps and bounds. If nothing else, the experience at UCLA indicates that excellence is not incompatible with a healthy concern for the problems of the larger community.

VII
Tranquility to Trashing: The Transition at Stanford

Stanford University stands out among all of the institutions studied as the most distinctive on almost all counts. Located in the foothills of the Santa Cruz Mountains thirty miles south of San Francisco on El Camino Real, The Leland Stanford Jr. University exudes a patrician atmosphere. Stanford was founded in 1885 by United States Senator Leland Stanford and was dedicated to the memory of his only son who had died at sixteen of typhoid fever. A multimillionaire who had made the major portion of his fortune as one of California's "big four" railroad kings, the senator was characterized by Upton Sinclair as a man "who for forty years or more plundered the people of California."[1] Part of Stanford's booty was spent indulging an interest in the breeding of championship trotting horses at the nine-thousand-acre horse farm that was later to become the campus of the university. Today Stanford

University still occupies this immense campus, hence its nickname—the "Farm."

Those who visit the Stanford campus are likely to feel that the farm is hardly an apt characterization for such an impressive campus. Stanford is probably unexcelled in opulence. A combination of old sandstone buildings (some reminiscent of Spanish castles) and impressive modern structures, are spread across the instructional portion of the campus. Whether it is true or not, it seems as if existing facilities could easily cope with an enrollment twice the size of the current 11,000 students. On a normal day, there are never crowds moving in a mass from one area to another between classes, only small groups of students meandering leisurely along the gardens and arcades.

In addition to its impressive instructional and research facilities, the campus has a variety of student housing, including fraternities and sororities, a lake for swimming and boating, a championship golf course, stables, and an impressive array of auxiliary recreational and living facilities. It is not unfair to describe the setting as much like a country club. The terrace of Tresidder Memorial Union is reminiscent of an estate patio in Bel Air. In fact, the surroundings are so pleasant, that they sometimes make one feel ill at ease when comparing Stanford to campuses in other areas.

But all of this is not out of character, for Stanford's students match its facilities. The students are among the very brightest in the country by all of the conventional measures. Entering freshmen rank among the highest in the nation on Scholastic Aptitude Test scores. Although there are "no rigid requirements" for entry, a premium is placed on excellence in previous academic performance.[2] Most of its entering students are very near the top of their high school graduating classes. Of the 7,700 applicants for 1969–70, nearly 5,800 were not offered admission. Among these rejects were a substantial proportion whose predicted grade point average at Stanford, according to the Office of Admissions, would have been in excess of 2.79.[3] Of the 1,900 students who sought admission and were invited, 1,300 came,[4] suggesting that the institution ranked very near or at the top of the list of a large number of academically talented youth.

The high level of academic excellence demanded of the students aspiring to Stanford should not be taken as an indication that their interests are scholarly to a fault. Indeed, as is true with most distinguished institutions, a premium is placed on the student who exhibits a variety of desirable qualities including creativity, social maturity, and varied outside interests.[5] The result is a student who exhibits not only scholarly interest and competence, but an array of other interests including varying degrees of political involvement and activism. In this regard, the Stanford student appears to be at least as inclined toward political activism, if not more so, than his celebrated counterpart at Berkeley, although the object of his activism until recently was less often the university.[6]

Until late 1969, the situation at Stanford with regard to the student's relation to the institution itself was one which appeared to differ radically from that at Berkeley, San Francisco State, or for that matter from any of the other institutions studied. One got the definite impression that the feelings of the student toward the institution, even among student activists, rarely reached the level of hostility felt at these other schools. The interesting question here, of course, is why this was the case. Along this same line is the question of what precipitated the shift from the tranquil internal atmosphere that prevailed during most of the decade to the extensive trashing of the campus in February and May of 1970?

Attempting to compare Stanford with the other institutions studied presents a problem in some ways comparable to the proverbial comparison of apples and oranges because in many respects Stanford is a different world. It is private. It is wealthy. Its resources are magnificent, and its students overwhelmingly upper middle and upper class.[7] Although heavily endowed, it recently received a one-million-dollar Ford Foundation grant to "foster innovation." It has what are often circumspectly referred to as the "amenities." Behavior on campus usually reflects the life-style and behavioral norms of its constituents. Strident denunciations and vicious hostility have rarely emerged, even in the course of the most difficult controversies. A classic example of the kind of deference paid to "form" on the campus can be seen in the events surrounding the spring 1969 sit-ins at the Applied Electronics Laboratory. One San Francisco newspaper headline, describing the impasse between students and administrators, delivered the message—"Both Sides Polite, But Firm." It is probably safe to say that no California newspaper ever described disturbances at other institutions in the state in such neutral if not outright complimentary terms. The general atmosphere of the student meetings at the sit-in, seemed to be one of calm assurance that the administration, and ultimately the trustees, would respond affirmatively to the reasonable student demands. The tactic in this case, as opposed to many others, seemed not so much to be pitting the students' power against that of administrative forces, although there was surely some of that, as it was a demonstration of the students' seriousness of purpose. The student body president at the time, a central figure in the sit-in, added that "Student activists are convinced that they can win with reason." Although this air of calm and assurance obviously was not characteristic of later marches on the Stanford Research Institute (located off-campus), informants suggested that this style had usually prevailed. There appeared to be a different set of norms and tactical principles governing conduct at Stanford than at many of the other institutions.

Part of the explanation for the differences at Stanford lies with the fundamentally different nature of the institution. It is not only intellectually demanding, it is private and very expensive and, therefore, tends to draw students from a more homogenous background than does San Francisco State College or even, for that matter, Berkeley. Furthermore, the Stanford student's feelings about the institution may be quite different than those of the student of state schools because if he is going to Stanford he conceivably had his choice of any institution in the country. This is not as uniformly true of a school like the University of California where excellent students who have aspirations for other schools often attend because of the fact that there is no tuition. Stanford tuition is well in excess of $2,000 a year. We would only suggest here that one can reasonably argue that there is likely to be a much greater commitment to the institution per se in a place like Stanford than at a Berkeley, a UCLA or certainly a San Francisco State College. One might further argue that Stanford, in a sense that is true of none of the other institutions, "belongs to its students." Demands interpreted as illegitimate in a free public institution might well be cast in a different light here.

Assuming that such assumptions have merit, it is not difficult to conceive of an entirely different set of ground rules with regard to the resolution of internal conflicts,[8] not that such ground rules will prevent the eruption of serious difficulties but rather that they might temper enthusiasm of both sides for tactics which might be more readily employed in those cases where students have less commitment to the institution. In effect, there is some restraint here that does not appear to operate in institutions like Berkeley and San Francisco State.

Social conventions and restraints notwithstanding, the type of student attending an institution like Stanford is not likely to sit idly by if the institution does not respond to what he perceives as important needs. At some point, if the situation is bad enough from his perspective, he is likely to take some action. Apparently the situation became bad enough in 1965.

The Experiment and Its Failures

By 1965, Stanford, like Berkeley and San Francisco State, began to hear criticism about the nature of instruction and curriculum, especially the undergraduate curriculum. As in other institutions, the primary criticism centered around the issue of relevance. Many students saw what was happening in the classroom as irrelevant to their lives and aspirations. The critical issues of the time were not being addressed, nor were alternative approaches to their solution being discussed. The solution of some of the university's most vocal critics was to begin what was called the Experiment.

The Experiment was essentially a counterpart to the Experimental College at San Francisco State. It incorporated the idea of the free university within the confines of the institution. Apparently, the idea was initially successful and enrolled fairly large numbers of students in its courses. It received some national attention along with the Experimental College at San Francisco State, especially when one of its founders David Harris was elected student body president. Harris's platform was one of educational reform, but his radical position on other issues was a focal point of interest on the Stanford campus. His later activities as a leader in the draft resistance movement have kept him in the national news. The Experiment reached its zenith on campus during his time in office.[9]

At the time of its founding, the university administration had given only minimal support to the Experiment, according to a past student body president. After a series of verbal confrontations with the founders of the program, facilities were allocated in the old student union building. At the time, according to one student, "nothing else was happening on the campus." Although the right of the program to exist had been conceded, a series of later episodes undermined the ability of the organization to operate on the campus. The first was the reclaiming of the space allocated earlier. Arguing that the university required the space for administrative offices, the administration asked the Experiment to vacate its quarters. Although alternative quarters were requested, they were not received.

Aside from the lack of campus support and facilities, there were other factors which worked to undermine the Experiment. One of these, according to a student at the time, was the fact that many of the best courses were being incorporated into the regular university curriculum. A faculty member commented that Stanford was the most laissez-faire institution in this regard with which he had ever been associated. He observed that "any professor can teach virtually anything he wants," and he noted further, that this applied to courses considered a part of his teaching load. While other observers contend that this is an overstatement and that there is great variation among the several departments and schools, it does appear that the curriculum procedures are far more flexible than at most other institutions so that new courses can be added with comparative ease. There is no curriculum committee as such so that primary responsibility for decisions regarding curriculum lies with the department, making introduction of new courses faster than in most public institutions. Because of this kind of flexibility and the co-optation of the best Experiment courses, it was argued by some informants that attention was being diverted from its programs.

In addition to the fact that courses were being co-opted into the regular curriculum, other procedures were available for securing university credit for student-initiated courses. Approved in 1964 by the Committee on Undergraduate Education, the Undergraduate Specials Program was designed to meet the needs for special categories of courses which could not be offered under the regular provisions of the university. Among the kinds of things that might be done under the Specials Program are the provision of certain courses from the graduate professional schools for the undergraduate. As described in the *Bulletin,* these courses would not be technical in nature, but could draw on the resources of the professional schools to "enrich the curriculum for undergraduates." [10] Also included, however, were provisions for experimental and interdisciplinary courses.

Using the Undergraduate Specials option, the student can submit a proposal for any course which he or she feels worthwhile. Then the proposal is reviewed by a joint faculty-student-administration committee and, if approved, listed in the course announcement as an Undergraduate Special. Although it is considered the responsibility of the student to find someone willing to teach the course, the committee, if it approves the course, will often take it upon itself to find an instructor where the student has been unsuccessful. More often than not, according to the assistant to the provost, this turns out to be an advanced graduate student.

One of the problems with the Undergraduate Specials Program, like similar programs at other institutions, is that it has no independent funds with which to underwrite the costs of instruction of any course which means that the instructor must assume the course in addition to the normal load which he has already undertaken. As in other institutions, the enthusiasm of faculty for this arrangement is not overwhelming. Perhaps for this reason, and because the arrangements for offering courses are left to the discretion of individual departments, courses are not initiated in this fashion as often as they might be. Although an average of perhaps ten to fifteen courses are offered per term, it was estimated that in fact probably fifty per cent of the faculty and an even greater proportion of the students do not even know that the program exists. It was suggested that part of the reason undoubtedly lies in the fact that it is so easy for the professor to introduce a course, at least in some departments, that if a student convinces him it is worthwhile, he will offer it without going through the circuitous Undergraduate Specials procedure. Besides, no increase in course load is involved if he goes through regular departmental channels.

It has also been suggested that a third factor, university worry over its responsibilities for exotic courses such as sensitivity training or encounter groups may have had something to do with the university's withdrawal of the Experiment's facilities. If this was an issue, however, it was apparently never officially verbalized.

Whatever the feelings of the university, David Harris eventually resigned the student body presidency in despair of ever moving it, and the Experiment eventually withdrew from the campus in 1967. It did not stop its activities, however. The Experiment now functions as the Mid-Peninsula Free University, perhaps the most successful free university in the country. It has also shifted its emphasis somewhat, generating the greatest enthusiasm in the area of encounter group activities.[11] One dean noted that Mid-Peninsula served a very important function in this respect for the university. Specifically, it offered those courses considered "too far out" for Stanford. He estimated that as many as 2,500 students enrolled in encounter groups alone in the course of a year. The two institutions then, have reached a situation of mutual accommodation, each meeting a need for which it is particularly suited.

Both Stanford and the Free University seem relatively satisfied with the current arrangement. Although some of the founders of the Experiment might be unhappy at the turn of events, it seems to have met the needs of the students, at least as they perceived them. In this sense, the Free University appears to serve as a safety valve, partly relieving student pressures for curricular change and thereby avoiding the internal political battles and trustee reaction which have been so much a part of other institutions. The 1968–69 student body president, an activist, noted that there was little or no enthusiasm in the student body at large for the issue of educational reform. Although there was some criticism, he did not see it as "the issue that [would] mobilize the masses." The more compelling issues, he suggested, were those which involved questions of secret research and other kinds of involvement of the campus with the outside world. His prognosis in this regard seems to have been quite correct as we shall see when we return to this issue in the last section of the chapter.

Despite the lack of what might be termed a massive interest in curricular innovation, Stanford students, especially student politicos, have not been totally quiescent in this regard. Their efforts though, have been typically low key. In October 1969, a group of students and faculty submitted a proposal to the Committee on Undergraduate Studies for a Student Center for Innovation in Research and Education. The essence of the proposal was to create a committee of six students and five faculty which would facilitate student-initiated and student-managed "educational projects" by aiding students in their contacts with faculty who might be helpful, "allowing students to experiment with subject matter which is not of traditional academic interest," and encouraging them to engage in an examination of current university policies, procedures, and programs.[12]

In view of the fact that Stanford had been traditionally quite flexible in the allocation of academic credit for independent work and sometimes "off-beat" courses, the proposal was not a particularly radical one. Nevertheless, it did constitute a distinct departure from previous programs in that it provided greater opportunities for student freedom from direct faculty control and encouraged students to take advantage of the opportunity that such a program offered.

The response of the Committee on Undergraduate Studies was a relatively quick and enthusiastic endorsement of the proposal.[13] In order to implement the proposal, the committee simply established a Subcommittee on Student Innovation which was to be the student-faculty governing board of the Center for Innovation in Research and Education. The guidelines for the subcommittee's operation were simply the rules incorporated in the original proposal. By the 1970-71 academic year, the center was in full operation, and, according to one campus administrator, there were a number of courses being generated under its auspices.

Study of Education at Stanford (SES)

Of the five schools studied in addition to Stanford, four have undertaken a major study of the institution during the past few years.[14] Each of these has, in its own way, addressed questions of curriculum, long range planning, institutional goals, and internal government of the institutions. None, however, has been as comprehensive, or as ambitious as the Study of Education at Stanford.[15]

The Study of Education at Stanford, SES as it is generally called on the campus, grew out of a series of addresses delivered by former Stanford President J. E. Wallace Sterling in which he noted a need for a "fresh review of the educational programs at Stanford."[16] The last time that such a review had been undertaken was more than ten years before and then the focus had been entirely on undergraduate education. Even in this sphere the previous study had not included many questions which would have been considered relevant in this decade (e.g., institutional governance)[17] and had a distinctly different approach to the problems of undergraduate education than does the SES. Whereas the SES can generally be described as suggesting extensive revisions in the form of lessening or removing requirements, the 1954-57 study was characterized by its attempts to build in assurances of a liberal education by extending previous requirements or adding new ones. In this area, the earlier report had recommended that the English requirement be extended from two terms to three, that the requirement of a language or mathematics sequence be retained, and that area requirements be used to assure some additional exposure in the humanities, social sciences, and natural sciences.[18]

The Study of Education at Stanford was actually begun early in the fall of 1966. Preliminary work and planning continued until the winter of 1967 when the Steering Committee, which assumed the responsibility for conducting the investigation and the publication of the final reports and recommendations, was appointed.[19] This committee was chaired by Vice Provost and Professor of Law Herbert L. Packer. In addition, the committee included two department chairmen, professors from engineering, history, and physics, one graduate student each in medicine and physics, an undergraduate student in philosophy, and an associate dean who assumed the role of Staff Director for the Study. Insofar as possible for such a committee, it had been composed to give representation to the professional schools as well as the College of Liberal Arts, to the humanities as well as the sciences, and to students as well as faculty and administrators.

The Study of Education at Stanford (SES), as pointed out earlier, was far more comprehensive than the last study that had been conducted. Topics included in its ten-volume *Report to the University* comprise: undergraduate education; university residences and campus life; undergraduate admissions and financial aids; advising and counseling; the extra-curriculum; graduate education; teaching, research, and the faculty; international education; and government of the university. In addition to its broader scope, SES differed from the previous study in its most basic assumptions. The accent was on freedom where earlier emphasis had been placed on institutionalized mechanisms for insuring educational breadth in the liberal arts. The Steering Committee, in referring to its most basic premises, makes the following comments:

> Education at Stanford demands great freedom of choice and independent decision. This demand is less a mark of rebellion than a mark of success. A prescriptive academic program is founded on pretensions of eternal truth that we do not share. We hope that the students who come here have enough curiosity and independence of mind to suspect any "eternal" truths, and "infallible" methods, and "indispensible" knowledge.
>
> This freedom to choose what knowledge and what disciplines to learn may be Stanford's greatest gift to the student. For to choose he must think about himself and about the world in which he is involved. And this process of thought may contribute more to the student's educational development than any number of required University courses. His education is not imposed; it is his own.[20]

The committee then goes on to point out that the ultimate goal of such a philosophy is to develop an undergraduate whose work is characterized by independence. The process described again reflects the commitment to increasing freedom rather than restriction of the undergraduate:

> The undergraduate years should be a time apart, in which the student can reflect on his values and interests, guided by his own intellectual goals. At the same time the undergraduate years may involve for the student some degree of preparation for graduate school or for a more immediate career. In our attempt to resolve these somewhat antithetical goals we have been guided by the belief that, among other things, the undergraduate curriculum should lead the student to independence in his work. This independence will lead not only to personal involvement in subject matter, but to knowledge and to the variety of intellectual experiences as well.[21]

The recommendation in the volumes which follow reflect, to a great degree, this commitment to a philosophy of freedom from intellectual constraint for the student. As one might imagine, the principle is not one that is likely to meet with uniform and universal approval among the faculty of the institution.

Even before the *Report to the Faculty* had been released to the university community, feedback in the way of criticism of the principles outlined in the last few pages had begun to emerge. In an interview printed in *The Arena,* a professor of French blasted the SES as a "propaganda pamphlet."[22] The substance of his critique reflected a serious disagreement in philosophy with the Steering Committee of SES. His position, one that is undoubtedly shared by a portion of the academic community, was that whatever the goals of the institution, the "system should impose strong requirements."[23] He went on to charge that "SES is a panicky attempt to pacify violent change. It was not conceived as a long-range problem. . . . If this report is accepted, voted on favorably and instituted, it will cheapen the Stanford diploma."[24]

This debate over "standards," or variations on a similar theme, is characteristic of all of the institutions studied. The intensity of the debate varies, but it is an almost universal feature of contemporary American higher education. While the opinions in the student community are as varied as those in the faculty or administration camps, there are clear indications of an emerging consensus in favor of liberation from constraints and extended freedom of choice. Part of this emerging consensus can be seen in the nature of student body governments elected and in the platforms on which student elections are contested. At all of the six schools in this study, student body officers have expressed a strong commitment to the ideals of freedom and educational change. Indeed, no serious candidate for a student body office expresses opposition to either of these principles. At Stanford, the students have supported moves toward educational reform embodied in the SES with active involvement in the formulation of the report and a detailed plan for securing passage of faculty legislation incorporating the SES recommendations into the policy of the institution.

From the very beginning students were involved in the preparations and planning of the Study of Education at Stanford. Although three students, only one of whom was an undergraduate, were on the Steering Committee, the general level of student involvement was much higher. Student officers and others interested in the study participated in discussions out of which all of the various reports emerged. According to one member of the Council of Presidents,[25] some of the students were impatient with the time required in the development of the study and the consideration of its recommendations, but most were happy with the extent of student involvement and with many of the recommendations. On the other hand, there were many recommendations which were points of contention and which have undoubtedly prevented the implementation of many of the report's recommendations.

The procedure for consideration of the recommendations of the various reports has been that the Student Education Council (SEC) considers each of the reports and its recommendations along with the Academic Senate, a representative group of the Faculty Council (full faculty) which acts as the faculty's policy-making body. The Academic Senate is a body of fifty-three faculty while the Student Education Council has forty-four student members. Each of the groups is elected and there is a distribution of positions in each case to provide some assurance of representativeness.

Originally the Academic Senate had been planning to be the sole deliberative body regarding the Study of Education at Stanford. A group of students calling themselves the SES coalition argued, however, that such a procedure was unacceptable to students and that no decision should be made without some vote by the students. Out of this group came many of the students serving on the Student Educational Council.

Once the Student Education Council had been formulated, it had been decided that because of the combined size of the faculty and student groups (ninety-seven) they should hold separate meetings to discuss the recommendations. If there were disagreements in the votes regarding the proposals, then they were to be returned to the Academic Senate for further deliberation. When the first set of recommendations was considered in the spring of 1969, the Academic Senate approved all of them, but the SEC unanimously rejected half. Following the student rejection, deliberations began anew, but progress was slow and very little was accomplished. Then, in April, the deliberations were interrupted by sit-ins at the Applied Electronics Laboratory and Encina Hall (administration). Nothing more was accomplished during the spring of 1969.

In the interim the students adopted a new strategy for pushing recommendations they considered important. A system of floor managers was worked out so that blocks of recommendations could be handled by a floor manager and a small group of students and faculty whose views on a recommendation coincided. Each of these groups is responsible for formulating the presentation of the particular block of recommendations and for otherwise rounding up votes in the Faculty Senate in order to secure its passage. Given the system and the students' strategies for pushing proposals, there appears to be a good chance of passage for many of the recommendations which the students consider critical, but progress to date has been slow. While all this may be important, however, its consequence is limited by two factors: first, that final decisions are the prerogative of the Faculty Senate; and, second, that many of the recommendations fall far short of what some students consider ideal and may later be points of more serious divisiveness.

The first of the above problems is self-explanatory. The student committee, in the last analysis, serves in an advisory capacity. The distaste of students for advisory positions has been one of the most frequently articulated complaints on university campuses. While the faculty may finally accept most of the SES recommendations, it is unlikely that they will accept all of them, and it is precisely in those cases where the students are asking for the greatest change that the faculty is most likely to balk. Beyond the rejection of existing SES proposals is the potentially more serious problem of the shortcomings of existing proposals. As we shall see further on, many of the recommendations of the SES fell far short of the objectives of the student membership; this was particularly true of the report on the government of the university. Although the progress reports on the implementation of the recommendations of SES indicate quite a surprising amount of progress, few, if any, of the changes can be considered radical departures from existing institutional policy.[26] How students will react to the newly developing policy is a moot question at this point.

The areas where there are most likely to be serious disagreements are undergraduate education and university government. The problems which might arise in the area of undergraduate education are not likely to result from student rejection of the study's recommendations for liberating the student from some traditional constraints. Rather, some student leaders feel that the recommendations do not provide sufficient alternatives to existing educational opportunities. The new kinds of alternatives for which students may press are outlined in a series of proposals drafted by an Associated Students committee headed by a former student body president.[27] Included in the proposals were two experimental colleges, a white racism project, an urban extension college, and an institute for the study of higher education.

The proposed experimental colleges would provide the opportunity for approximately two hundred students to be freed from *all* of the constraints of the conventional university structure, for example, courses, grades, and structured classes; these students would join with a group of approximately twenty professors, ten from the regular faculty and ten from the community to "attempt to re-kindle the curiosity of childhood, to eliminate the dichotomy between living and learning, and to demonstrate that learning can be enjoyable."[28] Decisions about what is to be studied and how to go about it would be the prerogative of the student body, but the accent would be on new and different techniques and approaches.

The Urban Extension College is not so different in its fundamental principles from the experimental colleges except that it would be located in the city and would limit its focus to the problems presented in coping with the urban environment and the more general problems generated by this environment. The White Racism Project is another variation on the same theme in that it would be oriented toward giving the student practical experience in attempting to cope with a single problem, in this case white racism, and through the experience provide a preparation otherwise unavailable for teaching and similar kinds of positions.

The Institute for the Study of Higher Education would incorporate many of the principles of the other projects except that its focus would again be restricted to a particular area. In this case, however, enrollment would not be limited to Stanford students, but would include students from public and private universities around the country. Furthermore, it would use fewer resident faculty and more faculty with a broad range of perspectives from other institutions. The goal is to turn the students' talents and perspectives toward the major problems in higher education and to try to bring their peculiar insights to bear on them.

While none of these proposals is outside of the realm of possibility and while any or all might gather considerable support from a portion of the faculty, each of them is a radical departure from the kinds of recommendations incorporated in the SES report. It is one thing to suggest that "The Dean and Committee on Undergraduate Studies should be given responsibility for encouraging the whole area of independent studies and honors work" [29] and quite another to approve the kinds of programs advanced in the student proposals. Although the report goes on to suggest that opportunities for field work be established, it strongly emphasizes a selectivity of students and academic rigor that is absent from student proposals.[30]

Difficulties in the area of financial aids and admissions might have been expected over the issue of minority programs. Stanford, which has been an all-white campus for most of its history,[31] recently moved to change this situation. As is almost universally true, the expressed commitment of the institution and the actual program for increasing minority enrollments and special programs differ somewhat, but Stanford's performance has been better than most. Part of the usual discrepancy can be traced to the variety of reactions from the faculty, ranging from unrestrained enthusiasm for such programs to rigid opposition. Although the reasons for opposition vary, e.g., lack of funds, lowering of standards, and importation of problem students, the combined resistance to the extensive expansion of such programs is often formidable. The SES report recommends that priority with regard to financial aid resources be ordered so that minority students who qualify in the open competition be given top priority, with minority students admitted by special arrangement to come next.[32] After the minority students will come those students who rank highest in the open competition. Among traditionalists such an alignment of priorities is rarely well received though the SES progress report indicates that this is simply a continuation of existing policy; and, in fact, minority student recruitment does seem to be progressing at a comparatively fast pace.[33] As long as the number of students gaining admission under the special programs remains relatively modest, informants felt that opposition would not gain widespread support. The important question is the limits to which such programs might be extended. No one would speculate on what these limits might be, but they have apparently failed to reach a point which might generate any backlash.

Finally, there is the area that is likely to be the source of greatest disagreement, university government. Even before the SES report had been discussed, the recommendations in the area of institutional government were scored by the current student body president. We can assume that since he was elected and presumably his views were reasonably well known that he spoke for some constituency and that one might expect similar criticism of recommendations in this area from other students.

Of all of the recommendations of the Study of Education at Stanford, perhaps those related to university government were the most timorous. At a time when students are clamoring for increasing recognition in the form of participation in the decision-making procedures, the recommendations of the study clearly prescribe an advisory and secondary role for the student which is most clearly spelled out in the following recommendations:

> An appropriate number of students, *as determined by the Senate*, should be members of the Senate *without vote*. . . .
>
> It should be presumed, in the absence of good cause shown to the contrary, that students have a contribution to make to the work of each University-wide, school, and departmental committee and therefore should be eligible for membership on each such committee. *This eligibility should not extend to committees dealing with the appointment and promotion of faculty members.* . . .
>
> The appropriate number of students on such committees *should be determined* in the case of committees of the Academic Council *by the Senate's Committee on Committees* and in the case of school and departmental committees *by the faculties of the schools and departments.* [Emphasis added.] [34]

The committee which made these particular recommendations supported their suggestions with the rationale that the emphasis should not be on formal legislation, but should recognize also the importance of "informal consultation" and "post audits." [35] In a more general statement of the philosophy of institutional government which guided the subcommittee preparing the report, they comment:

> The title of this section ("Student Participation in Faculty Committees"), deliberately narrow in scope, may disappoint those members of the University who think that the spirit of the times requires some sweeping or even apocalyptic statements about the role of students in the governance of the University. We have no statements of that sort to make. In particular, we find no basis at the present time for opining about the concept of "community government," a vague phrase, quite without operational content, whose very vagueness makes it a rallying cry for some and a source of disquiet for others.[36]

This statement and the ensuing section drew a heated response from the student body president that expressed both his personal outrage and the sentiment that might have been expected from most activist or concerned students:

> I am one of the disappointed. This section is one of the most paternalistic pieces of nonsense which has been written on this topic in the last several years; it endeavors to sweep the major governmental problem of our times under a corner of the rug.
> What students are asking for today is not the right to give advice, but rather the right to help make decisions. We do not want to be dependent upon some all-faculty group which will set up committees, and review the student nominees to committees. This becomes particularly insulting when you realize that those committees are merely advisory to an exclusively faculty body which will review their recommendations and then make the final decision by exclusive vote of the faculty.[37]

It seems obvious from the foregoing, that student reaction to this kind of suggested arrangement for university governance will not be altogether sympathetic. On the other hand, it is not entirely clear to what extent the views expressed by the subcommittee in this case will be shared by the larger faculty. It is probable though that faculty sentiment is more likely to fall somewhere nearer this position than that of the students, especially in the very highly charged area of personnel matters. Whether or not this will become an issue at which there will be an impasse remains to be seen. For example, in 1970 students served on the Presidential Selection Committee, but sensed the tokenism and their lack of potency. It does seem, however, that this whole issue of university governance presents the greatest potential for impasse of all of the current issues.

All of the recommendations that have been covered in the preceding pages are simply illustrative of the kinds of issues over which there are likely to be fundamental disagreements. This is no guarantee, however, that events will erupt similar to those typical of the recent history of Berkeley. Quite the contrary, one would not expect them given the history of faculty-student-administration relations at Stanford. It does suggest, though, that the period of relative quiescence over such issues is at an end.

One of the students on the Council of Presidents remarked in 1969 that the very existence of SES may have acted as a palliative for students because they felt that something was being done on important institutional problems. She estimated further that as many as one thousand students, primarily undergraduates, were involved in one way or another with some phase of the study. This, too, may have had its tranquilizing effect. But now the study is finished and there are going to be many on the campus who will want to see some results. To the extent that these results fall short of what some had anticipated, there will develop a potential source of conflict. It seems clear that the mood of Stanford students, like that of students on other campuses, is one that is rejecting the alternative of further study of the problems. They are beginning to demand action, and they will be increasingly difficult to put off.

Black Studies at Stanford

Stanford is reputed to enjoy the distinction of having the nation's first degree program in Afro-American Studies. A former student body president points out that the Stanford program precedes Harvard's by one week. The interesting point is not so much that the program was first but that it was instituted at Stanford, an institution which had virtually no Black students enrolled until the last six years.

With the recent spurt in Black student enrollment, especially during the last three years with the inception of special admission procedures, there had been an increasing pressure for an Afro-American Studies program. Given the time it has taken other institutions to respond to similar requests, Stanford's quick response is surprising in some respects. In other ways, though, it is understandable.

The surprise comes because of the relatively small Black enrollment and the comparative recency of such requests on the Stanford campus. The speed with which the institution moved, on the other hand, is not surprising when one recognizes its comparative flexibility, especially when contrasted with state institutions having far more cumbersome procedures for establishing any new degree program. In essence, approval by the Faculty Senate was all that was needed. Comparable moves on any of the University of California's campuses would require approval by a variety of senate committees, a vote by the full faculty, approval by the president of the university, and finally, and also most critical, approval by the regents.

It is important, however, to keep Stanford's commitments in the area of Afro-American Studies in perspective when comparing their action with other institutions. They have provided for an interdisciplinary degree program in African and Afro-American studies but not for an autonomous department or college which would likely meet resistance at Stanford as it has at other institutions because of the kinds of implications that many associate with the principle of autonomy. For many, the notion conjures up an image of a sanctuary from which periodic forays and guerrilla attacks on the outside community will be launched. For others less paranoid, there are still fears that such programs will downgrade the standards or in some other way reflect adversely on the institution. The inclusion of African Studies, long recognized as an academically legitimate area of interest, has undoubtedly helped to pacify such fears.

In addition to its less complex bureaucratic apparatus, Stanford seems to have had other favorable conditions. In the first place, many of the African Studies courses involved in the current program were already being offered before the degree was approved. What was involved then was simply the establishment of a committee to oversee a new interdisciplinary degree. Furthermore, since most of these courses had already been offered, many for a number of years, the academic legitimacy of the program was not a serious issue as it has been on other campuses, and new faculty recruitment was not the key to establishing the program. It was suggested that any attack on the program would have been an implied attack on distinguished members of the faculty as well as the program itself. Given the absence of major barriers, then, the establishment of the program was not a difficult problem. The student body president at the time the program was established suggested that administrative enthusiasm for the program was heightened by the fact that there was always the implied threat that the Black students would walk out leaving Stanford an all-white institution once again. He pointed out that the threat was perhaps more serious here because students qualifying under procedures employed at Stanford could literally have their choice, "not only of any school in the country, but any school in the world."

Inasmuch as the institution has shown sufficient commitment to implement an Afro-American Studies degree program and to move ahead on special admissions programs, one might reasonably expect relatively cordial relations between the school's Black student body and the administration. There are, however, mixed reports on this question. An article in the *Wall Street Journal* highlighted what the reporter interpreted as some fundamental problems in the program from the point of view of the Black students.[38] According to the article, discontent seemed to revolve around two basic issues. The first of these was the "academic" as opposed to "action" orientation of the courses. The second was the fact that most of the courses were taught by white instructors.

The extent of the discontent is very hard to estimate. Although some students may feel very real discontent it has been suggested that the pervasiveness of this discontent is somewhat masked by the fact that the Black Student Union leadership is the most vocal on the issue and, given the hierarchical nature of the organization, one rarely hears from the rank and file. There was agreement though, that it is very probable that the feelings of the leaders are shared to some extent by the rest of the organization. On the other hand, a *Stanford Daily* report suggests a fairly widespread satisfaction.[39] If the discontent alluded to is genuine, the eventual push will apparently be for courses of an applied nature as opposed to highly abstract and theoretical frameworks.

At Stanford, this kind of package may be difficult to accomplish, at least at first. While the institution has initiated a program, it shows no signs of yielding on the issue of demanding the standard credentials (Ph.D. usually) for program faculty. One dean told us, for instance, that "Black Studies will develop at Stanford just like any other department." Another administrator is quoted as saying that the Black students "see the Black studies program mainly as a lever to get the school involved in local political action." [40]

In the meantime, however, African and Afro-American Studies is not a separate department. Students receive their degrees from established departments with an emphasis in African and Afro-American studies. Since instructional personnel are also housed in traditional academic departments, it would seem that a change in the posture of the university on the issue of credentials is not likely to obtain widespread faculty sympathy. Given the fact that individuals, then, will be screened by departments for those qualities which will enhance their general standing nationally, it is not likely that the kinds of faculty which the Black students are requesting will be recruited.

The problem of obtaining Black faculty to staff the program does not appear to be one that is insurmountable. The university is actively recruiting. That it has not done as well as some others is primarily a function of a late start. One observer felt that their commitment and resources are sufficient in this regard that the issue will lose its force in the relatively near future.

The news article in the *Journal* noted that students were skeptical about the director of Afro-American Studies, a well known Black scholar. Students were described as feeling that he would not be the type of individual appropriate to such a program because of a combination of age and scholarly reputation.[41] On the other hand, a former student described him as "very militant," a characterization which, if apt, has probably helped to allay some of the discontent of student militants. This does not mean that there may not be difficulties in store from time to time, but it does suggest that Stanford's position in this regard is almost certain to be better than other institutions where progress has been virtually nil.

Self-Satisfaction and the Absence of Urgency

One of the pervasive aspects of Stanford as late as the spring of 1969 was an unmistakable air of self-satisfaction. This does not suggest that individuals did not recognize problems which needed attention, rather that there was not the sense of urgency which one found on other campuses. Perhaps more than on any of the other campuses, except Berkeley, there is a habit of engaging in self-congratulation even in the midst of criticism. Any critique of the institution is almost invariably tempered by an allusion to the excellence which characterizes most of its programs.

In its own way, the Study of Education at Stanford attempted to overcome this institutional conceit by suggesting that the most important outcome of the study would be to establish mechanisms which would insure that the process of self-evaluation and constructive change would become integral features of the life of the university. The Steering Committee noted that the "first and most important recommendation that we have to make to the University is this one: The University should seek to sustain a spirit of self-examination and self-renewal, which can be supported by a variety of institutional devices" as contrasted to "a convulsive once-a-decade effort, followed by a lapse into accustomed ways." [42]

In the past, it may have been that the program of periodic examination was sufficient to address the critical problems on the campus. Now, as in the rest of the society, the demands for change on the campus will not tolerate such a leisurely pace. Until very recently Stanford had enjoyed a more peaceful atmosphere than has been true of many other institutions. While it had had more than one sit-in, it is only recently that hostilities have reached the point where the police were called to the campus. In the first confrontation of this sort, the Encina Hall sit-in over the issue of Stanford Research Institute (SRI), students left the building voluntarily without being subjected to arrest. Although some students were later arrested in an attempt to close SRI, activities were kept off-campus, a move which was interpreted as designed to maintain campus sympathy. The failure to push campus confrontations beyond the point of peaceful demonstration was interpreted by a past student body president as a purposive attempt to keep tactics from becoming counterproductive. He felt that activist students believed the bulk of the student body could be won over by reasonable tactics and that the administration was more receptive than is often the case. That pervasive student rationality was summed up in a piece of graffiti reputed to have been found on a wall at Stanford which declared, "None of us is infallible—not even the youngest of us!" [43] Nevertheless, it was felt that the institution was not moving fast enough in many areas to avoid difficulties in the future. Perhaps the most fundamental of these areas was institutional government. Unlike other institutions, this had not yet been a major issue at Stanford, partly because, although little has been granted in the way of substantive power, the institution continues to be further ahead than others with which it might compare itself. Students do serve on virtually all faculty committees and the Study of Education at Stanford used students throughout. There is not, however, a lack of issues which might provoke confrontation.

Undoubtedly the most inflammatory issue at Stanford has been the controversy surrounding the Stanford Research Institute (SRI). Stanford students, like students everywhere, had been pushing for a severance of university ties with military research and training. The Stanford Research Institute, though located off-campus, became the focus of student hostility shortly after the sit-ins at the Applied Electronics Laboratories in the spring of 1969. Since SRI was engaged in extensive secret research for the Department of Defense, some of it reportedly in the areas of biochemical and counterinsurgency warfare, students pressed the university to sever all ties with the institute.[44] In the considerations which followed, students marched on SRI several times and were engaged by local police agencies with some major routings, arrests, and confrontations.[45] Although the university did finally sever its ties with SRI, there were, in the meantime, attacks on the university aimed at accelerating the process of disengagement.

Later, even though ties had been severed, students engaged in extensive trashing of the campus on the day after the verdict in the Chicago conspiracy trial and during the events of early May 1970 in response to the U.S. invasion in Cambodia. SRI trashings have continued in the fall of 1970. One source of continued antipathy was the fact that SRI continued to function, ostensibly with some participation by university faculty, even though there was no longer any formal relation between the two enterprises. Another was the investment of university funds in enterprises offensive to many students. As a result of these events students had also begun to exert pressure for a reconstitution of the Board of Trustees (including student membership) and a role for students in determining the allocation of university investment funds. Stanford University President Kenneth Pitzer resigned due to "pressures that tend to distract or disrupt the educational process."[46] During his tenure in office, Stanford, a campus which had enjoyed comparative tranquility during most of the 1960s, had been occupied by the police on thirteen different occasions.

Although the ties with SRI have now been severed and the ROTC program is to be phased out, the issues of student participation on the Board of Trustees and in the determination of university investments have not been resolved. Although the trustees have been reconstituted to allow for more alumni positions and there are now some younger more liberal members, the extent of student participation is negligible.

While students are on some of the committees of the board, the extent of their influence remains questionable.

It has been suggested that the focus of the student activists may shift in the future to the areas of low-cost housing for minorities and low-income whites. Students contend that Stanford as the major landholder in the area has an obligation to these people especially considering the impact of the Stanford Industrial Park which has meant an influx of research personnel and junior executives leading to the destruction of much of the low-cost housing in the area and forcing low-income families to vacate. While the university trustees have indicated that they do not wish to become involved in this issue, it appears that it may be next on the student agenda. In effect, this problem, along with the issue of Stanford Research Institute and others like it, is only peripherally related to the internal life of the university. As these are resolved or fail to be resolved, however, it has been suggested that the students will look inward more critically than they have in the past.

As this introspective movement continues, it may be better handled, but it will probably be no less traumatic for Stanford than for other universities. Among the various constituencies, there are mixed views regarding which groups provide innovative leadership and which serve as barriers to change. None, except perhaps the faculty, appears to be particularly inhibitive but then neither do any of the groups appear to exercise vigorous leadership. The general ethos that continues, despite difficulties, is one of disinterest. While one administrator was severely critical of the trustees, a former student body president characterized them as no more conservative than anyone else. From his point of view, the faculty were the chief barrier to extensive change. He argued, though, that the difference between an institution like Berkeley and one like Stanford is that relations between the various constituencies are not as strained at Stanford. "Students at Stanford," he said, "are not willing to attack the faculty." Unlike Berkeley, all of the professors at Stanford who are not associated with a graduate professional school have some responsibility for teaching undergraduates. Furthermore, the faculty-student ratio is much better so that exposure and interaction are qualitatively different. These are important considerations on all the campuses, and few have so favorable a situation in this regard as Stanford. This in itself might not be enough to maintain the general good will of students, but it appears that Stanford's capacity to institute change and its willingness to consider alternatives are perhaps equal to those of any other university.[47] It has the added advantage of a considerably less bureaucratized system and enjoys immunity from the worst plague of all—legislative interference.

The importance of this last consideration cannot be overemphasized. Given the nature of the political climate regarding students, there is almost no possibility of a reconciliation between the government and the academic community in some states. In most others, where the situation has not deteriorated to the extent that it has in California, developments are leading in that direction. Private institutions like Stanford are compelled, however, to assume a different position regarding students and their demands. Although the trustees may be conservative, they are usually interested in the institution in ways not characteristic of many state boards whose role is becoming increasingly defined as a protector of community interests. In the case of Stanford, the trustees' role includes doing everything that they can to insure that the general level of excellence is not only preserved but enhanced. In this respect, students are viewed as an asset to be recruited for virtues that often characterize the student activist. In the public institution, these same characteristics are viewed as a liability, and there appears to be a more uniform policy of suppressing students when they press grievances rather than of meeting such grievances relatively straightforwardly and attempting to deal with them to the students' satisfaction. Perhaps the major factor which could alter the nature of the relationship at Stanford would be a serious cut in income from private donors specifically because of a negative response to student activism or the university's posture vis-a-vis the students. At the moment there does not appear to be such a mood among Stanford patrons. Furthermore, the institution and its benefactors alike may look to the north for lessons in how not to deal with students. To the extent that they do, perhaps there is the potential for flexibility in the approach to the solution of problems that would allow Stanford to emerge comparatively unscathed.

VIII
Political Processes and Institutional Change

In the popular literature as well as in scholarly commentary on the contemporary university crisis, there are certain common features which are addressed as key contributors to the current problems in colleges and universities. Among these are rapid growth, size, and impersonality of the institutions along with a shift in emphasis from undergraduate education. It is argued, for instance, that the mammoth size of contemporary institutions and the attendant phenomena of huge classes and relative impersonality of the institutions have been prime factors in contributing to student rancor. While the statement certainly has elements of truth, an examination of the institutions in this study suggest that the extent to which it is true is vastly overstated. A comparison of almost any of the institutions in question will indicate the extent to which this is the case. UCLA, for instance, the largest of the institutions, appears to have achieved the best record in dealing with the broad range of student concerns among the six colleges and universities studied.

Graduate enrollment per se would seem to have equally little bearing on what happens. Stanford, for instance, has by far the largest percentage of graduate students of any of the institutions studied with forty-seven per cent. Berkeley and UCLA are almost identical with thirty-six and thirty-four per cent respectively, yet their problems, though similar, have been dealt with in widely divergent ways, with considerably different results. Berkeley remained rigid and inflexible and has paid the price with a continuing crisis. UCLA has been able to maneuver effectively within the broad limits imposed on the institution by statute and therefore has met its most significant problems with only minor difficulties, while at Stanford the issues have been slightly different because of a considerably different constituency and quite a different allocation of resources.

Even the extent of minority enrollments does not appear to be a crucial factor in contributing to institutional difficulties, except insofar as the institution is unwilling or unable to address the grievances or the issues raised by students. Again, UCLA, the school with the largest minority enrollment, has succeeded in dealing with the special needs of the minority student in perhaps better fashion than any of the other institutions.

While the gross characteristics of institutions certainly have some implications for colleges and universities, it seems clear that other factors such as the nature of institutional government, faculty commitments and policies, the institution's image of itself and its mission, administrative leadership, and larger political considerations are all more fundamentally important in determining the nature of the internal processes in the institution and the extent to which these will be characterized by gross problems and general enmity or relative tranquility. The difficulties of institutions of higher education are largely a consequence of the conscious choices and commitments of those in positions of authority and control rather than a function of processes over which they have little or no control. The extent to which this is the case is central to the discussion which follows.

Organization and the Innovational Process

No campus in this study was free of the problems that highlight the complaints of activist students outlined initially. Indeed, perhaps no campus in the nation is entirely free of such problems and probably few have escaped the attendant efforts of student activists to seek redress, not only because they seek change in the institution, but because they wish increasingly to have an impact on the larger society. In each case, the amount of student activism and concern have been rising steadily. These students are part of a phenomenon which Harold Taylor describes as nationwide and which is affecting to varying degrees each of the six colleges and universities studied. He says:

> Each new generation of future freshmen, white and black, men and women, will contain a higher proportion of socially sensitive, activist, and articulate youth who in high school have already begun to follow in the steps of those recent high school graduates who have now become college activists. Already a new generation of activists has been bred in the suburban and urban high schools, and has begun to develop tactics and strategies in educational and social reform which parallel the actions of those immediately ahead of them in college. With the introduction of more ghetto youth into the stream of precollege education through Upward Bound and similar programs, public and private, it will not be long before the joint and separate efforts of black and white youth in high school and college will produce a much more radical point of view about the character and necessity of social change than any we have seen in the present generation.[1]

While there has been no absence of student activism in any of the institutions studied, there has been a wide degree of variation in institutional response to student demands and in the mechanisms available within institutions for coping with such demands. There has also been considerable difference in the way that institutional leaders have operated with regard to manipulating the internal system in order to bring about a solution to student problems.

In no case was there an institution which could entertain and respond to issues or problems posed by students with quick and decisive action, excluding the mobilization of police or national guard. Indeed, a major dilemma in the structural organization of most colleges and universities is caused in part at least not by oppressive bureaucratic machinery, but by the democratic or quasidemocratic procedures which have become increasingly characteristic of college and university government. A number of observers allude to this dilemma of institutional democracy when they speak of the extent to which institutional executives are compelled to share their decision-making authority, if not legally, then at least by convention.[2] In each of the institutions studied, power to make decisions in many respects has gravitated toward the faculty.

The extent of this gravitation of authority, however, is extremely unclear because it rests, not on legal prescription, but on informal delegation by administration and governing boards. Only in the case of the University of Oregon is the authority of the faculty prescribed by law, and then it is limited to the curriculum, with the caveat that decisions are subject to review by the State Board of Higher Education.[3] In all other cases, responsibility for even the curriculum is delegated by the governing body. Other authority which the faculty enjoys in the internal operation of the institutions is a function of administrative delegation. This fact introduces an element of ambiguity in assessing responsibility and, in turn, in obtaining action on controversial or contentious issues. Often in such cases, the administration, because of its political acumen and an interest in avoiding faculty wrath, refers the matter to the faculty for deliberation and a decision, even though legal authority for making the decision rests with the institutional executive.

In such circumstances, the mechanisms for deliberation and decision by the faculty are usually exceedingly complex. They include study by ad hoc and standing committees and a faculty advisory body with decisions then rendered by the collective faculty or whatever proportion of it is interested enough to turn out for the faculty meeting which in our study frequently constituted less than fifteen per cent of the faculty unless there was a clear-cut crisis.

In only two of the institutions studied were faculty decisions delegated by the faculty to an executive committee or deliberative body. Surprisingly, these were the smallest institutions Stanford and Western Washington State College. At all of the other institutions there were reports of periodic decisions to begin considering alternative forms of faculty government, but none of them had taken any steps in this direction. The result of the cumbersome organization of faculty has been that even in those cases where they are basically sympathetic to student initiatives or concerns (apparently a rare event), their ability to act with dispatch is grossly inhibited. It should also be remembered that, at each step in the process of deliberation, parliamentary maneuvering and extended debate may further delay what is at best an extremely inefficient process. In any event, swift action, as nearly as could be determined, was limited to those times when institutions were under siege and the "normal" activities of the institution were called off or otherwise brought to a halt.

Interestingly, administrators have taken the brunt of abuse regarding the immobility of the institutions studied, although the administrative bureaucracy appeared, in all cases, to be far more capable than faculty of response to demands for action in areas where it has assumed jurisdiction. But these areas, usually having to do with the pedestrian affairs of clerical procedures (e.g., paperwork and registration), are the least sensitive in the current context. The most sensitive issues, those having to do with curricular reform and institutional priorities, have been delegated to the faculty, or at least no administrative decisions will be rendered without faculty action.

In those cases where the administration has taken the initiative on issues of critical importance, such as in the appointment of the President's Committee on Racism at the University of Oregon, or the Vietnam Convocation at San Francisco State College, there was a strong negative reaction among many of the faculty. The result of this kind of reaction is a growing reticence on the part of administration to assume a leadership role or to take the initiative without first going through the tedious and often futile procedure of consulting the faculty which often casts the administration in a role as the faculty lackey rather than one of decisive leadership. Those who interpret the administration's role as a more powerful one are, in the face of such administrative impotence, likely to focus their criticism on the administration rather than on other constituents in the organization. The result is that the administration has what is approaching an impossible task.

There is a genuine dilemma in any democratic or quasi-democratic system with multiple interests. Competing constituencies, with fundamental, and perhaps irreconcilable, conflicts of interests may effectively veto any administrative action. To the extent that this is true, moving the organization in any direction that involves altering the status quo may be very nearly impossible. To the extent that faculty interests are at odds with those of the student, there is little likelihood that faculty would respond differently even if the machinery would allow speedy action. Given that this is the case, the highly democratized, and in this case highly inefficient structure, acts as a barrier fostering the conservative interests of those hiding behind it. It is this situation to which the phrase "Hamletic strategy," [4] mentioned earlier, refers. The strategy of avoiding decisions through the construction of elaborate deliberative mechanisms is an integral feature of almost any action taken at the faculty level. In this respect, it has often been the case that institutions have given the appearance of taking action while, in effect, nothing was happening. Such action was taken on the grand scale at Berkeley in the forms of the Select Committee on Education and the Committee on University Governance, at UCLA with the Committee of Academic Innovation, and at Stanford with the Study of Education at Stanford. On a lesser scale, the strategy is an integral feature of most decisions rendered by faculty bodies. The interim between the time that committees are convened and the time which they act often serves as a cooling-out period during which hostilities ebb and a restoration of the status quo is achieved. The nature of this organization makes the institution inherently conservative to an extent rarely true of other organizations.

The difference between the colleges and universities in question is essentially one of the nature of the distribution of power within the organization. Although universities and colleges were rigidly hierarchical in their early history,[5] there has been a progressive transition away from this model toward a more democratic mode of organization. Among the major reasons for this, as discussed elsewhere, have been the professionalization of the various constituents of the organization and the leverage for expanding their power to control the organization because of the greater dependency of the society on their particular skills.

The conservatism of the organization in terms of its ability to meet the demands for change is not unique. A certain amount of conservatism is inherent in all organizational forms whether they are democratic or hierarchial in arrangement.[6] It appears, however, that democratic organizations may be less adaptable inasmuch as decisions cannot be rendered by fiat except insofar as organizational democracy is undercut by the development of oligarchical leadership. While bureaucratic organizations all have points of resistance when innovations are introduced, these can be more or less successfully challenged by an exercise of administrative power. While there are functional limitations to the exercise of executive authority, even in a bureaucracy, these would appear to be less formidable than in an organization where power and authority are decentralized. In higher education, although authority remains primarily in the hands of administrators, the growing power of constituencies severely limits their ability to provide effective leadership for change.

From the perspective of those who adopt a conservative position on the issue of institutional change, the deliberative mechanisms of the faculty are interpreted as institutional safeguards preventing rash decisions in the heat of emotional controversy. It is clear, however, that rigid organization and institutionalized incapacity for action, as well as being institutional safeguards, act as catalysts for the escalation of difficulties. Students in each case have become increasingly wary of operating through "appropriate channels" because their cumulative experience over the past few years has been what they interpret as less than adequate action. As negative experiences of this sort accumulate among the student body, attempts by administrators or faculty to submit demands or grievances to the "deliberative process" are increasingly rejected. Furthermore, as the position of faculty and administration is increasingly defined as intransigent, students have not only escalated tactics in the pursuit of goals, but in some cases, such as San Francisco State College, have expanded demands during the course of a controversy rendering the resolution of differences even more difficult.

Initially, student interests have rarely been radical in their character or in their implications. A comparison of the histories of institutions in the study suggest further that accession to "moderate" requests of student activists has not necessarily led to an increase in demands. The history of these institutions suggests, too, that students are not rallied to the support of confrontation tactics where they have interpreted the positions of the institutional leaders as ones that will accommodate requests which are both reasonable and for which they have the resources. Although one can counter that there are distinct differences in the student bodies which reduce the possibility of amicable relations between constituencies considerably, it can be argued that the extent to which this is true has been vastly overstated. Groups of students at all of the institutions have, in fact, demonstrated their willingness to engage in confrontation politics when the adversary is perceived as unwilling to entertain alternatives.

With respect to the gross differences which are often believed to characterize students in different areas, there is evidence to indicate a growing "student culture" emerging on a national scale.[7] Not only have college students formed a number of national political or quasi-political organizations such as the National Students Association and Students for a Democratic Society, they have become an important force in the realm of national politics, as witnessed in the 1968 national elections with the withdrawal of Lyndon Johnson, and the strong showing for Eugene McCarthy until the National Democratic Convention. Unlike a past age also, the students are no longer divided into small, relatively isolated groups. They are extremely mobile and can coordinate activities on a statewide or even a national scale without tremendous difficulties. Furthermore, their activities are well-publicized in the media so that students everywhere are aware of the activities taking place on other campuses throughout the country. In this respect, events which capture the imagination of the student community can take on the character of a mass national movement in relatively short order.

Aside from the different ideological configurations of student bodies which may be real to the extent that some have larger "pockets of radicalism" than others, there is a kind of social, psychological dynamic operating in which a great deal depends on how the contestants define the nature of the adversary. In each case radical activists were continually characterized as small minorities, yet their appeals were persuasive enough to generate widespread support where institutional response to popular issues was rigidly negative.

A further example of the importance of constituent perceptions of each other can be seen in consequences of leadership styles at various institutions. In those cases where the history of response to demands for change has been one of rhetoric without action, the consequences have been predictable. There is a situation not unlike that used to describe the "revolution in expectations" among minority communities.[8] Problems are compounded when the hopes of constituents are raised considerably and then disappointed. The history of educational reform at Berkeley has been one of expressed commitment without action, of study without follow-through and of a facade of innovation in what may be one of the most thoroughly conservative institutions in the nation. On the other hand, without notoriety UCLA has responded in a much more direct fashion to the aspirations of the various student constituencies. The same can be said to some degree when comparing other institutions in the study. At Oregon, candor with students and an attempt to convey problems from the administration to student dissidents at a person-to-person level succeeded in maintaining an amicable atmosphere over a considerable period of time. In this respect, it appears that the importance of administrative style, even given insurmountable difficulties in delivering on student requests, is of some consequence. An administration which provides some support or otherwise facilitates innovation may reduce the probability of confrontation to some extent. Access to those in a position to make decisions has been a hallmark of all of the administrations of institutions studied except Berkeley, and until recently San Francisco State. Not that this kind of style in and of itself could have prevented what happened at Berkeley over the past six years or at San Francisco State during the past three, but it might have helped considerably to reduce the frequency and the intensity of conflict. Sooner or later, however, the substantive demands of dissident students must be dealt with. Whether or not many of these can even be seriously entertained given the relation of the institutions of higher education to the larger community will be discussed further on.

Observations on Experimental Colleges

Experimentation in American higher education has ranged from minimal curricular reform to total reconstitution of learning environments. Some of the more exciting developments have occurred in the past few years as more and more educationists and students have reappraised their positions in light of massive criticism. After reading *How Children Fail,* most persons are excited to read John Holt's thoughts on *How Children Learn.*[9] Herbert Kohl's initial commentary on the feelings of conventional school environments led him to explore and experiment with alternative school settings.[10] Ivan Illich has extended the thoughts of writers such as Paul Goodman and examined the process of what he calls "de-schooling."[11] In most academic communities there are now a number of experimental schools ranging from those patterned after A. S. Neill's Summerhill to Montessori schools and behavior modification centers based on principles of operant conditioning. What is common to all such endeavors is an agreement that what now passes for education is inadequate, that the full creative potential of students is underdeveloped, if not totally atrophied, and that the learning context must be radically altered.

In higher education there has been an intriguing history of experimentation. Black Mountain College in North Carolina is perhaps the best known effort to alter the ownership-employee-client structure of American colleges. An interesting recent experiment is the offshoot of Reed College faculty and students now loosely affiliated with Antioch and functioning in Portland, Oregon as "The Learning Community." The Learning Community is experimenting with an environment that makes no distinction between living and learning. Other experimental efforts abound around the country, sometimes as adjuncts to existing schools and other times as autonomous efforts.

One important thrust in recent years has been to leave the mainstream of American higher education and to create counterinstitutions and independent alternatives which have partly come from a resignation on the part of innovators who feel change of any magnitude cannot be achieved within an existing college or university. Other times the innovative effort is forced away from the school or denied legitimacy. Interesting as these efforts are, our concern has been primarily to focus upon developments within the existing institutions, to note the efforts for innovation, and to discern trends and possible future directions.

Experimental colleges emerged with three primary points of emphasis. First was the call for relevance in the curriculum as defined by students, hence the stress on student-initiated courses. Second was the challenge for drawing instructors from on-campus and from the community who did not possess the conventional academic credentials, but who did meet the needs generated by the new demands. Third, there was an early call for translating campus experiences into community action. From this initial emphasis came a number of issues articulated in various forms. At Berkeley, the Free Speech Movement was followed by the development of a countercurriculum as students began to be concerned about the purpose of the university. Similarly, the resistance to student-initiated curriculum on the part of faculty and administration gave impetus to the cries for student power. The interrelationship between the various issues in educational innovation on the campus was such that initial concerns for experimental colleges later became translated into other issues.

At San Francisco State College the early community action programs and experimental college gradually shifted their focus from community and curricular "relevance" to internal issues such as colleges changes, student power on campus, and governance of the institution.

The experience at San Francisco State paralleled that at Berkeley with initial attention off-campus and a subsequent emphasis on-campus. In fact, the responses by the Muscatine committee and later by the governance committee reveal a pattern of shifting attention from the role of the university in the society to the matter of internal operations of the institution. We might observe that the Teach-In Movement sparked by activities against the Vietnam policy in 1965, followed a similar route. Attention was first focused on the war and U.S. foreign policy. The issue then became one of university complicity with that policy through military training, defense research, and direct involvement such as the CIA-related programs at Michigan State University. Out of such issues came increased demands for changes within the colleges and universities, and many groups of faculty and students were founded around the country as the initial solidarity generated by the issue of the war was reoriented in the direction of governance and other university matters.

Overall, experimental colleges appear to have taken essentially two paths. One has been to move outside the normal curricular offerings and sometimes away from the college or university. This has created free universities, structures which provide no academic credit but which exist as the result of student and faculty curricular concern so that people are able to "do their thing" individually and collectively. The evidence is that such efforts generated minimal pressures for change in the established colleges and universities. In some cases, such as the Mid-Peninsula Free University near Stanford, some of the residue of discontent on the campus has drained away. Of course, these free schools have not just siphoned off persons from the campus concerned with curricular alternatives; they appeal in large part to the community. Free schools in Bellingham, Washington and Eugene, Oregon have primarily non-university students. In short, the thrust of the movement to create counterinstitutions or free schools away from established colleges and universities has been to create parallel educational institutions and a modicum of energies—direct or indirect—have been spent on reforming the mainstream institutions.

In contrast, some experimental colleges have operated consistently on the premise that they are a source of leverage to create change within established colleges and universities. They have insisted on trying to maintain legitimacy, to assure that their curriculum was accepted as normal degree-winning work, and to affect the larger institutional curriculum.

The history of the campuses we intensively examined over several years is varied. At San Francisco State the experimental college is dead; at Berkeley it is nearly dead. At UCLA the effort remained on-campus, but assumed the character of off-campus enterprises. At Western Washington the free university followed the direction of Stanford and became a non-credit unit away from the college. Only at Oregon has the experimental college remained viable and active, and even there substantial assaults have been launched against it. Yet, there remains a structure for student-initiated courses with provision for student and community instructors and community involvement. This is all within the academic program of the university, although an off-campus free school also exists. The impact of the experimental college at Oregon on the total institution is difficult to measure. To date original student-initiated courses have been adopted in the permanent curriculum and with ethnic studies courses are leading the way for additional permanent curricular offerings.

What this brief overview suggests is that innovational efforts which have consciously operated to reform established schools seem to have a more pronounced impact on the colleges and universities. Yet, the reactions on some campuses have been severe. In many cases experimental innovations such as student-initiated curricula have been eliminated by faculty, administrative, or trustee action. The probability that off-campus experiments will have any impact for reform on established schools appears remote indeed. Reform efforts on campus may have an effect, but there is the problem of how to initiate change and sustain the effort to the point of success. While some efforts are short-lived and are still significant, others have not survived long enough to have created real change. What direction the future will bring is not really clear. Reactionary responses to student demands for curricular change should be expected as part of a societal pattern reflected within higher education. But we would observe that the radical slogan "Dare to struggle, dare to win" has much truth. Innovative efforts to create curricular change must be made within the mainstream if established higher education is to experience such reform and change. The history of experimental colleges suggests that this is one important vehicle which might bring about some changes in higher education.

The Innovation in Ethnic Studies: An Assessment

The recent development of ethnic studies has been one of the most significant developments in higher education. The growing recognition of the legitimacy of the endeavors is apparent with the introduction of such programs in secondary and elementary schools. As of 1970, nearly 300 colleges and universities had initiated or planned Afro-American courses.[12] Other minority studies programs relevant to the Chicano, Native-American and Oriental-American have been emerging in regions where these groups are a substantial portion of the population. The push for special programs of admission and academic offerings has been greatest, however, among Black students.

Political Processes and Institutional Change 249

The stimulus for educational change in recent years has come in large part, as a result of the Black liberation movement. The growth of CORE and SNCC and later the university following of Malcolm X brought the struggle for racial justice to the campus. It was obvious that Blacks were largely excluded from higher education; many campuses (e.g., University of Michigan and UCLA) had a far larger number of foreign students than American Blacks.[13] But the impetus for and leadership of the civil rights movement came to a considerable extent from college students, white and Black.

The primary arena of activity was off-campus. The focus was in the rural South and urban North where attention was placed on de facto school segregation, residential segregation, occupational discrimination, and the realities which locked Blacks out of the bastions of white privilege. In the wake of organizing efforts and urban uprisings, Black Power became the battle cry. This was translated to mean real control over one's life in all spheres, essentially a challenge for a remade America.

Although much effort continued in the ghettos and rural areas of the country, there was a reemphasis on the campus. The Black Panther Party joined campus radicals, such as Newton, and the articulate spokesmen of the Black proletariat, such as Eldridge Cleaver. In 1967 and 1968, over ninety per cent of the sit-ins and demonstrations by Black students were not in the community but on the campus.[14] The organization of Black student unions indicated the changed mood and objective among students on the campuses. The push was first for an end to the isolation felt by Blacks on campus which had been enhanced by racist practices in dormitories and classrooms and the total range of activities affecting the Black student's life. There was a growing recognition of the fact that Blacks "have been *in* America longer than 95% of all of the other ethnic groups represented in this society, and they still lie at the bottom . . . they are still not *of* America."[15] Black students had begun to ask why. What is more, they began to press for redress.

The emerging consciousness of Black students was not a regional phenomenon. By the mid-1960s, virtually all college youth had been socialized in a period of civil rights struggle, and many had been recruited into the movement in high school or even before. All over the country Black students on the college and university campuses were organizing in an effort to expand their control over their educational experiences and their lives and to relate their campus to community life.

This last point became increasingly an issue. Black students began to appreciate the fact that their life experiences were not considered intellectually relevant at the university. In turn, they found that the abstractions of the classroom had little meaning for their lives in terms of prior exposures in the community. The challenge was put to the university.

> If a university is truly interested in educating undergraduates, it must take them as they are upon matriculation. This no way endangers "standards", for in many ways the young black students are raising questions far more basic than many scholars have lately asked one another. Moreover, until the content of the students' lives is accepted as a valid part of the university learning experience, it will be impossible to teach students the abstract concepts by which they can go about solving their problems and those of society.[16]

This point was as significant in major metropolitan areas where the universities existed in the shadows of the Black ghettos as it was in typical small-town, isolated campuses. In fact, the assumptions that the size of the community and ethnic population would affect the integration of Blacks into the schools and reduce discrimination were revealed as demonstrably false.[17]

In addition to the strategic importance of locating the Black liberation struggle on the campus from the viewpoint of the students, a strong logical argument can be made in support of the strategy of choosing the campus as a focal point of effort by those deliberating methods of inducing societal change. In a particularly cogent argument, Immanuel Wallerstein contends that the liberals and upper-class conservatives who run American universities are most likely to be radicalized by issues of Black militance.[18] The point is that the total style and tradition of the university is in fundamental conflict with the press for racial justice. In addition, there is strong evidence to support Wallerstein's contention that the battles are more likely to be won on the campus, and that the Black Power movement has, for good strategic reasons, pressed demands on the colleges and universities.

Historically, ethnic studies got their first boost from student activists who had been involved in civil rights battles and who wished to use the campus for recruiting and support. The Free Speech Movement created a base for demands directed at the University of California. At San Francisco State College, the Institute for Community Services attempted to link the academy with the community and to increase the number of Third World students. But the prime push came with Upward Bound, the federal government program to support college and university admissions of minority and poor youth who otherwise would not obtain college educations. The program allowed universities to actively recruit ghetto youth who would normally not be college bound and to provide support services and programs to facilitate their completion of normal college work.

The Upward Bound program involved special curricular efforts, oftentimes in the summer prior to official enrollment. Basically these programs, part of the Office of Economic Opportunity's War on Poverty and the U.S. Office of Education programs, were extensions of the philosophy that urged compensatory social, economic, and educational programs to allow locked-out segments of the American population to get into the mainstream. The idea was to invest in some minority youth and allow them to pursue college careers with the idea that extending such opportunities would have a long-term impact on the ghettos of the country.

Some variations among institutions which had Upward Bound programs did exist, but they were at hundreds of colleges and universities all over the country.[19] In general, there were concessions made in such programs for so-called disadvantaged youth, and special admissions procedures were used to admit students whose pre-entrance achievement would normally have failed to qualify them. As a result minority youth in college in the late 1960s included more low-income ghetto students than ever before.

In the 1970s, there has been a continuing shrinkage of programs supporting minority students. In some cases total institutional programs have been jeopardized or eliminated as in the case of Oregon's Project 75 or UCLA's High Potential program. As federal funds were cut back with the escalation of the war in Vietnam, the constituency of minority students shifted back to more middle class youth.[20] Current projections of the Nixon Administration suggest that such cuts will continue and lead to the prediction that the push to admit low-income minority students into the colleges and universities is over, at least for the time being. In the earlier period of prosperity, and in the face of immense urban upheavals, the government and universities could accommodate subsidized specially-admitted minorities students. But with the subsequent escalation of the war, serious recession, and growing financial crisis in the university, things were bound to change. In any case it is important to note that the difficult consequences of admitting more students have become clear to administrators, trustees and state legislators. With the massive escalation of on-campus demonstrations, there was a growing awareness of the role of Third World demands. The image of Blacks with guns walking out of Cornell buildings was probably far more vivid in its impact than that of academically-oriented Blacks who had been given the opportunities of gaining college educations. The shooting of Blacks at UCLA, the long strike at San Francisco State, and hundreds of other incidents made it clear that the campuses were increasingly to be the battleground for the grievances of growing numbers of minority students.

The push for ethnic programs has seen a number of critical substantive problems. The first of these is the problem of developing academic programs designed to remedy community problems. One analyst says that students "enrolled in black studies programs to develop an appreciation of their black identity and heritage and to help other black people solve immediate community problems," but they became frustrated because they realized that "because of their inexperience, their resources were limited to little other than understanding the problems." [21] Afro-American studies are obviously not a panacea for solving the needs of a population suffering the results of institutionalized racism.

Another problem centers on the issue of separatism and the failure of ethnic studies programs to lessen the barriers and burdens for blacks. John Hatch maintains that:

> If, as seems certain, a great deal of charlatanry develops within the black study programs as untrained faculty are pressed into service or take the opportunity to jump on the bandwagon, black students will find that they have created another institution to emphasize their inferiority, another cause for intellectual derision. And the inclination, already so apparent, toward cultural separatism in black studies can only deepen the trauma of self-contempt within a closed community.[22]

The counterargument advanced is that a Black Studies program is designed to compensate for the traditional educational experience rooted in the culture and value system of the white middle class which are so foreign to the Black student. This argument calls for a separate program of study, one which opens the doors of the institution to community

Blacks now excluded, and was central to the events which precipitated the San Francisco State strike.[23]

The variation in viewpoints is real, and the questions of whether Black studies are a boon or bane and whether there is an intellectual crisis have not been resolved with any unanimity.[24] We can make some observations, however, about what seems to have happened in the half-dozen years or so since the first major programs have developed to admit more minority students and create ethnic studies curricula.

When ethnic programs began, there was an obvious scarcity of faculty resources. But the first push coincided with the broader demands by students calling for increased curricular relevance, student determination of curricular offerings, and the utilization of instructors lacking in traditional academic credentials, all of which led to a crisis in recruitment. This crisis was exacerbated by the rigidity of colleges and universities who refused to follow the lesson of schools such as UCLA which did not lower standards but raised opportunities. Their efforts included the cultivation of their own Ph.D.s or the facilitation of the educational advancement of persons considered assets and worthy faculty additions. It is interesting to reflect, in this regard, on the question of how often professors attempt to place outstandingly qualified Black graduate students, while simultaneously serving on faculty recruitment committees which are "unable" to attract Black faculty. Where there was a shortage of Blacks considered qualified for faculty appointments, the situation was acute for administrators. Roosevelt Johnson argues:

> I will contend that it is contradictory to pass legislation, appropriate funds, recruit and enroll black students who, for some asinine reason, have been tagged "high risk," if no instrument is available whereby their needs can be communicated to the higher echelon of the college administration and, for heaven's sake, the faculty. Where this instrument is lacking, turbulences are in the making and some type of "undesirable" confrontation will enure in a subtle or blatant fashion, depending upon the severity of the incident which triggers the charge. The conspicuous exclusion of blacks from the viable and legitimate administrative roles is one of the central, underlying forces which have detonated most of the campus explosions where black students were involved.[25]

The tight labor market for minority faculty played a critical role in the tensions surrounding the early development of ethnic studies programs. White administrators and faculty were on the defensive as minority students, and in some cases community members, pressured them to enlist non-faculty instructors to upgrade student instructors and to allow students to play a major part in curricular development. Over the past few years, however, there has been a decrease in such pressures. In part, we suspect that this is a function of the growing numbers of minority faculty and a concomitant reduction of pressures to recruit community persons who may tend to be more activist and radical.

A number of colleges and universities have recruited their own minority student leaders into positions on the administrative staff—assistant deans of students and the like. Such students have increasingly adopted university values and mellowed. As programs become established and legitimized they have shifted from community action and service orientations and adopted more traditionally academic and distinctly non-radical characteristics.

All of the phenomena described are illustrated in the institutions we studied. Although UCLA made a more concerted and successful initial effort to recruit minority faculty, other institutions have added their former ethnic student leaders to their staffs. This suggests a theory of organizational accommodation in which colleges and universities develop avoidance strategies to cope with pressures from minority students for radical community-oriented ethnic programs. The first step is to uphold traditional criteria for faculty recruitment while adding some student dissidents to the staff. Early calls for radical programs are rejected, but alternate programs identified as legitimate and academic are developed. Concessions, then, are token and made as much as possible within the customary operating framework of academic institutions.

Some complementary developments have helped to reduce the pressures for ethnic studies. First, there have been other outlets addressing student demands for relevance in the curriculum, including student-initiated courses (which typically include white racism material) and shifts in normal academic department offerings. At Oregon, for example, there is no ethnic studies program, but there are a wide range of relevant student-initiated courses in SEARCH, including white racism, Chicano studies, and politics and the Black community. In addition, the regular curriculum has been altered substantially to stress racism and materials tied to the Third World struggles domestically and internationally.

More important, perhaps, is that minority students over the past years have conceded to faculty on some curricular decisions, especially as more minority faculty are recruited. Such concessions have probably

Political Processes and Institutional Change

been facilitated as students have lost battles and recognized where the real power lies in the institution. The lesson was perhaps most vivid at San Francisco State. The Black Studies department head was ultimately impotent, as were the other Black faculty and administrators. At Western Washington State College, leadership came from minority faculty and white faculty allies. Students largely followed faculty initiatives. On each of the campuses studied, most students, whether minority members or not, came to realize the amount of work involved in curricular development. With some assurances of support from liberal white faculty, students pushing for ethnic studies and curricular change were content to defer decision making to faculty members. It is not possible to talk in terms of the push for ethnic studies having crested, but surely the reduction in student demands has come with an increasing reliance on faculty and administration to move ahead. This development has paralleled changes in the curriculum resulting in increased relevance and expansion of ethnic studies, the loss of student power battles, and the addition of more minority members on faculties and administrations.

We have already observed that cutbacks in federal government support have severely affected minority student programs. The return to the traditional admissions standards means Black students who make it to the university will come from the middle classes. It is not really possible to predict if the class shift means a simple reduction in the potential for militant leadership. However, as some concessions have been made by the institution, early demands have become displaced. Evidence from the history of social movements suggests that as people come closer to their objectives their militancy increases. This has been the history of the struggle for racial justice in the United States and accounts for the events of the past decade, and as colleges and universities accommodate the demands of Black students, they may well find a rise in their militancy. It seems more likely, however, that this militancy will be fashioned by the external events in the society in much the same way as the militancy of white students. Harry Edwards observes:

> With the militant at the helm, means become less radical, the immediate issues around which he organizes programs of action become less relevant to the Black community, and a premium is placed upon threatening rhetoric and cultural exhibitionism while meaningful political action of significance in achieving the long-range goals of freedom and justice for the Black masses is minimized. In adopting such

tactics, militants seek both to participate in the Black student movement and simultaneously to protest their own personal educational goals. But straddling this fence is not an easy task, because constant pressures tend to push militants toward more radical action.[26]

There is no question about the significance of Black student protest in recent years. At the end of the 1968–69 academic year, 72 presidents had resigned from colleges or universities in the wake of demonstrations initiated and/or led by Black student organizations.[27] Nationally there were 292 major student protests on 232 campuses during the first six months of 1969. In a very large percentage, Black students were involved, and the issues included ethnic studies and racism on campus.[28] In the period since, however, there has been an apparent decline in student militancy over the issue of ethnic studies. Following the Third World strike at Berkeley, there was the most severe outbreak ever over People's Park. Although the Oregon campus has experienced a considerable amount of turmoil during the past year, minority students are concentrating on recruiting, developing curricula, and improving minority services in the university and community action efforts. May 1970 saw campuses all over the country explode, but there have not been democratic confrontations and demonstrations in the past year comparable to those of 1968 and 1969, in which ethnic studies, minority student enrollment, and racism were key issues on campuses. Whether or not we will see a return to the earlier high level of activity over ethnic studies is not clear, but at the present there is little reason to expect such a development.

Perhaps one of the reasons that ethnic studies proposals have met with such success is that the major constituencies have been traditional white college and university students. In most cases ethnic studies, not ethnic colleges, have developed. Separate Black units have not taken hold, possibly because the NAACP challenge that it would initiate legal proceedings against such a segregationist approach curtailed them. Perhaps it was just the reluctance of administrators and faculty to allow the extra autonomy of a college structure; surely this was true of the Berkeley case, and UCLA opted for another approach. The College of Ethnic Studies at Western Washington State College was created in line with an existing movement toward the development of cluster college units. Generally the thrust of ethnic studies has been to create curricular offerings but not within separate and racially homogeneous colleges or degree-granting departmental units. While the 1960s created a sensitivity and a fear on the part of White America and with it the movement for ethnic studies in colleges and universities and while such programs were proposed by angry minority students, the resulting modest curricular developments were designed largely for white students. A minority equivalent to white higher education was never a serious possibility.

Another conclusion generated by our study has been that the community context appears to have played an important role in the ethnic studies experience. Western Washington State College and the University of Oregon have small ethnic populations in the immediate surrounding communities. On the other hand, at San Francisco State, Berkeley, and UCLA there are substantial ethnic populations nearby. In no case is there an ecological arrangement comparable to such private urban universities such as Columbia, Chicago, and Case Western Reserve or to such public institutions as Wayne State, which all border on or are surrounded by Black ghettos. Nevertheless, the California colleges and universities take on more of the character of enclaves of intellectuals, largely white and middle class, surrounded by diversified communities including minority groups. This does appear to be important in explaining some of the response patterns. Correctly perceived threats, coupled with the induced white guilt and accusations of institutional racism, led to more dramatic efforts to open doors at UCLA than at Oregon. Yet this alone is not an adequate explanation, for Berkeley and UCLA were not comparable. The commitment to minority student and faculty recruitment was measurably greater at UCLA. The long-standing positive relationships between the university and minority populations in Los Angeles was a key factor in this difference.

No complete and clear pattern seems to emerge. There is some suggestion that gradual reformist efforts are more likely to affect change without too much reaction. Some structural arrangements are more acceptable for ethnic studies—such as the cluster college or ethnic studies institutes—while others such as Third World colleges and departments of ethnic studies seem to engender greater hostility and resistance. Community pressure plays a part, especially in the consciousness of white administrators and faculty.

The reformist trend is most obvious in the direction in which ethnic studies programs seem to be going all over the country. With the recruitment of more minority faculty, recruitment of minority students to the faculty and staff, and the addition of academic offerings in ethnic studies, the turbulence associated with the demands of the mid-1960s has shifted to a posture of working within the system. What this has meant is a reduction in community pressures, the return to earlier admissions standards, and an increase in minority enrollments, but with a cutback in low-income and special students. The ethnic studies courses are more and more nearly approximations of regular offerings in terms of rigor and content, while the total curriculum has been radicalized to some extent.

In the area of ethnic studies, college and university administrators and faculty seem to have retreated from the challenges initially posed, and counterposed a gradualist reform effort which is reflected in curricular change and the shifting ethnic composition of student bodies—but all within traditional academic boundaries. In this sense the substantial changes witnessed have contributed to the longer-range stability of the traditional university structure. Where this effort will lead in further educational innovation is not clear, but the first round would suggest that the issue of ethnic studies in the 1960s and thus far into this decade, has not proven adequate to remake the American college or university.

Catalysts for Change: Who Are the Innovators?

One of the central interests of this study has been to identify the sources of innovation and change on the various campuses, to compare these in order to determine whether a particular campus constituency has taken the lead in this respect, and to compare the roles of various constituencies in this regard. The question of the source of innovations is the one with probably the least ambiguous answers of all that concerned us.

There is no question that on all of the campuses, the students have taken the lead in innovation in recent years. Among the most active, as we have seen, have been the minority students because of the growing interest in ethnic studies programs. On occasion administrators have occupied a central role but usually as facilitators of innovation rather than as leaders. The main contribution of faculty to the innovative process has been where it has not acted as a reactionary force. In no case has it exhibited superior leadership in innovation.

In the early stages of the development of experimental programs at San Francisco State College, the impetus came largely from students who were older and whose experience often included some sort of work outside of the university in activities like the Peace Corps or VISTA. The impetus shifted considerably, however, and there appears to be a more general support of the types of educational reform envisioned by early student reformers. Innovative activities now engage a wide range of undergraduate students at various stages in their academic careers.

Although students have been largely responsible for taking the lead in matters of educational reform, there are indications of their ambivalence toward it. It would seem that the ambivalence is a consequence of being forced to operate in the context of an institution which, while it may have made minor commitments to reform, still operates on essentially the same principles as it always has. The result then is that the student operates in a milieu which offers some opportunities to escape from the conventional pressures of the college environment, but he appears unsure that he will not be penalized for exercising such an option. A case in point is grading. All of the institutions which we studied offer some opportunities for taking courses without being graded on the conventional scale. Many of the students who express commitment to the objectives of educational reform, however, do not enroll on a pass/no-pass basis. The rationale they usually advance is that they feel they will be put at a competitive disadvantage at some point if they exercise this option with any great regularity. In this respect, the larger institutional system has an inhibiting effect on innovation at the level of individual colleges and universities. Since many of these students aspire to graduate or professional school, they are caught between their commitment to educational reform on the one hand, and what they see as the pressures to enroll under the normal procedures on the other. Often, too, the pressures to avoid the pass/no-pass option are strong within the individual institution. The pressures may be formal in the sense of strictly limiting the ability of the student to enroll under such an option but more often they are informal and entail warnings from administrative officials or faculty that the student jeopardizes his future by opting in favor of the new arrangements.

The problem of the cross-pressures on students is not limited to the area of pass/no-pass grading. Many graduate students, usually the mainstay of the teaching staff of the experimental colleges, have been "advised" not to teach or otherwise participate in them. Often this advice comes in the form of suggesting that participation will "delay progress," and some who receive such advice feel that it is a veiled threat. Others choose simply to ignore it as irrelevant. Some students who have been active at the various campuses have been disappointed in student performance in some of the new curricula because it has often reflected an interest in using the curricula as a mechanism for building their grade point average or as a place to "slough off" while concentrating efforts in the more traditional academic areas. The net result has often been that the new curricula have been something less than a complete success. There are, of course, many students who do not use the courses this way, but the problem is that student leaders don't want any of them used as padding. As long as the pressures continue at their present intensity, however, or increase in the name of "rising standards," the problem is likely to persist.

Separated from the student by the podium—a distance symptomatic of a wider gulf—is the professor.[29] To attempt to speak of him in collective terms is necessarily an oversimplification. There are countless exceptions to everything that will be said here, but this should not deter us from generalizing where individuals are sufficiently alike in their behavior to merit such generalization. Although their interests and specialties make for gross differences among them, faculty members nevertheless exhibit a number of similarities to each other. One of the similarities appears to be their conservatism in regard to educational reform or innovation. In each of the institutions visited, the faculty was at best a neutral force in educational innovation. More often, though, they constituted the center of the resistance to change. Where there was organized resistance to new programs, it was usually the faculty who provided it. Furthermore, in many cases, the resistance was not token but strong.

Faculty resistance to innovation appears to have grown in each case almost in direct proportion to the success of the innovative program. Where participation was token or limited by institutional constraints, there was little overt reaction once a program had begun. Where programs enrolled large percentages of the student population, however, they invariably drew adverse criticism and reaction, especially when instruction was handled by, or shaped with, individuals without the "appropriate" academic credentials. In such cases it appears that faculty saw the growth of the innovative program as a threat, usually verbalized in terms of academic legitimacy or institutional standards. The threat to faculty interests, however, appears to play an important role.

It should be pointed out here that college professors are similar to other professional groups having a vested interest in promoting their par-

Political Processes and Institutional Change

ticular service. While no organization of the collective faculty has been particularly strong in this regard, individual professional organizations connected with the different disciplines represented in the university have been forceful in pursuing the interests of their constituencies and have been instrumental in advancing the proposition that a greater and greater proportion of the young adult population should be subjected to their instruction for longer and longer periods. While pressing the argument for the extension of education to ever greater numbers, these same organizations and their constituencies have been the source of increasing pressures for the "appropriate" credentials among faculty, for increasing specialization, and for an increasing restriction of the measure of professional competence to the professor's research activities.

Most professional organizations with which the academic community is allied have advanced their arguments without any real consideration of the issues involved. They have regarded as axiomatic the proposition that "if some [education] is good more must be better." [30] The argument has been advanced with little or no examination of what is a debatable issue; namely, whether education, either for its own sake or with the end of developing esoteric professional or technical skills, especially in the form in which it is currently conducted in most of the major institutions in this country, has real merit. It may or may not. A number of critics argue that the continued attendance of inner-city black and poor children in the public schools has a demonstrably negative impact.[31] The same argument might be extended to higher education. The academic community has never really come to grips with this possibility.[32]

It is in the context of an unexamined faith in the desirability of higher education that college faculty have seen their prestige and their material rewards steadily increase in the past few decades. As Paul Woodring points out, college professors are as much given to status seeking as any other segment of the community.[33] To the extent that this is true, it may account for much of the conservatism with regard to their position on internal university issues. The tightening up of requirements in the way of formal credentials has at the same time strengthened the bargaining position of those with the Ph.D. (often referred to as the union card) and buttressed claims to prestige. The claims of esoteric knowledge, which only those who have passed the most rigorous educational screening mechanisms possess, further accentuates the prestige and bargaining position of faculty. It is not surprising with this type of professional emphasis and the growing prestige consciousness of all of the institutions in question, that there was a faculty reaction which, as pointed out earlier, appeared not so much when controversial courses were offered nor when they were taught by the "unlettered," as when they began to enroll very large numbers among the student body. The enrollment in such cases focused attention on innovative programs in ways which threatened to undermine the legitimacy of the kinds of claims that faculty have traditionally advanced in order to support the retention of a range of prerogatives regarding curricular and other educational matters. The root of the problem, then, would not seem to be so much in any direct objection to the courses taught in the name of innovation so much as it is in the fact that when such programs grow, they threaten the rationale which is the undergirding for faculty claims to both status and pecuniary rewards. As in all organizations, there appears to be a critical point in each institution beyond which such programs cannot go without inviting reaction.

Beyond the threat which curricular innovations pose in the realm of claims to expertise and control, there is another problem with innovation to which many faculty are sensitive, that is, the reaction of the outside community. To the extent that there have been threats or actions against the academy which have been rationalized by allusion to the nature or content of innovative courses or programs, there has been a negative faculty reaction. While they are occasionally willing to defend the principle of academic freedom, such willingness appears limited to those areas where the outside world threatens to encroach on the "normal activities" of the academic community. When the activities to be defended are in any sense radical, the harbingers of academic freedom tend to withdraw as seen on separate occasions at Berkeley, San Francisco State, and in its nascent stages at the University of Oregon. Harold Taylor gets to the center of the issues when he argues that:

> There is no tradition within their [faculty and administration's] academic communities, and very few people there who are capable of teaching radicals except by denying their premises and thereby denying out-of-hand their interpretations of history and contemporary politics. Because the colleges and universities have been operating a system of cultural and social paternalism, they have appointed to their faculties and administrative staff the experts in academic studies and administration whose talents and values are those of the academic profession and the managerial class.[34]

The withdrawal from the defense of academic freedom is prompted by additional factors, among them the threat to economic security posed by a potential cutback in support by state legislatures and a widespread conflict-avoidance syndrome which rejects the notion that there may be fundamental conflicts of interest between students and faculty. We saw direct rejection of the "conflict model of organization" [35] at the University of Oregon when the faculty passed a policy resolution barring "negotiation" as a method of resolving disputes with students. Although not so explicitly rejected in the other institutions studied, there is a similar rejection of the idea that negotiation may be an appropriate mechanism for the resolution of institutional conflict. The combination of shared values to which Taylor alludes and the interest in protecting and enhancing a position which has risen sharply in the past twenty-five years, combine to make the faculty one of the principal retardants in the area of educational innovation.

This leaves only the administrators who present a much less homogeneous facade than do the faculty. In many respects, the inclinations of administrators are masked by maneuvers in other sectors which supersede their ability to act or which are used to give the appearance of such an effect. In this respect, it is often possible for an administrator to shift responsibility for unpopular decisions to other sectors of the academic community. This is true even where decisions reflect administrative views. An illustrative case is Berkeley where informants have argued that the administration had, in the recent past, appeared to have a more liberal viewpoint regarding community action involvement by the university than was true of the faculty. This impression was projected because the faculty had traditionally overruled such involvement and the administration had given the impression that while not opposed, it was bound by the faculty decision. Later, however, when the faculty reversed its position during one of the periodic crises, the administration stepped in and overruled the faculty arguing that its position was taken out of an interest in restoring peace, rather than because of adherence to any coherent principles or guidelines. This type of action on the part of the administration points out the extent to which it is in a strategic position to manipulate appearances in order to circumvent pressures from other sectors of the academic community. What often happens in fact is that the principle of democracy in the institution is operant as long as decisions are made in accord with administrative interests or perspectives. As in other organizations, when decisions begin to violate these parameters, it is often the case that the administration will invoke its legal authority to overturn the decision. The administration often presents a sympathetic facade to student interests and demands on the one hand, while pleading that they have neither the prerogatives or decision-making power on the other. Only in rare instances is this actually the case, as with the power to control the curriculum at the University of Oregon or to establish new departments within the University of California, but even here there are mechanisms available for circumventing these restrictions to some extent where the administration is attuned to the point of view of the constituency seeking change. It is exactly these kinds of alternatives for instance which allowed the formation of the Institute for the Study of American Cultures at UCLA or the development of the SEARCH program at Oregon.

While the particular episode at Berkeley used as an illustration casts the administration in a conservative light, this is certainly not always the case. There appears to be a far greater response by administrators to the pressure for reform than is true of faculty. This is undoubtedly due in part to the fact that the identification of administration with faculty interests is abridged to some extent when faculty opt for an administrative role. It is those features of the system which have most contributed to the rising position of the faculty, and in some respects to a denigration of the administrative role, which students or other reformers are most interested in changing. These objectives include increasing professionalism and the departmental system, the heavy emphasis on formal credentials, increasing competition and "standards" with their accompanying elitism, and the withdrawal of faculty into research. The administrator, by virtue of his position in the system, is often forced to assume a broader perspective regarding overall institutional interests and therefore may be constrained to at least attempt to provide some relief from the problems attendant to departmental parochialism, specialization, and failure to come to grips with the issues which students define as pressing. While interested in the prestige of the institution and valuing all of the features which bring such prestige, the college and university executive's enthusiasm for the kinds of change which have been occurring in the university within the past several years appear to be more often tempered by the fact that he is at the center of the forces pushing for countermeasures. In this sense, administrators at the institutions studied appear to be more sensitive to the problem of meeting the needs of the range of constituencies, not just the faculty. They also appear to be aware that their methods of dealing with serious issues may ultimately make the difference between a state of open warfare like that which periodically bursts forth at Berkeley and the relative tranquility of a UCLA.

The difficulties involved in meeting the needs of the range of constituencies to which the university president or administrator answers are manifest in the problems of past presidents at San Francisco State College and the University of Oregon. Both were subjected in varying degrees to faculty pressures because they assumed a style of leadership which was interpreted in many sectors as an alliance with the students against the faculty. In the case of San Francisco State, efforts to retrench or to salve the hurt of the group which felt that it had been violated bred an escalation of hostility from the student or radical sector because of what they then interpreted as a sellout. At Oregon, the president resigned before hostilities reached that level. The point here is that the administration, because their position is so sensitive in attempting to moderate the conflicting demands of a range of constituencies, may exhibit a greater sensitivity to the wide range of institutional problems and issues than is true of the faculty, but balancing the interests of these factions is increasingly difficult and may well be impossible for an extended period. The possibility of maintaining such a balance is further limited by personal commitment, the mission and resources of the institution, and a variety of other factors.[36]

Curricular Innovation and the Problem of Institutional Governance: Substantive vs. Procedural Issues

In an article discussing the legitimacy of student participation in curricular decisions, Carl Cohen draws a distinction between substantive and procedural issues.[37] Substantive issues are those having to do with the nature of requirements, form of examinations, decisions on promotion and tenure, and so on. Procedural matters are those having to do with the question of how decisions will be reached. The distinction was drawn in the context of an argument for student involvement in advisory capacities and against their inclusion in the process of rendering a decision. This distinction is also useful in another context.

In the recent history of educational development on the campuses included in the study, early student activism appears to have focused almost entirely on substantive rather than procedural issues. The thrust toward emphasis on procedural issues seems to come primarily in those cases where attempts to innovate have met with administrative and/or faculty resistance. Rather than developing as an issue in its own right, procedural issues appear, more often than not, to emerge in the process of bringing about substantive change. Demands for participation in the decision-making process of the institution are partly a consequence of concern over the nature of the educational experience. Although there were cases where student involvement was initiated prior to the establishment of experimental programs, it was almost invariably on a small scale. In the process of development of experimental programs and the ensuing growth in resistance to innovation, procedural issues have gained in salience. To the extent that the administrative and faculty response on substantive issues is positive from the students' viewpoint, procedural matters do not assume a critical dimension. While students may still be interested in moving on procedural matters, especially given the growing national movement for student power, they are not as willing to push in this arena if substantive concerns are being addressed. But, as in the larger society, questions of change cannot be separated from questions of the decision-making process. Just as one cannot hope to alter the quality of life in the larger society and to begin to seriously address pressing issues without having some mechanism for imposing pressures at every decision-making level, neither can one hope to alter the nature of the educational experience in the university unless there is substantial involvement in the decision-making process. In this respect, students are not likely to reduce their pressures for participation in institutional governance, but to increase them. The speed with which the pressures are escalated will be a function of the speed with which they recognize the links between decision-making power and curricular reform. In every one of the institutions in this study, there has been a varying degree of recognition of the need for power and authority among student reformers. While the extent of this recognition will undoubtedly vary among institutions across the country, it is doubtful that there are many where it is not present to some extent.

    The history of educational reform at all of the institutions studied has been one of mixed success and failure. Limited objectives which provide outlets for some of the peculiar needs of small groups of students have usually been introduced with relatively little difficulty. When the objectives have been more general, and when the emphasis shifts from providing opportunities to "do your own thing" to one of altering the nature of the institution, the problems become formidable.

The idea of "doing your own thing" is usually facilitated in the larger institutions by the general anonymity and lack of interaction among the constituents. As long as what is being done is not interpreted as having implications for the larger university or college community, there is likely to be relatively little reaction. Substantive programs may not gain the active support of large sectors of the faculty, but neither do they generate active resistance. Implementation of such programs is facilitated by the general disinterest in affairs transpiring outside of the narrower confines of the individual department or school.

When programs have implications for the larger community, however, as when they threaten to take resources from existing programs, or to divert potential resources from established programs into new ones, there is an invitation to reaction. Depending on the extent of the program implications, faculty interest groups of greater or lesser magnitude are mobilized. While these interest groups may sometimes take on an ad hoc character, more often they are existing caucuses with relatively stable constituencies. Such groups are periodically activated by one or another issue. In the continuing caucuses one usually finds the "faculty politicians," those faculty members (a very small minority) who regularly participate in the affairs of the institution. When a particularly sensitive issue arises, what appear to be ad hoc interest groups are often rallied around a core of the continuing caucuses. The reaction usually takes the form of an appeal to the principle of "upholding institutional standards" or rests on the arguments that available resources simply will not allow the institution to move into the new areas.

The appeal to standards is one which particularly nettles students with a range of experience because they realize that the argument is based on a fallacious assumption that any course taught by regular faculty must have high academic standards (usually left undefined or meaning a certain proportion of the grades are bad or failing). Students also recognize that the assumption that all regular faculty uphold high standards is, at best, perfunctory. They realize that most faculty would concede the fallacy if the assumption were ever verbalized. Nevertheless faculty often act as if the assumption were true. While the rationale might not hold up under close scrutiny, it serves the purpose in the short-run of protecting faculty interests in autonomy and freedom from the interference of "non-academic" personnel. Translated into this form, the issue cannot be argued on purely rational grounds but becomes a highly politicized development which will require action at the institutional level for its resolution. Given existing conflicts of interest described earlier, it has rapidly become apparent to students that they cannot depend on faculty or administration to look out for what are perceived by them to be their best interests. What generally follows is a move by the students to assert the legitimacy of the principle of "student power."

In every case presented, there has been a transition during the past few years from informal mechanisms for student participation in institutional governance on a very limited scale, to more formal mechanisms for participation involving an increasing scope of shared responsibility. The amount of participation varies from one institution to the next with Berkeley, the institution which has experienced the most prolonged and serious disturbances by students, having the least in the way of student participation. In all cases, the principle of student power, a procedural issue, has become both an end in itself and a necessary adjunct if students are to be successful in bringing about curricular change or educational reform.

Although there has been a development of a move for formal inclusion in the decision-making process at each of the institutions studied, there remains a wide gulf in every case between what the students and each of the other units see as an appropriate role. Faculty and administrative responses run the gamut from one extreme to the other. They encompass full endorsements of the principle of community government as well as total resistance to any form of participation by students in the decision-making process. Most fall somewhere between these extremes but lean in the direction of the conservative, nonparticipation position. The most general perspective appears to be one which grants the legitimacy of student participation but in an advisory capacity or, at most, in the position of a voting member of committees but with a substantial minority position. While this is true of both faculty and administration, every indication is that collectively the faculty are more conservative on this issue than the administration. Members of the administration have taken the lead in all cases in inviting student membership on administrative committees while membership is often barred on faculty committees. At UCLA, for instance, students have held substantial voting membership on a number of important administrative committees during the tenure of the last two presidents. During the summer of 1968, they even chaired the important committees of the Summer Task Force on Urban Problems. Only recently, however, have they been invited to membership on Faculty Senate Committees, and then only in an advisory capacity with one graduate and one undergraduate participating in each case. The interpretation of the faculty action by the students is predictably that it is tokenism. They have chosen, however, to pursue the matter cautiously because to date the administration has delivered on major student requests almost entirely. At the moment, student leaders exhibit a real trust in the ability and inclination of the administration to continue to honor "reasonable" requests.

Such trust in the administration is a relatively rare commodity in two of the institutions, Berkeley and San Francisco State, but one sees traces of such trust in the other four institutions although it is fading in some cases. The reaction of students against the faculty has usually been less hostile initially with antagonisms developing when students begin to realize goals or objectives and subsequently meet faculty resistance. The general hostility toward faculty is often allayed however, if the administration acts in the capacity of translator of faculty fear or as an agent of the faculty in imposing restraints on the students. In institutions where student antagonism has been directed primarily toward administrators, many observers indicate that it is only a matter of time until student activists recognize the faculty as the major block to innovation and reorient their hostilities.

If faculty reaction does not reorient the students, then lack of action will. In those cases where the faculty have been generally disinterested, students are increasingly looking to them for support, not because they have demonstrated a willingness in the past to provide such support, but because students are beginning to perceive the faculty as potential valuable allies given their strategic position in the institutional structure. Activists are beginning to interpret the faculty role as one which should include an alliance with students to pursue the issue of educational reform. In addition, there appears to be a growing appeal among radical and reform-oriented students of the idea of a "community of scholars." [38] In such a community, the conventional authority relations of educational systems would be broken down and the roles of both faculty and student would be consolidated into a single role of student. The only difference in the new context would be that some of the students would be more advanced than others.

The recent history of the university, however, has not been one of unconscious drift but of conscious choice which has been exercised largely by faculty and not by administrators or state legislators. In the final analysis, it is faculty who develop the criteria by which they will judge the excellence of the academy, and the choices they have made are being interpreted by growing numbers of students as antithetical to their interests. While legislators have shown increasing enthusiasm for intervention, it is still the faculty who must reorder their priorities or convince the students that they should share the perspective of the faculty member on what is important and what is unimportant. Maintenance of the status quo by faculty will continue to invite student enmity.

The issues leading to divisions between students and faculty are not limited to what is going on inside of the academy. They apply as well to faculty action, or lack of action, in the larger political arena. Seymour Melman speaks eloquently to this issue in an appeal to "the 800 faculty members who have identified themselves with an appeal to reason and order at Columbia and other universities." [39] He says:

> Until now, as a group, you have not made your weight felt on the side of peace, on the side of reducing the power of the military, on the side of changing American priorities. This is precisely what needs to be done if American society and American universities are to have a serious option in economic development as an alternative to race war.[40]

It is the faculty who are in the most strategic position to bring about change in higher education because they are such a vital cog in the machine that is now education. Their actions, however, cannot be highly individualistic and be successful. The individual exerts relatively little influence, even if he is a Nobel laureate. This is especially true in the public university where the final decision-making power rests directly or indirectly in the hands of the politician who has increasingly chosen to use the university as a ticket to political fame and fortune. Although they have lost a few distinguished faculty, the threat of a faculty exodus has not been one which has alarmed California political forces. In addition, individual resignations are often ambiguous in their meaning. Collective actions with clearly defined issues are not. But collective action by faculty is a rare event in American higher education and the prospects of such action in the future, while growing, do not appear to be growing rapidly. It is conceivable that faculty might mobilize under the impetus of some cataclysmic or catastrophic campus event, but the history of faculty action at Berkeley and San Francisco State College suggests that this is unlikely. Anything short of collective faculty action, however, can be expected to generate student antipathy and result in an increasing cleavage between faculty and the student body.

Student Power and Its Potential

Given what appears to be an almost certain lack of response on the part of the faculty, at least to the degree that the students would interpret as satisfactory, the only alternative is to gain an equal measure of power with the faculty. Most students are confident that if they had an equal voice in critical institutional affairs, they would be able to achieve the objectives which they seek. There is some evidence to indicate, for instance, that while the students are divided on some issues, they represent a relatively uniform front on many issues. Observations in this study suggest that this is particularly true of students in leadership positions. To the extent that this is true, many students feel that a coalition of reformist students and faculty could, in theory, transform the institution.

Some administrators, faculty, and governing board members have opined that they cannot understand why a voice in running the institution is not sufficient, why the student finds it necessary to demand equal participation.[41] It seems that the answer to this question is relatively simple. Students want to win. They are not interested in being heard and then having their petitions discarded or rejected as they have been in many cases in the institutions studied. Until they can achieve their major objectives, in whole or in part, they are likely to interpret their participation as hollow ritualism or a form of co-optation. Most students are becoming relatively sophisticated in the organizational mechanisms for siphoning off their energies or enthusiasm for change and have become wary of being given a voice in the decision-making process where they do not have power equal to achieving their substantive objectives. To the extent that such power continues to be denied, and to the extent that fundamental conflicts of interest persist, it is likely that students will continue to fail in the achievement of important reform objectives.

One final point in this area needs to be addressed. Many student leaders seem to feel that the incorporation of students into the decision-making process as equals will essentially resolve major problems. This position, however, ignores the fact that even the elements of democratic procedure involving faculty in all of the institutions studied are, in fact, spurious. In the last analysis, decisions rendered via the democratic process, even in areas supposedly reserved to faculty, can be overruled by administrative or trustee action. That this has not been a frequent occurrence reflects not so much the power of faculty, as it does a general faculty willingness to operate within the confines dictated by boards and administrators. In this sense, educational institutions take on the characteristics of what have been described as "guided democracies," where the "sense of electoral potency is high but mistaken." [42] As pointed out earlier, institutional democracy is not fully developed even now among those who "share" the decision-making power. The result is that any decision arrived at collectively is tentative inasmuch as it is subject to the approval of an executive head or board of trustees.

Introducing students into the deliberative process will not alter the basic structure insofar as alternative actions will be circumscribed by those in whom legal authority is vested. To the extent that this is true, the introduction of students as equals, if it leads to a change in the general thrust of decisions, might well expose the lack of substance of current institutional democracy. If this happens, the roles of constituencies would almost certainly revert to their previous adversary character. Under such circumstances, students are more likely than ever to resort to tactics such as strikes, boycotts, or disruption which are defined as illegitimate by institutional and extra-institutional authorities and which harden cleavages and escalate mutual hostility. What threatens then is a cyclical process of escalation. Student pressures are followed by moves to co-opt the student. Once the student recognizes that he has been co-opted, there is an escalation of the original pressures and tactics. Interestingly, as this process develops, the long-range developments may lead to a displacement of procedural goals by substantive goals once again. While the procedural issues have taken on a life of their own in that power becomes an important goal, even more important substantive goals within the institution and the larger society are more likely than ever to occupy the center of students' attention.

By now the issue of student participation in college and university decision making has been universally recognized and considered. In a study of 875 institutions in the fall of 1969, Earl McGrath found that eighty-eight per cent have some students on at least one policy-making body.[43] Although most institutions have not experimented with community government in the tradition of Antioch [44] or similar avant-garde institutions, the overwhelming majority of colleges and universities have recently reappraised the nature of their institutional government.

A number of institutions have developed self-study commissions on the matter of governance, occasionally because of some initiatives for creative exploration but more often in response to crises.[45] Our evidence, as well as that of others, suggests that pressure politics are necessary for change. In most cases, innovation follows from an expressed commitment to change in the fact of pressure rather than as a consequence of self-study. In short, self-studies rarely generate change unless great outside pressure is brought to bear or a majority of faculty genuinely desire change.[46]

The experiences of colleges and universities with reference to the issue of governance are varied, but one reform gaining widespread attention is a push for the re-consideration of trustee membership—that is, including students or other younger persons on boards.[47] College and university trustees are typically male, over fifty (with more than a third over sixty), white, Protestant, well-educated, wealthy (over half report incomes over $30,000), and Republican.[48] The concern with trustee membership is indicative of the extent of the demands for change in governance ranging all the way to the most important and powerful of governing elements. While there are often formidable legal barriers in the case of public institutions, the trustee concern is especially important in private institutions—even those as prestigious as Harvard and Stanford.[49]

The issue of governance is clearly complex, especially when addressing the thousands of institutions of higher learning. Among the prime issues have been the issue of *in loco parentis*—the conception of the university as a surrogate parent where there is substantial evidence that the traditional conception has been eroded and altered—and the issue of the curriculum—an area in which surveys suggest a considerable amount of student participation in decision making.[50] In other crucial areas, however, the amount of student involvement is miniscule. In particular, the proportion of schools in which students participate in faculty and personnel matters is substantially less than the number in which students participate in curricular matters.[51] While some would play down the importance of the participation of students in institutional governance, the issue is fundamentally linked to the more basic question of whom the university serves and in what way, a crucial issue, not only for the institutions in question, but for the society which they ostensibly serve.[52]

The question of governance has been addressed by scores of individuals including prominent educators from prestige universities. By and large, their analyses indicate a lack of sensitivity to the actual power contests, conflicts of interest, and organizational structure that are a part of contemporary universities.[53] One renowned observer comments, for instance, that:

> The claim that students should have a major role in actual governance is based upon a false premise: that students can plan, with reasonable awareness of the outcomes, the essentially professional service they receive from the college and university.[54]

With such views as a frequent point of departure for the consideration of student involvement, it is no mystery why efforts to develop institutional governments based on a concept of the creative participation of all members of an intellectual community have failed. There is an explicit assumption that faculty are more committed to institutional welfare, more sensitive than students, and possess a monopoly on wisdom and truth. In the long run, the essence of the contest is one of who knows what is better for the student, the student himself or the faculty and administration. While no serious advocate of radical change denies that faculty generally possess more of certain kinds of knowledge and have had more of certain kinds of experiences than students, there is a feeling that traditional views of faculty-student relations fail to give serious consideration to the positive potential of alternative learning communities with experimental approaches to decision making in academic and administrative matters.

The barrage of material on the matter of governance is understandable. The issue *is* one of fundamental prerogatives, power, and the sharing of privilege. The debate goes to the heart of traditional versus alternative conceptions of education. After the Berkeley Select Committee on Governance issued their report, a counterreport was advanced. As an addendum to the Cornell governance report, one professor made the case for academic education and against participatory education which he saw as political involvement and a threat to free inquiry and expression.[55] The diversity of viewpoints aside from the conventional liberal-conservative distinctions is illustrated by the debate between a liberal college professor and a radical professor, in which the radical professor's model is one based on the slogan "power to the people" rather than "student power" or "faculty power"—a people's university using the Chinese model.[56] No single piece is definitive nor can any argument speak for all constituencies in higher education; however, our observation is that efforts in the area of educational innovation inevitably open up the larger questions of governance. Furthermore, every indication is that the modes of participation will continue to develop and expand.

Although it is argued by some that student participation is unwarranted because of their short tenure and lack of commitment and wisdom, there are effective counterarguments. Wallerstein contends, for instance, that "Wisdom is maximized by the fullest participation of those who desire to participate" and that "Commitment is increased by involvement in decision-making."[57] At the schools intensively examined in this study, we have noted the degree to which participation in the curricular experiments has served an educational function. Designing curriculum in the Experimental College at San Francisco State, participating in a Task Force at UCLA, and planning the ethnic studies programs at Berkeley were significant experiences for students involved. At the University of Oregon, the participation of students in university and departmental functions during the past couple of years has heightened student awareness, commitment, and the degree to which they could relate their own educational experiences and needs to those of others within the university.

As suggested earlier, the impetus for change has usually been external pressure and dramatic events or crises. The Berkeley Free Speech Movement created a mood for change, though temporary in character. The Cambodian invasion in May 1970 created a climate of concern across the country leading many faculties to pass legislation concerning ROTC or governance on the campus. Often such decisions were rescinded shortly thereafter. The pattern of immediate response in the face of a crisis followed by later retrenchment is not an infrequent one. Typically the major concessions and changes made are altered shortly afterwards, or agreements are ignored or abrogated by higher authorities. The strike at San Francisco State College perhaps best illustrates this dynamic. While schools around the country were exploring new cooperative student-faculty-administration relationships, San Francisco State became increasingly polarized. The 1968 efforts for a constitutional convention to revise governance gave way to the strike, the appointment of S. I. Hayakawa as President, and the entrenchment of a no-nonsense autocratic administration.[58]

One of the recurrent questions in educational reform has to do with the method of approach. Typically the perspective is to ameliorate tensions, improve conditions, grant changes as pressures increase, and gradually reform or modify existing structures and procedures. In part this is due to the institutionalized conservatism of higher education. As we have observed, change is most frequently a response to pressures or events. Innovation is often a defensive phenomenon. Changes usually come only grudgingly.

The alternative approach to the problem of change, that is, developing conceptions of new educational environments and then devising the best way to achieve the new deal, is one that is rarely found. Although the strategy is rare, there are some provocative arguments for adopting such perspectives. In an extremely provocative book, Robert Paul Wolff argues that appeals to the principle of participatory democracy, on the grounds that students should participate in decisions which affect them, should be abandoned. He insists, instead, that students should participate because they are part of the academic community and community governance is the only logical form of government for a real community. In advocating the implementation of Paul Goodman's idea of the community of learning, Wolff is arguing that we should bring university decision making into the open for full scrutiny, criticism, and review and that decision-making procedures should be developed which maximize the natural growth of a university community.[59]

Although one might take issue with some of the details in Wolff's proposal, his argument articulates, in many ways, our position that some affirmative model or concept of the university is required to successfully meet the challenges now facing the university. The matter of governance cries out for systematic effort to alter the existing structures of colleges and universities to fit a more ideal model.

Experiences of the past few years lead us to the conclusion that most efforts to change are reactive in character. Faculty-administration response to demands for student power has largely been to assume a defensive posture. Radical innovations in curriculum have challenged the total governance of the academy. Response has been piecemeal and predicated on the position of minimal change to ward off the assaults. To the extent that there is a real crisis in the university, we see the cries for student power as misdirected. The question is increasingly seen by students, faculty, and administrators as one of the nature of decisions made, not merely who makes them. To be sure, the argument might be made that power should lie in the hands of faculty and students rather than regents or trustees and administrators.[60] But power is not shared by those who have it, and what is ultimately critical is what changes might be created in the colleges and universities. A changed conceptualization of what the institution ought to be will naturally enough lead to an expression of how decisions should be made. In this climate it would be well to address the matter of governance. In the meantime, demands for change in student participation will likely circle about the controversial issues on the campus—such as student-initiated curricula, ethnic studies programs, and the wider issues of student admissions and the functions of the college and university particularly regarding corporate and military training.

The Politics of Higher Education

The previous section focused on questions of the internal politics of educational institutions. If their internal difficulties were the only ones to be resolved, then perhaps the task before higher education might not be so formidable. But the internal conflicts and hostilities are only a part of the picture. Universities and colleges, including private institutions, are affected directly and indirectly by what goes on in the outer political arena. Their ability to resolve their internal problems is mitigated considerably by the nature of their relationship to the outside community. In the case of the private institution, this is considerably less true than in the case of the public, but even here there is no escaping the impact of political pressures and decisions. Stanford is a case in point.

A great portion of Stanford's resources, especially its research money, comes from federal agencies. The extent to which this plays a part in the internal decisions of the institution can be seen in the fact that Stanford's president felt that it was necessary to go to Washington immediately following the decision to phase out secret research on the campus and assure the government that this did not mean that Stanford would no longer accept defense contracts, only that it would not be able to accept them if they were secret. Students at the institution who played a prominent role in the sit-in leading to the new policy argue that the president and others in the Stanford community were worried about the possibility of a government backlash or reprisals taking the form of a cutback in grants and appropriations to the institution. As long as this threat exists, and as long as the institution feels that it is compelled to take it into account in determining internal policies, then the influence of the government on what happens internally will be formidable.[61]

It is interesting to speculate in this regard what the reaction of the university community would be in the event that the government did choose to engage in reprisals against institutions refusing secret research. Perhaps such an eventuality is unlikely because of the potential of alienating a large sector of the scientific community whose talents are required in other enterprises, but the problem presents an interesting dilemma. As things now stand, the freedom and autonomy of even the private institution are jeopardized in this regard inasmuch as rising costs have made them increasingly dependent on the federal government for an important part of their operating resources.

If the problem of outside governmental interference in the affairs of private institutions presents a serious problem, it has taken on an acute character in the case of public institutions. Public institutions, because of their total dependence on government resources, have been compromised throughout their history. In California, despite the officially apolitical character of the governing boards of the university and state college systems, the politics of higher education have become the most salient issue in the state political arena. There is every indication, too, that as long as public response to political interference in the affairs of the colleges and universities continues to be supportive, it will increase. The kinds of direct intervention described in earlier chapters increased during 1969 and have continued to increase. As long as such intervention continues, the potential for a reconciliation of internal conflicts in higher education is rendered nearly impossible. Part of the reason for this is not simply that constant interference limits the alternatives open to constituencies within the university to maneuver but because the state agencies have shown that they will not only interfere periodically, they will overturn or overrule decisions which are not in accord with their own carefully circumscribed interests. In such cases, decisions of the faculty or administration, where they do not reflect the educational philosophy or political ideology of the governing boards, may very well be overturned.

The interference of the regents and the trustees in California indicate that it is relatively easy to maintain a facade of democracy even in a fundamentally authoritarian institution, as long as there are no serious disagreements. In the past there were fewer disagreements. In no case have disagreements ever been as thoroughgoing or as widespread as in the recent past. The result has been that decisions democratically arrived at through approved procedures have been overruled at every level. Student decisions have been overruled by faculty and administration, and administrative decisions by regents, trustees or by political pressures from the office of the governor and the State Superintendent of Schools.

The problem in California has been exacerbated by the fact that incidents and goals have taken on a symbolic character which effectively eliminates the possibility of resolution of differences. Rational solutions to the differences at San Francisco State, for instance, were made impossible because any concessions on the part of the administration were interpreted by political forces as capitulation and therefore unacceptable. Compromise has become effectively impossible. One can point to the resolution of the strike and suggest that it represented a compromise of sorts, but it should be kept clearly in mind that the strikers were conceded nothing that had not been conceded before the strike and faculty participants without tenure were subsequently dismissed despite the fact that administrative rigidity and the subsequent escalation in hostilities led to an exodus by both students and faculty and increased tension and fear in the college community. The president made it clear that he was not going to be bound by any amnesty negotiated by the faculty committee charged with negotiating a settlement. Resolution of difficulties in any other way short of repression was, therefore, rendered extremely unlikely. Furthermore, the cause of educational reform in other areas was severely set back with the confiscation of the fiscal power of the student body government which had previously underwritten the major innovational programs on the campus.

Such an ethos often leads to the further escalation of hostilities between the students and the state. Where such an escalation can lead was seen in the case of the People's Park in Berkeley. Interest groups inside and outside of the education institutions in California have become so polarized that there appears to be little possibility at this point in finding any common interest which might lead to a productive resolution of problems. In many respects, the conflicts of interest at every level are irreconcilable. Students cannot enjoy a more intense relationship with, and a greater contribution from, faculty if the faculty are progressively withdrawing from the educational aspects of their institutions into research. In any event, the faculty could not turn out the kind of student which the larger public appears to demand—one that is docile but has a variety of technical skills and can man the roles which industry and government have carved out for him—because the student increasingly rejects these roles. In the end, it would appear that the goals which the governing bodies such as those in California have in mind for higher education have nothing to do with liberating the student but are oriented toward further molding him to fit into a preconceived notion of what the end product of a college education ought to look like.[62]

While not all of the institutions have been plagued by the kind of interference that has been characteristic of Berkeley and San Francisco State, the limits of governmental oppression are not at all obvious. While one or two institutions may be singled out more frequently than others, the California experience indicates that both the capacity and the appetite of governmental figures for interference is immense. While an astute administration may save an institution from the degree of intervention that has characterized Berkeley and San Francisco State, it cannot be avoided altogether. If the potential for interference is limited by the capacities of the governing boards, it is clear that the limits of these capacities have not yet been reached. It appears likely that any institution with any internal activism will be subjected to political repression either directly or indirectly. To the extent that this is the case, the crisis to which the nation must address itself is not in the university but in the larger community.

The University in the Larger Political Arena

In a nation where technocratic demands have placed primary emphasis on the universities' role as supplier of trained manpower to buttress the research capacity of the country, it is somewhat surprising to hear, on occasion, the argument that universities should remain isolated from the society in order to retain their neutrality. It should be absolutely clear by now that there is no such thing as a neutral college or university. The political concerns and protests of those in the universities have exposed the issue of the political posture of the academy and destroyed the myth of the ivory tower.

Colleges and universities of the United States are fully implicated in the society's achievements and its atrocities, its creativity and its violence. Although institutions of higher learning may wish to claim an aloofness from the society, they can be divorced from the real world only in relative terms. More importantly, it is not a question of *whether* the college or university is involved, it is a matter of *how*. Does the administration turn over student records to intelligence agencies or not? Will the college accept federal funds contingent upon loyalty oath signatures? Does the university accept Department of Defense research contracts? Will the college have military training as part of its institution? Are lists of campus speakers given to Congressional committees? Does the college allow military recruiters on the campus? Will the university develop minority student programs with governmental funds? The list of questions can be extended almost indefinitely. Whether we are talking about public or private institutions, virtually all colleges and universities are involved directly with various agencies of government. What is important, of course, is the nature of those relationships at any particular point.[63]

There are any number of appeals, from both inside and outside the academic community, for the university to return to what is alleged to have been its former neutral position. Some of these are simplistic efforts to link student protest primarily to demands for curricular change while ignoring the broader issues. They usually take the form of a plea for the retention of appropriate standards.[64] Other critiques are more sophisticated, usually attempting to sidestep the issues. Former Assistant Secretary of State and Columbia Professor of Philosophy Charles Frankel fears politicization of the academy which he sees as "abandonment of free inquiry and criticism, and the negation of individual rights." [65] This argument comes from a man who served the foreign policy objectives of Lyndon Johnson even as university faculties and students around the country were protesting the complicity of academy with that policy in Indochina. Such intellectual schizophrenia is widespread. It takes the form of accepting, but defining as nonpolitical, those academic enterprises which support the interests of the government. It is only contrary political arguments that such defenders of the status quo find threatening the open and free nature of our centers of learning.

Some analysts are convinced that it is the indulgence of liberal administrators which has ceded to New Left students all the vestiges of academic integrity. Former Leftist and now conservative critic Sidney Hook, in a spirit of self-congratulation, says, "Shortly after the riotous events at the University of California at Berkeley in 1964, I predicted that in consequence of the faculty's refusal to condemn the student seizure of Sproul Hall, the administration building, American higher education would never be the same again. . . ."[66] University administrators in the past few years have seen the extension of this position to the point where Governor Reagan of California, in the spring of 1970, indicated his willingness to see a bloodbath at the universities if that was what was required to bring tranquility.

It is not that students are speaking to, and reacting to, issues in the real world that is threatening, it is *how* they are reacting. Who decried the politicization of American institutions of higher learning when they made total accommodations in mobilizing for the Second World War? Yet protests generated by the war in Vietnam, leading to disavowals of university military training and defense research, have generated reactionary and accusatory challenges to the alleged new politicization of the campuses.

The concern of those who are offended by recent campus events is not solely a function of the intensity of protests. More people are attending colleges and universities. Growth is fastest at the state institutions and the size of universities and colleges is growing dramatically, so that the "small" state universities often enroll well over 20,000 students. If the radicalization of the college population is real, the implications for the future are indeed threatening to the system's defenders.

In another sphere, the campus crisis poses a threat because of the role of the university in research and development; the university is an important resource to those who control the nation. Of course, this is a two-way street. The importance of governmental monies in the university budgets—private or public—grows continually greater. Private institutions such as Johns Hopkins and MIT have gigantic annual allotments from the Department of Defense for contract research. In institutions not considered especially elite, there is a strong mission-oriented thrust in DOD programs such as Project Themis which was an effort launched a few years ago to increase the number of universities doing research for the military. The service station concept of a university, much discussed since Clark Kerr's commentary on the development of the multiversity,[67] leads inevitably to a posture of institutional accommodation to governmental, military, and corporate interests. Even private universities are not independent, for they too are dependent to a large extent upon government and corporate work as sources of support. Such dependency explains ROTC on campus. It explains a great deal of research activity, whether for the Department of Defense or private industry. It also explains a good deal of the curriculum and why substantial university resources are used for recruitment—military and civilian. That universities have retained some real sense of autonomy and neutrality with regard to the larger political and economic structures of the society is a canard thoroughly discredited by recent events.

The problem is presented because the past few years have seen a dramatic increase in the numbers of students who have gone to college and who have subsequently become radicalized. The struggle for racial justice and against militarism and American imperialism have attracted larger and larger numbers of students. The college or university that has not experienced some turmoil is rare indeed! The threat that this imposes *is* considerable. There is a widespread challenge to legitimacy that is expressed in a variety of forms from the student skepticism over the authority of faculty on the campus to the rejection of the legitimacy of the draft. The experimentation with life-styles indicates a rejection of the consumerism and traditional concerns with occupational and social mobility. Richard Flacks has recently suggested that one-half of all voters in the U.S. by 1975 will be under 35 years of age. Obviously a large percentage will have had a college experience.[68] Of the eight million students in colleges and universities today, there is considerable evidence that a substantial number are participants in, and an even more substantial number supporters of, the student protest movement.

There has been a rash of congressional and state legislative action or proposed action designed to curtail the protest movement and curb student and faculty political activity. In part this intervention has resulted in the radicalization of increasing numbers of academics. But if there are those who have been radicalized, there are also those who have become so profoundly cynical as a result of their impotence that they have withdrawn even further into their esoteric academic shells. Whether or not they will muster the enthusiasm and the courage to rejoin the battle in the near future is a moot question. If they do not, however, if the lesson we have learned really is that repression works, then the future of the academy will be bleak indeed.

Postscript: An Admonition

Throughout its history, higher education in America has assumed a defensive position with regard to its role vis-a-vis the larger society. It has been characterized as the ivory tower, ostensibly because of its withdrawal from the affairs of the larger community. The academy was a place where men engaged in reflection and intellectual frivolity which had little or nothing to do with the rest of the world.

The ivory tower image is one that has been waning for a considerable period. This is especially true in the wake of the 20th century's scientific and technical revolution.[69] But while higher education has enlisted itself in the service of the society, it has never assumed a role of leadership. Growing numbers of scholars and critics are becoming aware of the necessity of the academy to assume such a role. These men speak of the critical function of the academy and of its inherently subversive character. It is a role, however, which many if not most academicians reject or would prefer to ignore.

Traditionally, higher education could ignore its critical functions because only an occasional isolated individual was prompted to prod the educational community into action. This was true in no small measure because the university served a distinctly elite community. The bulk of the constituents of higher education came from the traditional bulwarks of the status quo, the upper and upper-middle class. The composition of the academy has been changing rapidly, however, and its constituents represent a range of interests previously unrepresented in higher education. Today the academy is constantly reminded of its failure to assert itself as a critic of society and as a positive force attacking social and world problems.[70] It is not being prodded gently either. A generation of politically active, sophisticated, and morally sensitive youth are more and more stridently calling on the university to recognize its obligation and to assume a position of leadership. In a sense, it seems that this is what the demand for relevance is all about. It is a demand for more than an intellectual leadership; it involves a moral commitment, a commitment which it must largely shape itself.

Moral leadership in the secular society has passed out of the hands of religious institutions, but no one seems quite sure where it has gone. It is certain at this point that it is not in the college and university. In the guise of neutrality, the university has willingly lent itself to the advancement of the most reprehensible activities of the society of which it is a part. The president of one state university, arguing that the myth of neutrality is both "corrupting and cowardly," calls upon the academic community to abandon the facade.[71] Increasing numbers of college students are coming to recognize what he says:

> The federal government knows, the State Department knows, the Pentagon knows, the CIA knows, [and] our adversaries around the world know—that American universities are and have been agents for research and recruitment in support of America's world policies and military efforts.[72]

A rarity among college administrators, he calls upon the university to enlist itself in the cause of a humane politics.[73] In a sense, this is what the students are demanding, and every indication is that they will be tenacious in their demands. Until the university becomes an active agent of social and political change, it is unlikely that it can expect anything but increasing difficulties and crisis. In effect, higher education must address itself to the crisis outside its walls, as well as inside, or there will be little chance of a reconciliation in the academic world. Other responses have been attempted and they have failed. Repression has simply confirmed the students in their objectives. It is possible that the academic world might still resolve its problems, but there is every indication, unfortunately, that the teacher has not learned his lesson.

APPENDIX
A Note on Methodology

As suggested in the prefatory and introductory remarks, this investigation was prompted by asking questions which have basically not been researched. From the beginning we saw our inquiry as exploratory in nature, as we attempted to understand the dynamics of the major educational innovations in American higher education since the mid-1960s. We hoped that a research strategy could be developed which would allow some ability to generalize and which would indicate the critical dimensions of developments in colleges and universities; we wished to maximize our understanding of the problem, identify the critical issues, and discern the questions which our study could make clear as well as some of the important research and programmatic needs. We decided very early to employ a strategy best described as a series of comparative case studies.

The techniques employed were what the anthropologist Jules Henry

Appendix

referred to as a "natural history," using a combination of strategies including an examination of records and written materials, focused interviews, and participant observation.[1] The idea of the natural history is quite simple in that it reconstructs contemporary events in a fashion which will allow the reader to gain some picture of the process of development of a particular phenomenon or issue. In the context of this study, such an approach represents a compromise between the intensive case study of a single institution, which is characteristic of much of the work done in the past on complex organizations, and the massive survey research study which is currently used by many in the social sciences.[2] A number of recent studies have utilized the case study approach. Some have focused exclusively on a particular campus; others have been comparative.[3] The one thing that appeared obvious, however, was that quantitative data accessible through the use of survey techniques would not have provided the kinds of information or insight that we wanted.

For a study such as this, we considered it necessary to move beyond the scope of a single institution to gain a clearer perspective from which to suggest possible generalizations applicable to a range of institutions. We attempted to maximize the potential for extrapolation beyond the schools studied by choosing institutions which represented, insofar as possible, a range of prototypes of American colleges and universities. Similar strategies have been used successfully in a number of excellent studies focusing on different facets of the university including studies by Jencks and Riesman,[4] Burton Clark,[5] Harold Taylor,[6] and Education and World Affairs.[7] An inherent limitation to selecting a variety of institutions was that the central issue—that is, the process of implications of educational change—required that the study be focused on institutions which have attempted educational experimentation and innovation on a scale that could be considered to have a potential impact on the entire institution. Many institutions were thus eliminated from consideration simply because they had made virtually no recent attempts to implement educational change or reform at the institutional level.

In making the final selection of the institutions to be included in the study, there were obviously other considerations. Financial and time constraints affected the decision to limit the study to institutions on the West Coast. Given these parameters, then, the institutions finally chosen were the Universities of California at Berkeley and Los Angeles, Stanford University, San Francisco State College, the University of Oregon, and Western Washington State College. To the extent that it was possible given the limitations discussed, we felt that they represented at least a partial range of the types of institutions found in American higher education. Each institution is described in detail in a separate chapter, but, in capsule form, the list includes a range of sizes from the very large to relatively modestly sized institution; elite and non-elite schools with the full range of graduate and professional studies; varying degrees of commitment to graduate education as opposed to undergraduate education; a variety of locales ranging from huge urban centers to suburban residential areas to comparatively small cities; and varying degrees of emphasis on the strictly educative functions of higher education versus a broader range of commitments including research and service. Each was chosen also because it had attained some reputation for having greater than average commitment to educational innovation and constructive change.

In order to analyze the processes of educational change in any detail, we decided that it was essential to use an approach which would facilitate a thorough understanding of the character of the various institutions and the internal dynamics of change. It was necessary, for instance, to speak with a range of individuals in key places in the organizational structure, individuals who might not show up in a random sample.[8] Furthermore, we considered it essential to gather as much as possible of the wealth of documentary material available which could clarify the chronology of events, provide clues to the issues involved, and elaborate the conflicts, intrigues, and decisions which are a part of the innovational process.

In the case of the institutions involved in the study, there is a vast amount of material in the form of proposals, working papers, memoranda, reports, institutional records, assessments, and historical data which are important sources of information regarding the development of particular programs and the general process of change on the various campuses. These documents range from reports issued at the very highest administrative levels, including the trustees or other governing bodies of the institutions, to various subunits of the student body pursuing a relatively narrow interest. They range from the official to the unofficial; from the published to the unpublished; from documents for general dissemination to in-house papers; and from technical proposals to critical attacks on institutional policy and personalities. Each, in its own way, contributes to an understanding of the processes underlying educational developments in the particular institution. In fact, one recent book has been devoted solely to a study of university self-study reports, including those of three campuses we examined.[9]

We suggested earlier that interviews with key informants in administrative, faculty, and student positions is a more efficient method of obtaining information than many other alternatives, a fact that has long been recognized by anthropologists but often disdained by sociologists because of the risks involved in relying on informant data.[10] Barzun and Graff reconstruct the negative arguments of the skeptic who observes that "Most people are notoriously bad observers; some are deliberate or unconscious liars; there is no such thing as the perfect witness." [11] While they concede that there is no such thing as the "perfect witness," they go on to point out that the issue is not whether or not one exists but that we must take precautions to cross-check information, to corroborate the observations of informants, and to ascertain, insofar as possible, that we have separated the fact from the fancy or the truth from the lie.[12] We have accomplished this kind of cross-checking by relying not on one or two key informants but on a range of informants representing a variety of perspectives on each of the issues which is of central concern. Similarly, much of the documentary data provides a further cross-check, helping to minimize the distortion involved. It should also be recognized, though, that the distortions of informants, insofar as they can be identified, also provide valuable insights into the political processes involved in the kind of organizational change under examination. Indeed, differing perceptions and interpretations of the same events by those occupying radically different roles in the institutions are among the most interesting features of such a study and often provide some of the most important insights. In this respect, it seemed to us that the choice of alternative methods to those employed might well have obscured partially, if not totally, much of the most important information which eventually emerged.[13]

Gathering Data

The institutions involved in the study were visited systematically from 1968 to 1971, sometimes for a day at a time, other times for several weeks. Dozens of documents including memos, reports, position papers, technical programs, long-range plans, evaluation reports, and a variety of others were gathered. In addition, we talked at varying lengths with more than 140 faculty, students, and administrators at the six campuses. These individuals included members of governing boards, presidents and vice presidents, deans and program directors, faculty and staff, and student leaders and program participants.

In addition to general historical information, each informant was interviewed with regard to such items as the sources of support for or resistance to innovation from faculty, administrative, or student constituencies; support for or antipathy toward innovation from institutional governing boards, politicians, state government, the outside community or its organized constituencies; financial arrangements and future commitments for innovative programs; general campus interest in particular programs; the extent to which programs are considered possible models for the larger institution; the organizational relationship of experimental programs to each other and to the larger system; prognosis for the maintenance and extension of experimental programs; changes in the roles of various campus constituencies in the governing of the institution; and their perceptions of the impact of radical pedagogical changes or experiments in the realm of governance and decision making.

Recently some researchers indicated that at the time they initiated their inquiry into the dynamics of academic reform in 1967 they "could detect little overt student influence on most academic changes."[14] In our study we initiated our inquiry precisely because we wanted to examine the changes in student-initiated curricula and the developments in governance, as well as the experimental colleges and ethnic studies programs. The logic of our inquiry dictated the range of campus constituencies in our interviews. Initial interviewees helped to identify other informants. Students directed us to faculty and administrators who in turn often steered us to students.[15]

We did employ the device of telephone interviewing after initial interviews. Since we interviewed many of the same persons repeatedly over the years of the study, we obtained later interviews by telephone, having established relationships with them. This is a device relatively little discussed in the literature on social science research methodology,[16] and one which we felt was very useful and appropriate, especially for the latter part of our study.

The myth of value neutrality in social science research has been the butt of a substantial assault in the past few years.[17] During this period it has become increasingly clear that social researchers have rarely considered the impact of their own human qualities and experience on their field research and on the formulation of their social theories.[18] In this respect, we came to the problem having both been considerably involved in the curricular and governmental activities at one of the institutions studied. There is no question that our experiences very much shaped our perspectives and sensitivities regarding student initiatives in curriculum and participation in governance.[19]

At this point, perhaps a final precautionary note is in order. Although our research strategy was chosen as the most appropriate to our particular problem, there are inherent limitations. The number of institutions included is small though it is representative of a large portion of the institutions of higher learning in the United States. There are, however, no church-related sectarian institutions and no small colleges. In addi-

Appendix

tion, the six institutions included in the study are among the scholastically superior colleges and universities in the country. These limitations should be taken into account in extrapolating our conclusions or attempting to fit them to particular institutions.

NOTES

CHAPTER I

1. An overview of the 1960s and the thrust of the student mood is presented in Jonathan Eisen and David Sternberg, "The Student Revolt Against Liberalism," *Annals of the American Academy of Political and Social Science,* 382 (March 1969), pp. 83–94. For an interesting assessment see Richard Flacks, "The New Left and American Politics: After Ten Years," paper presented at the American Political Science Association meetings, Los Angeles, September 1970.

2. Jack Newfield, "In Defense of Student Radicals," in Gary R. Weaver and James H. Weaver (eds.), *The University and Revolution* (Englewood Cliffs, N.J.: Prentice-Hall, 1969), p. 49.

3. Immanuel Wallerstein, *University in Turmoil: The Politics of Change* (New York: Atheneum, 1969), p. 11.

4. Ibid., p. 9.

5. Robert Ross, "The University and the Future," *Social Policy,* 1 (November-December 1970), p. 37.

6. Roger Kahn, *The Battle for Morningside Heights: Why Students Rebel* (New York: Wm. Morrow & Co., 1970), p. 17.

7. Ibid.

8. See, for example, the American Council on Education survey as reported by Gene Currivan, "Poll Finds Shift to Left Among College Freshmen," *New York Times,* December 20, 1970, p. 42.

9. See Milton Mankoff and Richard Flacks, "The Changing Social Base of the American Student Movement: Its Meaning and Implications," *Annals of the American Academy of Political and Social Science,* May 1971, pp. 54–67.

10. Joseph Axelrod, "New Organizational Patterns in American Colleges and Universities," in Lewis B. Mayhew (ed.), *Higher Education in the Revolutionary Decades* (Berkeley: McCutchan, 1967), pp. 161–83.

11. Thorstein Veblen, *The Higher Learning in America* (New York: Huebsch, 1918).

12. Ibid., pp. 148–69. For an excellent discussion showing that Veblen's analysis is contemporary, see Thomas Sowell, "Veblen's Higher Learning after Fifty Years," *Journal of Economic Issues,* 3 (December 1969), pp. 66–78.

13. Upton Sinclair, *The Goose-Step* (Pasadena: Published by author, 1922), pp. 16–17.

14. Robert Hutchins, *The Higher Learning in America* (New Haven: Yale University Press, 1936).

15. James Wechsler, *Revolt on the Campus* (New York: Covici-Friede, 1935).

16. Clark Kerr, *The Uses of the University* (New York: Harper and Row, 1963), p. 48.

17. Harold Orlans, *The Effects of Federal Programs on Higher Education,* quoted in Kerr, op. cit., p. 64.

18. These issues have been important in confrontations at institutions like Columbia, Chicago, City College of New York, Berkeley, San Francisco, Cornell, and a number of others. See Harry Edwards, *Black Students* (New York: The Free Press, 1970) for a general discussion.

19. James A. Perkins, *The University in Transition* (Princeton, N.J.: Princeton University Press, 1966), Chapter 1; and Kerr, op. cit.

20. Although student disturbances are not new phenomena in America, as already noted, a review of their history makes it clear that the recent student disorders in this country are unparalleled. For an elaboration of the early history of student rebellions, see Frederick Rudolph, *The American College and University* (New York: Random House, 1962), Chapters 5 and 6.

21. Some notable examples of such reports are the Report of the Select Committee on Education, *Education at Berkeley* (Muscatine Report) (Berkeley: University of California Press, 1966); Study Commission on University Governance, *The Culture of the University: Governance and Education* (Berkeley: University of California, 1968); Committee on Academic Innovation and Development, *The Kneller Report* (Los Angeles: University of California, 1968). In each of these cases, a few of the many items have been adopted. In almost all cases of adoption, there is little more than an approval in principle rather than any development of mechanisms for implementing the program in the proposal.

22. For detailed descriptions of such programs and their functions, see any of

the following: Joseph Axelrod, "An Experimental College Model," *Educational Record*, 48 (fall 1967), pp. 327–37; John H. Bunzel, "Black Studies at San Francisco State," *The Public Interest*, 13 (fall 1968), pp. 22–38; Marjorie Carpenter, "The Role of Experimental Colleges in American Higher Education," in W. Hugh Stickler (ed.), *Experimental Colleges* (Tallahassee: Florida State University, 1964); John E. Dietrich and F. Craig Johnson, "A Catalytic Agent for Innovation in Higher Education," *Educational Record*, 48 (summer 1967), pp. 206–13; Kenneth J. Hallam (ed.), *Innovations in Higher Education* (Baltimore: Towson State College, 1966); Joseph Tussman, *Experiment at Berkeley* (New York: Oxford, 1969).

23. Report of the Select Committee on Education, op. cit.

24. Study Commission on University Governance, op. cit.

25. Kerr, op. cit.

26. See Harold Taylor, *Students Without Teachers* (New York: McGraw-Hill, 1969).

27. Rudolph, op. cit., p. 491.

28. Kerr, op. cit., p. 46.

29. Ibid., pp. 46ff.

30. For an elaboration of the most recent liberal and radical critiques of the university, see Taylor, op. cit.

31. Kalman Goldberg and Robin C. Linstromberg, "The University as an Anachronism," *Journal of Higher Education*, 40 (March 1969), pp. 193–204.

32. The best discussion of this tradition in the social sciences is found in Alvin Gouldner, "Anti-Minotaur: The Myth of a Value-Free Sociology," in Irving Louis Horowitz (ed.), *The New Sociology* (New York: Oxford, 1965), pp. 196–217. A more general discussion is found in a brilliant piece by Noam Chomsky, "The Responsibility of Intellectuals," in Theodore Roszak (ed.), *The Dissenting Academy* (New York: Random House, 1968), pp. 255–98. An illustration of the argument that favors the alleged neutrality of the university is Joseph Schwab, *College Curriculum and Student Protest* (Chicago: University of Chicago Press, 1969).

33. For a discussion of the problems related to the confrontation of moral issues in the university, see Andrew M. Greeley, "The Teaching of Moral Wisdom," in G. Kerry Smith (ed.), *Stress and Campus Response* (San Francisco: Jossey-Bass, 1968), pp. 209–13.

34. Ibid., pp. 85–123.

35. Much of the rhetoric of the student movement in this country alludes directly to the issue of the massive, impersonal, and irrelevant character of the students' education. Even if one is willing to challenge the merits of these arguments, the fact that they are perceived as real problems by significant numbers of students makes it imperative for the institution to deal with them. For an elaborate discussion of the problem of size, see Warren B. Martin, *Alternative to Irrelevance* (Nashville: Abingdon, 1968).

36. See Dwight R. Ladd, *Change in Educational Policy* (New York: McGraw-Hill, 1970).

37. Robert H. Somers, "The Berkeley Campus in the Twilight of the Free Speech Movement: Hope or Futility?" in James McEvoy and Abraham Miller

(eds.), *Black Power and Student Rebellion* (Belmont, Cal.: Wadsworth Publishing Co., 1969).

38. Hilary Putnam, "From 'Resistance' to Student-Worker Alliance," in Priscilla Long (ed.), *The New Left Reader* (Boston: Porter-Sargent, 1969), p. 326.

39. Kerr, op. cit., p. 99.

40. John J. Corson, *Governance of Colleges and Universities* (New York: McGraw-Hill, 1960); Herbert Stroup, *Bureaucracy in Higher Education* (New York: Free Press, 1966); Corson, "From Authority to Leadership," *Journal of Higher Education*, 40 (March 1969), pp. 181–92.

41. Ralf Dahrendorf, *Class and Class Conflict in Industrial Society* (Stanford: Stanford University Press, 1959).

42. Edward H. Litchfield, "The University: A Congeries or an Organic Whole?" *AAUP Bulletin*, 45 (September 1959), pp. 374–79. These problems are certainly not absent from industry, but the greater authority often vested in management allows manipulation of a type not possible in the academic world to limit its effects. See Theodore Caplow, *Principles of Organization* (New York: Harcourt, 1964), Chapter 7.

43. See for instance Charles E. Bidwell, "The School as a Formal Organization," in James G. March (ed.), *Handbook of Organizations* (Chicago: Rand, 1965), pp. 979–1022; Alvin W. Gouldner, "Cosmopolitans and Locals: Toward an Analysis of Latent Social Roles," *Administrative Science Quarterly*, 2 (1957–58), pp. 281–306 and 444–80; Harold L. Wilensky, *Intellectuals in Labor Unions* (Glencoe: The Free Press, 1956), pp. 129–44.

44. Edward Gross, "Universities as Organizations," *American Sociological Review*, 33 (August 1968), pp. 518–44.

45. Ibid., pp. 536–37.

46. Martin Trow, "Bell, Book, and Berkeley: Reflections Occasioned by a Reading of Daniel Bell's *The Reforming of General Education*," *Experiment and Innovation*, 1 (January 1968), p. 9.

47. Ibid. Also see Somers in McEvoy and Miller, op. cit., Henry F. May, "Living With Crisis: A View from Berkeley," *The American Scholar*, 38 (autumn 1969), p. 601.

48. Ibid.

49. Morris Keeton and Conrad Hilberry, *Struggle and Promise: A Future for Colleges* (New York: McGraw Hill, 1969).

50. Burton R. Clark, *The Distinctive College* (Chicago: Aldine Publishing Co., 1970).

51. John A. Howard and H. Bruce Franklin, *Who Should Run the Universities?* (Washington, D.C.: American Enterprise Institute, 1969).

52. For a full discussion of the assaults, response pattern, and questions about universities and change, see Julian Foster and Durward Long, "The Dynamics of Institutional Response," in Julia Foster and Durward Long (eds.), *Protest! Student Activism in America* (New York: Wm. Morrow & Co., 1970).

53. J. B. Lon Hefferlin, *Dynamics of Academic Reform* (San Francisco: Jossey-Bass, 1969), p. 146.

54. Ibid., pp. 10–16.

55. Ibid., p. 79.

56. Ibid., pp. 131–32.

57. Ibid., pp. 118–46. For a discussion of the role of faculty in university change, see Nevitt Sanford, "Whatever Happened to Action Research?" *Journal of Social Issues,* 26 (autumn 1970) pp. 3–23.

58. For an analysis of the change process in the public schools, see any of the following: Paul R. Mort, "Studies in Educational Innovation from the Institute of Administrative Research: An Overview," in Matthew B. Miles (ed.), *Innovation in Education* (New York: Columbia, 1964), pp. 317–28; Richard I. Miller, *An Overview of Educational Change* (New York: Appleton-Century-Crofts, 1967), pp. 1–20; Goodwin Watson (ed.), *Change in School Systems* (Washington D.C.: NEA, 1967); Goodwin Watson, "Resistance to Change," in Goodwin Watson (ed.), *Concepts for Social Change* (Washington, D.C.: NEA, 1967), pp. 10–25; Richard C. Carlson, "Barriers to Change in Public Schools" (Eugene: University of Oregon, 1965), p. 308; Thomas M. Barrington, *The Introduction of Selected Educational Practices into Teachers Colleges and Their Laboratory Schools* (New York: Columbia, 1953); Matthew B. Miles, "Planned Change and Organizational Health: Figure and Ground," in Carlson et al., pp. 11–34; Matthew B. Miles, "Some Properties of Schools as Social Systems," in Watson, *Change in School Systems,* pp. 1–24; Sloan B. Wayland, "Structural Features of American Education as Basic Factors in Innovation," in Miles, *Innovation in Education,* pp. 587–613.

59. Samuel P. Capen, *The Management of Universities* (Buffalo: Foster & Stewart, 1953), Chapter 2.

60. Corson, "From Authority to Leadership," op. cit.

61. Rudolph, op. cit., Chapter 1.

62. *The Experimental Colleges Within the California State Colleges,* The California State Colleges, Office of the Chancellor, Division of Academic Planning, June 1968 (mimeograph).

63. See Paul Goodman, *The Community of Scholars* (New York: Random House, 1962) for a cogent argument in favor of such a structure.

64. See Erving Goffman, "On Cooling the Mark Out: Some Aspects of Adaptation to Failure," *Psychiatry,* 15 (November 1952), pp. 451–563.

65. One need only look at Berkeley for the classic example of such an approach to problems. See Nathan Glazer, "What Happened at Berkeley," in S. M. Lipset and Sheldon S. Wolin (eds.), *The Berkeley Student Revolt* (Garden City: Doubleday, 1965); Somers, op. cit.; Ladd, op. cit.

66. Alvin Gouldner, "Explorations in Applied Social Science," in Alvin W. Gouldner and S. M. Miller (eds.), *Applied Sociology* (New York: Free Press, 1965), pp. 16–17. The strategy is labeled as the "Hamletic strategy" after the "Great Procrastinator."

67. See Paul Potter, "Student Discontent and Campus Reform," in Mayhew, op. cit., pp. 251–68; Carl Davidson, "University Reform Revisited," *Educational Record,* 48 (winter 1967), pp. 5–10; Martin Meyerson, "The Ethos of the American College Student: Beyond the Protest," *Daedalus,* 95 (summer 1966), pp. 713–39; Henry Mayer, "No Peace in Our Time," *Change in Higher Education,* 1 (January–February 1969), pp. 22–25.

68. Daniel Bell, *The Reforming of General Education* (New York: Columbia, 1966), p. 106.

69. Joseph Katz and Nevitt Sanford, "The Curriculum in the Perspective of

the Theory of Personality Development," in Nevitt Sanford (ed.), *The American College* (New York: Wiley, 1962), pp. 418–44; Joseph Katz and Associates, *No Time for Youth* (San Francisco: Jossey-Bass, 1968).

70. For examples see Taylor, op. cit.; or Paul Goodman, *People or Personnel* and *Like a Conquered Province* (1 volume) (New York: Random House, 1968), especially "A Causerie at the Military Industrial," pp. 423–37.

71. For an elaboration of the nature of institutional conservatism, see Joseph C. Palamountain, "Power Structures in the University," *Antioch Review,* 26 (fall 1966), pp. 299–306; Michael Rossman, Morris Abram, Seymour M. Lipset and Michael Vozick, "Violence and Power on Campus," *Change in Higher Education,* 1 (March–April 1969), pp. 28–41.

72. See Mervyn Cadwallader, "The Cybernetic Analysis of Change in Complex Social Organizations," in Walter Buckley (ed.), *Modern Systems Research for the Behavioral Scientists* (Chicago: Aldine, 1968), pp. 437–41; Chadwick J. Haberstroh, "Control as an Organizational Process," in Buckley, pp. 445–49; Walter Buckley, "Society as a Complex Adaptive System," in Buckley, pp. 490–513; Joseph Katz and Nevitt Sanford, "The New Student Power and Needed Educational Reforms," *Education Digest,* 32 (September 1967), pp. 37–40.

73. Robert K. Merton, "Bureaucratic Structure and Personality," in R. K. Merton et. al., *Reader in Bureaucracy* (Glencoe: Free Press, 1962), pp. 361–71.

74. Master Plan Survey Team, *A Master Plan for Higher Education in California, 1960–1975* (Sacramento: California State Department of Education, 1960), Chapter 3.

75. Meyerson, op. cit.

CHAPTER II

1. The organizations through which students channeled their energies included the Student Non-Violent Coordinating Committee (SNCC) in the South, the Northern Student Movement, and the Congress of Racial Equality (CORE). Others left the campus to join in efforts such as the SDS Educational Research and Action Project working in lower class Black and white communities in cities like Cleveland and Newark.

2. The teach-in strategy began as a strategy for educating university communities about the Vietnam War in 1965, while the suspension of classroom activities was first used on a large scale as a response to the Cambodian invasion and the killing of students at Kent State and Jackson State.

3. For a comment on the failure to change at Berkeley see Nathan Glazer, "Student Power in Berkeley," *The Public Interest,* 13 (fall 1968), pp. 3–21.

4. Allan M. Cartter, *An Assessment of Quality in Graduate Education* (Washington D.C.: American Council on Education, 1966). Some dispute Berkeley's claim since Harvard has no engineering school.

5. The hostilities over the park began on May 16, 1969 and continue. See Sheldon Wolin and John Schaar, "Berkeley: The Battle of the People's Park," *New York Review of Books,* 12 (June 19, 1969), pp. 24–31; Frederick Berry, Thomas Brooks, Eugene Commins, "The Berkeley Park: Terror in a Teapot," *The Nation,* 208 (June 23, 1969), pp. 784–88; "Special Report from Berkeley," *Ramparts,* 8 (August 1969), pp. 34–58.

6. The events at Berkeley during the Free Speech Movement in 1964 are probably among the most studied and written about events in the history of student activism. See S. M. Lipset and Sheldon S. Wolin (eds.), *The Berkeley Student Revolt* (Garden City: Doubleday, 1965); Hal Draper, *Berkeley: The New Student Revolt* (New York: Grove Press, 1965); Kathleen Gales, "Campus Revolution," *British Journal of Sociology,* 17 (March 1966), pp. 1–19.

7. Nathan Glazer, "What Happened at Berkeley," in Lipset and Wolin, op. cit., pp. 285–303.

8. Max Heirich and Sam Kaplan, "Yesterday's Discord," in Lipset and Wolin, op. cit., pp. 10–35.

9. Ibid., p. 27.

10. Ibid.

11. William A. Watts and David Whittaker, "Profile of a Nonconformist Youth Culture: A Study of Berkeley Non-Students," *Sociology of Education,* 41 (spring 1968), pp. 178–200.

12. Heirich and Kaplan, op. cit., pp. 29–33. For a discussion that shows that students' rights were not lost but never really existed, see C. Michael Otten, "Ruling Out Paternalism: Students and Administrators at Berkeley," in Carlos E. Kruytbosch and Sheldon L. Messinger (eds.), *The State of the University: Authority and Change* (Beverly Hills, Cal.: Sage Publications, 1970).

13. Ibid., pp. 29–30.

14. Select Committee on Education, *Education at Berkeley* (Berkeley: University of California Press, 1968), p. iii.

15. Ibid., p. 4.

16. Ibid., p. 5.

17. Ibid., p. 11.

18. Ibid., pp. 11–12. A number of other studies have touched on issues, but the Select Committee's seems to be the most thorough with a sample of more than 2,200 students. See also Robert H. Somers, "The Mainsprings of the Rebellion," in Lipset and Wolin, op. cit., pp. 530–57; and Gales, op. cit.

19. Select Committee on Education, op. cit., p. 21.

20. Ibid., pp. 195–203.

21. Martin Trow, "Bell, Book, and Berkeley: Reflections Occasioned by a Reading of Daniel Bell's *The Reforming of General Education,*" *Experiment and Innovation,* 1 (January 1968), p. 9. See also Martin Trow, "Conceptions of the University," in Kruytbosch and Messinger, op. cit.

22. Select Committee on Education, op. cit., p. 241.

23. For a detailed look at the differences see Select Committee on Education, op. cit., pp. 149–55 and Special Committee on Academic Program, *The Undergraduate Program in Letters and Science* (Berkeley: University of California, 1967), pp. 25–47.

24. Richard Brown et al., "A Student Proposal for an Undergraduate Program in Letters and Science," Associated Students, University of California, December 1967 (mimeograph).

25. Division of Interdisciplinary and General Studies, "CAL PREP information concerning the freshman-sophomore course sequence Humanities 1A-1B-1C-1D-1E-1F (mimeograph), p. 2.

Notes

26. Study Commission on University Governance, *The Culture of the University: Governance and Education* (Berkeley: University of California Press, January 15, 1968).

27. For an elaboration see Joseph Tussman, *Experiment at Berkeley* (New York: Oxford, 1969), pp. 46–68, or "The Collegiate Rite of Passage," *Experiment and Innovation*, 2 (July 1968), pp. 1–19.

28. Tussman, *Experiment at Berkeley,* op. cit., p. 42.

29. Select Committee on Education, op. cit., p. 245.

30. Board of Educational Development, "Report of the Board of Educational Development," *Minutes of the Berkeley Division* (Berkeley: University of California, May 15, 1967), pp. 26–37; "Report of the Board of Educational Development," Berkeley, University of California, February 21, 1969 (mimeograph).

31. For a comprehensive review of the Berkeley situation from a number of perspectives, see Kruytbosch and Messinger, op. cit.

32. Board of Educational Development, "Report of the Board of Educational Development," Memorandum from the Chairman of the Board of Educational Development to the Berkeley Division of the Academic Senate, September 25, 1968 (mimeograph), pp. 3–4.

33. Ibid., p. 4.

34. Senate Concurrent Resolution No. 18, January 20, 1969. Reproduced in full in the *Center for Participant Education Catalogue* (spring 1969), pp. 8–9.

35. James L. Bess and John L. Bilorusky, "Curriculum Hypocrisies: Studies of Student-Initiated Courses," *Universities Quarterly,* 24 (summer 1970), pp. 291–309.

36. Afro-American Student Union, "Proposal for Establishing a Black Studies Program," Berkeley, University of California, spring 1968 (mimeograph).

37. Assistant Chancellor for Academic Affairs, "Statement on the Proposal for a Department of Afro-American Studies at the University of California," Berkeley, University of California, fall 1969 (mimeograph).

38. "Proposal for a Third World College," Berkeley, University of California, spring 1969 (mimeograph).

39. Douglas Davidson, "The Furious Passage of the Black Graduate Student," *Berkeley Journal of Sociology,* 15 (1970), pp. 192–211.

40. *The Berkeley Academic Plan Revealed* (Berkeley: Center for Educational Change, April 30, 1969), p. 11.

41. Sheldon S. Wolin and John H. Schaar, *The Berkeley Rebellion and Beyond* (New York: New York Review, 1960), p. 17. Another study has shown that students know that the FSM failed to create structural changes and that this heightened student alienation at Berkeley. See Robert H. Somers, "The Berkeley Campus in the Twilight of the Free Speech Movement: Hope or Futility?" in James McEvoy and Abraham Miller (eds.), *Black Power and Student Rebellion* (Belmont, Cal.: Wadsworth Publishing Co., 1969).

42. See results of polls in Jeremy Main, "Reinforcements for Reform," *Fortune,* 79 (June 1969), pp. 73–74; Daniel Seligman, "A Special Kind of Rebellion," *Fortune,* 79 (January 1969), pp. 66–71 and 179–81; George Gallup, "College Curriculum Say So By Students Shows Age Gap," *Portland Oregonian,* January 10, 1969.

43. Board of Educational Development, "Report of the Board of Educational Development," Berkeley, University of California, May 28, 1968 (mimeograph).

44. Wolin and Schaar, "The Battle of People's Park," op. cit., p. 25.

45. Ibid., p. 26.

46. Berry et al, op. cit., p. 785.

47. Wolin and Schaar, "The Battle of the People's Park," op. cit., p. 26.

48. Ibid. For one perspective on the posture of the Berkeley administration, see Henry F. May, "Living with Crisis: A View from Berkeley," *The American Scholar*, 38 (autumn 1969), pp. 588–605.

49. As visitors to the campus on the day the hostilities broke out, we were confronted outside the chancellor's office by a highway patrolman replete with riot gear (e.g., helmet with face mask, riot stick, and so forth). This was at 8:30 in the morning more than three and a half hours before the student rally began. Underneath the windows of the chancellor's office on the outside of the building were a cordon of riot police. The chancellor was prepared for trouble.

50. The governor had used these "emergency powers" in the case of strikes emanating both from the Cleaver controversy and the Third World College.

51. Rich Brown, "Limits of the Faculty-Student Alliance," *Liberation* (June 1970), pp. 13–18.

52. Jim Brann, "Guest Opinion," *Edcentric* (September–October 1970), p. 3.

53. Wolin and Schaar, *The Berkeley Rebellion and Beyond*, op. cit., pp. 157–58.

54. Mary Levine and John Naisbitt, *Right On!* (New York: Bantam Books, 1970).

55. A University of California survey, for example, showed that eighty-six per cent of students in a national study were involved in or in sympathy with the protest movement against the Vietnam War. As reported in *Edcentric* (September–October 1970), p. 13.

56. David Kemnitzer, "Educational Reform—Revolution," *Edcentric* (June–July 1970), p. 12.

57. Carl Davidson, "Program for the Berkeley SDS and the University" (mimeograph) n.d., p. 9.

58. For a discussion of how the shifts in recent times make these inseparable, see Seymour Melman, *Pentagon Capitalism* (New York: McGraw-Hill, 1970).

59. Wolin and Schaar, *The Berkeley Rebellion and Beyond*, op cit., pp. 153–54.

60. The articles by Wolin and Schaar, *"Battle of Berkeley and Beyond,"* op. cit., and Berry et. al., op. cit., point to the recent referendum in which 15,000 Berkeley students, an overwhelming record in any student election, voted eighty-five per cent in favor of the retention of the park as it existed before—perhaps the most significant omen for the future to emerge from the May events.

61. Cited in *Edcentric* (September–October 1970), p. 8.

62. For an analysis of this phenomenon, see John R. Howard, "The Flowering of the Hippie Movement," *The Annals of the American Academy of Political and Social Science,* 382 (March 1969) pp. 43–55; David Whittaker and William A. Watts, "Personality Characteristics of a Nonconformist Youth Subculture: A Study of the Berkeley Non-Student," *The Journal of Social Issues,* 25 (April 1969) pp. 65–89.

63. For some interesting commentary on these themes see Theodore Roszak,

Notes

The Making of a Counter-Culture (New York: Doubleday, 1969); Charles Reich, *The Greening of America* (New York: Random House, 1970); Philip Slater, *In Pursuit of Loneliness* (Boston: Beacon Press, 1970).

CHAPTER III

1. See Master Plan Survey Team, *A Master Plan for Higher Education in California, 1960–1975* (Sacramento: State Department of Education, 1960), prepared for the Liaison Committee of the State Board of Education and the Regents of the University of California.

2. Ibid., pp. 27–44. The *Master Plan* clearly spells out the nature of the institutional functions.

3. Ibid., p. 73.

4. For a detailed analysis of the appeal of State for faculty, see Christopher Jencks and David Riesman, "The Viability of the American College," in Nevitt Sanford (ed.), *The American College* (New York: Wiley, 1962), pp. 74–192; or Herbert Wilner, "Zen Basketball, etc. at San Francisco State," *Esquire*, 68 (September 1967), pp. 99, 47–60; Ralph M. Goldman, "San Francisco State: The Technology of Confrontationism," in Julian Foster and Durward Long (eds.), *Protest! Student Activism in America* (New York: William Morrow & Co., 1970).

5. Ibid., p. 162.

6. Ibid.

7. Ibid.

8. Technical Committee on Costs of Higher Education in California, *The Costs of Higher Education in California, 1960–1975* (Berkeley: University of California Press, 1960), p. 27. Expenditures for the ten-year period up to the time that the *Master Plan* was prepared are included.

9. Master Plan Survey Team, op. cit., pp. 64, 166. The projected enrollments and projected allocations respectively are presented.

10. Arthur G. Coons, *Crises in California Higher Education* (Los Angeles: Ward Ritchie Press, 1968), p. 155; Kingsley Widmer, "California: Why the Colleges Blew Up," *Nation*, 208 (February 24, 1969), pp. 237–41.

11. Jencks and Riesman, op. cit., pp. 182–83.

12. Coons, op. cit.; Goldman, op. cit.

13. Scrue Pherson, "No 69 Valedictory for H———K———," *Daily Gator*, June 20, 1969, p. 2.

14. Karen Duncan, "What Makes the Revolution Quiet?" in *Experimental College*, San Francisco State College, spring 1966 (mimeograph), pp. 6–10.

15. See the prospectus "Community Services Institute," San Francisco State College, fall 1968 (mimeograph).

16. From a draft of a proposal, "The Community Services Institute," San Francisco State College, 1967 (mimeograph).

17. Donald L. Garrity, "Response to Student Demands for Relevance," in G. Kerry Smith (ed.), *Stress and Campus Response* (San Francisco: Jossey-Bass, 1968), pp. 214–19.

18. Russell Bass, James Nixon, and Ian Grand, "Some Notes on the Experi-

mental College," in *Experimental College,* San Francisco State College, October 1967 (mimeograph).

19. Ibid., p. 3.

20. Ibid.

21. Mike Rossman, "On Learning and Social Change," Washington D.C.: Center for Educational Reform, 1968 (mimeograph); Ralph Keyes, "The Free Universities," *The Nation* (October 2, 1967), pp. 294-99.

22. Most of those interviewed who had been at State when the Experimental College was founded were administrators. Their assessments, however, are corroborated by the written appraisals of student organizers. See Rossman, op. cit.; Bass et. al., op. cit. For a faculty view which was essentially the same, see Wilner, op. cit.; also see Terry F. Lunsford, "Educational Innovations in Response to Student Activism," Paper read at Conference on Innovation in Higher Education, State University of New York at Albany, June 19, 1967.

23. Russell Bass et. al., op. cit., p. 1.

24. Wilner, op. cit.

25. Ibid., pp. 59-60.

26. Russell Bass et al., op. cit., p. 7.

27. Peter Janssen, "Free U. and Old U.," *Change in Higher Education,* 1 (November-December 1969), p. 12.

28. Wilner, op. cit.

29. Ibid., p. 56.

30. Keyes, op. cit., p. 296.

31. *The Experimental Colleges Within the California State Colleges,* prepared by the California State Colleges Office of the Chancellor, Division of Academic Planning, June 1968 (mimeograph).

32. Ibid., p. 111.

33. Ibid., pp. 12-15.

34. Peter Shapiro and Bill Barlow, "San Francisco State," *Leviathan,* 1 (April 1969), p. 4-11.

35. For a detailed account of the debate see the *Daily Gator,* October and November 1968.

36. Smith made a special point in our interview to indicate that both in informing Murray of his dismissal and in making the general announcement he made it absolutely clear that it was the chancellor, not he, who had taken the action.

37. Steve Toomajian, "An Overview: The Strike at SF State," in Howard Finberg (ed.), *Crisis at San Francisco State* (San Francisco: Insight Publications, 1969), pp. 6-10.

38. Ibid., p. 8.

39. As quoted by James McEvoy and Abraham Miller, "San Francisco State: 'On Strike . . . Shut it Down,'" in McEvoy and Miller, op. cit., p. 19.

40. See Nathan Hare, "The Case for Separatism: 'Black Perspective,'" in James McEvoy and Abraham Miller (eds.), *Black Power and Student Rebellion* (Belmont, Cal.: Wadsworth Publishing Co., 1969); Nathan Hare, "A Conceptual Proposal for a Department of Black Studies," Appendix 4 in William H. Orrick, Jr., *Shut It Down! A College in Crisis,* A Report to the National Commission on

the Causes and Prevention of Violence (Washington, D.C.: U.S. Government Printing Office, 1969).

41. S. I. Hayakawa, "Statement on Plans and Policies," *On the Record* (San Francisco: San Francisco State College, March 21, 1969).

42. Robert Chrisman, "Observations on Race and Class at San Francisco State," in McEvoy and Miller, op. cit.

43. *San Francisco Chronicle,* March 3, 1970, p. 1.

44. Some of this history is traced by George S. Rothbart, "The Legitimation of Inequality: Objective Scholarship vs. Black Militance," *Sociology of Education,* 43 (spring 1970), pp. 159–74.

45. Bill Barlow and Peter Shapiro, "The Struggle for San Francisco State," in McEvoy and Miller, op. cit.

46. Todd Gitlin, "On the Line at San Francisco State," in McEvoy and Miller, op. cit.; Barlow and Shapiro, op. cit.; Chrisman, op. cit.

47. Rothbart, op. cit., p. 173.

48. As suggested, a number of things have been written on various facets of the strike and the events at San Francisco State College. Among the collections of materials are: Bill Barlow and Peter Shapiro, *An End to Silence* (Washington, D.C.: Pegasus, 1970); Arlene Daniels and Rachel Kahn-Hut (eds.), *Academics on the Line: The Faculty Strike at San Francisco State* (San Francisco: Jossey-Bass, 1970); Robert Smith, et al., *By Any Means Necessary* (San Francisco: Jossey-Bass, 1970).

49. David Swanston, "How to Wreck a Campus," *The Nation* (January 8, 1968), p. 41. For a further discussion on this theme during the strike, see the analysis of a San Francisco State professor, Mervin B. Freedman, "Urban Campus Prototype," *The Nation* (January 13, 1969), pp. 38–42.

50. Orrick, op. cit., p. 141.

51. Roger Rapoport and Laurence J. Krishbaum, *Is the Library Burning?* New York: Random House, 1969), p. 144.

52. Widmer, op. cit., p. 238.

53. Ibid.

54. Hayakawa, "Statement on Plans," op. cit.

55. See Philip Selznick, *TVA and the Grass Roots* (New York: Harper, 1966), pp. 259–66; Robert L. Kahn, "Field Studies of Power in Organizations," in Robert L. Kahn and Elise Boulding (eds.), *Power and Conflict in Organizations* (New York: Basic Books, 1964), pp. 67–72.

56. See Janssen, op. cit.; Keyes, op. cit.; Widmer, op. cit.

57. Christopher Jencks and David Riesman, *The Academic Revolution* (Garden City: Doubleday, 1968), pp. 35–60.

58. S. I. Hayakawa, Letter to the students, faculty, and staff at San Francisco State, April 24, 1969. For an analysis of Hayakawa's role, see Orrick, op. cit.

59. Hayakawa, "Statement on Plans," op. cit.

60. Swanston, op. cit.

CHAPTER IV

1. Charles Reich, *The Greening of America* (New York: Random House, 1970).

2. Headline of article by Douglas E. Kneeland, *New York Times,* December 20, 1970, pp. 1, 37.

3. David Smothers, "Campuses Relatively Peaceful As Many Have Second Thoughts," UPI National Column "1970 In Review," Eugene, Oregon *Register-Guard,* December 31, 1970, p. 2.

4. Aaron Novick, et. al., *A Report of the Committee on the Future of the University* (Eugene: University of Oregon, 1970).

5. Allan M. Cartter, *An Assessment of Quality in Graduate Education* (Washington: American Council on Education, 1966).

6. Novick Report, op. cit.

7. Ken Metzler, "A Few Observations on the World's Most Thankless Job," *Old Oregon,* 49 (July-August 1969), p. 2.

8. "Student Conduct Code," *Student Handbook* (Eugene: University of Oregon, 1968).

9. Oregon State Board of Higher Education, *Statement by the Oregon State Board of Higher Education Relating to Faculty Conduct and Amendments to the Board's "Administrative Code,"* September 8, 1970.

10. Irrelevant here would be such committees as Personnel Welfare.

11. One author (Joseph Fashing) was a member of the Faculty-Student Council in 1966–67 and served as President of the Graduate Student Council (68–69), a member of the Presidential Search Committee, and a member of several other university committees. It should also be pointed out that although the graduate students formed a graduate student organization in 1965–66, it remains a subunit of the Associated Students. The Student Senate, legislative body for the student government, is comprised of both graduates and undergraduates and acts primarily on matters of general concern.

12. Phil Semas, "1965–66—A 'Student Voice,'" *Oregon Daily Emerald,* September 20, 1966, p. 1.

13. Ibid.

14. Ibid.

15. "Student Movement(s) to Establish a 'Free University,'" memorandum from the Dean of Men to President Flemming, University of Oregon, September 30, 1966, p. 1.

16. Ibid., p. 2.

17. Ibid.

18. Ibid.

19. Committee on the Curriculum, Memo addressed to the members of the faculty, University of Oregon, December 12, 1966.

20. Ibid.

21. Committee on the Curriculum, "400–410 and 500–510 Courses in the

Notes

University of Oregon Curriculum," University of Oregon, May 29, 1967 (mimeograph), p. 1.

22. Ibid., Appendix A.

23. Ibid., p. 2.

24. During registration students fill out IBM cards on which course marks will later be recorded. In each case, they check whether they are registering for the course for a letter grade or on a pass/no-pass basis.

25. Dean of Faculties, "Memorandum to Deans and Department Heads re: SEARCH Courses," University of Oregon, July 7, 1969.

26. *Oregon Summer Emerald,* July 29, 1969, p. 3.

27. Robert Clark, "Prospectives," Keynote Address, Conference on Educational Innovations in Higher Education, University of Oregon, July 24, 1969. Reprinted in *Oregon Summer Emerald,* July 29, 1969. For a comprehensive discussion of this issue and a variety of views see John Minter and Ian Thompson (eds.), *Colleges and Universities as Agents of Social Change* (Boulder: Western Interstate Commission on Higher Education, 1968).

28. Arthur S. Flemming, "Memorandum to Chairmen of Committee on Racism," University of Oregon, April 24, 1968.

29. President's Committee on Racism, "Proposal for a School of Black Studies," University of Oregon, spring 1968 (mimeograph); Academic Affairs Sub-Committee of the President's Committee on Racism, "Recruitment Procedures for Black Faculty and Graduate Students," University of Oregon, spring 1968 (mimeograph).

30. The most famous contemporary exponent of the principle is Paul Goodman. For a detailed discussion, see *The Community of Scholars* (New York: Random House, 1962).

31. Martin Acker, Herbert Bisno, Daniel Goldrich, Aaron Novick, Frank Stahl, George Streisinger, Lee Bolinger, Joe Fashing, Gary Feuerberg, Marvin Feuerberg, and Gerald Selzer, "Guidelines for Faculty-Student Participation," *Oregon Daily Emerald,* January 23, 1968, pp. 5–6.

32. Metzler, op. cit.

33. "Board Policies Relating to Institutional Governance—With Particular Reference to Student Participation," (Eugene: Oregon State System of Higher Education), adopted by the State Board of Higher Education, December 9, 1968.

34. Ibid., p. 2.

35. Ibid., p. 3.

36. Ibid., p. 4.

37. Committee on Academic Affairs, Oregon State Board of Higher Education, *A Discussion of Student Unrest* (Eugene: Oregon State System of Higher Education, November 1968).

38. Ibid., p. 1.

39. Ibid., p. 38. The discussion of student revolutionaries is developed extensively in pp. 1–18, 33–51.

40. "Policy Change Concerns Faculty," *Oregon Daily Emerald,* May 8, 1969.

41. Task Force on Higher Education, *Report to the Fifty-Fifth Legislative Assembly* (Salem: Oregon Legislative Assembly, April 1969), p. 1.

42. Ibid., pp. 29–30. Similar warnings are voiced on pages 17, 49, and throughout the text.

CHAPTER V

1. *A Long-Range Plan for Western Washington State College* (Bellingham: Western Washington State College, 1968), pp. 84–85.

2. *Western Washington State College: A Plan for the Future* (Bellingham: Western Washington State College, 1966), p. 3.

3. Paul Woodring, *The Higher Learning in America: A Reassessment* (New York: McGraw-Hill, 1968).

4. *Fairhaven College* (Bellingham: Western Washington State College, 1969), p. 2.

5. Ibid., p. 7.

6. "Progress Report," Fairhaven College, August 18, 1970 (mimeograph).

7. Ibid.

8. Ibid.

9. Ibid.

10. "Tentative Constitution," Fairhaven College, June 2, 1969 (mimeograph).

11. Jim Hansen, "Proposed Constitutional Amendment," Fairhaven College (mimeograph).

12. "Progress Report," Memorandum from Fairhaven dean to the president, Western Washington State College, December 31, 1968.

13. 1970 "Progress Report," op. cit.

14. "Second Progress Report," Memorandum from Fairhaven dean to the president, Western Washington State College, May 12, 1969; 1970 "Progress Report," op. cit.

15. "Huxley Requirements," 1970 (mimeograph).

16. During 1970 Vine DeLoria, author of *Custer Died For Your Sins,* was a visiting faculty member in the College of Ethnic Studies. An OEO-funded structure, Small Tribes Organization of Western Washington has also had an impact upon Native-American college student recruitment.

17. Quoted in John Haigh, "Western Washington State College," *Seattle Times Magazine* (December 6, 1970), p. 8.

18. It was reported in fall 1970 that the mean entrance year to college for faculty was 1968.

CHAPTER VI

1. Christopher Jencks and David Riesman, *The Academic Revolution* (Garden City: Doubleday, 1968), pp. 50–60.

2. Ibid., p. 52.

3. Allan M. Cartter, *An Assessment of Quality in Graduate Education* (Washington: American Council on Education, 1966).

4. The university sponsors periodic conferences organized around every con-

Notes

ceivable topic and mission at its special retreat on Lake Arrowhead in the mountains near Los Angeles. These conferences are uniformly referred to as Arrowhead Conferences because of the locale.

5. UCLA social scientists have been conducting an extensive research program on the 1965 Watts riots since their occurrence.

6. *Daily Bruin,* January 9, 1966, p. 7.

7. Raymond Orbach, "Request for Funding for the Committee for the Study of Education and Society," UCLA, March 1969 (mimeograph).

8. One of the requirements for credit in the University of California system is that it be given through a full-fledged department. Research institutes and other similar non-academic units cannot act as sponsors. One of the few bodies outside of individual departments that can legally offer a course is the College of Letters and Science. Because of the interdisciplinary nature of the courses and because CSES itself was not legally constituted to give courses, official sponsorship was from the college. The legal impediments to course sponsorship were one of the chief issues in the Cleaver controversy at Berkeley.

9. Quoted in R. Baker, "Summary of the Activities of the Committee for the Study of Education and Society," UCLA, 1969 (mimeograph).

10. John Egerton, *State Universities and Black Americans* (Atlanta: Southern Education Foundation, 1969), p. 51.

11. Charles E. Young, "Report on UCLA's Response to the Urban Crisis," memorandum to UCLA faculty, November 25, 1968.

12. Task Force on Student Entry Programs, "Selection Criteria and Procedures," UCLA, summer 1968 (mimeograph).

13. Task Force on Curriculum Development, "High Potential Student Curriculum," UCLA, summer 1968 (mimeograph).

14. Task Force on Urban Research and Action, "Urban Research and Problem Solving," UCLA, summer 1968 (mimeograph); also, "Proposal for a Board of Urban Research and Development," UCLA, summer 1968 (mimeograph).

15. Ibid.

16. The new chancellor Charles Young assumed office in the spring of 1968. His administration has taken on a kind of activist character that was not characteristic of the previous administration. It should not be assumed that the previous chancellor was opposed to any of the kinds of activities currently being developed on the campus, only that the current chancellor seems to be more active in this regard. An indicator of the general agreement of the two on policy matters is the fact that Young was former Chancellor Murphy's chief assistant and reputed to have been his personal choice as his successor.

17. For some of the background of this shoot-out, see Ray Rogers, "Black Guns on Campus," *The Nation* (May 5, 1969), pp. 558–60.

18. See "Proposal for the Creation of the Center for the Study of Afro-American History and Culture," UCLA, September 1968 (mimeograph).

19. Committee on Academic Innovation, "The Kneller Report," *Daily Bruin,* January 4, 1968, pp. 13–20.

20. Ibid.

21. See for instance, Larry Weinstein, "The Powerlessness of a UCLA Student," *Daily Bruin Spectra,* February 17, 1970.

22. See Educational Policy Commission, *UCLA Renewal,* April 1969.

23. For an example of the kind of course which is causing difficulties, see Community for Awareness and Social Education, "The Humanistic and Educational Needs of the Academic Community," UCLA, winter 1969 (a proposed CSES course).

CHAPTER VII

1. Upton Sinclair, *The Goose-Step* (Pasadena: Published by author, 1922), p. 152.

2. *Stanford University Bulletin,* (Stanford: Stanford University Press, January 2, 1969).

3. Study of Education at Stanford, *Report to the University: Undergraduate Admissions and Financial Aid,* Volume 4 (Stanford: Stanford University Press, December 1968).

4. Ibid.

5. Ibid., Part 2, "Selection Criteria and Procedures," pp. 27–53.

6. Joseph Katz and Associates, *No Time for Youth* (San Francisco: Jossey-Bass, 1968).

7. Study of Education at Stanford, Volume 4, op. cit., pp. 15–24.

8. Obviously such ground rules were not of overriding importance at Harvard or Columbia in the 1968–69 disorders. In spite of this, however, a comment on a recent newscast by one Harvard student who was a participant in the activities surrounding the ROTC episode illustrates the kind of sentiment we are referring to. "These things," he said, "just do not happen at Harvard." In the same way, "these things" just do not happen at Stanford. Even where there is a serious escalation of tactics and the lines of dispute become very rigid, one has the distinct impression that reconciliation will be simpler at an institution like Stanford than at one like Berkeley.

9. For an in-depth portrait of Harris, see Gina Berriault, "The New Student President," *Esquire,* 68 (September 1967), pp. 95, 153–56.

10. *Stanford University Bulletin: Courses and Degrees 1968–69* (Stanford: Stanford University Press, May 19, 1968), pp. 437–38.

11. Keith Power, "Midpeninsula: The Jivy League," *The Nation,* 208 (April 14, 1969), pp. 463–64.

12. Joyce Kobayashi et al., "Proposal for a Student Center for Innovation in Research and Education at Stanford," Associated Students, Stanford University, October 27, 1969 (mimeograph).

13. Committee on Undergraduate Studies, "Charge to the Subcommittee on Student Innovation," Stanford, February 1970 (mimeograph).

14. The studies referred to here and discussed in other sections are Select Committee on Education, *Education at Berkeley* (Berkeley: University of California, 1968); *Western Washington State College: A Plan for the Future* (Bellingham: Western Washington State College, 1966); Committee on Academic Innovation, "The Kneller Report," *UCLA Daily Bruin,* January 4, 1968, pp. 13–20; *Report of the Committee on the Future of the University of Oregon,* 1970 and a Student-

Notes

Faculty Committee on governance also appointed in 1970 at the University of Oregon.

15. Steering Committee for the Study of Education at Stanford, *Report to the University*, Volumes 1–5, 7, 9–10, (Stanford: Stanford University Press, 1968). Volumes 6 and 8 have not yet been completed and will be released sometime next year.

16. Study of Education at Stanford, *Report to the University: The Study and Its Purposes,* Volume 1 (Stanford: Stanford University Press, November 1968), p. 8.

17. Robert Hoopes and Hubert Marshall, *The Undergraduate in the University* (Stanford: Stanford University Press, 1957). The volume is a report to the faculty by the Executive Committee of the Stanford Study of Undergraduate Education, 1954–56.

18. Ibid., pp. 84–105.

19. Study of Education at Stanford, *The Study and Its Purposes,* op. cit., p. 9.

20. Ibid., p. 13.

21. Ibid., p. 15.

22. "Professor Blasts SES Report," *The Arena,* April 11, 1969, p. 1, 4.

23. Ibid.

24. Ibid.

25. Instead of one student body president in 1969 Stanford had a council of four. This is not a formal change; they simply ran as a group and won. Three of the students are undergraduates; one is a graduate. This pattern has been followed since.

26. SES Progress Reports, Stanford, 1970 (mimeograph).

27. Denis Hayes et al., "Educational Innovation," Associated Students of Stanford University, 1969 (mimeograph).

28. Ibid., "Stanford Experimental College—Proposal A," p. 1.

29. Study of Education at Stanford, *Report to the University: Undergraduate Education,* Volume 2 (Stanford: Stanford University Press, 1968), p. 31.

30. Ibid., p. 33.

31. Study of Education at Stanford, *Report to the University: Undergraduate Admissions and Financial Aids,* Volume 4 (Stanford: Stanford University Press, 1968), p. 59. The breakdown on the admission of Black students since 1960 is presented. As recently as 1960 there were only two Black students admitted in the freshman class. In the four year period ending in 1967 only about a hundred Black students entered. According to the figures of the registrar, in 1969 there were 232 Black students enrolled, representing less than two per cent of the student body.

32. Ibid., pp. 10–11.

33. SES Progress Reports, op. cit.

34. Study of Education at Stanford, *Report to the University: Government of the University,* Volume 10 (Stanford: Stanford University Press, 1968), p. 8.

35. Ibid., p. 13.

36. Ibid., p. 36.

37. Ibid., p. 36.

38. Norman Sklarewitz, "Rating Black Studies," *Wall Street Journal*, June 11, 1969.

39. Fred Mann, "Afro-American Studies," *Stanford Daily*, January 29, February 12, 1970.

40. Sklarewitz, op. cit.

41. Ibid.

42. Study of Education at Stanford, *The Study and Its Purposes*, op. cit., p. 16.

43. Art Seidenbaum, "Testing Tomorrow at Stanford," *Los Angeles Times, West Magazine*, June 22, 1969, p. 14.

44. For a discussion of Stanford's Hoover Institute and the larger issue, see Peter S. Stern, "Cold-War Scholarship," *The Nation* (September 1, 1969), pp. 176-80.

45. The flavor of disruption of tranquility is captured by the headline, "Police Break-up Palo Alto Jam-In by Stanford Mob," *Palo Alto Times*, May 16, 1969.

46. As reported in the *New York Times*, December 20, 1970, p. 67.

47. Consider the following: of 230 SES recommendations, approximately 90 have been implemented, 40 partially implemented, and 15 delayed by insufficient funds. The remaining 85 are recommendations lost, rejected, or still under review. See Sally Main, "A Progress Report on Recommendations From The Study of Education At Stanford," *Campus Report Supplement*, No. 15, January 28, 1971.

CHAPTER VIII

1. Harold Taylor, *Students Without Teachers* (New York: McGraw-Hill 1969), p. 42.

2. John J. Corson, "From Authority to Leadership," *Journal of Higher Education*, 40 (March 1969), pp. 181-92; Herbert Stroup, *Bureaucracy in Higher Education* (New York: Free Press, 1966); Clark Kerr, *The Uses of the University* (New York: Harper & Row, 1966); James A. Perkins, *The University in Transition* (Princeton: Princeton University Press, 1966); Joseph C. Palamountain, "Power Structures in the University," *Antioch Review*, 26 (Fall 1966).

3. *Oregon Revised Statutes*, 352.010.

4. Alvin W. Gouldner, "Explorations in Applied Social Science," in Alvin W. Gouldner and S. M. Miller (eds.), *Applied Sociology* (New York: Free Press, 1965), pp. 5-22.

5. Frederick Rudolph, *The American College and University* (New York: Random House, 1962).

6. Among the range of materials dealing with this issue, see Seymour Martin Lipset, Martin A. Trow, and James S. Coleman, *Union Democracy* (Glencoe, Ill.: Free Press, 1949); Robert K. Merton, *Social Theory and Social Structure* Glencoe, Ill.: Free Press, 1957), pp. 195-224; Warren G. Bennis, *Changing Organizations* (New York: McGraw-Hill, 1966).

7. See Jeremy Main, "Reinforcements for Reform," *Fortune*, 79 (June 1969), pp. 73-74; Daniel Seligman, "A Special Kind of Rebellion," *Fortune*, 79 (January 1969), pp. 66-71 and 179-81; Taylor, op. cit.

8. See National Advisory Commission on Civil Disorders, *Report of the*

Notes

National Advisory Commission on Civil Disorders (New York: Bantam, 1968); William McCord, John Howard, Bernard Friedberg, and Edwin Harwood, *Life Styles in the Black Ghetto* (New York: Norton, 1969).

9. See John Holt, *How Children Fail* (New York: Pitman Publishing Corp., 1967), *How Children Learn* (New York: Pitman Publishing Corp., 1969).

10. Herbert Kohl, *36 Children* (New York: New American Library, 1967), *The Open Classroom* (New York: New York Review Books, 1970). Also see Steven E. Deutsch and John Howard (eds.), *Where It's At: Radical Perspectives in Sociology* (New York: Harper & Row, 1970), Section on Education.

11. Ivan Illich, "Schooling: The Ritual of Progress," *New York Review of Books* (December 3, 1970), "Education Without School: How It Can Be Done," *New York Review of Books,* (January 7, 1971).

12. William J. Waugh, "Black Studies Winning Strong Scholarly Support," AP Report, Eugene, Oregon, *Register-Guard,* July 19, 1970, p. 13D.

13. John Egerton, *State Universities and Black Americans* (Atlanta: Southern Education Foundation, 1969).

14. Harry Edwards, *Black Students* (New York: The Free Press, 1970), p. 61.

15. Ibid, p. 68.

16. Robert F. Engs and John B. Williams, "Integration by Evasion," *The Nation* (November 17, 1969), p. 540.

17. See, for example, Clyde E. Deberry, Joseph Fashing, and Calvin Harris, "Black Power and Black Population: A Dilemma," *The Journal of Negro Education,* 38 (winter 1969), pp. 14–21.

18. Immanuel Wallerstein, *University in Turmoil: The Politics of Change* (New York: Atheneum, 1969), pp. 120–21.

19. For an analysis of the history of Upward Bound and an examination of university features associated with the development of such programs, see Mary D. Adams Howard, "A Study of Organizational Innovation: Sponsorship of the Upward Bound Program Among Institutions of Higher Education," unpublished Ph.D. dissertation, Department of Sociology, University of Oregon, 1970.

20. For a general discussion of the problem, see Thomas Sowell, "Colleges Are Skipping Over Competent Blacks to Admit 'Authentic' Ghetto Types," *The New York Times Magazine* (December 13, 1970), pp. 36–37, 39–40, 42, 44, 46, 49–50.

21. Charlayne Hunter, "Confusion Feared in Black Studies," *New York Times* (March 8, 1970), p. 58.

22. John Hatch, "Black Studies: The Real Issue," *The Nation* (June 16, 1969), p. 758.

23. The general arguments and how they relate to the particular case are presented in Nathan Hare, "The Case for Separatism: 'Black Perspective,'" in James McEvoy and Abraham Miller (eds.), *Black Power and Student Rebellion* (Belmont, Cal: Wadsworth Publishing Co., 1969); Robert Chrisman, "Observations on Race and Class at San Francisco State," in ibid.

24. See Clement E. Vontress, "Black Studies—Boon or Bane?" *The Journal of Negro Education,* 39 (summer 1970), pp. 192–201; John W. Blassingame, "Black Studies: An Intellectual Crisis," *The American Scholar,* 38 (autumn 1969), pp. 548–61. It is instructive to note the variations in perspective and opinion; for

example, see Armstead L. Robinson, et al. (eds.), *Black Studies in the University: A Symposium* (New Haven: Yale University Press, 1969).

25. Roosevelt Johnson, "Black Administrators and Higher Education," *The Black Scholar*, 1 (November 1969), p. 71.

26. Edwards, op. cit., p. 82.

27. Ibid, p. 201.

28. These data come from national analyses of the protest movement. See Mary Levine and John Naisbitt, *Right On!* (New York: Bantam Books, 1970).

29. Edward Gross, "Universities as Organizations: A Research Approach," *American Sociological Review*, 33 (August 1968), pp. 518–44; Max Ways, "The Faculty is the Heart of the Trouble," *Fortune*, 79 (January 1969), pp. 94–97, 161–64.

30. Paul Woodring, *The Higher Learning in America: A Reassessment* (New York: McGraw-Hill, 1968), p. ix.

31. See Paul Goodman, *Growing Up Absurd* (New York: Random House, 1960); Jonathan Kozol, *Death at an Early Age* (Boston: Houghton-Mifflin, 1967); Herbert Kohl, *Teaching the Unteachable* (New York: New York Review, 1967).

32. See Paul Goodman, *The Community of Scholars* (New York: Random House, 1962).

33. Woodring, op. cit.

34. Taylor, op. cit., p. 57.

35. For the best elaboration on inherent conflict of interest in organizations, see Ralf Dahrendorf, *Class and Class Conflict in Industrial Society* (Stanford: Stanford University Press, 1959).

36. See Clark Kerr, *The Uses of the University* (New York: Harper & Row, 1966); Roger Heyns, "The University as an Instrument of Social Action," in W. John Minter and Ian M. Thompson (eds.), *Colleges and Universities as Agents of Social Change* (Boulder: Western Interstate Commission on Higher Education, 1968), pp. 25–38.

37. Carl Cohen, "Democracy and the Curriculum," *The Nation*, 208 (March 17, 1969), pp. 334–38.

38. Goodman, *The Community of Scholars*, op. cit.

39. Seymour Melman, "Economic Development or Race War," *Columbia Daily Spectator*, April 30, 1969.

40. Ibid.

41. Michael Miles, "Whose University?" *The New Republic*, 160 (April 12, 1969), pp. 17–19.

42. Robert E. Agger, Daniel Goldrich, and Bert E. Swanson, *The Rulers and the Ruled* (New York: Wiley, 1964), pp. 82–90.

43. Earl J. McGrath, *Should Students Share the Power?* (Philadelphia: Temple University Press, 1970).

44. See ibid. for a discussion of the history of experimentation with governance at Antioch and other institutions. For a discussion of Antioch, also see Burton R. Clark, *The Distinctive College* (Chicago: Aldine Publishing Co., 1970); Morris Keeton and Conrad Hilberry, *Struggle and Promise: A Future For Colleges* (New York: McGraw-Hill, 1969).

45. Dwight R. Ladd, *Change in Educational Policy* (New York: McGraw-Hill, 1970), reviews some of the self-study commissions.

46. Ibid. This is a major conclusion from the survey of self-studies.

47. "Reforms in Governance," *Time* (September 26, 1969), p. 47.

48. "What the Trustees Think," *Saturday Review* (January 10, 1970), p. 62.

49. See Rodney T. Hartnett, "College and University Trustees: Their Backgrounds, Roles, and Educational Attitudes," in Carlos E. Kruytbosch and Sheldon L. Messinger (eds.), *The State Of The University* (Beverly Hills, California: Sage Publications, 1970).

50. M. S. Handler, "Gain By Students on Rights Found," *New York Times* (December 13, 1970), p. 62.

51. Ibid. Also see McGrath, op. cit.

52. See the analysis by former president of the National Student Association, Robert S. Powell, Jr., "Participation Is Learning," in the symposium, "Who Runs The University?" *Saturday Review* (January 10, 1970).

53. See J. Douglas Brown, *The Liberal University: An Institutional Analysis* (New York: McGraw-Hill, 1969), Chapter 6, for the views of a Princeton University provost.

54. Lewis B. Mayhew, *Colleges Today and Tomorrow* (San Francisco: Jossey-Bass, 1969), p. 78.

55. Robert S. Morrison, *Students and Decision-Making* (Washington: Public Affairs Press, 1970). See the commentary to this report of the Cornell University Commission on Student Involvement in Decision Making by Professor Ian Macneil.

56. John A. Howard and H. Bruce Franklin, *Who Should Run The Universities?* (Washington, D.C.: American Enterprise Institute, 1969).

57. Immanuel Wallerstein, *University in Turmoil: The Politics of Change* (New York: Atheneum, 1969), p. 91.

58. Robert Paul Wolff, *The Idea of the University* (Boston: Beacon Press, 1969), Part Three.

59. Ibid., p. 134.

60. Ibid. For a provocative discussion suggesting that the past decade has been unique and, contrary to surface indicators, students have become disenfranchized and less potent, see J. B. Lon Hefferlin, *Dynamics of Academic Reform* (San Francisco: Jossey-Bass, 1969), pp. 148–49.

61. The president of one large private institution is reputed to have preferred the designation "independent" rather than "private." The extent of this "independence" was manifest later when in the face of cutbacks in appropriations for research as a consequence of the escalation of the Vietnam War, this "independent" institution was forced to terminate more than one-third of the non-tenured members of the mathematics and physics departments because of a lack of funds.

62. Goodman, *Growing Up Absurd*, op. cit.; Taylor, op. cit.

63. This point is well examined by Immanuel Wallerstein, *University in Tumoil: The Politics of Change* (New York: Atheneum, 1969), p. 11.

64. For example, Joseph J. Schwab, *College Curriculum and Student Protest* (Chicago: The University of Chicago Press, 1969). The matter of curricular relevance is discussed in a journalistic account by Donald L. Rogan, *Campus*

Apocalypse: The Student Search Today (New York: The Seabury Press, 1969), Chapter 6.

65. Charles Frankel, *Education and the Barricades* (New York: W. W. Norton, 1968), p. 82.

66. Sidney Hook, *Academic Freedom and Academic Anarchy* (New York: Cowles Book Co., 1970), p. 232.

67. Kerr, *The Uses of the University,* op. cit.

68. Richard Flacks, "The Roots of Radicalism," *Playboy* (March 1969), p. 180. For a discussion of the growth of the student movement, see Chapter 1 this book.

69. See Kenneth Boulding, *The Meaning of the Twentieth Century* (New York: Harper and Row, 1965).

70. See Theodore Roszak (ed.), *The Dissenting Academy* (New York: Random House, 1968).

71. Harris L. Wofford, Jr., "Agent of Whom?" in W. John Minter and Ian M. Thompson, op. cit., p. 12.

72. Ibid.

73. Ibid.

APPENDIX

1. Jules Henry, *Culture Against Man* (New York: Random House, 1965), pp. 322–88.

2. For an example of this type of study, see Edward Gross, *Academic Administrators and University Goals* (Washington, D.C.: American Council on Education, 1968); or "Universities as Organizations: A Research Approach," *American Journal of Sociology,* 33 (August 1968), pp. 518–44.

3. For example, a single campus study is Walter L. Wallace, *Student Culture* (Chicago: Aldine Publishing Company, 1966) and a comparative study is Morris Keeton and Conrad Hilberry, *Struggle and Promise: A Future for Colleges* (New York: McGraw-Hill, 1969).

4. Christopher Jencks and David Riesman, *The Academic Revolution* (Garden City, N.Y.: Doubleday, 1968).

5. Burton Clark, *The Distinctive College* (Chicago: Aldine Publishing Company, 1970).

6. Harold Taylor, *The World as Teacher* (New York: Doubleday, 1966).

7. Education and World Affairs, *The University Looks Abroad* (New York: Walker, 1965).

8. Claire Selltiz, Marie Jahoda, Morton Deutsch, and Stuart W. Cook, *Research Methods in Social Relations* (New York: Holt, Rinehart, and Winston, 1964), pp. 50–71.

9. Dwight R. Ladd, *Change in Educational Policy* (New York: McGraw-Hill, 1970).

10. See Philip Selznick, *TVA and the Grass Roots* (New York: Harper and Row, 1966), pp. 249–59; Matilda White Riley, "Sources and Types of Sociological Data," in R. E. L. Faris (ed.), *Handbook of Modern Sociology* (Chicago: Rand McNally, 1964), pp. 978-1026.

Notes

11. Jacques Barzun and Henry F. Graff, *The Modern Researcher* (New York: Harcourt, 1962), p. 140.

12. Ibid., pp. 140ff.

13. There are numerous illustrations. In another study, survey data was gathered from a sample of representative colleges and universities, and the design was seen as appropriate for tapping questions about international dimensions of higher education, as distinct from the ethos on a particular campus as in the case study by Education and World Affairs, op. cit. See Steven E. Deutsch, *International Education and Exchange: A Sociological Analysis* (Cleveland: The Press of Case Western Reserve University, 1970).

14. J. B. Lon Hefferlin, *Dynamics of Academic Reform* (San Francisco: Jossey-Bass, 1969).

15. The technique of informants identifying leadership and persons in critical positions of decision-making power is well developed in the political sociology literature. See, for example, Floyd Hunter, *Community Power Structure* (Chapel Hill: University of North Carolina Press, 1953) as the first major study built upon the so-called reputational technique.

16. See Chapter Five of Seymour Sudman, *Reducing the Cost of Surveys* (Chicago: Aldine Publishing Company, 1967). Telephone surveying was used to obtain data from 110 campuses in the study by Hefferlin, op. cit.

17. For some provocative positions see Steven Deutsch and John Howard (eds.), *Where It's At: Radical Perspectives in Sociology* (New York: Harper & Row, 1970), especially Part One.

18. This problem is brilliantly analyzed in Alvin Gouldner, *The Coming Crisis in Western Sociology* (New York: Basic Books, 1970). The book's implications are discussed at some length in a review essay by Steven Deutsch in the April 1971 *American Sociological Review,* pp. 321–26.

19. For example, Ladd, op. cit., was on the Educational Policies Committee of the University of New Hampshire, which stimulated his interest in examining the impact of self-studies of colleges and universities. His own university is one of several in his study of select institutions.

Index

Academic Council (Western Washington), 164, 170, 174, 175
Academic Plan Steering Committee (Berkeley), 58
The Academic Revolution, Jencks and Riesman, 181
Academic Senate (Berkeley), 35, 42, 46, 48, 49, 50, 52, 62; Emergency Executive Committee, 37
Academic Senate (San Francisco State), 84
Academic Senate (Stanford), 223, 224
Academic Senate (UCLA), 189, 190, 194, 201, 202, 203, 209; Committee on Educational Policy, 189-90; committees, 202-03
Ad Hoc Committee for Programs on Minority Cultures (Western Washington), 169-70
Administrative Council (Western Washington), 175

Afro-American History and Culture Center (UCLA), 196, 200, 205
Afro-American Student Union (Berkeley), 54, 55
Afro-American studies programs, 199, 248, 252; degree for, 229-32
Alumni Association (Oregon), 148
American Association of University Professors (AAUP), 105
American Council on Education, 72; study by, 117-18
American Federation of Teachers (AFT), 105; strike of San Francisco State Local, 98, 99, 100, 105, 106, 107, 112
American Imperialism course (Oregon), 136
American Indian students: Oregon, 145; Western Washington, 171. *See also* Native-American studies program

Index 317

American Legion, 7; Portland convention, 115
Antioch College, 11, 18, 245, 273
Applied Electronics Laboratory (Stanford), sit-in, 214, 224, 234
Aptheker, Bettina, 112
The Arena (Stanford), 222
Argonne Laboratory (University of Chicago), 8
Arrowhead Conference (UCLA), 184
Assistant Dean of Student Activities (UCLA), 189
Associated Students (San Francisco State), 82, 89
Associated Students (Western Washington), 173, 175
Associated Students of Stanford University, 225
Associated Students of the University of California (Berkeley), 47; survey by, 36
Associated Students of the University of California at Los Angeles, 188, 194, 204
Associated Students of the University of Oregon, 124, 128, 134, 145
Astoria, Ore., 139
ASUCLA. *See* Associated Students of the University of California at Los Angeles
ASUO. *See* Associated Students of the University of Oregon

BED. *See* Board of Educational Development
Bellingham, Wash., 156; free schools, 247; hippies, 173
Bellingham Northwest Passage, 174
Berkeley campus, 8, 9, 18, 31-75, 122, 170, 180, 181, 209, 215
Birmingham, Ala., 2
Black administrators, 96, 97, 98
Black faculties, 253, 254; at Berkeley, 55, 56, 57; at Oregon, 143, 145; at San Francisco State, 93, 96, 97, 98, 103, 271; at Stanford, 232; at UCLA, 200-01; at Western Washington, 173
Black graduate students, 253, 254, 255
Black liberation movement, 249
The Black Man in a Changing American Context course (UCLA), 191
Black Mountain College, 245
Black Panther Party, 48, 64, 146, 154, 249

Black Panther Party Paper, 146
Black Power, 249, 250
Black Student Union (Oregon), 143, 145, 146
Black Student Union (San Francisco State), 93, 95, 96, 98, 99, 100, 106, 112
Black Student Union (Stanford), 231
Black Student Union (UCLA), 191, 194, 197, 205
Black Student Union (Western Washington, 170
Black students, 31, 181, 195, 248, 249, 250, 252; at Berkeley, 54, 55; at Oregon, 139, 143, 146; at San Francisco State, 93-98 passim; at Stanford, 226, 229-32 passim; at UCLA, 181, 195; at Western Washington, 171. *See also* Afro-American History and Culture Center (UCLA); Militants, Black; Black studies programs; Ethnic studies programs
Black students assassinated (UCLA), 198, 206, 210, 252
Black Studies Department. *See* Department of Black Studies (San Francisco State)
Black studies programs, 252-53; at Berkeley, 256; at San Francisco State, 95-99 passim; at UCLA, 191, 196, 199, 200, 205. *See also* Afro-American studies programs; Ethnic studies programs
Board of Educational Development (Berkeley), 40, 43, 45, 46, 50, 53, 70, 190; administration and, 62; Center for Participant Education and, 47, 48, 49, 51, 52; duties of, 46; faculty evaluation by, 59-60; regents and, 50-51
Board of Trustees (Stanford), 234-35, 236
Board of Urban Research and Development (UCLA), 196, 197
Boeing Aircraft industry, 169
Bombings (Oregon), 115, 116, 121
Brown, Rick (Berkeley), 48
BSU. *See* Black Student Union (of various schools)
Budget Committee, Chairman (UCLA), 194
BURD. *See* Board of Urban Research and Development (UCLA)
Burns, Hugh, 36
Burns Report, 36

California, anti-Communist employment policy, 210
California educational system, 76-79; State Colleges, 27, 28, 90, 111, 113; *Master Plan for Higher Education*, 76, 77, 79, 80, 99, 117; and political pressures, 270, 278, 279, 280
California legislature, and Berkeley campus, 34-35, 36, 37, 52, 69, 70, 71-72, 73, 74, 103
California State Superintendent of Schools, 73, 94, 279
Cambodian invasion, 17, 64, 65, 234, 275; demonstrations against, 113, 115, 127, 155
Carmichael, Stokely, 146
Carnegie Foundation, 164
CASE. See Community for Awareness and Social Education (UCLA)
Case Western Reserve, 257
Castro, followers of, 36, 70
CED. See Committee on Educational Development (UCLA)
Center for Innovation in Research and Education (Stanford), 220
Center for Participant Education (Berkeley), 42, 53, 54; Board of Educational Development and, 49, 51, 52; function of, 47, 48
Chicago Eight Conspiracy Trial, 65, 115, 121, 146, 154, 206, 234
Chicano students: Oregon, 145; Western Washington, 171. See also Mexican-American students (UCLA); United Mexican-American Students (UCLA)
Chicano studies programs, 248, 254; Oregon, 138. See also Mexican-American studies program, Berkeley; Mexican Culture program (UCLA)
CIA, 246, 285
City College of New York, 4; Free University, 129
Civil rights struggle, 2, 81, 183, 249, 250. See also Racism
Clark, Burton R., 18
Clark, Robert, President of University of Oregon, 151
Cleaver, Eldridge, 51, 146, 249; course controversy, 43, 48, 51, 52, 53, 89, 94, 203, 205
Cohen, Carl, 265
Cold War, 2
College of Ethnic Studies, 169-70, 171, 256, 257

College of Letters and Science (UCLA), 189
Columbia University, 4, 7, 17, 257; faculty, 270; research project, 157
Committee for the Study of Education and Society (UCLA), 186, 187, 188, 189, 190, 191, 204, 205
Committee of Academic Innovation (UCLA), 203, 242
Committee on Educational Development (UCLA), 190
Committee on Educational Policy (UCLA), 204
Commitee on Ethnic Studies (Oregon), 145
Committee on Housing and Environment (Berkeley), 63
Committee on Student Affairs (Berkeley), 48
Committee on the Future of the University (Oregon). See Novick Report (Oregon)
Committee on Undergraduate Education (Stanford), 217, 226
Committee on Undergraduate Studies (Stanford), 219
Committee on University Governance (Oregon), 121, 127
Communist Party, 210
Communists, 7, 36, 70
Community action programs (San Francisco State), 80-82, 139, 258
Community Arts Program (UCLA), 184
Community for Awareness and Social Education (UCLA), 204, 205
Community issues, 13, 26, 31-32, 48, 63, 64, 66, 137, 183, 193, 239, 245-63 passim, 280-85
Community Services Institute (San Francisco State), 81-82, 99, 102, 111
Compton College Project, 196
Conant, James, 2
Conference on the Curriculum (Oregon), 131-32, 133
Congress of Racial Equality (CORE), 145-46, 249
Connor, Bull, 2
Convocation on Undergraduate Education (UCLA), 185-86
Coordinator of Special Educational Programs (UCLA), 184
CORE. See Congress of Racial Equality
Cornell University, 84; governance report, 274

Index

Corruption course (UCLA), 189
Council of Department Chairmen (Western Washington), 174
Council of Presidents (Stanford), 223, 229
Council for Educational Development (UCLA), 202, 203
CPE. *See* Center for Participant Education
CSES. *See* Committee for the Study of Education and Society (UCLA)
Cuban crisis, 2
The Culture of the University: Governance and Education, 42
Curriculum Committee (Western Washington), 174

Dahrendorf, Ralf, 15
Daily Bruin (UCLA), 186, 187
Daily Emerald (Oregon), 126, 130.
Daily Gator (San Francisco State), 93
Daughters of the American Revolution, 7
Davis, Angela, 64, 146, 210
Dean for Academic Affairs (Western Washington), 164, 167
Dean of Graduate Division (UCLA), 189
Dean of Letters and Science (UCLA), 189
"death of God" controversy, 1
Declaration of the Berkeley Liberation Front, 74
Defense research, 3, 7, 8, 12, 13, 33, 59, 66, 67, 68, 234, 235, 282; federal funds for, 8, 10, 157, 277-85 passim
Demonstrations, 4, 7, 10, 18, 66, 283. *See also* Defense research; Draft issue; Educational reforms; Free Speech Movement; People's Park episode; Vietnam war controversy
Department of Black Studies (San Francisco State), 95, 96, 99, 112
Department of Ethnic Studies (Berkeley), 56, 57
"Discussion of Student Unrest," 152-53
Division of Experimental Courses (Berkeley), 52, 53
Division of Interdisciplinary and General Studies (Berkeley), 42
Dow Chemical recruiters, 120
Draft issue, 3, 66, 126, 216

Dumke, Chancellor Glenn (San Francisco State), 113

Educational Opportunities Program (UCLA), 195
Educational reforms, 239, 244, 245. *See also* Center for Participant Education; Ethnic studies programs; Experimental colleges; Free University; Students' Exploratory Actions Regarding Curricular Heterodoxy program (Oregon); Third World College
Educational Research and Action Projects (ERAP), 3
Edwards, Harry, cited, 255-56
Encina Hall (Stanford), sit-in, 224, 233
ERAP. *See* Educational Research and Action Projects
Esalen center, 138
Ethnic studies programs, 5, 23, 248-58; Berkeley, 54-55, 56, 57, 257, 275; Oregon, 143, 145, 146, 254; San Francisco State, 93-100, 106, 112, 255; UCLA, 195, 203, 211; Western Washington, 173. *See also* Black studies programs; Chicano studies programs; Mexican-American studies programs; Native-American studies programs; Oriental-American studies programs
Eugene, Ore., 116, 145, 146; bombings in, 115; City Council, 127; free schools, 247; minority groups, 139, 257
Evergreen State College (Olympia, Wash.), 46
the Experiment (Stanford), 186, 216-19
Experimental College (Berkeley), 43-46, 138, 165, 186, 202
Experimental College (San Francisco State), 78, 82, 83-93, 101, 102, 109, 112, 186, 216, 247, 275
Experimental College (Stanford). *See* the Experiment (Stanford); Mid-Peninsula Free University
Experimental College (UCLA), 174, 186-90, 247
Experimental colleges, 5, 10, 11, 18, 23, 138, 186, 204, 216-19, 225, 245-48
Extension programs (UCLA), 184-85

320   Index

Faculty Advisory Council (Oregon), 121, 124, 127
Faculty Committee on Academic Innovation (UCLA), 201
Faculty Committee on Courses (Berkeley), 53
Faculty conduct code (Oregon), 121, 155
Faculty Council (Stanford), 223
Faculty Council (Western Washington), 174
Faculty Curriculum Committee (Oregon), 130, 131, 132, 135
Faculty Hiring Committee (Western Washington), 165
Faculty Legislative Assembly (UCLA), 201
Faculty Rehiring, Promotion and Tenure Board (Western Washington), 165
Faculty Renaissance group (San Francisco State), 104
Faculty Senate (Oregon), 124, 127
Faculty Senate (Stanford), 224, 227, 230; Committee on Committees, 227
Faculty Senate Committees (UCLA), 269
Faculty-Student Council (Oregon), 122, 125
Fairhaven College, 160, 161-68; community government, 165; Policy Board, 167; purpose of, 163-64; seminars, 163-64
the "Farm." See Stanford University campus
Farm Workers boycott, 150
Fleming, Arthur, President of University of Oregon, 123, 129, 139, 140; Committee on Racism, 140-43, 241
Flora, Charles, President of Western Washington State College, 159
Foote Report on University Governance (Berkeley), 58
Ford Foundation, 53; grants, 184, 214
Foreign students, 249
Flacks, Richard, 283
Frankel, Charles (Columbia), 281
Franklin, H. Bruce, 18
Free School (Oregon), courses offered, 138-39
Free schools, 247-48
Free Speech Movement (Berkeley), 3, 9, 11, 17, 37, 43, 44, 47, 58, 63, 102, 112, 119, 122, 210, 246, 250, 275; issues of, 34-35; Kerr's denunciation of, 36, 70; purpose of, 32, 33
Free University, 129, 130; defined, 82-83; at San Francisco State, 82-83; at Stanford, 216, 218, 219. See also Northwest Free University
Fresno State College, 89
Froines, John, 121, 146, 154
FSM. See Free Speech Movement (Berkeley)
Full-time equivalencies (FTEs), 189

Gay Liberation Movement, 137
Glazer, Nathan, cited, 11
Goodman, Paul, 245, 276
Graduate Student Association (UCLA), 194, 204
Graduate students, 117, 238; at Berkeley, 33-34, 38, 39, 66, 75; at Huxley, 169, 170; at Oregon, 116, 117, 118; at San Francisco State, 78, 79; at Stanford, 238; at UCLA, 181, 182, 204, 238; at Western Washington, 157, 158
GSA. See Graduate Student Association (UCLA)
Guerrilla warfare, 89-90, 120, 126
"Guidelines for Faculty-Student Participation" (Oregon), 148

Haggard, President of Western Washington State College, 159
Hare, Nathan (San Francisco State), 96, 97, 98
Harris, David (Stanford), 216, 218
Harvard University, 66; Afro-American Studies degree, 229; trustees, 273
Harwood, Charles (Fairhaven), 164
Hatfield, Senator Mark, bill to end war, 121, 155
Hayakawa, S. I., President of San Francisco State, 90, 96, 97, 99, 105, 110, 111, 113, 276
Hayden, Tom, 52
Hefferlin, J. B. Lon, 18-19
Heirich, Max, 36
Herr Report (Berkeley), 42
Heyns, Roger (Berkeley), 72
High Potential Program (UCLA), 194-95, 198
High School Equivalency Program (Oregon), 139
The Higher Learning in America, Veblen, 6

Index

The Higher Learning in America: A Reassessment, Woodring, 161
Hippies, 73-74, 87, 91, 109; courses for (Oregon), 138-39; culture, 114, 115; at Western Washington, 173, 177
Hitch, Charles, President of UCLA, 50, 193, 198
Hitch resolution (Berkeley), 49-50
Hook, Sidney, 281
House Foreign Relations Committee, 64
House Task Force on Higher Education (Oregon) Report, 153-54
House Un-American Activities Committee, 31; California counterpart of, 36, 70, 210
How Children Fail, Holt, 245
How Children Learn, Holt, 245
Howard University, 96
HUAC. See House Un-American Activities Committee
Human Sexuality course (Oregon), 137
Hutchins, Robert, 7
Huxley College, 168-69, 170, 171; environmental studies, 168, 169

Illich, Ivan, 245
Indochina war. See Cambodian invasion; Vietnam war controversy
Innovations. See Educational reforms
Institute for Community Services (San Francisco State), 250
Institute for Defense Analysis, 4
Institute for Social Change (San Francisco State), 85
Institute for the Study of American Cultures (UCLA), 195, 199, 264
Institute for the Study of Higher Education (Stanford), 225-26
Introduction to Frisbee course (San Francisco State), 84

Jackson State College, 65; killings at, 64, 113, 127, 155
Japanese-American students (UCLA), 181, 192
Jarrett, James, President of Western Washington State College, 159-60
Jencks, Christopher, 78, 79, 181
Johns Hopkins University, 282
Johnson, Charles, President of University of Oregon, 150-51
Johnson, Lyndon B., 243, 281
Johnson, Roosevelt, 253
Junior colleges, 9, 77, 99

Kaplan, Sam, 36
Kennedy, John F., 2
Kennedy, Robert: assassination of, 4; "children's campaign," 150
Kennedy-Johnson liberalism, 2
Kent State College, 65; killings at, 64, 113, 127, 155
Kerner Commission Follow-Up (UCLA), 204
The Kerner Report, 134, 144
Kerr, Clark, President of Berkeley, 8, 12, 35-37, 44, 70, 282; dismissal of, 36, 37, 71, 72
Kesey, Ken, 114
King, Martin Luther, assassination of, 4, 54, 140, 150, 204
Kneller Report (UCLA), 190, 201, 202
Kohl, Herbert, 245
Kurweil, Jack, 112

Lawrence Radiation Laboratory (Berkeley), 8
"The Learning Community," 245
Leland Stanford Jr. University. See Stanford University campus
Lincoln Laboratory (Massachusetts Institute of Technology), 8
Long Range Planning Committee (Western Washington State College), 162
Los Angeles, Calif., 95, 180, 211; minority groups, 257; Watts area, 184, 185, 186
Loyalty oaths, 281

Malcolm X, 249
Mao, followers of, 70
Marin County Courthouse murder, 210
Massachusetts Institute of Technology, 8, 282
Master Plan for Higher Education, California, 76, 77, 79, 80, 99, 117
McCarthy, Eugene, 243; "children's campaign," 150
McCarthy era investigations, 2, 35-36, 70
McGovern, Senator George, bill to end war, 121, 155
McGrath, Earl, 272
Meiklejohn, Alexander, 43
Melman, Seymour, cited, 270
Mexican-American History and Culture Center (UCLA), 196
Mexican-American students (UCLA),

Mexican-American students (*cont.*) 181, 195. See also Chicano students; United Mexican-American Students (UCLA)
Mexican-American studies program (Berkeley), 55
"Mexican Culture" program (UCLA), 184
Michigan State University, 246
Mid-Peninsula Free University, 219, 220, 246
Militants, 89-90; Black, 4, 8, 57, 72, 113, 146, 250, 252, 255-56. See also Black Panther Party; Black Power
Minority students. See American Indian students; Black students; Chicano students; Mexican-American students; Oriental-American students
Mississippi Freedom Summer, 3
MIT. See Massachusetts Institute of Technology
Montessori schools, 245
Morrill Act of 1862, 12
Mosser, John, 124
Mosser Plan (Oregon), 124
Murphy, Franklin (UCLA), 184
Murphy, Senator George, 73
Murray, George (San Francisco State), controversy over, 93, 97, 98, 103
Muscatine, Charles (Berkeley), 37, 47
Muscatine Report (*Education at Berkeley*, 1966), 11, 17, 37, 38, 40, 46, 58, 201-02, 246; recomendations of, 39-40

NAACP. See National Association for the Advancement of Colored People
Narcotics, 114, 120
National Association for the Advancement of Colored People, 256
National Democratic Convention, 4, 150, 243
National Guard, 239; on Berkeley campus, 34, 63, 69, 71; on Oregon campus, 115, 155
National Student Association, 126, 243
Native-American studies program, 248; at Berkeley, 55
"The Negro and the Arts" program (UCLA), 184
Neill, A. S., 245
"New American Community," 115
New American Revolution course (Berkeley), 52

New Left, 2, 4, 31, 153, 281
New York Times, 4
Newfield, Jack, 2
Nixon, Richard M.: administration, 251; and Cambodian invasion, 64, 65; and Vietnam war, 150
North Vietnam, students travel to, 126
Northwest Free University, 172-76; "Course Critique," 176; Teacher of the Year, 176
Novick Report (Oregon), 117, 118

Oakland, Calif., 146
Office of Economic Opportunity's War on Poverty, 251
"Old Bahstud" (O.B.), 192
Oregon State Board of Higher Education, 121, 124, 142, 240
Oregon State University, 124
Oriental-American Cultural Center (UCLA), 192
Oriental-American History and Culture Center (UCLA), 196
Oriental-American students (UCLA), 181
Oriental-American studies programs, 248; at Berkeley, 55
Orlans, Harold, 8

Packer, Herbert L. (Stanford), 221
Paris, students travel to, 126
Pass/no-pass grading, 125, 134, 259-60
Patriot Party, 146
Peace Corps, 2, 81, 259
Pentagon, 285
People's Army Jamboree, 115
People's Park episode, 34, 62, 63, 72, 74, 127, 256, 279
"People's Peace Treaty," 126
Pimentel, Professor, 39
Pitzer, Kenneth (Stanford), 234
Police, 239; on Berkeley campus, 34, 69, 71; on Oregon campus, 115, 155; on Stanford campus, 233, 234
Political pressures, 3, 210, 236, 238, 270, 277-80; on Berkeley, 34-35, 36, 69, 70-71; on Oregon, 150-55, 178; on San Francisco State, 71-72, 73, 74, 90-91, 102, 110, 111, 113, 279, 280; on Stanford, 236, 277; on UCLA, 193
Political Science Department (UCLA), 186
Poor People's Campaign, 48
Port Huron Statement, 32

Index

Portland, Ore., 115, 139; "The Learning Community," 245
Portland State University, 116
Presidential Search Committee (Oregon), 147
Presidential Selection Committee (Stanford), 228
President's Committee on Racism (Oregon), 140-44 passim, 241
Project 75, 141-42, 144, 251
Project Themis, 282
Publishing, faculty and, 101-02, 108

Racism, 1, 2, 13, 63, 74-75, 126, 127, 170, 225, 249, 254, 256, 257. *See also* Black Panther Party; President's Committee on Racism (Oregon); Watts riots
Radical Collectives Union, 146
Rafferty, Max, 73, 94
RAT Troupe (Oregon campus), 120
Reagan, Governor Ronald: austerity plan, 198; and Berkeley disorders, 36, 69, 70, 71, 73, 74, 282; and San Francisco State strike, 88-89, 95, 110, 111, 113; and San Jose State, 151
Reality of the Ghetto course (Western Washington), 173
Reed College, 18, 245
Regents (Berkeley), 36, 48, 51, 52, 54, 64-65, 70-71, 88, 192; members of, 69-70; and Social Analysis 139X course, 49-50
Regents (UCLA), 195, 206, 210
Reich, Charles, 114
Report of the Faculty Committee on University Governance (Berkeley), 11
Report of the Select Committee on University Governance 1968 (Berkeley), 58, 274
Report on the Future of the University, Novick, 117
Report to the Faculty (Stanford), 222
Report to the University (Stanford), 221
Resurrection City, 48
Riesman, David, 78, 79, 181
Rock music, 114; festivals, 115
ROTC, 7, 275, 283; on Berkeley campus, 33, 64, 67, 68; on Oregon campus, 115, 120, 121, 151, 154; on Stanford campus, 234
Rudolph, Frederick, cited, 12

San Francisco, Calif., 31, 76, 77, 99, 211; Bay area schools, 119, 123; Haight-Ashbury district, 114; minority groups, 257; newspaper cited, 214
San Francisco State College campus, 4, 11, 30, 70, 76-113, 119, 172, 181, 215, 246
San Jose State College, 46, 112; Black militants, 151; Governor Reagan and, 151
San Juan Islands, Wash., 156
Satellite schools. *See* College of Ethnic Studies; Fairhaven College; Huxley College; Mid-Peninsula Free University; Northwest Free University
Saturday Review, 161
Schaar, John (Berkeley), 58, 65; cited, 68-69
Scholastic Aptitude Test scores (Stanford), 213
School Desegregation Institute (Oregon), 139
School of Community Service and Public Affairs (Oregon), 130
School of Education (San Francisco State), 78
School of Ethnic Studies (San Francisco State), 99, 112
SDS. *See* Students for a Democratic Society
Seale, Bobby, 146
SEARCH. *See* Students' Exploratory Actions Regarding Curricular Heterodoxy program (Oregon)
Seattle, Wash., 156
SEC. *See* Student Education Council (Stanford)
Select Committee on Education (Berkeley), 37, 38, 39, 41, 42, 242
Seminar in Guerrilla Warfare (San Francisco State), 89-90
Seminar on Drug Use (Oregon), 131
Senate Foreign Relations Committee, 64
SES. *See* Study of Education at Stanford
Sinclair, Upton, 212; cited, 6-7
Sit-ins, 2, 249, 256; at Berkeley, 210; at Oregon, 147, 148, 149, 150, 154; at Stanford, 214-15, 224, 234; at Western Washington, 176
SLATE, 36
Smith, Robert, President of San Francisco State, 94, 95, 110
SNCC. *See* Student Nonviolent Coordinating Committee

Social Analysis 139X course (Berkeley), 43, 48, 51, 52, 62; Hitch resolution on, 49-50
Sociology Department (Oregon), bombing of, 115
Sociology Department (San Francisco State), 92
South Vietnam, students travel to, 126
Southeast Asia, 2, 120. *See also* Vietnam war controversy
Special Committee on Academic Program (Berkeley), 41, 42
Special Education Coordinator (UCLA), 184
Sproul Hall (Berkeley), seizure of, 282
SRI. *See* Stanford Research Institute
Staff Council (Western Washington), 175
Stanford, Senator Leland, 212
Stanford Daily, 231
Stanford Industrial Park, 235
Stanford Research Institute, controversy, 215, 233, 234, 235
Stanford University *Bulletin*, 217
Stanford University campus, 18, 30, 172, 212-36
State Board of Higher Education (Oregon), 121, 124, 133, 142, 148, 149, 150, 154, 155; Committee on Academic Affairs, 152; policy statement of, 151-52
State Colleges, California system of, 27, 28, 90, 111, 113. *See also* San Francisco State College campus; Western Washington State College campus
State system of higher education (Oregon), 133
Sterling, J. E. Wallace (Stanford), 220
Student Center for Innovation in Research and Education (Stanford), 219-20
Student Conduct Code (Oregon), 119-20
Student disorders. *See* Bombings (Oregon); Demonstrations; Free Speech Movement; Militants; People's Park episode; Sit-ins; Student strike (San Francisco State)
Student Education Council (Stanford), 223, 224
Student involvements. *See* Educational reforms
Student Nonviolent Coordinating Committee, 249

Student Political Movements course (Oregon), 131
Student revolutionaries, international, 153
Student Senate (Oregon), 124
Student strike (San Francisco State), 93, 95-107 passim, 110-13, 206, 252, 253, 254, 275
Student-Faculty Coalition (Oregon), 127
Students' Exploratory Actions Regarding Curricular Heterodoxy program (Oregon), 128-38 passim, 145, 147, 254, 264
Students for a Democratic Society, 2, 3, 52, 67, 130, 136, 137, 151, 153, 243; Labor Committee, 138
Study Commission on University Governance (Berkeley), 41, 242, 247
Study of Education at Stanford, 220-29, 232, 233, 242; *Report to the Faculty*, 222; *Report to the University*, 221; Steering Committee comments, 221, 222, 223
Subcommittee on Student Innovation (Stanford), 220
Summer Task Force (UCLA), 193-94, 197, 199, 275
Summerhill school, 245
Summerskill, John, President of San Francisco State, 84, 96, 100, 102, 104, 132
Swarthmore College, 18

Task Force on Curricular Development (UCLA), 194, 195
Task Force on Financial Aid (UCLA), 198
Task Force on Higher Education (Oregon) Report, 153-54
Task Force on Student Entry (UCLA), 194
Task Force on Urban Research and Action (UCLA), 194, 196, 269
Taylor, Harold, 63, 239, 262, 263
Teach-In Movement, 3, 127, 246
Teacher of the Year (Western Washington), 175
Third World College, 252, 254, 257; at Berkeley, 54-56; at San Francisco State, 93, 95, 98, 251
Third World Liberation Front, 95, 99, 100, 109, 256
"Time Out for University-Wide Evaluation" (Oregon), 144

Index

Tongue Point Job Corps., Astoria, Ore., 139
Topanga center, 138
Tresidder Memorial Union (Stanford), 213
Trow, Martin, 17; cited, 40-41
Trustees (San Francisco State), 103, 111, 112, 113
Trustees (Stanford), 273
Tussman, Joseph, 43, 44, 45, 46
Tussman program. *See* Experimental College

UCLA campus, 30, 80, 179-211, 215; Afro-American Studies degree, 229-30
UMAS. *See* United Mexican-American Students (UCLA)
Undergraduate Course Committee (UCLA), 189, 190
Undergraduate Specials Program (Stanford), 217, 218
Undergraduate students, 6-7, 8, 9, 13, 16, 27, 28; at Berkeley, 40, 41; at Oregon, 124; at San Francisco State, 78, 79; at Stanford, 216, 235; at UCLA, 182, 185, 189, 190, 193; at Western Washington, 157-58. *See also* Junior Colleges
United Mexican-American Students (UCLA), 194, 205
University College (UCLA), 202
University of California, 48, 54, 66, 78, 99, 119, 177, 178, 209, 230. *See also* Berkeley campus; UCLA campus
University of California, Berkeley campus. *See* Berkeley campus
University of California, Los Angeles campus. *See* UCLA campus
University of California at Santa Cruz, 171
University of Chicago, 4, 7, 8, 257
University of Michigan, 117, 249
University of Oregon campus, 114-55
University of Rochester, 12
Upward Bound program, 239, 251; at Oregon, 138; at UCLA, 184; at Western Washington, 171
Urban Communities studies (San Francisco State), 85, 87

Urban Extension College (Stanford), 225
U.S. National Commission on Causes and Prevention of Violence, 101
U.S. Office of Education programs, 251
U.S. State Department, 285
The Uses of the University, Kerr, 8

Vancouver, B.C., 156
Veblen, Thorstein, 6
Vice Chancellor for Academic Innovation (UCLA), 192, 203
Vice Chancellor for Educational Planning (UCLA), 194
Vietnam Convocation (San Francisco State), 84, 241
Vietnam war controversy, 3, 10, 64, 66, 84, 118, 123, 126, 127, 246, 251, 282; bill to end war, 121, 155
VISTA, 259
VOICE (UCLA group), 186

Wall Street Journal, 231, 232
Wallerstein, Immanuel, 3, 250, 275; cited, 4
Washington, D.C., Resurrection City, 48
Washington, state of, educational system, 162
Watts riots, 185
Watts-Compton area, 184. *See also* Los Angeles, Watts area
Wayne State University, 257
Wechsler, James, 7
Western Washington State College campus, 30, 123, 156-78, 188; Satellite schools, 160-76, 247
Westwood community episode, 206
Weyerhaeuser Corporation, 120
White Racism Project (Stanford), 225
Wolff, Robert Paul, 276
Wolin, Sheldon, 58, 65; cited, 68-69
Woodring, Paul, 161, 172, 261
Work-Study degree program (San Francisco State), 87
World War II, 8, 12, 282

Young, Charles (UCLA), 193, 206

Zen Basketball course (San Francisco State), 84
Zurich, Switzerland, 115